Communicating Through Behavior

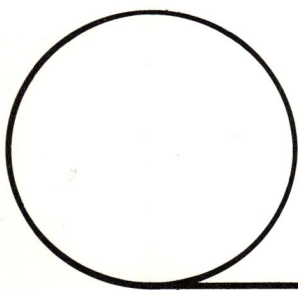

Communicating Through Behavior

William E. Arnold *Arizona State University*

Robert O. Hirsch *Arizona State University*

West Publishing Company ■ St. Paul ■ New York ■ Los Angeles ■ San Francisco

Library of Congress Cataloging in Publication Data

Main entry under title:

Communicating through behavior.

Includes index.
1. Interpersonal communication. I. Arnold,
William E., 1940– II. Hirsch, Robert O.
BF637.C45C64   153   76-52409
ISBN 0–8299–0133–7
2nd Reprint 1978

Preface

We live in a time when communication seems to be both the cause of problems and the solution to them. In politics, business, education, and even in our relationships with one another, we hear that communication has broken down and barriers have been created. On the other hand, when we are asked for solutions to these problems, we are told, generally, that better communication can solve the dilemmas. This book cannot solve all of your communication problems nor can it answer all the questions you may have about communication. However, it is intended to provide you with a basis for understanding the process of communication.

Each chapter is devoted to a major component of the communicative process. The first chapter examines what is meant by communication and why one seeks to interact with another person. Chapters Two, Three, Four, and Five explore the essential elements of the communication process—perception, verbal, nonverbal, and listening behaviors. The remainder of the text investigates the uses of communication in a variety of settings. It begins by looking at the relationship that we find ourselves in most often—interpersonal communication.

We spend most of our time communicating with one or two other people. When we expand our interaction, we begin looking at the impact of communication in a small group setting. On less frequent occasions, we are asked to communicate with an audience of fifteen or more people. This setting, called public communication, offers some unusual challenges for the speaker. Our relationship to the mass media is also examined, and finally in Chapter Ten, we look at the application of all types of communication to a variety of settings—political, crisis, and cross-cultural.

Each reading has been carefully selected to provide information yet avoid the usual textbook approach. Readings have been selected from popular magazines, books, and other materials in order to provide content yet make the reading enjoyable.

Contents

① Elements of Communication

(2) Communication Settings

Ten Applying Communication 263

†

1

Elements
of Communication

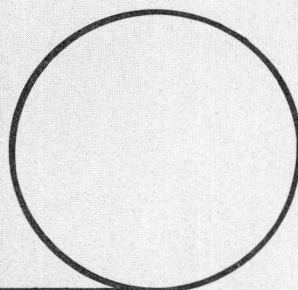

One
Process of Communication

Introduction

In this chapter, we will present an overview of the process of communication. In addition to introducing the readings in this chapter, we will answer three basic questions about communication: (1) Why do we communicate? (2) What is the goal of communication? (3) What is communication?

We will begin with the rather simple assumption that you communicate to satisfy self-interest. We believe that every behavior that a person engages in is done on the basis of self-interest. Brooks and Emmert (1976) suggest that we communicate to survive (get the fullest adjustment to our environment). You attend this class, you read this text, you go to college in order to satisfy your self-interest. You might say, "I am going to college because my parents gave me the money" or "I didn't want to go out and find a job because there aren't any." While these sound like valid reasons, we think that you engage in these behaviors because they satisfy your self-interest.

Each of the answers that you have given as to why you behave the way you do ultimately rests on the satisfaction of your own needs. In fact, the only time that you might not be satisfying self-interests is when something occurs as the result of an accident. Granted, when you trip on a rock and fall and break your leg, you are probably not doing so because of a need unless, of course, you are looking for the sympathy that goes along with the injuries. We assume that accidents are not perpetrated out of self-interest. Returning to our initial point, then, we communicate with each other because it satisfies our own self-interest. Chapanis suggests that we converse with one another to impress, cajole, threaten, influence, inform, shape, deceive, conceal, etc. We maintain that underlying all of these reasons for communication is our concept of self-interest. You communicate because it does something for you.

While this approach may sound selfish and even crass, a knowledge of the underlying motivation for our communication and the rest of our behavior makes the process of communication more understandable. To explore this point, let's look at the relationship of communication to self-interest when we are interacting with another person. When you call up a friend to go to the movies with you, you are either trying to find company to go to a film or you are seeking the companionship of another individual. In both cases, you are satisfying your own self-interest. If we extend this concept further, you will see that your friend is not likely to attend the film with you except in his or her self-interest. The two of you may have the same motivations for attending the film. If not, you would be in the process of trying to convince your friend that it really is in his or her self-interest to go to the film. We are sure that you have heard or used many of the standard arguments for seeking companionship for a film or some other activity. Thus, there is no reason to list them all here.

Although we have yet to define the word *communication*, you should begin to recognize the role of self-interest in that definition. When one communicates with another person, there is an attempt on the part of both parties to satisfy their own self through that interaction. We will elaborate on a definition later.

With the brief understanding of why we communicate, let us now turn our attention to the goals of communication. We believe that the primary goal of most communication is to influence the behavior of the receiver in some way. Behavior can be influenced in three basic ways. First, a speaker can try to get us to stop doing something that we are currently doing. For instance, you have all seen ads on television by the American Cancer Society to get us to stop smoking.

If you remember those ads, you may also remember the American Cancer Society's attempt to relate the idea of stopping smoking to our self-interest. For those who were parents, the ad suggested that if you did not stop smoking, your children were going to pick up the habit. If you did not have children, they encouraged you to stop smoking because you were going to get varicose veins if a woman or lose your sexual virility if a man. They were assuming that beauty and sexual virility were both concepts within the receiver's self-interest. In summary, a speaker can seek to have us stop engaging in an existing behavior.

As a second way to influence behavior, the speaker can try to get us to continue what we are already doing. This is called strengthening or reinforcing existing behaviors. The American Tobacco Institute spent $450,000 to encourage those who were smoking to continue the smoking habit. In fact, a number of bumper stickers were printed that read "Continue to Enjoy Tobacco Products." Magazines are filled full of advertisements designed to get those who do smoke to continue.

Finally, the speaker can encourage us to engage in a new behavior. For example, if you watch much television, you can see combinations of these various forms of behavior being promoted by media advertising. Sponsors of soap products will encourage you to stop using one product and try new Brand Z. If Brands A, B, and C deodorants do not work, one should use Brand Q. The message is, "One should stop certain behaviors and start brand new ones."

While we believe that the primary goal of all communication is to influence the behavior of the recipient, there are other reasons for communicating. Chapanis suggests later in this chapter that communication can serve noninformation functions. In our discussion of verbal messages, we talk about phatic communication: It helps maintain friendships and improves our social interaction with others. To pass a friend on the street and not speak would indicate a lack of interest.

So far, we have looked at motivation for communicating and the outcomes that we desire from our communication interaction. Now we will focus your attention on some of the mechanics of communication itself by answering the third question: What is communication?

To understand communication, let us look at a rather basic model of the communication process.

The model of communication (labeled the SMCR Model) was developed in the early 1960s by David K. Berlo. The "S" stands for all of the components of the source of the communication. "M" stands for the message and its components. "C" stands for the channel of communication which is represented by the various sense organs. Finally, "R" stands for the receiver. The only difference between the source and the receiver is that one is sending a message and the other is listening to the message. In fact, the listener or receiver might be sending nonverbal messages to the source. Although this model comprises many of the components of communication, it does not include them all. One key component of the model that is missing is the concept

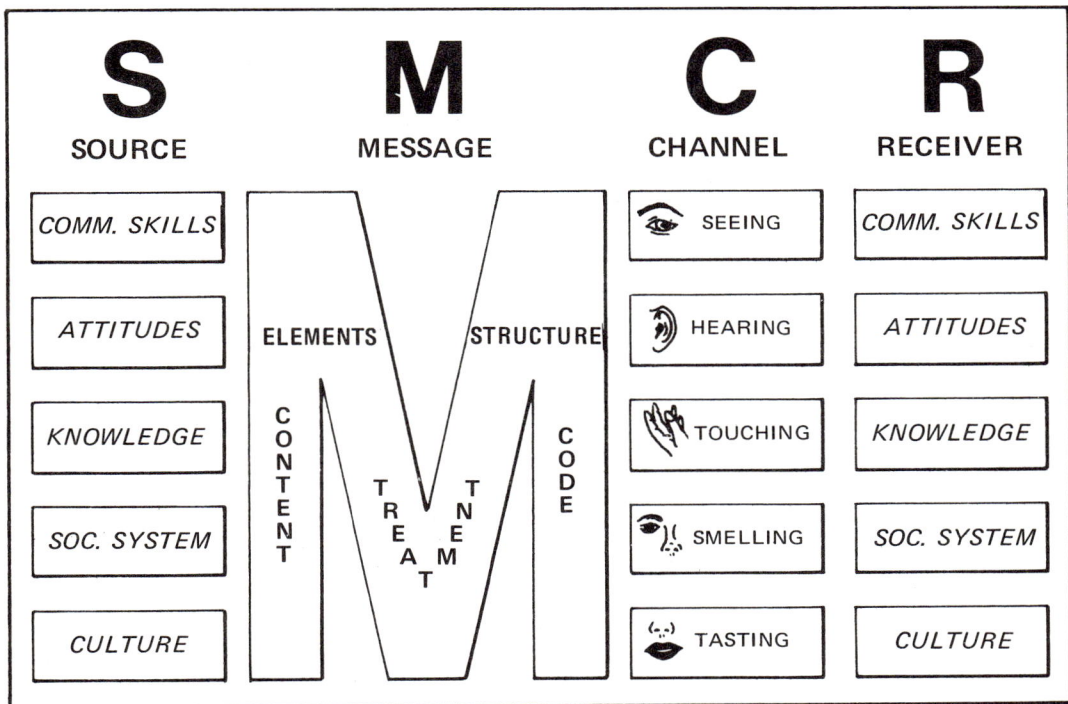

A model of the ingredients in communication.

From *The Process of Communication: An Introduction to Theory and Practice* by David K. Berlo. Copyright © 1960 by Holt, Rinehart and Winston, Inc. Reprinted by permission of Holt, Rinehart and Winston.

of feedback. If you look just at the model, it assumes that a message goes from source to receiver. Feedback is the response that the receiver makes to the source of that communication. The feedback can take the form of both verbal and nonverbal response. If we like what a source has said, we may do nothing more than nod our head in agreement. If we don't, we may give catcalls or walk out.

Each model of communication adds additional insight into communication, yet at the same time must leave out other essential components. A second model of communication developed by Schramm introduces another important aspect of communication.

In Schramm's model, you see the two circles labeled Field of Experience. The assumption that he makes about communication is that there must be overlapping fields of experience in order for communication to take place. In other words, we need something in common with another person in order to communicate. When you travel abroad, there may be little overlap of the fields of experience with the person in his native country, especially if you cannot speak his language or he yours. Without overlapping fields of experience, no communication can take place. On the other hand, the presumption that we have much in common may cause us to assume that the person we communicate with knows what we mean. Husbands and wives spend a great deal of time together, and therefore, know a lot about each other. Occasionally, a spouse will assume

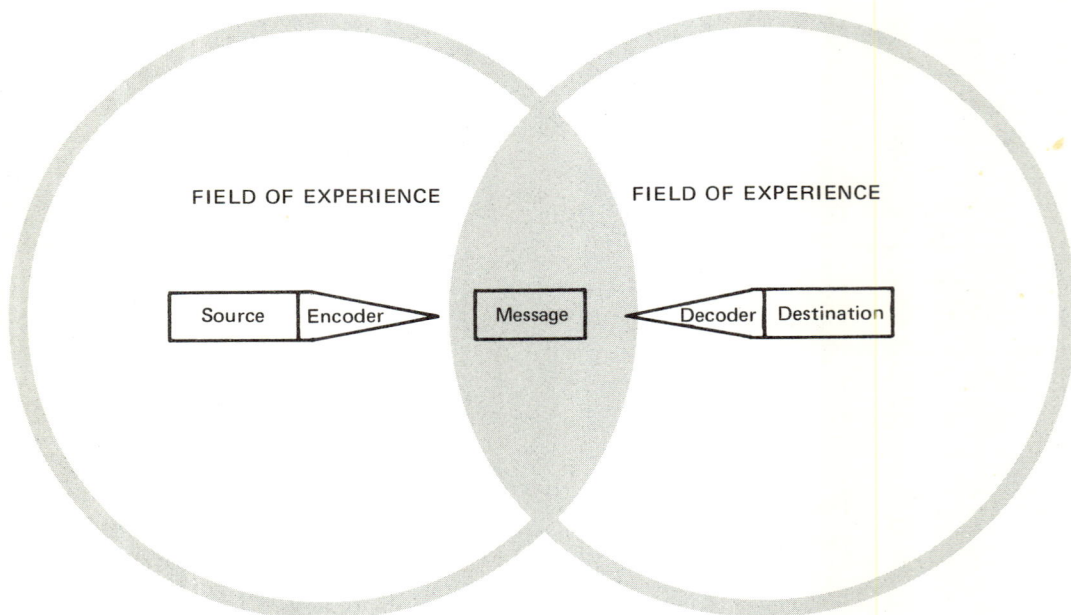

FIELD OF EXPERIENCE   FIELD OF EXPERIENCE

| Source | Encoder | | Message | | Decoder | Destination |

Schramm model.

that the other person knows what is going on when, in fact, that person does not. Such a conclusion can cause a breakdown in communication.

The last model that we will introduce was developed by Dance. He calls his the Helical or Interactive Model of Communication.

It may be easier to think of the Helical Model as that of a slinky. In essence, the model suggests that communication is an ongoing, continuous process. The source sends a message which is received, responded to as feedback, and this process continues. Seldom do we communicate with another person by making a statement and then receiving feedback and ending the communication. Most of our interaction occurs in a continuous process relationship. We will communicate, we will be responded to, we will communicate again, and this process will go on and on. In fact, in some of our communication interactions, the process continues for years with occasional interruptions. The Helical Model allows us to view the nature of the process of communication.

We have looked at the essential elements of communication: source, receiver, message, channel, feedback, and process. Each of the articles in this chapter relates to the basic introduction that we have provided here.

Articles

Toffler provides a psychological perspective on the nature of communication in our society by talking about how we, as individuals, are constantly bombarded by

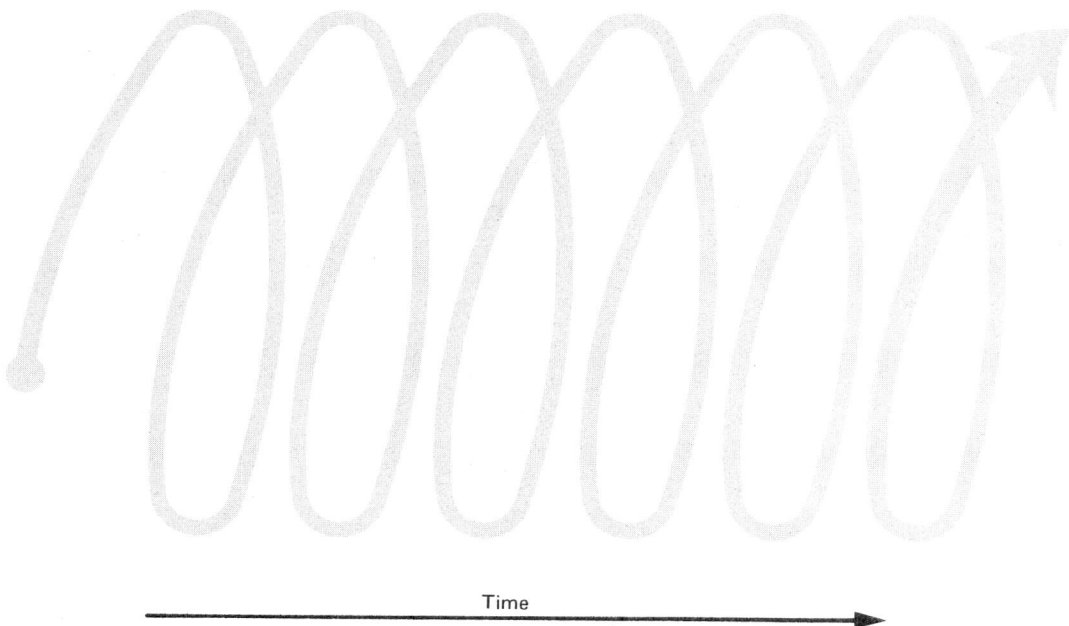

Helical model.

communication stimuli. This bombardment of our senses through various means of communication creates what he calls "culture shock," an individual disorientation with society, and perhaps even some other forms of distortion. We are forced, through an information overload, to process more information at ever-increasing rates of speed. If you go to the library, you will note the number of different magazines, journals, books, and other related educational materials. Toffler also looks at the impact of this future shock on our personal decision making. He describes the kinds of victims that result from future shock. While Toffler does not deal directly with communication or the process, you will be able to see the role of communication in his analysis of the environment around us.

Chapanis offers a traditional analysis of communication. Since he is a psychologist, his comments that communication is a field for psychological inquiry should be overlooked. Both he and Toffler suggest new systems of handling information and of finding new ways to communicate for our future.

We conclude with a final article by Menninger which discusses some of the language that we use to cloud our communication. He asks that we examine our language and listen to what we are saying.

References
W. Brooks and P. Emmert, *Interpersonal Communication* (Dubuque: William C. Brown, 1976).

Future Shock: The Psychological Dimension

Alvin Toffler

If future shock were a matter of physical illness alone, it might be easier to prevent and to treat. But future shock attacks the psyche as well. Just as the body cracks under the strain of environmental overstimulation, the "mind" and its decision processes behave erratically when overloaded. By indiscriminately racing the engines of change, we may be undermining not merely the health of those least able to adapt, but their very ability to act rationally on their own behalf.

The striking signs of confusional breakdown we see around us—the spreading use of drugs, the rise of mysticism, the recurrent outbreaks of vandalism and undirected violence, the politics of nihilism and nostalgia, the sick apathy of millions—can all be understood better by recognizing their relationship to future shock. These forms of social irrationality may well reflect the deterioration of individual decision-making under conditions of environmental overstimulation.

Psychophysiologists studying the impact of change on various organisms have shown that successful adaptation can occur only when the

From Alvin Toffler, *Future Shock* (New York: Random House, Inc., 1970), pp. 295-315. Reprinted with permission.

level of stimulation—the amount of change and novelty in the environment—is neither too low nor too high. "The central nervous system of a higher animal," says Professor D. E. Berlyne of the University of Toronto, "is designed to cope with environments that produce a certain rate of ... stimulation ... It will naturally not perform at its best in an environment that overstresses or overloads it." He makes the same point about environments that understimulate it. Indeed, experiments with deer, dogs, mice and men all point unequivocally to the existence of what might be called an "adaptive range" below which and above which the individual's ability to cope simply falls apart.

Future shock is the response to overstimulation. It occurs when the individual is forced to operate above his adaptive range. Considerable research has been devoted to studying the impact of inadequate change and novelty on human performance. Studies of men in isolated Antarctic outposts, experiments in sensory deprivation, investigations into on-the-job performance in factories, all show a falling off of mental and physical abilities in response to understimulation. We have less direct data on the impact of overstimulation, but such evidence as does exist is dramatic and unsettling.

The Overstimulated Individual

Soldiers in battle often find themselves trapped in environments that are rapidly changing, unfamiliar, and unpredictable. The soldier is torn this way and that. Shells burst on every side. Bullets whiz past erratically. Flares light the sky. Shouts, groans and explosions fill his ears. Circumstances change from instant to instant. To survive in such overstimulating environments, the soldier is driven to operate in the upper reaches of his adaptive range. Sometimes, he is pushed beyond his limits.

During World War II a bearded Chindit soldier, fighting with General Wingate's forces behind the Japanese lines in Burma, actually fell asleep while a storm of machine gun bullets splattered around him. Subsequent investigation revealed that this soldier was not merely reacting to physical fatigue or lack of sleep, but surrendering to a sense of overpowering apathy.

Death-inviting lassitude was so common, in fact, among guerrilla troops who had penetrated behind enemy lines that British military physicians gave it a name. They termed it Long Range Penetration Strain. A soldier who suffered from it became, in their words, "incapable of doing the simplest thing for himself and seemed to have the mind of a child." This deadly lethargy, moreover, was not confined to guerrilla troops. One year after the Chindit incident, similar symptoms cropped up en masse among the allied troops who invaded Normandy, and British researchers, after studying 5000 American and English combat casualties, concluded that this strange apathy was merely the final stage in a complex process of psychological collapse.

Mental deterioration often began with fatigue. This was followed by confusion and nervous irritability. The man became hypersensitive to the slightest stimuli around him. He would "hit the dirt" at the least provocation. He showed signs of bewilderment. He seemed unable to distinguish the sound of enemy fire from other, less threatening sounds. He became tense, anxious, and heatedly irascible. His comrades never knew when he would flail out in anger, even violence, in response to minor inconvenience.

Then the final stage of emotional exhaustion set in. The soldier seemed to lose the very will to live. He gave up the struggle to save himself, to guide himself rationally through the battle. He became, in the words of R. L. Swank, who headed the British investigation, "dull and listless . . . mentally and physically retarded, preoccupied." Even his face became dull and apathetic. The fight to adapt had ended in defeat. The stage of total withdrawal was reached.

That men behave irrationally, acting against their own clear interest, when thrown into conditions of high change and novelty is also borne out by studies of human behavior in times of fire, flood, earthquake and other crises. Even the most stable and "normal" people, unhurt physically, can be hurled into antiadaptive states. Often reduced to total confusion and mindlessness, they seem incapable of the most elementary rational decision-making.

Thus in a study of the responses to tornadoes in Texas, H. E. Moore writes that "the first reaction . . . may be one of dazed bewilderment, sometimes one of disbelief, or at least of refusal to accept the fact. This, it seems to us, is the essential explanation of the behavior of persons and groups in Waco when it was devastated in 1953 . . . On the personal level, it explains why a girl climbed into a music store through a broken display window, calmly purchased a record, and walked out again, even though the plate glass front of the building had blown out and articles were flying through the air inside the building."

A study of a tornado in Udall, Kansas, quotes a housewife as saying: "After it was over, my husband and I just got up and jumped out the window and ran. I don't know where we were running to but . . . I didn't care. I just wanted to run." The classic disaster photograph shows a mother holding a dead or wounded baby in her arms, her face blank and numb as though she could no longer comprehend the reality around her. Sometimes she sits rocking gently on her porch with a doll, instead of a baby, in her arms.

In disaster, therefore, exactly as in certain combat situations, individuals can be psychologically overwhelmed. Once again the source may be traced to a high level of environmental stimulation. The disaster victim finds himself suddenly caught in a situation in which familiar objects and relationships are transformed. Where once his house stood, there may be nothing more than smoking rubble. He may encounter a cabin floating on the flood tide or a rowboat sailing through the air. The environment is filled with change and novelty. And once again the response is marked by confusion, anxiety, irritability and withdrawal into apathy.

Culture shock, the profound disorientation suffered by the traveler who has plunged without adequate preparation into an alien culture, provides a third example of adaptive breakdown. Here we find none of the obvious elements of war or disaster. The scene may be totally peaceful and riskless. Yet the situation demands repeated adaptation to novel conditions. Culture shock, according to psychologist Sven Lundstedt, is a "form of personality maladjustment which is a reaction to a temporarily unsuccessful attempt to adjust to new surroundings and people."

The culture shocked person, like the soldier and disaster victim, is forced to grapple with unfamiliar and unpredictable events, relationships and objects. His habitual ways of accomplishing things—even simple tasks like placing a telephone call—are no longer appropriate. The strange society may itself be changing only very slowly, yet for him it is all new. Signs, sounds and other psychological cues rush past him before he can grasp their meaning. The entire experience takes on a surrealistic air. Every word, every action is shot through with uncertainty.

In this setting, fatigue arrives more quickly than usual. Along with it, the cross-cultural traveler often experiences what Lundstedt describes as "a subjective feeling of loss, and a sense of isolation and loneliness."

The unpredictability arising from novelty undermines his sense of reality. Thus he longs, as Professor Lundstedt puts it, "for an environment in which the gratification of important psychological and physical needs is predictable and less uncertain." He becomes "anxious, confused and often appears apathetic." In fact, Lundstedt concludes, "culture shock can be viewed as a response to stress by emotional and intellectual withdrawal."

It is hard to read these (and many other) accounts of behavior breakdown under a variety of stresses without becoming acutely aware of their similarities. While there are differences, to be sure, between a soldier in combat, a disaster victim, and a culturally dislocated traveler, all three face rapid change, high novelty, or both. All three are required to adapt rapidly and repeatedly to unpredictable stimuli. And there are striking parallels in the way all three respond to this overstimulation.

First, we find the same evidences of confusion, disorientation, or distortion of reality. Second, there are the same signs of fatigue, anxiety, tenseness, or extreme iritability. Third, in all cases there appears to be a point of no return—a point at which apathy and emotional withdrawal set in.

In short, the available evidence strongly suggests that overstimulation may lead to bizarre and antiadaptive behavior.

Bombardment of the Senses

We still know too little about this phenomenon to explain authoritatively why overstimulation seems to produce maladaptive behavior. Yet we pick up important clues if we recognize that overstimulation can occur on at least three different levels: the sensory, the cognitive and the decisional.[1]

The easiest to understand is the sensory level. Experiments in sensory deprivation, during

---

[1] A bit is the amount of information needed to make a decision between two equally likely alternatives. The number of bits needed increases by one as the number of such alternatives doubles.

which volunteers are cut off from normal stimulation of their senses, have shown that the absence of novel sensory stimuli can lead to bewilderment and impaired mental functioning. By the same token, the input of too much disorganized, patternless or chaotic sensory stimuli can have similar effects. It is for this reason that practitioners of political or religious brainwashing make use not only of sensory deprivation (solitary confinement, for example) but of sensory bombardment involving flashing lights, rapidly shifting patterns of color, chaotic sound effects—the whole arsenal of psychedelic kaleidoscopy.

The religious fervor and bizarre behavior of certain hippie cultists may arise not merely from drug abuse, but from group experimentation with both sensory deprivation and bombardment. The chanting of monotonous mantras, the attempt to focus the individual's attention on interior, bodily sensation to the exclusion of outside stimuli, are efforts to induce the weird and sometimes hallucinatory effects of understimulation.

At the other end of the scale, we note the glazed stares and numb, expressionless faces of youthful dancers at the great rock music auditoriums where light shows, split-screen movies, high decibel screams, shouts and moans, grotesque costumes and writhing, painted bodies create a sensory environment characterized by high input and extreme unpredictability and novelty.

An organism's ability to cope with sensory input is dependent upon its physiological structure. The nature of its sense organs and the speed with which impulses flow through its neural system set biological bounds on the quantity of sensory data it can accept. If we examine the speed of signal transmission within various organisms, we find that the lower the evolutionary level, the slower the movement. Thus, for example, in a sea urchin egg, lacking a nervous system as such, a signal moves along a membrane at a rate of about a centimeter an hour. Clearly, at such a rate, the organism can respond to only a very limited part of its environment. By the

time we move up the ladder to a jellyfish, which already has a primitive nervous system, the signal travels 36,000 times faster: ten centimeters per second. In a worm, the rate leaps to 100 cps. Among insects and crustaceans, neural pulses race along at 1000 cps. Among anthropoids the rate reaches 10,000 cps. Crude as these figures no doubt are, they help explain why man is unquestionably among the most adaptable of creatures.

Yet even in man, with a neural transmission rate of about 30,000 cps, the boundaries of the system are imposing. (Electrical signals in a computer, by contrast, travel billions of times faster.) The limitations of the sense organs and nervous system mean that many environmental events occur at rates too fast for us to follow, and we are reduced to sampling experience at best. When the signals reaching us are regular and repetitive, this sampling process can yield a fairly good mental representation of reality. But when it is highly disorganized, when it is novel and unpredictable, the accuracy of our imagery is necessarily reduced. Our image of reality is distorted. This may explain why, when we experience sensory overstimulation, we suffer confusion, a blurring of the line between illusion and reality.

Information Overload

If overstimulation at the sensory level increases the distortion with which we perceive reality, cognitive overstimulation interferes with our ability to "think." While some human responses to novelty are involuntary, others are preceded by conscious thought, and this depends upon our ability to absorb, manipulate, evaluate and retain information.

Rational behavior, in particular, depends upon a ceaseless flow of data from the environment. It depends upon the power of the individual to predict, with at least fair success, the outcome of his own actions. To do this, he must be able to predict how the environment will respond to his acts. Sanity, itself, thus hinges on man's ability to predict his immediate, personal future on the basis of information fed him by the environment.

When the individual is plunged into a fast and irregularly changing situation, or a novelty-loaded context, however, his predictive accuracy plummets. He can no longer make ·the reasonably correct assessments on which rational behavior is dependent.

To compensate for this, to bring his accuracy up to the normal level again, he must scoop up and process far more information than before. And he must do this at extremely high rates of speed. In short, the more rapidly changing and novel the environment, the more information the individual needs to process in order to make effective, rational decisions.

Yet just as there are limits on how much sensory input we can accept, there are in-built constraints on our ability to process information. In the words of psychologist George A. Miller of Rockefeller University, there are "severe limitations on the amount of information that we are able to receive, process, and remember." By classifying information, by abstracting and "coding" it in various ways, we manage to stretch these limits, yet ample evidence demonstrates that our capabilities are finite.

To discover these outer limits, psychologists and communications theorists have set about testing what they call the "channel capacity" of the human organism. For the purpose of these experiments, they regard man as a "channel." Information enters from the outside. It is processed. It exits in the form of actions based on decisions. The speed and accuracy of human information processing can be measured by comparing the speed of information input with the speed and accuracy of output.

Information has been defined technically and measured in terms of units called "bits."[2] By now, experiments have established rates for the

processing involved in a wide variety of tasks from reading, typing, and playing the piano to manipulating dials or doing mental arithmetic. And while researchers differ as to the exact figures, they strongly agree on two basic principles: first, that man has limited capacity; and second, that overloading the system leads to serious breakdown of performance.

Imagine, for example, an assembly line worker in a factory making childrens' blocks. His job is to press a button each time a red block passes in front of him on the conveyor belt. So long as the belt moves at a reasonable speed, he will have little difficulty. His performance will approach 100 percent accuracy. We know that if the pace is too slow, his mind will wander, and his performance will deteriorate. We also know that if the belt moves too fast, he will falter, miss, grow confused and uncoordinated. He is likely to become tense and irritable. He may even take a swat at the machine out of pure frustration. Ultimately, he will give up trying to keep pace.

Here the information demands are simple, but picture a more complex task. Now the blocks streaming down the line are of many different colors. His instructions are to press the button only when a certain color pattern appears—a yellow block, say, followed by two reds and a green. In this task, he must take in and process far more information before he can decide whether or not to hit the button. All other things being equal, he will have even greater difficulty keeping up as the pace of the line accelerates.

In a still more demanding task, we not only force the worker to process a lot of data before deciding *whether* to hit the button, but we then force him to decide *which* of several buttons to press. We can also vary the number of times each button must be pressed. Now his instructions might read: For color pattern yellow-red-red-green, hit button number two once, for pattern green-blue-yellow-green, hit button number six three times; and so forth. Such tasks require the worker to process a large amount of data in order to carry out his task. Speeding up

[2]The line between each of these is not completely clear, even to psychologists, but if we simply, in commonsense fashion, equate the sensory level with perceiving, the cognitive with thinking, and the decisional with deciding, we will not go too far astray.

the conveyor now will destroy his accuracy even more rapidly.

Experiments like these have been built up to dismaying degrees of complexity. Tests have involved flashing lights, musical tones, letters, symbols, spoken words, and a wide array of other stimuli. And subjects, asked to drum fingertips, speak phrases, solve puzzles, and perform an assortment of other tasks, have been reduced to blithering ineptitude.

The results unequivocally show that no matter what the task, there is a speed above which it cannot be performed—and not simply because of inadequate muscular dexterity. The top speed is often imposed by mental rather than muscular limitations. These experiments also reveal that the greater the number of alternative courses of action open to the subject, the longer it takes him to reach a decision and carry it out.

Clearly, these findings can help us understand certain forms of psychological upset. Managers plagued by demands for rapid, incessant and complex decisions; pupils deluged with facts and hit with repeated tests; housewives confronted with squalling children, jangling telephones, broken washing machines, the wail of rock and roll from the teenager's living room and the whine of the television set in the parlor —may well find their ability to think and act clearly impaired by the waves of information crashing into their senses. It is more than possible that some of the symptoms noted among battle-stressed soldiers, disaster victims, and culture shocked travelers are related to this kind of information overload.

One of the men who has pioneered in information studies, Dr. James G. Miller, director of the Mental Health Research Institute at the University of Michigan, states flatly that "Glutting a person with more information than he can process may . . . lead to disturbance." He suggests, in fact, that information overload may be related to various forms of mental illness.

One of the striking features of schizophrenia, for example, is "incorrect associative response." Ideas and words that ought to be linked in the subject's mind are not, and vice versa. The schizophrenic tends to think in arbitrary or highly personalized categories. Confronted with a set of blocks of various kinds—triangles, cubes, cones, etc.—the normal person is likely to categorize them in terms of geometric shape. The schizophrenic asked to classify them is just as likely to say "They are all soldiers" or "They all make me feel sad."

In the volume *Disorders of Communication*, Miller describes experiments using word association tests to compare normals and schizophrenics. Normal subjects were divided into two groups, and asked to associate various words with other words or concepts. One group worked at its own pace. The other worked under time pressure—i.e., under conditions of rapid information input. The time-pressed subjects came up with responses more like those of schizophrenics than of self-paced normals.

Similar experiments conducted by psychologists G. Usdansky and L. J. Chapman made possible a more refined analysis of the types of erros made by subjects working under forced-pace, high information-input rates. They, too, concluded that increasing the speed of response brought out a pattern of errors among normals that is peculiarly characteristic of schizophrenics.

"One might speculate," Miller suggests, ". . . that schizophrenia (by some as-yet-unknown process, perhaps a metabolic fault which increases neural 'noise') lowers the capacities of channels involved in cognitive information processing. Schizophrenics consequently . . . have difficulties in coping with information inputs at standard rates like the difficulties experienced by normals at rapid rates. As a result, schizophrenics make errors at standard rates like those made by normals under fast, forced-input rates."

In short, Miller argues, the breakdown of human performance under heavy information loads may be related to psychopathology in ways we have not yet begun to explore. Yet, even without understanding its potential impact, we are accelerating the generalized rate of change in society. We are forcing people to adapt to a new life pace, to confront novel situations and master them in ever shorter intervals. We are forcing them to choose among fast-multiplying options. We are, in other words, forcing them to process information at a far more rapid pace than was necessary in slowly-evolving societies. There can be little doubt that we are subjecting at least some of them to cognitive overstimulation. What consequences this may have for mental health in the techno-societies has yet to be determined.

Decision Stress

Whether we are submitting masses of men to information overload or not, we are affecting their behavior negatively by imposing on them still a third form of overstimulation—decision stress. Many individuals trapped in dull or slowly changing environments yearn to break out into new jobs or roles that require them to make faster and more complex decisions. But among the people of the future, the problem is reversed. "Decisions, decisions . . ." they mutter as they race anxiously from task to task. The reason they feel harried and upset is that transience, novelty and diversity pose contradictory demands and thus place them in an excruciating double bind.

The accelerative thrust and its psychological counterpart, transience, force us to quicken the tempo of private and public decision-making. New needs, novel emergencies and crises demand rapid response.

Yet the very newness of the circumstances brings about a revolutionary change in the nature of the decisions they are called upon to make. The rapid injection of novelty into the environment upsets the delicate balance of "programmed" and "non-programmed" decisions in our organizations and our private lives.

A programmed decision is one that is routine, repetitive and easy to make. The commuter stands at the edge of the platform as the 8:05 rattles to a stop. He climbs aboard, as he has done every day for months or years. Having long ago decided that the 8:05 is the most convenient run on the schedule, the actual decision

to board the train is programmed. It seems more like a reflex than a decision at all. The immediate criteria on which the decision is based are relatively simple and clear-cut, and because all the circumstances are familiar, he scarcely has to think about it. He is not required to process very much information. In this sense, programmed decisions are low in psychic cost.

Contrast this with the kind of decisions that same commuter thinks about on his way to the city. Should he take the new job Corporation X has just offered him? Should he buy a new house? Should he have an affair with his secretary? How can he get the Management Committee to accept his proposals about the new ad campaign? Such questions demand non-routine answers. They force him to make one-time or first-time decisions that will establish new habits and behavioral procedures. Many factors must be studied and weighed. A vast amount of information must be processed. These decisions are non-programmed. They are high in psychic cost.

For each of us, life is a blend of the two. If this blend is too high in programmed decisions, we are not challenged; we find life boring and stultifying. We search for ways, even unconsciously, to introduce novelty into our lives, thereby altering the decision "mix." But if this mix is too high in non-programmed decisions, if we are hit by so many novel situations that programming becomes impossible, life becomes painfully disorganized, exhausting and anxiety-filled. Pushed to its extreme, the end-point is psychosis.

"Rational behavior . . . ," writes organization theorist Bertram M. Gross, "always includes an intricate combination of routinization and creativity. Routine is essential . . . [because it] frees creative energies for dealing with the more baffling array of new problems for which routinization is an irrational approach."

When we are unable to program much of our lives, we suffer. "There is no more miserable person," wrote William James, "than one . . . for whom the lighting of every cigar, the drinking of every cup . . . the beginning of every bit of work, are subjects of deliberation." For unless we can extensively program our behavior, we waste tremendous amounts of information-processing capacity on trivia.

This is why we form habits. Watch a committee break for lunch and then return to the same room: almost invariably its members seek out the same seats they occupied earlier. Some anthropologists drag in the theory of "territorialtiy" to explain this behavior—the notion that man is forever trying to carve out for himself a sacrosanct "turf." A simpler explanation lies in the fact that programming conserves information-processing capacity. Choosing the same seat spares us the need to survey and evaluate other possibilities.

In a familiar context, we are able to handle many of our life problems with low-cost programmed decisions. Change and novelty boost the psychic price of decision-making. When we move to a new neighborhood, for example, we are forced to alter old relationships and establish new routines or habits. This cannot be done without first discarding thousands of formerly programmed decisions and making a whole series of costly new first-time, non-programmed decisions. In effect, we are asked to re-program ourselves.

Precisely the same is true of the unprepared visitor to an alien culture, and it is equally true of the man who, still in his own society, is rocketed into the future without advance warning. The arrival of the future in the form of novelty and change makes all his painfully pieced-together behavioral routines obsolete. He suddenly discovers to his horror that these old routines, rather than solving his problems, merely intensify them. New and as yet unprogrammable decisions are demanded. In short, novelty disturbs the decision mix, tipping the balance toward the most difficult, most costly form of decision-making.

It is true that some people can tolerate more novelty than others. The optimum mix is different for each of us. Yet the number and type of decisions demanded of us are not under our autonomous control. It is the society that basi-

cally determines the mix of decisions we must make and the pace at which we must make them. Today there is a hidden conflict in our lives between the pressures of acceleration and those of novelty. One forces us to make faster decisions while the other compels us to make the hardest, most time-consuming type of decisions.

The anxiety generated by this head-on collision is sharply intensified by expanding diversity. Incontrovertible evidence shows that increasing the number of choices open to an individual also increases the amount of information he needs to process if he is to deal with them. Laboratory tests on men and animals alike prove that the more the choices, the slower the reaction time.

It is the frontal collision of these three incompatible demands that is now producing a decision-making crisis in the techno-societies. Taken together these pressures justify the term "decisional overstimulation," and they help explain why masses of men in these societies already feel themselves harried, futile, incapable of working out their private futures. The conviction that the rat-race is too tough, that things are out of control, is the inevitable consequence of these clashing forces. For the uncontrolled acceleration of scientific, technological and social change subverts the power of the individual to make sensible, competent decisions about his own destiny.

Victims of Future Shock

When we combine the effects of decisional stress with sensory and cognitive overload, we produce several common forms of individual maladaptation. For example, one widespread response to high-speed change is outright denial. The Denier's strategy is to "block out" unwelcome reality. When the demand for decisions reaches crescendo, he flatly refuses to take in new information. Like the disaster victim whose face registers total disbelief, The Denier, too, cannot accept the evidence of his senses. Thus he concludes that things really are the same, and that all evidences of change are merely superficial. He finds comfort in such cliches as "young people were always rebellious" or "there's nothing new on the face of the earth," or "the more things change, the more they stay the same."

An unknowing victim of future shock, The Denier sets himself up for personal catastrophe. His strategy for coping increases the likelihood that when he finally is forced to adapt, his encounter with change will come in the form of a single massive life crisis, rather than a sequence of manageable problems.

A second strategy of the future shock victim is specialism. The Specialist doesn't block out *all* novel ideas or information. Instead, he energetically attempts to keep pace with change—but only in a specific narrow sector of life. Thus we witness the spectacle of the physician or financier who makes use of all the latest innovations in his profession, but remains rigidly closed to any suggestion for social, political, or economic innovation. The more universities undergo paroxysms of protest, the more ghettos go up in flames, the less he wants to know about them, and the more closely he narrows the slit through which he sees the world.

Superficially, he copes well. But he, too, is running the odds against himself. He may awake one morning to find his specialty obsolete or else transformed beyond recognition by events exploding outside his field of vision.

A third common response to future shock is obsessive reversion to previously successful adaptive routines that are now irrelevant and inappropriate. The Reversionist sticks to his previously programmed decisions and habits with dogmatic desperation. The more change threatens from without, the more meticulously he repeats past modes of action. His social outlook is regressive. Shocked by the arrival of the future, he offers hysterical support for the not-so-status quo, or he demands, in one masked form or another, a return to the glories of yesteryear.

The Barry Goldwaters and George Wallaces of the world appeal to his quivering gut through the politics of nostalgia. Police maintained order in the past; hence, to maintain order, we need only supply more police. Authoritarian treatment of children worked in the past; hence, the troubles of the present spring from permissiveness. The middle-aged, right-wing reversionist yearns for the simple, ordered society of the small town—the slow-paced social environment in which his old routines were appropriate. Instead of adapting to the new, he continues automatically to apply the old solutions, growing more and more divorced from reality as he does so.

If the older reversionist dreams of reinstating a small-town past, the youthful, left-wing reversionist dreams of reviving an even older social system. This accounts for some of the fascination with rural communes, the bucolic romanticism that fills the posters and poetry of the hippie and post-hippie subcultures, the deification of Che Guevara (identified with mountains and jungles, not with urban or post-urban environments), the exaggerated veneration of pre-technological societies and the exaggerated contempt for science and technology. For all their fiery demands for change, at least some sectors of the left share with the Wallacites and Goldwaterites a secret passion for the past.

Just as their Indian headbands, their Edwardian capes, their Deerslayer boots and gold-rimmed glasses mimic various eras of the past, so, too, their ideas. Turn-of-the-century terrorism and quaint Black Flag anarchy are suddenly back in vogue. The Rousseauian cult of the noble savage flourishes anew. Antique Marxist ideas, applicable at best to yesterday's industrialism, are hauled out as knee-jerk answers for the problems of tomorrow's super-industrialism. Reversionism masquerades as revolution.

Finally, we have the Super-Simplifier. With old heroes and institutions toppling, with strikes, riots, and demonstrations stabbing at his consciousness, he seeks a single neat equation that will explain all the complex novelties threatening to engulf him. Grasping erratically at this idea or that, he becomes a temporary true believer.

This helps account for the rampant intellectual faddism that already threatens to outpace the rate of turnover in fashion. McLuhan? Prophet of the electric age? Levi-Strauss? Wow! Marcuse? Now I see it all! The Maharishi of Whatchmacallit? Fantastic! Astrology? Insight of the ages!

The Super-Simplifier, groping desperately, invests every idea he comes across with universal relevance—often to the embarrassment of its author. Alas, no idea, not even mine or thine, is omni-insightful. But for the Super-Simplifier nothing less than total relevance suffices. Maximization of profits explains America. The Communist conspiracy explains race riots. Participatory democracy is the answer. Permissiveness (or Dr. Spock) are the root of all evil.

This search for a unitary solution at the intellectual level has its parallels in action. Thus the bewildered, anxious student, pressured by parents, uncertain of his draft status, nagged at by an educational system whose obsolescence is more strikingly revealed every day, forced to decide on a career, a set of values, and a worthwhile life style, searches wildly for a way to simplify his existence. By turning on to LSD, Methedrine or heroin, he performs an illegal act that has, at least, the virtue of consolidating his miseries. He trades a host of painful and seemingly insoluble troubles for one big problem, thus radically, if temporarily, simplifying existence.

The teen-age girl who cannot cope with the daily mounting tangle of stresses may choose another dramatic act of super-simplification: pregnancy. Like drug abuse, pregnancy may vastly complicate her life later, but it immediately plunges all her other problems into relative insignificance.

Violence, too, offers a "simple" way out of burgeoning complexity of choice and general overstimulation. For the older generation and the political establishment, police truncheons and military bayonets loom as attractive remedies, a way to end dissent once and for all. Black extremists and white vigilantes both employ violence to narrow their choices and clarify their lives. For those who lack an intelligent,

comprehensive program, who cannot cope with the novelties and complexities of blinding change, terrorism substitutes for thought. Terrorism may not topple regimes, but it removes doubts.

Most of us can quickly spot these patterns of behavior in others—even in ourselves—without, at the same time, understanding their causes. Yet information scientists will instantly recognize denial, specialization, reversion and super-simplification as classical techniques for coping with overload.

All of them dangerously evade the rich complexity of reality. They generate distorted images of reality. The more the individual denies, the more he specializes at the expense of wider interests, the more mechanically he reverts to past habits and policies, the more desperately he super-simplifies, the more inept his responses to the novelty and choices flooding into his life. The more he relies on these strategies, the more his behavior exhibits wild and erratic swings and general instability.

Every information scientist recognizes that some of these strategies may, indeed, be necessary in overload situations. Yet, unless the individual begins with a clear grasp of relevant reality, and unless he begins with cleanly defined values and priorities, his reliance on such techniques will only deepen his adaptive difficulties.

These preconditions, however, are increasingly difficult to meet. Thus the future shock victim who does employ these strategies experiences a deepening sense of confusion and uncertainty. Caught in the turbulent flow of change, called upon to make significant, rapid-fire life decisions, he feels not simply intellectual bewilderment, but disorientation at the level of personal values. As the pace of change quickens, this confusion is tinged with self-doubt, anxiety and fear. He grows tense, tires easily. He may fall ill. As the pressures relentlessly mount, tension shades into irritability, anger, and sometimes, senseless violence. Little events trigger enormous responses; large events bring inadequate responses.

Pavlov many years ago referred to this phenomenon as the "paradoxical phase" in the breakdown of the dogs on whom he conducted his conditioning experiments. Subsequent research has shown that humans, too, pass through this stage under the impact of overstimulation, and it may explain why riots sometimes occur even in the absence of serious provocation, why, as though for no reason, thousands of teenagers at a resort will suddenly go on the rampage, smashing windows, heaving rocks and bottles, wrecking cars. It may explain why pointless vandalism is a problem in all of the techno-societies, to the degree that an editorialist in the *Japan Times* reports in cracked, but passionate English: "We have never before seen anything like the extensive scope that these psychopathic acts are indulged in today."

And finally, the confusion and uncertainty wrought by transience, novelty and diversity may explain the profound apathy that desocializes millions, old and young alike. This is not the studied, temporary withdrawal of the sensible person who needs to unwind or slow down before coping anew with his problems. It is total surrender before the strain of decision-making in conditions of uncertainty and over-choice.

Affluence makes it possible, for the first time in history, for large numbers of people to make their withdrawal a full-time proposition. The family man who retreats into his evening with the help of a few martinis and allows televised fantasy to narcotize him, at least works during the day, performing a social function upon which others are dependent. His is a part-time withdrawal. But for some (not all) hippie dropouts, for many of the surfers and lotus-eaters, withdrawal is full-time and total. A check from an indulgent parent may be the only remaining link with the larger society.

On the beach at Matala, a tiny sun-drenched village in Crete, are forty or fifty caves occupied by runaway American troglodytes, young men and women who, for the most part, have given up any further effort to cope with the exploding high-speed complexities of life. Here decisions are few and time plentiful. Here the choices are narrowed. No problem of overstimulation. No need to comprehend or even to feel. A reporter visiting them in 1968 brought them news of the assassination of Robert F. Kennedy. Their response: silence. "No shock, no rage, no tears. Is this the new phenomenon? Running away from America and running away from emotion? I understand uninvolvement, disenchantment, even noncommitment. But where has all the feeling gone?"

The reporter might understand where all the feeling has gone if he understood the impact of overstimulation, the apathy of the Chindit guerrilla, the blank face of the disaster victim, the intellectual and emotional withdrawal of the culture shock victim. For these young people, and millions of others—the confused, the violent, and the apathetic—already evince the symptoms of future shock. They are its earliest victims.

The Future-Shocked Society

It is impossible to produce future shock in large numbers of individuals without affecting the rationality of the society as a whole. Today, according to Daniel P. Moynihan, the chief White House advisor on urban affairs, the United States "exhibits the qualities of an individual going through a nervous breakdown." For the cumulative impact of sensory, cognitive or decisional overstimulation, not to mention the physical effects of neural or endocrine overload, creates sickness in our midst.

This sickness is increasingly mirrored in our culture, our philosophy, our attitude toward reality. It is no accident that so many ordinary people refer to the world as a "madhouse" or that the theme of insanity has recently become a staple in literature, art, drama and film. Peter Weiss in his play *Marat/Sade* portrays a turbulent world as seen through the eyes of the inmates of the Charenton asylum. In movies like *Morgan*, life within a mental institution is depicted as superior to that in the outside world. In *Blow-Up*, the climax comes when the hero joins in a tennis game in which players hit a non-existent ball back and forth over the net. It is his symbolic acceptance of the unreal and irrational—recognition that he can no longer distinguish between illusion and reality. Millions of viewers identified with the hero in that moment.

The assertion that the world has "gone crazy," the graffiti slogan that "reality is a crutch," the interest in hallucinogenic drugs, the enthusiasm for astrology and the occult, the search for truth in sensation, ecstasy and "peak experience," the swing toward extreme subjectivism, the attacks on science, the snowballing belief that reason has failed man, reflect the everyday experience of masses of ordinary people who find they can no longer cope rationally with change.

Millions sense the pathology that pervades the air, but fail to understand its roots. These roots lie not in this or that political doctrine, still less in some mystical core of despair or isolation presumed to inhere in the "human condition." Nor do they lie in science, technology, or legitimate demands for social change. They are traceable, instead, to the uncontrolled, non-selective nature of our lunge into the future. They lie in our failure to direct, consciously and imaginatively, the advance toward super-industrialism.

Thus, despite its extraordinary achievements in art, science, intellectual, moral and political life, the United States is a nation in which tens of thousands of young people flee reality by opting for drug-induced lassitude; a nation in which millions of their parents retreat into video-induced stupor or alcoholic haze; a nation in which legions of elderly folk vegetate and die in loneliness; in which the flight from family and occupational responsibility has become an exodus; in which masses tame their raging anxieties with Miltown, or Librium, or Equanil, or a score of other tranquilizers and psychic pacifiers. Such a nation, whether it knows it or not, is suffering from future shock.

"I'm not going back to America," says Ronald Bierl, a young expatriate in Turkey. "If you can establish your own sanity, you don't have to worry about other people's sanity. And so many Americans are going stone insane." Multitudes share this unflattering view of American reality. Lest Europeans or Japanese or Russians rest smugly on their presumed sanity, however, it is well to ask whether similar symptoms are not already present in their midst as well. Are Americans unique in this respect, or are they simply suffering the initial brunt of an assault on the psyche that soon will stagger other nations as well?

Social rationality presupposes individual rationality, and this, in turn, depends not only on certain biological equipment, but on continuity, order and regularity in the environment. It is premised on some correlation between the pace and complexity of change and man's decisional capacities. By blindly stepping up the rate of change, the level of novelty, and the extent of choice, we are thoughtlessly tampering with these environmental preconditions of rationality. We are condemning countless millions to future shock.

Prelude to 2001: Explorations in Human Communication

"It is the thesis of this book that society can only be understood through a study of the messages and the communication facilities which belong to it; and that in the future development of these messages and communication facilities, messages between man and machines, between machine and man, and between machine and machine are destined to play an ever-increasing part [Wiener, 1950, p. 9]."

In the science fiction film _2001: A Space Odyssey_ and in the book based on that film (Clarke, 1968), one of the principal characters is a computer called HAL. HAL is quite a remarkable gadget. It directs and plots the course of an enormous vehicle traveling through deep space. It computes courses, speeds, and trajectories for satellite vehicles that leave and return to the mother ship. It monitors continuously the various subsystems of the space ship and displays the information it senses in a variety of forms. In anticipation of emergencies and equipment failures, it alerts the astronauts and suggests expedient courses of remedial action. It controls the physiological condition of astronauts who are in hibernation for the duration of the trip,

From Alphonse Chapanis, "Prelude to 2001: Explorations in Human Communication," 26 (November 1971), pp 949–61. Copyright 1971 by the American Psychological Association. Reprinted by permission.

as well as those who are in a normal physiological state and on duty. When the astronauts are bored, it plays chess with them and engages in other intellectual diversions upon request. Indeed, HAL even has some primitive human emotions and motivations, and it is those that eventually lead to a catastrophic end of the mission.

All these things that HAL did in the film are more fact than fiction, for computers today already do all the things enumerated or are at least capable of doing them. Computers guide space vehicles. They monitor complex assemblages of men and machines and warn of emergencies that are beyond human capacities to sense and comprehend. Computers keep watch over the physiological states of astronauts as well as comatose patients in intensive-care units. Computers play tolerably good games of chess and poker, and never lose in games of tick-tack-toe and matching pennies. Finally, most people who work with computers are convinced that they have personalities with some of the same perverse traits one can find in emotionally unstable persons.

What is unusual about HAL is the way in which it interacts with its human counterparts. The astronauts can and do insert data into the computer through pushbuttons and similar manual devices, much as we do today. That primitive kind of interaction, however, is the exception rather than the rule. HAL more typically interacts with the astronauts in humanlike terms. For the most part, HAL and the astronauts converse orally in idiomatic English, and what contributes to the eventual destruction of most of the crew is that HAL can even read lips.

That, you say, is pure fiction, and indeed it is—today. Still, some very able minds do not see it as unattainable fiction, but as a prophecy of things to come. Even if you do not believe that such things are possible, I ask you to go along with the fiction for a little while.

What Do We Need to Know to Build a Computer Like HAL?

The question I would like you to keep constantly before you while you read this article is the following: What do we need to know to build a computer that would communicate like HAL? Many of you will probably think immediately that this is a matter of engineering technology and not a psychological question at all. I do not agree. Engineers are very clever people, and it is axiomatic in engineering that if you can describe any phenomenon in precise quantitative terms, an engineer can build a machine to simulate it. Think about that for a moment. If we could specify in precise, quantitative terms exactly how we hear and recognize speech, engineers would have no difficulty in building a speech-recognition machine to do what we do. As psychologists, we believe that all human behavior is lawful, orderly, and measurable. But it is our inability to describe our behavior fully in exact mathematical terms that is the chief obstacle standing in the way of our attempts to design conversational computers. So, you see, my question really is a psychological one. If we *really* knew how people communicate, we would be able to build a computer like HAL.

Purpose of My Talk

Communication between computer and man is the focus of research efforts in my laboratory at the present time. I am happy to say that I think we have been able to make some significant inroads into this virtually unexplored area. Still, I am not going to give you many results. My purpose is rather to pose some questions and, in so doing, to show you how questions about an important practical problem can at the same time be fundamental ones about human behavior. In a more general way, the reason I would like you to consider my question about what we need to know to build a computer like HAL is that it provides us with a convenient vantage point, a hilltop, from which to see how some of us look at life, behavior, and the world in which both occur. I want to introduce you to an area of applied psychology that some of you may recognize only by name. I would like to try to convince you that problems in this area of applied psychology are at least as stimulating as, and often much more difficult than, those in basic areas of psychology. Finally, I would like to show you that trying to solve a practical problem can lead you to ask exciting basic questions, questions that might not otherwise be asked.

Philosophical Stance

The history of man is littered with labels that have been attached to various stages of it. You surely recognize the age of enlightenment, the age of reason, the golden age, and the roaring twenties. The years in which we find ourselves at present will in some future time, I suppose, be called the age of relevance. All of a sudden, psychologists are raising serious questions and entertaining nagging doubts about the relevance of their science. As an engineering psychologist, I do not have these doubts, because, you see, we have always been relevant. To be sure, you might not be excited by the things we have been relevant about, but we have been relevant.

Although I have just identified myself as an engineering psychologist, I also answer to the name of human factors engineer or ergonomist, depending on where I am and to whom I am talking. These contemporary labels are, however, not quite as descriptive of my philosophical position as a considerably older title that has now, unfortunately, been gradually dropping out of use. There was a time, you see, when I called myself an experimental psychologist, albeit a special sort of experimental psychologist, an *applied* experimental psychologist. Indeed, my first book written with Garner and Morgan (Chapanis, Garner, & Morgan, 1949) over 20 years ago coined the term applied experimental psychology.

As an applied experimental psychologist, or, if you will, as an engineering psychologist, I have little patience with most so-called theoretical or basic experimental psychology, a substantial amount of which I find trivial, turgid, and an appalling misuse of scarce and precious resources.[1] I say this not because I am opposed to basic research per se, but rather because I am completely unimpressed by certain kinds of basic research. You see, it is my firm belief that the best basic work in psychology starts not with psychological theory, but with attempts to solve questions posed by the world around us. The history of psychology is full of examples: reaction-time studies started with a practical problem in astronomy; the field of mental testing started with a problem put to a French elementary school teacher; the field of speech communication and its measurement started from some problems raised and first attacked by telephone engineers; information theory started from attempts to understand complex switching networks; and some of the best work in color vision has been done to construct a usable system of specifying colors for engineering, business, and industry.

So one of my purposes in writing about communication between computers and people is to try to convey to you some of the challenge and the excitement of starting with a practical problem and attacking it with all the intellectual skills you can bring to bear upon it. I mean to imply by that statement a much broader view of the science of psychology than is currently

taught in many graduate schools. Basic and theoretically oriented experimental psychologists typically spend a great deal of time playing intellectual games, called experiments, in their laboratories. Because laboratory experiments today are often elegantly formulated, intricately designed, and meticulously executed, it is easy to assume that they are thereby useful and powerful. This does not follow. In a recent methodological paper (Chapanis, 1967), I have called attention to the many technical, statistical, and philosophical difficulties one encounters when he tries to extrapolate from laboratory research to the solution of practical problems. The applied experimental psychologist, on the other hand, is not bound by an undeviating dedication to laboratory experimentation. He has in his repertoire a great many techniques of investigation, of which laboratory experimentation is only one. The object of his game, you see, is not to be elegant, but to be right.

Now that I have stated my biases and my reasons for writing this article, I suspect that I have either delighted or antagonized you. I doubt that you are neutral. Whatever the state of your affect at the moment, I hope that at the very least I have been able to capture your attention. If I have done so, perhaps I will be able to show you how some of us in psychology try to be relevant.

The starting point for an engineering psychologist is not a deduction from someone's theory or a self-generated hypothesis, but a real-world question, a question such as people asked some 10 years ago: What do we need to know to put men on the surface of the moon? or the question I am asking today: What do we need to know to build a computer that would communicate like HAL?

Communication as a Field of Psychological Inquiry

Having framed a question, the engineering psychologist next usually wants to know, Is it an important question? One thing that is characteristically different about our outlook on life as

[1] A point of view shared even by some basic experimental psychologists (see, e.g., Tulving & Madigan, 1970).

compared with that of the typical experimentalist is that we want our answers to make a practical difference. It is not enough that our results be statistically significant. We want them to be practically significant as well. Basic research scientists are fond of pointing out the difficulties of making judgments about the importance of any particular research question or any area of research. Although I certainly agree about the difficulty of making such judgments, I do not admit that they are impossible. As a practical matter, the resources available for research in this country, and the time and talent that can be dedicated to this kind of activity, are not sufficient for us to undertake research on anything and everything with equal commitment or justification. Like it or not, the research man himself, is forced to make value judgments about the comparative importance of problems and programs. We recognize implicitly that we should not fritter away our time on problems that do not or will not make much difference. Life is too full of big things that need doing for us to waste our time in that way.

How important is communication as a subject for psychological study? Not very, if we were to

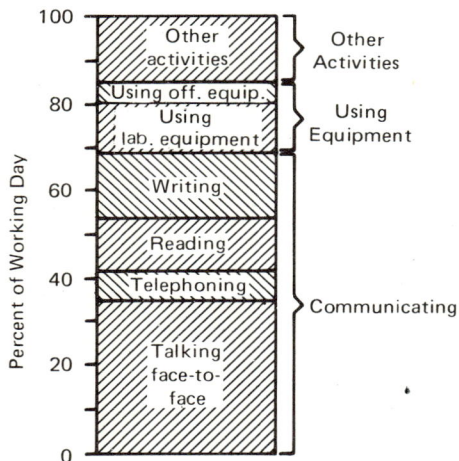

Fig. 1. Proportion of the working day spent in various activities by clerks, secretaries, technicians, professional people, and supervisory personnel. (E. T. Klemmer, personal communication, March 20, 1970.)

judge from the amount of work that has been devoted to it by psychologists. After all, the word started to appear regularly in the index to *Psychological Abstracts* only with Volume 16 (1942). Even then, entries under the heading of *communication* were sparse until Volume 23 of the *Abstracts* appeared in 1949.

The situation has changed since that time, to be sure. The semiannual index of the *Abstracts* for the first half of 1970 contains 171 entries under the word communication. This means that communication has finally nosed out dissonance, eyelid conditioning, galvanic skin response, paired-associates learning, and parapsychology. Still, it is by no means as popular a topic as conditioning, rat, and reinforcement. Indeed, there are well over 1,000 entries under *rat* in that index. To keep things in their proper perspective, too, one should bear in mind that the 171 communication entries are only 1.8% of the total of 9,485 items abstracted during the period I am considering.

A substantial fraction of the current and recent literature one finds under the heading of communication is concerned with what has come to be called communication theory or information theory. That literature is essentially useless for our purposes. I have yet to find a single instance in which psychological research on communication theory has contributed to the solution of any practical psychological problem. For one thing, the bits, bytes, or chunks of communication theory are like mouthfuls of sawdust. They are as mindless as they are tasteless. Communication theory is concerned only with the randomness or, conversely, with the statistical organization of messages. It ignores completely their sense or content. The kinds of communication we are concerned with when we talk about men and computers are meaningful communications.

The impressions I have tried to convey about the relative importance of communication as a psychological process are supported by what one finds in contemporary textbooks of psychology: A survey of some of the most popular books in the field reveals that communication has been, and still is, a topic of some minor interest to psychologists.

An Activity Analysis of a Work Day

Is this as it should be? In worrying about communication, are we indeed concerned with a kind of behavior that occurs only infrequently in life? Not at all. Klemmer[2] and his associates at the Bell Telephone Laboratories recently completed a careful activity analysis of how clerks, secretaries, technicians, professional people, and supervisory personnel spend their time. Observations were made on over 3,000 persons at carefully chosen intervals throughout the work day. Some of Klemmer's findings are summarized in Figure 1. On the average, the people in Klemmer's study spent over two-thirds of their time in some form of communication.

However surprising these figures may be, they are almost certainly not atypical. Other smaller studies by Burns (1954) on four managers in a single manufacturing company, Hinrichs (1964) on chemists and chemical engineers, and Stewart (1967) on 160 managers in several British companies all agree in showing that technical and supervisory personnel spend considerably more than half their time in some form of communication activity.

Communications in Our Society

If we look at communications in a slightly different way, it is clear that efficient networks of communication are as vital to a modern society as the nervous system is to a living body. Even a partial breakdown of communications, such as occurs during a newspaper or telephone strike, can cripple a society as effectively as a crushed nerve can cripple a man. Wars have been lost and empires destroyed by poor communications. Indeed, communication problems of one kind or another seem to be at the root of what many of us see as the disintegration of our contemporary way of life. Therein lies a kind of paradox, for communications are so much a part of

everyday living that it is easy for us to forget how pervasive and extensive they really are.

Take, for example, postal communications. No official estimates are available on the total amount of work done by the United States Post Office Department prior to 1847, but in that year the service handled some 124 million pieces of mail. That was only a trickle. In the following century the volume of mail increased over 100 times (see Figure 2). It is expected to reach 84 billion pieces this year and to increase another 50% by the end of the decade. When the data are converted to pieces of mail handled per person, the rate of growth is no less impressive.

Postal communications are, of course, concerned primarily with the transmission of written, printed, or hard-copy messages. Telephonic communications, by contrast, are almost exclusively concerned with the transmission of oral messages. Despite this important difference between them, certain statistics for the two kinds

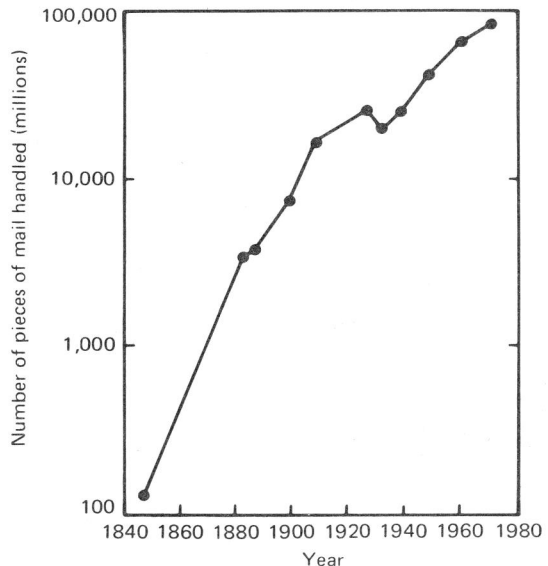

Fig. 2. Selected data on the yearly volume of mail handled by the United States Post Office Department from 1847 to the present. (Sources: United States Department of Commerce, 1960, 1970.)

[2] E. T. Klemmer, personal communication, March 20, 1970.

of communication parallel one another very closely. From the time of the introduction of commercial telephones in 1884, the yearly volume of telephone conversations in the United States has grown to a total that is about as far beyond our ordinary comprehension as is the national debt. In Figure 3, I have plotted the average number of telephone calls per day made in the United States from 1880 to 1969. For comparison, I have plotted population figures for the United States on the same graph. Especially dramatic is the way in which the divergence between the slopes of the two curves is increasing decade by decade.

On the Flood of Written Communications

I could now turn to still another kind of communication and tell you about the total number of different printed pieces of writing available

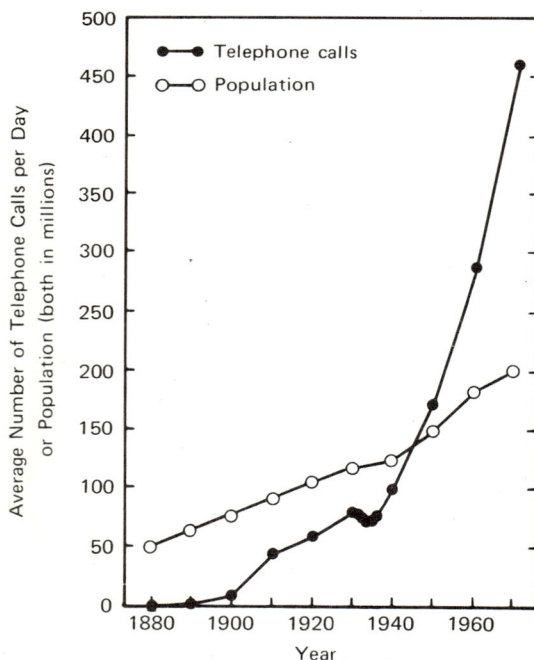

Fig. 3. Selected data on the average daily number of telephone calls made in the United States from 1880 to the present and population figures for the same period. (Sources: United States Department of Commerce, 1960, 1970.)

to an avid reader today. Since Licklider (1966) among others has already described the situation dramatically and since I myself have written about this elsewhere (Chapanis, 1965), let me make just one observation about the volume of literature in my own highly specialized subfield of psychology. A compulsive, well-versed engineering psychologist would have to read, I estimate, somewhere on the order of 30–40 articles, books, theses, and technical reports every day of the year merely to keep abreast of the current literature, much less catch up with things that have been published in the past. This is a communication problem of staggering proportions. And the worst is yet to come!

Communication and Computers

In writing about these aspects of communication, perhaps I have been able to convey to you my feeling that communication is a central problem in our society and that it will continue to be so for the indefinite future. Never in the history of society has communication been so abundant, so freely available, and so much used. Yet on all sides we hear that the major faults of society can be traced to insufficient communication. I submit that the reverse may be true. We have too much communication; that is, we have far more communication that it is possible for mortal man to assimilate by himself. In coping with these problems of communication we shall need, among other things, to make use of the enormous information-handling capacities of modern computers. I see no other rational alternative. The ways in which computers are harnessed for our use is what I am concerned with today.

On Computers and People

One of the most dramatic and impressive developments in the technology of American society during the past 20 years has been the growth in the number of computers and in the uses to which they have been put. In fact, it would probably be more economical to list those areas in which computers have not been applied than it would be to list those in which they are being applied. So far, government agencies, business and industrial organizations, and large scientific laboratories have been the chief beneficiaries of these advances. Most of us still have little direct contact with computers. Nonetheless, they already affect our lives in varied and often unexpected ways. Not only do computers prepare our utility bills, credit card bills, and bank statements, but they also control our traffic, assist us in making travel and theater reservations, and help diagnose our bodily ills.

Although most computers still require an intermediary between the ultimate user and the computer, the advent of time sharing and other interactive computer systems is almost certain to produce a radical change in current practices. The physician concerned with proper drug dosages and side effects, the student needing help on some math homework, the young couple trying to decide how to spend an infrequent night on the town, and the householder ordering merchandise from a large mail order house, all may soon rely for help on a computer and do so directly through their own terminals.

Even though modern computers admittedly have many limitations, the last two decades have already seen a fantastic increase in the number of computer users. Computer users today are, however, different from those who have been the principal companions to computers during their childhood and adolescence. These new users are not computer programmers, nor are they interested in computer technology per se. This new breed of users sees the computer as a tool, a terribly expensive and complicated tool, to be sure, but a tool nonetheless. They are interested primarily in what the computer can do for them, and not in how the computer does it. The typical user today is no more interested in understanding or getting into the guts of a modern computer than he is in tearing down the engine of his high-powered automobile. He wants both machines to do what he asks them to do, when he asks them to do it, in the way he wants the job done. Trying to find out how best to meet these human demands is at the

heart of the question about how we could build a computer like our fictitious HAL.

On the Nature of Man-Computer Interactions

The interactions between man and modern computers may, in a manner of speaking, be thought of as conversations. They are characterized by commands, statements, questions, answers to questions, and sundry other messages that go from man to computer and vice versa. These conversations are all carried out in one of several different foreign languages called programming languages. This means that the computer user has to learn a foreign language with all of the difficulties associated with that learning task. To be sure, programming languages are continually being improved in attempts to develop those that are most convenient for the user and most efficient for the computer. At the present time, programming languages compromise between the requirements of man and machine, and even computer experts admit freely that it is the user who has to adapt to the computer rather than vice versa.

For all practical purposes, these interactions are all written or, to be more precise, typewritten. Although significant attempts are being made to broaden the channels of communication between man and computer, the fact remains that the bulk of the messages that go from man to computer, or vice versa, are printed messages produced by some sort of a keyboard device. When messages are not printed, they are often painted onto television-like screens, but however you describe them, the channels of communication between man and computer are, at present, highly limited.

It is also important to recognize that for all the successes we have had with computers, we can probably find equally impressive and expensive failures. No one likes to talk about failures, and there is no incentive in writing them up for posterity to see in print. Still, it is not hard to find examples of computer systems and applications that have scarcely survived their conceptions. Very often these failures are not due to any defect in the mechanical or electrical features of the machine itself, but are instead due to a failure to match the computer to the needs of the people who need and want to use it. However apt it may be to say that the interaction between man and computer is a conversation, we have in all fairness to add that most of these conversations are stilted, esoteric, and frustrating. Perhaps even more important, communication with computers requires thought patterns and processes that are, at best, unfamiliar for most people and, at worst, unnatural.

Human Communication as the Starting Point

If we are to know how to build computers so that they can converse with their human users in efficient, human-like terms, we need to know first how people naturally communicate with each other. When we can describe how people communicate with each other most effectively, we will then be able to formulate general principles that can be used in the design of truly conversational computers for the future.

Let me tell you two reasons why I see the problem this way. The first has to do with a fanciful way I think about computers. In my mind's eye, I sometimes think of a computer as a huge, compliant, and versatile slave from another planet. The slave has arrived and is here waiting to serve me. Unfortunately, his whole life, from birth to adulthood, was spent alone on a space ship. As a result, this poor chap has never had the experience of communicating with earth people and, indeed, he does not even know how one goes about the business of communicating. It is my job to teach this underprivileged fellow the language of conversation. But, even more important than the mere language itself, I have to teach him the rules of conversation. And there is the rub: Before I can teach him how to communicate, I have to understand how I myself carry on conversations with my fellow man. I have to be able to describe the rules, the essence of human communication.

My second reason for saying that we need to know first how people communicate is a more realistic one. You know, of course, that no one teaches computers anything. Computers are just pieces of hardware, designed, built, and programmed by people. Human communication is often characterized as having intent, or intention. Messages from computers have no intent. Whatever intent is there is the intent of the man who built and programmed the computer. So, if we want to have truly conversational computers, we have to be sure that the people who design, build, and program these computers know and understand the rules of human communication. This is entirely a psychological problem. As psychologists we have to be able to describe human communication in precise terms and convey the rules of human communication to other people—the people who are ultimately responsible for the computers with which we will interact. Indeed, let me put that last statement even more strongly. Unless we psychologists tell engineers and technicians how to design computers, they will go about the job as they have in the past, using their own intuitions, hunches, and guesses. If that happens, and if we later grumble because computers are badly designed for human needs, we should remember that we have only ourselves to blame.

On the Value of Interactive Communication Systems

Why do I place so much emphasis on computers that will converse in human-like ways? Or, more generally, is it really important to have communication systems that respond to us in our terms? I think so, and there is some evidence to support my opinion. Kinkade and his colleagues recently investigated a number of variables that affect the human use of an information clearinghouse (Kinkade, Bedarf, & Van Cott, 1967; Kinkade & Bedarf, 1967). For their studies, they set up a specialized information retrieval system in cooperation with the Federation of American Societies for Experimental Biology. In one study, the subjects were 50 biological scientists working in universities in the Washington, D.C., area; 46 of the same scientists served as subjects for a second study.

The procedure was straightforward enough. Scientists with questions were invited to telephone their requests to a central office where the requests were recorded. Answers were returned to the initiators of the request at a later time. In one experiment, requests were received either by a biologically trained scientist or a tape recorder. Requests were tape-recorded in all instances, but the presence of the biologically trained receptionist in half the trials provided human feedback and interaction with the requester. The users of the system were free to choose either the human or the machine receptionist, and they knew precisely when each would be on the channel. . . . Users of this information retrieval system more often preferred to interact with a human rather than an impersonal machine.

In another study, scientists had the option of telephoning their requests to a scientifically trained receptionist or to an intelligent, but scientifically unsophisticated receptionist. Both receptionists provided human interaction and feedback, but the scientifically trained one could, of course, interact more meaningfully with the originator of the request. The results of this study, conducted over a period of 30 days, yielded curves something like those above with the scientifically trained receptionist receiving the greater number of calls.

There were some exceptions to these general findings. Some scientist users deliberately chose to communicate with what you might regard as the less desirable kind of receptionist. The data from these exceptions are, in some ways, as interesting and as informative as the data from those who were in the majority.

Users had to work harder when they placed their requests with the machine or with the less sophisticated receptionist. Requests had to be more precise, and the requesters had to spend more time organizing their questions before they reached for the telephone. Relatively simple, structured requests—such as a request for a specific document—were placed about equally with the untrained and trained receptionists. In both studies, scientist users preferred scientifically trained receptionists for more complex queries, for bibliographic searches, and for requests that were less well structured. Indeed, for these more complex kinds of requests, users made conscious efforts to telephone into the more knowledgeable receptionist.

To conclude, then, there is some evidence that human, or human-like, interaction in information retrieval systems is desirable. As is true of most things, that simple statement does not tell the whole story. People prefer to communicate with people, or people-like systems, when the information to be communicated is complex or unstructured. Moreover, the communications themselves take on different forms depending on the purpose of the communication. This, I think, leads us naturally into my next question.

Why Do People Communicate?

Some of the most basic questions we might ask about human communication are: Why do people communicate? and What function does communication serve? Why? is such a fundamental question that you might suppose people would have spent a great deal of time searching out answers to it. Oddly enough, that is not the case at all. To be sure, most people who write about communication have some general things to say about why we communicate: such as, to persuade or to convey information. What I have in mind, however, is something much more detailed and precise. What I am looking for is a kind of taxonomy of communication much like the one that Miller (1969) tried to provide us for problem solving.

A precise statement of the *why* of human communication has not only great significance for the understanding of human behavior itself, but relevance to the design of computers as well. Briefly, communication serves different human purposes, and to serve these several purposes, the very nature of communication takes on different forms. We had a glimpse of this in the results of the Kinkade studies to which I have just referred. I would like now to amplify that theme. In so doing, we shall see, I think, that communication for some purposes is easily served by interactive computers; other purposes are not so easily adapted to intelligent machines.

Human conversations and communications run the gamut from the sublime to the ridiculous, from the profound to the silly, from the formal to the intimate. In the most general sense, I suppose one could say that we engage in communication to impress, cajole, threaten, influence, inform, shape, deceive, conceal, alert, warn, question, query, explain, demonstrate, argue, and perhaps a few hundred other things as well. As far as I know, no one has ever made a comprehensive catalog or a sensible grouping of all the reasons why we communicate with our fellow man. Most of the purposes implied in the verbs I have listed above suggest an interpersonal relationship between two particular people, one of whom is trying to impress, cajole, threaten, influence, etc., the other through his communications. The very large, impersonal purpose of communication—and the primary general purpose for which computers are being designed—is the transmission of factual information. In confining our attention to this more circumscribed purpose we can exclude things like gossip, lovers' quarrels, family conversations, psychiatric interviews, and what are generally referred to these days as "meaningful dialogues."

Communications whose sole purpose is the transmission of factual information still include a very large group of functions that have never been systematically cataloged, described, or investigated. Let me talk about a couple of such functions to illustrate the kind of thing I have in mind.

The Communication of Specific Facts

Perhaps the most obvious function served by factual communication is the transmission of very specific information in response to simple inquiries. In some cases, you may not only phrase the inquiry, but you may also find your own answer. You do this when you consult a timetable to find out about plane schedules from one city to another, when you consult a newspaper to find the feature times of a movie you want to go to after dinner, or when you thumb through a dictionary for the definition of a word.

In other cases, you may phrase the inquiry but obtain the answer from another communicator or a machine. This is what happens when you consult the central directory service for a telephone number, when you call your broker for the latest quotation on your favorite growth stock, or when you telephone a machine to find out the exact time of day.

Who? When? Where? How long? How many? are some of the forms that simple inquiry may take. The objects of these inquiries may be any of the thousand of entities with which we come in contact during our daily lives or about which we need to know. They include such things as stock numbers, model numbers, stock quotations, selling prices, departure times, transit times, arrival times, route numbers, flight numbers, names, addresses, distances, sizes, and weights.

Although many inquiries and communications require highly sophisticated communicators and are technical in content, they are still classifiable as simple communications. Examples are the following: What is the product-moment coefficient of correlation between these two sets of numbers? What is the chemical formula for chlorpromazine? What is the simplest diode transistor logic circuit for representing "Not (A and B and C)"? Understanding these questions requires a considerable amount of technical sophistication. Nonetheless, I still call them simple inquiries. To the person who understands each question, there is a simple, direct, and unequivocal answer. In response to the first question, one has merely to insert the numbers into the appropriate formula and do the computations correctly. In the case of the latter two questions, one has merely to consult the appropriate books, documents, or files, or, perhaps, the memory of a sufficiently knowledgeable human communicator.

Since speed is one important requirement of this kind of communication, it is probably better served by the auditory rather than the visual channel. Spoken requests are easier to make than written, printed, or typewritten requests. Similarly, spoken replies are usually quicker to make and easier to assimilate unless the reply is so complex that it might exceed the immediate memory span of the listener. A time of arrival, flight number, or route number is probably best conveyed through the auditory channel. Even a coefficient of correlation is probably best communicated that way. On the other hand, if the reply is a 15-digit stock number or a circuit diagram, the reply may be better communicated in some other way.

Computers can generally do a superb job at this kind of communication because they can search rapidly through enormous files of data for precisely the information that is desired. Further, communications of this kind usually involve no hidden assumptions, ambiguities, or judgments to complicate the reply.

Free Browsing

Free browsing is, in a manner of speaking, at the other end of the continuum from simple inquiry and the communication of simple facts, for in browsing you are generally not looking for anything in particular. When you pick up the morning newspaper and scan the headlines, you are usually searching for things that satisfy an exceedingly vague criterion: The items must pique your curiosity, stir your imagination, or otherwise excite your interest. Some articles may be read thoroughly, some skimmed lightly, and others passed over entirely. The particular set of items that falls into each of these categories will differ for each reader according to his profession, his level of education, his avocations, and his idiosyncratic interest patterns.

For all its indefiniteness, browsing is probably an extremely important form of intellectual activity. You browse through the new book offerings in a bookstore or at professional meetings to find out what is new in your field. You browse through the titles of papers in professional journals to get ideas for new research projects. You browse through advertisements to get ideas about the latest in fashions, automobiles, and houses. You browse through exhibits of garden equipment, boats, camping equipment, and machine tools for much the same reason. Although no one appears to have made any attempt to measure the amount of time that is consumed by browsing, I suspect that it is a highly productive source of new ideas and of catching up with the world.

The psychological requirements for communications that can be used in effective browsing are quite different from those that are used for the communication of simple facts. For one thing, the material to be scanned has to be grouped in some sort of organizational scheme. Although any one person's browsing is a free-ranging activity, it is bounded. Some people never look at the business and financial pages of a newspaper, others never look at the sports section, while still others have no interest in the women's section. Neither physician nor physicist has enough time to browse through all the medical and physical journals available to him. So free browsing is both free ranging and selective. Other characteristics undoubtedly occur to you.

As far as I can tell, there has been almost no psychological research on free browsing. The problems here are sufficiently numerous to support at least a dozen doctoral theses. For example, we seem to do most of our free browsing visually, but I know of no studies to show this sensory channel to be either better or worse than the auditory channel. Suppose one were to use the auditory channel for free browsing, how could material be best presented? How should material for visual free browsing be most effectively organized? Are the free-browsing habits of scientists different from those of lawyers, businessmen, government officials, and other citizens? What are the constellations of interest patterns that characterize these various groups of individuals, and how can browsing material be selected to make them match those interest patterns? How could a computer like HAL best assist us in free browsing? Other questions I leave to you.

Other Functions of Communication

I do not have time to enumerate all the other functions served by communication, nor, indeed, am I entirely sure how many other functions there are. Let me merely mention a couple of others.

Directed browsing is considerably more restricted than free browsing. Directed browsing is what a scientist does when he compiles a bibliography or what a patent attorney does when he searches patent files. There is browsing, to be sure, but the browsing has a much more definite goal.

Briefing and status reporting are important functions of communication in such things as weather reporting, reviewing the state of the economy, monitoring patients in hospitals, and planning military campaigns. Briefing and status reporting are, in a sense, much more complicated than any of the functions I have enumerated above because in presenting a report on the status of the weather, business, a patient in an intensive-care unit, or a battle, there always has to be some selection and condensation of data. Insuring that the condensation does not at the same time bias or distort the status report is something that not even psychologists know how to do at the present time. How then are we to instruct HAL to do this kind of communicating?

On Channels of Communication

Repeatedly throughout what I have said so far, I have had occasion to refer to channels of communication. This is a general area in which our own studies at Johns Hopkins have been primarily concentrated. To be sure, people were studying information transmission through various media long before the advent of the computer. For example, questions that educators raised about effective teaching methods have stimulated over the years a very large number of experiments comparing aural and visual forms of presentation. Almost without exception, all this earlier work has treated the human subject as a passive recipient of information. None of it has been concerned with truly interactive communication of the kind that characterizes human conversation or man-computer communication such as our fictitious astronauts engaged in with HAL.

Let's start with fundamentals and ask about how many different kinds of communication skills are common and widespread enough to be serious candidates for man-computer communication. The list is surprisingly short. Almost everyone can speak and understand one of the natural languages—perhaps not correctly, but fluently. In addition, most people these days seem to know how to write, at least in some rudimentary way. Many people know how to type, and those that do not know how to type can almost intuitively peck out acceptably comprehensible messages. But there the list ends.

The aim of our research so far has been to describe what happens when people communicate naturally through each of these several channels. Briefly, our subjects are asked to solve complex problems by communicating with one

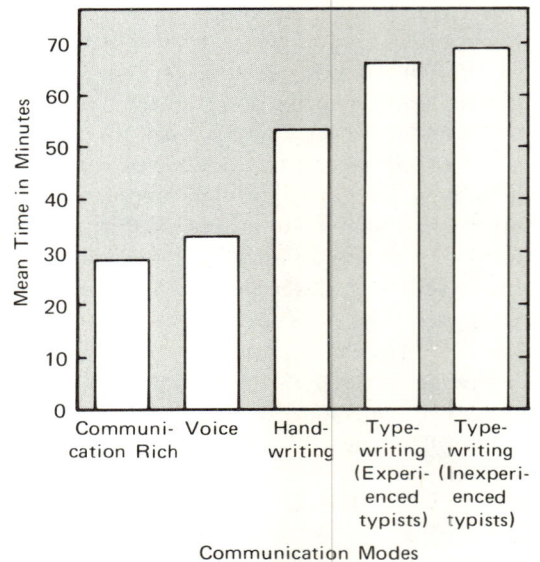

Fig. 4. Average times required by teams of subjects to solve complex problems using various modes of communication.

another. As you might expect from my professional orientation, our problems are real problems; that is, they are problems of the kind that already have been, or could be, programmed into computers. Our communication channels, or "modes" as we have been calling them, do not simulate any particular system but rather model computer systems that are, in a certain sense, ideal ones.

As so often happens with research, after you see the data, the findings seem obvious. We have to force ourselves to recall the predictions that we and other people made before our experiments to recapture the feelings of surprise we experienced as our summary tables and graphs took shape.

Figure 4 gives some results from one of our experiments. It shows the times required to solve our problems in four different modes of communication. In the typewriting mode, subjects communicated through special slaved typewriters. Whatever one subject wrote on one machine appeared simultaneously on his partner's in an adjoining room. In the handwriting mode, subjects wrote messages back and forth to one another. In the voice mode, subjects were able to talk freely but were not able to see each other. In the communication-rich mode, subjects sat side-by-side and were able to converse naturally using voice, gestures, and handwriting.

I call to your attention first the range of the differences represented in these data. In the typewriting mode, subjects took, on the average, about two and one-half times as long to solve problems as in the communication-rich mode. This is a difference of some considerable magnitude. One of our first surprises was the small difference between the results for our experienced and inexperienced typists. For the kinds of communication we are concerned with, typing skill seems to make much less difference than we and most other people assumed it would. Our second surprise was the small difference between the communication-rich and the voice modes. Gestures, facial expressions, and handwriting appear to contribute little extra to pure oral communication.

One of our biggest surprises, when we first saw the data, is illustrated in Figure 5. This shows the number of messages that subjects exchanged in the solution of problems. A message is a single uninterrupted utterance, or written or typewritten sequence of words. The data in the preceding figure become all the more impressive in the light of these. The voice and communication-rich modes, which turn out to be so fast, are also characterized by an enormous number of interchanges, or messages. One's first inclination is to guess that the lengths of the messages must also be different. I do not have data on that point to show here, but let me say that the story is not quite that simple. Typewritten messages do indeed tend to have somewhat more words per message than do voice messages, but this is true only of the sophisticated typists and at that the differences are surprisingly small. If you count the total number of words exchanged in the solution of problems, the data look almost exactly like those in Figure 5, except for a change in the numbers along the ordinate.

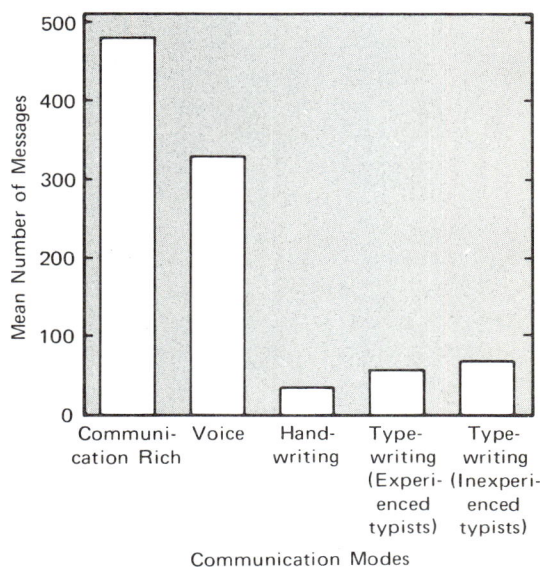

Fig. 5. Average number of messages exchanged by teams of subjects in solving complex problems using various modes of communication.

Another surprise came out of another study for which I do not show data. Feedback is such an important concept in psychology, we felt sure that problems would be solved much more efficiently if we allowed a subject to interrupt freely, rather than forcing him to wait until his partner had completed an utterance or message and released the communication channel to him. Not so. This is one of our variables that has no demonstrable overall effect.

On the Style of Communication

One of our biggest surprises, and the one with which I would like to close, is something that I think we knew intuitively but never really appreciated until we looked closely at our data. Almost all linguistic and psycholinguistic research today is being done with what I would call "immaculate" prose. Immaculate prose consists of messages that are grammatically pure and correct. They are sentences like:

John hit the girl with a ball.

It is true that I have two arms.

The man treats the boy and the girl in the park.

These are messages that have been carefully laundered, sanitized, starched, and pressed. Every word, phrase, and punctuation mark has been carefully selected, set into place, and then ironed out firmly on the printed page or writing tablet. It is literally immaculate writing.

When one looks at the typewritten protocols of what happened in our communication-rich and voice modes, one's first and almost immediate reaction is, What in the world were they talking about? At first glance, natural interactive communications between people convey the impression that they follow no grammatical, syntactical, or semantic rules. And yet obviously there are rules, for meanings do get across and problems do get solved. If we are ever to have computers that behave like HAL, we must somehow try to formulate those rules. Do you want

to have some real scientific fun? Join us in our attempts to unravel this important practical problem.

References

T. Burns, "The directions of activity and communication in a departmental executive group," *Human Relations*, 7 (1954), 73–97.

A. Chapanis, "Words, words, words," *Human Factors*, 7 (1965), 1–17.

A. Chapanis, "The relevance of laboratory studies to practical situations," *Ergonomics*, 10 (1967), 557–77.

A. Chapanis, W. R. Garner, and C. T. Morgan, *Applied experimental psychology* (New York: Wiley, 1949).

A. C. Clarke, *2001: A space odyssey* (New York: The New American Library, 1968).

J. R. Hinrichs, "Communications activity of industrial research personnel," *Personnel Psychology*, 17 (1964), 193–204.

R. G. Kinkade, and E. W. Bedarf, *Science information requirements of scientists: The need for an interacting request receiver in an information clearinghouse.* (American Institutes for Research Tech. Rep. No. 3) Silver Spring, Md.: American Institutes for Research, 1967.

R. G. Kinkade, E. W. Bedarf, and H. P. Van Cott, *Science information requirements of scientists: The need for a scientific request receiver and processor in an information clearinghouse.* (American Institutes for Research Tech. Rep. No. 2) Silver Spring, Md.: American Institutes for Research, 1967.

J. C. R. Licklider, "A crux in scientific and technical communication," *American Psychologist*, 21 (1966), 1044–51.

R. B. Miller, "Archetypes in man-computer problem solving," *Ergonomics*, 12 (1969), 559–81.

R. Stewart, "How managers spend their time," *Management Today* (1967), 92–160.

E. Tulving, and S. A. Madigan, "Memory and verbal learning," *Annual Review of Psychology*, 21 (1970), 437–84.

United States Department of Commerce, Bureau of the Census. *Historical statistics of the United States, colonial times to 1957: A statistical abstract supplement.* (Washington, D.C.: United States Government Printing Office, 1960).

United States Department of Commerce, Bureau of the Census. *Statistical abstract of the United States, 1970.* (Washington, D.C.: United States Government Printing Office, 1970).

N. Wiener, *The human use of human beings: Cybernetics and society* (Boston: Houghton Mifflin, 1950).

Do You Actually Realize What You're Saying?

Walter Menninger

"Man, you know, it was something else. You know, it was a gasser! Why, you know, what they said and what they did you wouldn't believe!"

No, I don't know. What I do know is that you say "you know" too much.

Why do people need to assume "you know"? Why, if we "know" it, are we told it? My father used to bug me when I would "you know" it too much. He called it a parasitic phrase, presumably because the words get used automatically, unthinkingly and seem to be a clinging part of the individual which one would be better off without. In the same vein as "you know" are phrases like "to be honest" and "in other words."

How People Communicate

In recent years, a lot has been said and written about how people communicate to one another, seeking to make people more aware of the subtle ways they express themselves. Body language is one aspect of this; we tell others quite a bit by our posture and gestures. Parasitic phrases are another aspect.

For some, "you know" may just be an auto-

matic "filler" to cover thinking time between sentences, a pause to keep control of the conversation and not let it get away from us. It can take the place of the old "uhhh" which was so prevalent in conversation.

"You know" is more educated and refined than "uhhh." The phrase may also be used to provide a bridge between the speaker and the listener. If "you know" it, we have something in common. Also, if "you know" it, you're more likely to agree with me and give me some positive strokes in return.

Control of Conversation

"In other words" may also be used to keep control of the conversation. Or it can be a kind of hedge, allowing us to repeat something to be sure we've gotten our point over to the listener. In every instance, the repetitive phrase has a purpose, although it may appear to be an unnecessary addition to the conversation.

Often, the purpose is not clear, like a hidden agenda; sometimes it is more obvious to the listener than the speaker.

One weekend, when working with a friend, I quickly noted that he began almost every sentence with the word, "bang!" He didn't usually do that. But with considerable emphasis, he would say, "Bang! What about the lighting? Bang!" When I asked him about it, he hadn't realized he was saying it.

Under Pressure

But I sure was. And so were others. His forceful "bangs!" made it clear he was under a good deal of pressure. While I didn't really expect him to explode, he was letting me know he felt like it.

I drew back a bit, but I also called it to his attention when it persisted. He was able to stop "banging" after it was called to his attention, and he admitted feeling under pressure.

On another occasion, I was talking with someone who repeatedly said in the course of the conversation, "I'll be honest with you," or "to be honest . . ." Of course, when you sit back and think about it, what does such a statement imply? First, I might assume that he hadn't been fully honest with me except when he prefaced his comment with that phrase. Or, perhaps he'd really prefer not to be honest with me.

As a listener, I think I do have a responsibility to tune into these things, and also to give the speaker some feedback of my impressions. Only then can I confirm whether the message I am getting is what the speaker really wants me to hear. Or, in the case of a conflicting message, only then can I determine what is the dominant intention.

Have you listened to yourself lately?

Two
Perception: What You See
May Not Be What Is

The following passage, written by Burrill (1948), is an ideal way to begin this chapter on perception:

> There is a story of two Greek sculptors who competed for the placing of a statue on a pillar in the public square. And one worked skillfully and well, until the features of his figure were smooth and polished to look as if living. But the other left his block of marble crude and jagged and uncouth, so that one could hardly tell if indeed it were a human being at all. And they put the statue of the first up on the pillar, where all might see; but high up on the pillar it was blurred by distance, and it could not be seen clearly from any angle. So they took it down, and put up the other's, and, behold, that which had not seemed true to life was now in its right perspective, and became life-like and beautiful, true to the imagination (Burrill, 1948, p. 139).

On one hand, you might expect the lifelike sculptor to be the best representation of the figure, as was apparently the case with the Greeks. After all, the smooth figure was the first one placed upon the pillars. However, what might appear to be true, on the first glance, is not always what is. The distorted figure took on lifelike characteristics when placed high upon a pillar for all to see.

Look at the picture on the next page for a couple of seconds. What do you think is taking place? Is the person giving a formal speech to a large group of people? Is it a small group of people? Are there any people present? Is this person presenting some information at a press conference? Or, was this person telling other friends of his date with a beautiful girl the evening before? Indicate below whether or not you think any of these statements would seem appropriate.

No	Yes	Statement
___	___	1. "Today I would like to formally announce my candidacy for the senate."
___	___	2. "Gee whiz, Sally, I don't think my mommy will let let me go out today."
___	___	3. "So, you're the punk who stole my wallet!"

___ ___ 4. "My second point is that there is enough money being wasted."

___ ___ 5. "And then he hit me on the head with his pistol."

___ ___ 6. "With your help we'll win in November."

___ ___ 7. "Sharon, I really do love you."

___ ___ 8. "Yes, I'll mow the lawn today, but quit bugging me."

___ ___ 9. "I really don't understand how you could be so stupid."

___ ___ 10. "You really are a chauvinistic pig!"

Did all of the above statements seem appropriate? We suspect that you probably discarded some in favor of others. Most people would probably indicate that statements 1, 4, and 6 seem appropriate for the picture. Did you pick these? Why? What information was revealed in the picture? In other words, what visual cues did you perceive (see) in the picture which permitted you to draw some conclusions, based on the specific information present?

1. The speaker was a male.
2. The speaker was standing behind a podium.
3. The speaker was smiling.
4. The speaker was gesturing with his right hand.
5. The speaker's gesture was in the form of a "V" made with his fore and middle fingers.
6. The speaker was dressed in a suit and wore a tie.
7. The podium had a microphone on it.
8. A television camera was in the background.
9. A male was looking through a camera.
10. The microphone was attached to the camera.

On the surface it appears as though someone is giving a formal speech or presentation to someone or some group of people. Did you assume that there was an audience other than the cameraman present? No audience was shown. Why were the camera and cameraman present? Did you further assume that the cameraman was focusing on the speaker? How might you have gained this impression? It is equally possible that the cameraman was focusing on someone or something beyond the speaker. But since you cannot see anything or anyone else in the picture, you undoubtedly assumed otherwise.

Perception refers to the process of becoming aware of objects, happenings, or qualities that stimulate the various sense organs and also determine the relationship between these objects, happenings, and qualities. Thus, in the preceding picture you used your eyes (one of your senses) to become aware of what objects were present. Did you actually see all things present in the picture? Turn back, look closely once again, and see if there was any detail you left out. What was the color of the speaker's and cameraman's hair? Were they clean shaven? What other things did you now notice?

What conclusions do you think might be reached by a person from the early 1400s? While this kind of person may have seen a speaker standing behind a podium before, do you think he would know what the cameraman was doing? Taking someone's picture was something a person from the 1400s would have never experienced. Thus, it is important that we realize that what we perceive to see happening is based upon our previous experience. The reason we would probably infer that the cameraman was taking the speaker's picture is because we have

seen such things happen before. While we may never have been in a television studio before, we have probably seen people taking other people's pictures with cameras. Therefore, not only do we look at the individual objects in situations, but based upon our previous experiences with these objects, attempt to assign some meaning to their relationship with each other.

After you have become aware of the objects, do you try to make sense out of what you see? This is another part of perception. We attempt to explain the relationship between and among these objects. We see a person standing behind a podium and a cameraman with a camera aimed in the direction of the speaker and posit a relationship between these two objects. We say that the cameraman is taking the speaker's picture. Therefore, we look not only at the individual objects and our previous experience with them but also at the other factors associated with it. Perception is truly an integrational process.

Perception is also an integral part of communication. What we see affects what we say. What we have experienced affects what we see. Thus, the way we perceive our world and the other people within it will directly influence the kinds of interactions we will have with other people. For example, the next time you are walking around on your campus, notice the different happenings which are taking place between people. Consciously identify what you think is happening. Then try to estimate other possibilities. See how many other possibilities you come up with. Why did you select the first possibility? How does it relate to your previous experiences? What is the likelihood that the other people being observed shared the same experiences?

Perception affects all aspects of the communication process. One thing we do while interacting with people is ascertain how they feel about an infinite variety of things. We like to think that we are discovering their attitudes. Actually, we are only taking bits and pieces of conversations and inferring, on the basis of this information, what their attitudes are. This is a perceptual process. If we hear people tell us that they went on a fantastic camping trip to the North Rim of the Grand Canyon, we may conclude that they enjoy camping and ask them to go on a backpacking trip into the Cascade Mountains. Actually, the person may simply be telling us that he or she enjoyed staying in a trailer house viewing the Grand Canyon, but hates hiking. We tend to select out things we want to hear and organize them in such a fashion as to make sense for each of us as individuals. Unfortunately, we are never the other person who has organized his or her thoughts differently and assigned different meanings to them. Thus, perception affects the bits of information we sort out from other people and attach meaning.

Articles

Three articles are included within this chapter on perception. They were chosen for three basic reasons. First, they provide some important information on perception. It is hoped that through your reading of these articles you will better understand just what perception is. Second, they are readable articles. The first article was taken from *Life* magazine and it explains how perception works. The second article, "Perceiving Real-World Scenes," calls attention to the fact that what we see takes place in the "real world." Finally, the last article explains how perception is related to communication. Remember, what we think we see and hear affects what we think of others and how we will act toward them. This is the power of perception as related to communication.

References

E. W. Burrill, "Perspective: View Points," in *Leaves of Gold*, C. F. Lytle, ed. (Williamsport, Pa.: Coslett Publishing Co., 1948).

In Search of the Mind's Eye

Rick Gore

A monkey's brain is being tapped. With a tiny tungsten electrode two Harvard scientists are intently monitoring the cryptic messages crackling along just one private line, one neuron, in its visual pathway. The men, David Hubel and Torsten Wiesel, immersed themselves in this world of neural chatter more than a dozen years ago. Since then they have been working with infinite patience, helping to resolve one of the human brain's most provocative mysteries: how can the neuron, that commune of chemicals which by themselves are cold and inert, permit man not just to see, but to perceive? In this mechanistic age any layman can at least dimly grasp how a jolt from the brain can order a muscle to bend an elbow; but how can this same kind of nervous energy give us a perception as grand and evocative as an autumn sunset, a spring rain—or for that matter the ability to recognize something as simple as the dot over an *i*?

A man walks in a park. Perhaps the aroma of a vendor's steaming chestnuts reaches him on a sudden breeze. The cool air touches his face and makes the leaves rustle behind him, while

Rick Gore, from Part II of *Life's* series on the brain. Copyright © 1971 Time Inc.

the gravel on the pathway crunches against his feet. A soft perceptual concert is being played by innumerable agitated neurons in all the sensory seats of his brain. But the busiest groups of neurons by far are those that deliver his visual messages and make him instantly and even unconsciously aware of the world around him. They tell him he is indeed in the park he sought. A thing darts past the corner of his eye and his brain says bird, then bluejay, and, noting the bluejay's constantly changing size and position, tells him which way the bird is flying. A boy with a bat hits a pop fly; somehow the man knows almost instantly just about where it will land. The green of the grass is succumbing to winter brown and a stranger is sitting on one of the park's benches. He's seen him there before— how does he know this? In fact, how does the man perform all these split-second perceptual tasks with such remarkable aplomb? Day after day we are all working out data-processing miracles like these, and research now points to the fact that we do so almost entirely through the elegant, often inscrutable organization of those remarkable neurons.

Neurons first begin to handle such visual perceptions in the retina of the eye. There is a familiar (but false) analogy that compares the eyes to a camera, projecting little pictures of the

41

outside world upside down on that rear part of the cortex that is our visual brain. Actually there is nothing like a little picture; instead each retina is sending the cortex about a million simultaneous, steady streams of electrochemical data, transmitted by the more than 125 million rods and cones behind it. A far better, though still crude, analogy of how we see is found on the printed page. Seen under a magnifying glass, the printed image turns out to be nothing more than a multitude of tiny dots which the naked eye combines to form a picture. In this analogy, each dot in the picture would correspond to the "on" or "off" message of a particular retinal cell.

This mosaic of dots from the retina must then be transformed into something that has meaning. Working with their cats and monkeys, Harvard scientists Hubel and Wiesel have uncovered important clues as to how the brain begins to do this. Most important, their experiments are showing we have neurons in our brains that respond to one certain stimulus, and to nothing else. Some, for example, respond only to a line at one particular place and one precise angle. Other cells, the two men find, are more complex. They will respond to any line anywhere in their limited field of view as long as it's at the proper angle. And there are still other cells, farther back along the visual pathway which Hubel and Wiesel call "hypercomplex." These respond to even more specific patterns, like curves or corners. Since everything we see can ultimately be reduced to a series of minute lines at angles to each other, and since most of the information we glean from our surroundings is concerned with edges and contours and corners, they call these basic sets of cells "the building blocks of perception."

In 1959, at about the same time that Hubel and Wiesel were making their initial discoveries at Harvard, an MIT group headed by Jerome Lettvin found what he called "bug detectors" in the retina of a frog. They consist of certain neurons that react to nothing but small dark objects that move through their receptive fields. The discovery may explain why a hungry frog will not eat dead flies set before him: because they are not moving he may not see them in terms of food. These cells are known as feature filters or pattern detectors.

Pattern detectors are no less vital to us than to the frog. We have developed a far greater repertoire of filters and use them for far more sophisticated purposes. As you read this page, for example, your retina and visual cortex are analyzing progressions of black lines, angles and curves on a white background. You come across the letter E—three parallel horizontal lines each forming a right angle with the same vertical line. How we perceive that this is indeed the letter E is yet unknown. But somehow we recognize E whether it is printed small or capital, fine or large, in flashing neon or chalked on a sidewalk and half scuffed out. Thus there inevitably must be a net of neurons that can extract this pattern whenever it occurs. And thus there must be a neural model for the letter E. The leading theory today is that each signal that comes into our visual system will be compared to that model and categorized as E or non-E. We perceive by an instantaneous matching process.

No one may ever be able to trace the actual nerves that make up the neural model. In simplistic terms one might compare it to a telephone which can reach any other far away, but only if a specific set of ten numbers is dialed. In the brain, of course, even the most basic of events involves tens of thousands of neurons. The model may exist in many places in our brain, each extension having its own battery of associations. Where the neural model is and how it got there is lost in the baffling question of how memory is laid down.

Pattern recognition so dominates all perception that the brain will even fill in visual gaps. Hans-Lukas Teuber of MIT has for years studied people with head wounds that made holes in their visual cortex. He finds that patients may be completely unaware of resulting gaps in their vision because their brains somehow complete straight lines, plain-colored surfaces and all sorts of patterns across these blind spots. Such spots, or scotomas, will sometimes occur briefly during migraine attacks. Teuber recalls how his teacher, the late Karl Lashley, used to describe unusual effects of his own migraine-produced scotomas. Once when he visually "beheaded" a colleague whose face fell within the scotoma's range, Lashley's brain still kept the wallpaper pattern behind the friend's head intact. Lashley once developed a scotoma while driving along a straight Florida road; he discovered that he could make a pursuing highway patrol car "disappear" without subjectively disrupting the road or landscape.

Actually, everyone has a perfectly normal hole in his vision—the blind spot where the optic nerve leaves the retina en route to the higher centers. Yet we routinely complete the patterns across it. To find the blind spot in your right eye, first close your left eye and stare at a word on this page. Then slowly move a pencil eraser to your right. At some point—the blind spot—the eraser will briefly disappear and then return near the corner of your eye. If you have trouble finding the spot, it's just because you are used to bridging the gap with an expected pattern.

Our interpretation of these patterns depends largely on our own patterns of expectations, and our perceptions are really no more than a hypothesis. We are always "guessing" on the basis of past experience. Thus people can see different shapes in the same ambiguous object and Hamlet could tease Polonius into admitting that a nearby cloud looked at once like a camel, a weasel and a whale. Thus a Rorschach ink blot looks to one man like a raging dragon, and to another like a playful puppy.

. . . We see the world as we have experienced it. At MIT, Richard Held has conducted experiments to demonstrate the importance of experience. With Alan Hein, Held raised kittens and monkeys from birth draped with cloth coverings so that they were never able to see their limbs though they could reach about with their paws and fingers. When the coverings were removed and they could at last see their limbs, there was no coordination at all between hand and eye.

For several weeks they could not reach out and locate objects they could clearly see. In another experiment, Held outfitted two men with prismatic spectacles that grossly distorted their vision. One man walked about, pushing the other in a wheelchair. The man who was active quickly adapted to his new view of the world, but his passive partner made no adjustment at all. This suggests strongly that in order to perceive an object properly we may have to establish some kind of pattern of movement in relation to it.

It is not always noticeable, but the eyes are constantly in movement. Because of the peculiar chemical requirements of the rods and cones, an image disappears if it stabilizes on the retina. So each eye has six muscles that not only focus it on the interesting object, but also keep it quivering to prevent a stabilized image. We are usually quite unconscious of our eye movements; they may be as rapid as 1/50th of a second.

There seems to be an intimate interaction between patterns of sensing and patterns of eye movement, whether it is the eyes, the rest of our bodies or the outside world that does the moving. And our brains must continually cope with all this change. A friend's face doesn't seem to shrink if he moves a few feet away—but it does, just as it would on film if you took his picture at both five and ten feet. The brain has intriguing but poorly understood mechanisms for smoothing out such transitions. If we tilt our heads to look up at a skyscraper, for example, we don't really see the skyscraper tilting back in perspective, even though what used to be its vertical lines on our retina are now sharply angled. This automatic adjustment to perspective may help explain why we are tricked by the famous Müller-Lyer arrow illusion. For decades scientists have debated why one line seems longer. A leading theory is that the angles evoke familiar, but misleading, patterns of perspective —like those an artist would use to make a line drawing seem either closer to us or farther away.

. . . In the everyday world, patterns change

frequently because we ourselves change position. To perceive this world properly our brains must take our own movements into account. Lightly tap the corner of your eye. The world seems to jump—and indeed the image on your retina is jumping. Yet if you move your eyes with your own eye muscles, there is a smooth transition. Why the difference? Because whatever center commands the eyes to move in the first place must also send a copy of its message to some crucial, but as yet unknown, way station in our sensory system. That station in turn tells the rest of our visual brain to compensate for the image change. Once again, as in the Held experiments, the act of moving our muscles ourselves seems to be essential to proper perception.

Movement of all sorts so affects our perception that many scientists are beginning to think we have a separate visual system devoted to it—centered in two little mounds, the superior colliculi, buried deeply in an old part of the brain (LIFE, Oct. 1). These mounds are evolutionary outgrowths of the optic tectum, which for lower animals, like birds and frogs, is an all-important visual center. Some superior colliculi cells respond to sound as well, and it is likely that the superior colliculi act as a kind of early warning system. A frog must move fast if it wants to catch a bug, so nature has wired in its tongue-flicking triggers close to its optic detectors. Man, too, must pay attention to rapid changes around him—after all, that bluejay in the park just might have been a bee. Some superior colliculi cells have recently been found that react not to angles and lines like the Hubel and Wiesel cortical cells, but to the direction and extent of eye movements. While this warning system tells us where things are and what we should be watching, a process known as "scanning" lets us perceive the scene as a whole. When you look at the park, for example, you take in one object at a time. Only a small part of our retina, called the fovea, can focus sharply. So you scan the area with the fovea moving with unconscious speed from one point to another, from tree to bench to sidewalk. You match up object after object to patterns stored in your memory bank until you distill, in this case, a park pattern. You recognize the stranger on the bench because just enough of his features—the shape of his head, the color of his hat, the cut of his clothes—fit a well-established pattern.

Your eyes jump quickly to follow any change or motion. If you try to fix them on an object, like a bush, you still find yourself breaking the bush down further, going from branch to leaf to flower, even from petal to stamen to pollen.

It is likely that each of us has characteristic scan paths. Different people will scan the same flower differently. And one person won't use the same path on flowers that he uses on trees. These scan paths, like the feature detectors and eye movements, must be controlled by some kind of neural network.

For years science has nibbled away at the whole area of human perception, broken it down into ever smaller units and subunits, like these feature filters and scan paths and neural mounds with tongue-twisting Latin names. But perception can never be fully explained in these clinical terms. It is already obvious that we must know more about how neurons learn and remember. We must know how we focus our attention. We must understand more, too, about human motivation: why is it we often do see just what we look for? And, of course, our emotions clearly color our perceptions, adding awe to those autumn sunsets and sweetness to the spring rains. Years ago the great neurophysiologist Sir Charles Sherrington called the brain the "great raveled knot." He knew the answers lay hidden in all its tortuous pathways that feed into each other. The disentangling will be slow and arduous, but it has begun.

Perceiving Real-World Scenes

Irving Biederman

Abstract. *When a briefly presented real-world scene was jumbled, the accuracy of identifying a single, cued object was less than that when the scene was coherent. Jumbling remained an effective variable even when the subject knew where to look and what to look for. Thus an object's meaningful context may affect the course of perceptual recognition and not just peripheral scanning or memory.*

In experiments on perceptual recognition, a subject typically sees either a single item surrounded by homogeneous space or an array of unrelated ("random") items. In the real world, such meager perceptual experiences are rare. Outside the laboratory, objects are almost always perceived in some setting or context.

ʻGiven conventional stimulus displays, it is not surprising that the results of much perceptual research can generally be reconciled with a class of models that hold that the various items of the display are treated as separate entities; that is, they are initially processed independently in a very short-term sensory store (lasting just fractions of a second), and then transferred serially to a longer-term storage system. It is in this longer-term storage system that meaningfulness and long-term memory are seen as having their effects (1).

In contrast to laboratory modeling is the following thought. If we glance at the world, even at a scene rich with detail that we have never experienced before, our subjective impression is of clear and almost instantaneous perception and comprehension of what we are looking at. That is, one feels that the various parts of a scene are simultaneously identified and related. One possible source of this discrepancy between the laboratory and the real world is the presence, in the real world, of a meaningful context. Creatures and things in the real world rarely appear, as they typically do in the laboratory, surrounded only by homogeneous space or unrelated entities. Instead, things occur in some predictable relation to other things, that is, in some setting.

The results I report show that meaningful context does affect perceptual recognition (2). A secondary purpose of this study was to advance a methodology whereby real-world scenes could be used as stimuli in experiments on perceptual recognition, so that context effects could be studied more systematically (3).

Subjects briefly viewed pictures of many

varied scenes: for example, streets, kitchens, desk tops, and so forth. Their task was to identify which object occupied a given cued position in the scene. The technique was derived from Averbach and Coriell (4). By requiring a report of only part of a complex display, memory and response factors were greatly reduced. The major experimental variable was whether the scene was coherent or whether it was jumbled—cut into sixths and rearranged (but never rotated) so as to destroy the natural spatial relations of the components. This jumbling was assumed to be a manipulation of the meaningfulness of the object's setting independent of the complexity of the scene.

The scenes were 35-mm black-and-white positive slides. For each scene, two versions—one coherent and one jumbled—were made by photographing a print, 20 by 25 cm, which had been cut into six sections (generally with one horizontal and two vertical cuts) so that at least four well-defined objects were left intact. The coherent slide was taken after the sectioning, so that the section lines appeared in both versions (5). When sections were arranged for the jumbled version, one was left in its original position. This section always contained at least one well-defined object. The position of the section remaining constant was balanced across the different scences; for example, for one-sixth of the scenes, the top left section was identical in both jumbled and coherent versions.

Subjects viewed slides in a three-channel tachistoscope (6). Slides were shown for 300, 500, or 700 msec, and they subtended visual angles of 5° horizontally and 3.5° vertically. An arrow was presented for 300 msec, immediately after the scene in half the trials and immediately before the scene in the other half. The arrow pointed to an area associated with an object. The subject's task was to indicate, by pointing to one of four object pictures, which object had been cued. These object pictures were cut from the original print used in making the scene and were mounted on index cards displayed in a photo album. The cued object was the same in both coherent and jumbled

versions of each scene and always came from the section of the scene that remained in its original position.

In addition to the jumbling and cue-order variables, the order in which the subject viewed the scene and the response alternatives was also varied. In the alternatives-before condition, the subject was allowed to peruse the four object pictures before the scene was shown. In the alternatives-after condition, the subject viewed the response alternatives only after he viewed the scene. Thus, in the latter condition a few seconds elapsed between presentation of the scene and presentation of the response alternatives.

Each of 24 subjects viewed four blocks of 32 slides each. Within each block, the slides were equally divided between jumbled and coherent scenes. The four possible combinations of alternative-order and cue-order variables were used, one combination in each block. The first eight slides in each block were considered practice trials and were not included in the data analysis. In the remaining 24 slides, the cued object occurred in each of the six sections an equal number of times (four). All variables were balanced across slides. Each subject viewed only the jumbled or coherent version of a given scene but never both.

. . . The experiment was designed to minimize peripheral-scanning effects (since the cued object was in the same position in both scene versions, and since brief durations and relatively small visual angles were used) and to minimize memory and response effects (by requiring the subject to simply point to one of a small set of well-defined and nameable objects). That jumbling remained an effective variable even when the subject knew where to look (when the cue preceded the scene) and what to look for (when the response alternatives preceded the scene) further limits the roles played by peripheral scanning and memory factors, respectively, in accounting for the jumbling effect. It is most likely that jumbling affected an early, but not peripheral, stage involved in the perceptual recognition of the cued object.

A number of theoretical issues present themselves when one attempts to account for the context effect, that is, the advantage of coherent over jumbled scenes. One issue concerns identification of the functional units involved in the perception of scenes. Is the functional unit an individual object, or does an observer have access to more global units or schema? A second issue is the determination of the locus, in the sequence of processing, where context has its effect. Is it in the initial manner in which objects are physically processed—in the initial segmentation, testing, and weighing of features? Or does the context influence a stage subsequent to that involved in the physical processing, so that physically ambiguous stimuli are interpreted to be consistent with other aspects of the scene already identified?

This experiment was not analytic for these issues, but Sternberg's additive factors method (8), coupled with reaction time measurements in the present task situation, might bring these issues under experimental scrutiny (9). For example, if jumbling is affecting a cognitive inferential stage, then an interaction would be expected between the magnitude of the effect of jumbling on reaction times and the magnitude of the effect of the probability of the cued object's being in the scene (10). (For example, this probability could be varied by cueing a bowl or a baseball glove on a formally set dining table.) In a similar manner, interactions between jumbling and (i) the size and contrast of the cued object or (ii) the presence or absence of background and contiguous areas would be expected if jumbling were affecting physical-feature testing or object segmentation, respectively.

References

1. D. E. Rumelhart, *J. Math. Psychol.* 7, 191 (1970).
2. In several studies with rigorous controls for guessing and memory effects, it was shown that an individual letter within a word is more perceptible than that same letter in a string of random-appearing letters, or even than the letter by itself [D. Aderman and E. E. Smith, *Cogn. Psychol.* 2, 117 (1971); G. M. Reicher, *J. Exper. Psychol.* 81, 274 (1969); D. D. Wheeler, *Cogn. Psychol.* 1, 59 (1970)]. A possible implication of these results, as well as the results I report, is that the functional perceptual unit can be something larger than the individual items (letters or objects).
3. Research with real-world scenes as stimuli has generally been limited to studies of eye movements or memory. The thrust of this report is the effect of an object's setting on its perceptibility in a single glance.
4. E. Averbach and A. S. Coriell, *Bell Syst. Tech. J.* 40, 309 (1961).
5. The end product of four photographic cycles was less-than-optimum clarity. Undoubtedly, performance would have been better if original positive slides had been used and the scenes had been larger.
6. Model GB Auto-Tach, Scientific Prototype Corp.
7. It could be argued that the effect of jumbling is due to the presence of a greater number of object segments, which created visual noise in the jumbled pictures. Since the fragments did not overlap the cued object, it is not clear how this factor could be operative. My observation is that literally adding external noise by scattering segments of other pictures over a photograph—compared to jumbling the photograph—does little to degrade the intelligibility of the scene. That jumbling is primarily affecting the relation of objects is, perhaps, evidenced by the minimum of 10 to 15 seconds of effort needed to determine how the sections of a scene were to be reassembled to the original. A more rigorous test of the noise interpretation would involve stimulus scenes that were made by either cropping out background objects that extended across the section lines or else by drawing scenes in which none of the objects would extend across the section lines.
8. S. Sternberg, *Acta Psychol.* 30, 276 (1969).
9. Reaction times could be measured by providing the subject with a target object before the scene was presented. When the scene and cue are presented, the subject would respond, "Yes," as quickly as possible if the cued object was the target, and, "No," otherwise.
10. The logic of the additive factors method (AFM) holds that if two factors, for instance jumbling and probability, are affecting the duration of separate and independent information-processing stages, then their combined effects on reaction time (RT) should be additive. That is, if jumbling adds 50 msec to the average RT and probability adds 25 msec, then the RT for a low-probability target in a jumbled scene should be, on the average, 75 msec longer than that for a high-probability target in a coherent scene. The AFM may also be applicable to error probabilities, but, in that case, if factors are influencing different information-processing stages, the logarithms of the errors should add.

A Phenomenological Approach to Discussion

Remo P. Fausti and Arno H. Luker

Phenomenology, or cognitive field psychology, has come into prominence only recently. Papers dealing with the phenomenological approach are being delivered at national speech and psychological conventions. Textbooks in pedagogy are including its techniques. A recent text, *Psychological Foundations of Education states*, "cognitive field has more to offer teachers than any other outlook."[1]

The origins of phenomenology extend back at least as far as Plato's analogy of the man-chained-in-a-cave comprehending life from shadows on the wall through Immanuel Kant's designation of the shadows and real objects as phenomena and noumena. Later, Edmund Husserl declared that the philosophy of phenomenology was "intended to provide a firm basis for the foundation of a new psychology and a universal philosophy. In the presence of a phenomenon (whether it be an external object or a state of mind), the phenomenologist uses an absolutely unbiased approach; he observes phenomena as they manifest themselves and only as they manifest themselves . . . the observer 'puts the world between brackets,' i.e., he excludes from his mind not only any judgment of value about the phenomena but also any affirmation about the existence of the object and of the observing subject."[2]

Phenomenology has been labeled, "cognitive field," "personal," and "perceptual."[3] In this paper the meaning of the term "phenomenology" is based on six premises:

1. Behavior is observed from the subjective point of view of the person behaving and not from the objective point of view of the empirical psychologist.

2. Behavior is seen as a problem of human perception.

3. Behavior is viewed at the holistic level, rather, that at the atomistic, molecular, or mechanistic level.

4. Behavior, from the point of view of the behaver, is always purposeful, lawful, and based on reason. "However capricious, irrelevant, and irrational his behavior may appear to the outsider, from his point of view, *at that instant*, his behavior is purposeful, relevant, and pertinent to the situation *as he understands it*."[4]

By permission of the authors and the Speech Communication Association. Vol. XIV, no. 1. January 1965, pp. 19–23.

[1] Morris Bigge and Maurice Hunt, *Psychological Foundations of Education* (New York: Harper and Row, 1962).

[2] Henri F. Ellenberger, "A Clinical Introduction to Psychiatric Phenomenology," *Existence* (New York: Basic Books, Inc., 1960), p. 96.

[3] Arthur Combs and Donald Syngg, *Individual Behavior* (New York: Harper & Row, 1959).

[4] *Ibid.*, p. 18.

5. "All behavior, without exception, is completely determined by, and pertinent to, the perceptual field of the behaving organism. The perceptual field has also been called the personal field, the private world, the psychological field, the individual's life space, and the phenomenal field. To each individual the perceptual field is reality for it is the only reality he can know."[5]

6. Phenomenology has its origins in Gestalt psychology as adapted by Kurt Lewin's field theory.

In general, phenomenology is an individualistic psychology that attempts to understand behavior from the behaver's point of view. Thomas Szasz supports this definition by accepting Bertrand Russell's definition: "Psychology is the science which deals with private data, and with the private aspects of data which common sense regards as public."[6]

Most teachers of speech are familiar with the definition and purposes of discussion as set forth by McBurney and Hance: "the cooperative deliberation of problems by persons thinking and conversing together in a face-to-face or coacting group under the direction of a leader for purposes of understanding and action."[7] The domain of discussion is basically the democratic solution of problems. Underlying discussion are John Dewey's "Steps in Reflective Thinking,"[8] which have been adapted to become the five steps in problem solving.[9] Because the objective of the democratic problem-solving process of discussion is usually (if not always) the ultimate "implementing of some form of action necessary to the existence, maintenance of equilibrium, or progress of a society,"[10] debate must of

necessity also be included as part of the "holistic" process.

The entire problem-solving process has as its essence a phenomenological referent. The individual seeks to maintain homeostasis or a state of equilibrium, which is never quite reached. The occurrence of a felt need (problem) disturbs the equilibrium of the person initiating the problem-solving process. In order to regain equilibrium, the problem must be differentiated as figure from ground. The problem must be brought into clear focus in a perceptual field. In other words, the individual must locate and define as figure the problem that had previously existed as ground in his life space.

Next, he explores the problem from his private frame of reference, for he can see the problem only the basis of his own perception. Solutions to the problem emerge into figure in his perceptual field. Some of these solutions are more enhancing (or threatening) than others to the reestablishment of his equilibrium. Privately he may develop an extreme preference for one of the possible solutions, but his selection of a final course of action must take into consideration another element in his perceptual field: his interrelationship with others, as he perceives the place he occupies in society. His perception of self is affected by his stable concept of self. Hence, he chooses the final solution (best solution), or mode of operation (behavior) on the basis of all of the factors that he perceives in his perceptual field.

The final mode of operation, or solution to the problem, is that one which in his perceptual estimation best satisfies all of the factors of his personality and is most enhancing to his continued maintenance of equilibrium. The implementation of the foregoing steps in problem solving are motivated by tension and the problem-solver's desire to remove the tension and return to equilibrium and self-adequacy. Often the individual does not follow the steps hierarchically. He may skip steps, or return to a previous step, depending on tensions that result from his participation in the solution of the problem.

[5]*Ibid.*, pp. 21–22.

[6]Thomas Szasz, *Pain and Pleasure* (New York: Books, Inc., 1957), p. 17.

[7]J. H. McBurney and K. G. Hance, *Discussion in Human Affairs* (New York: Harper & Row, 1950), p. 10.

[8]John Dewey, *How We Think* (Boston: D. C. Heath & Company, 1933), p. 12.

[9]Henry L. Eubank and J. J. Auer, *Discussion and Debate, Tools of a Democracy* (New York: Appleton-Century-Crofts, Inc., 1951), p. 5.

[10]Remo Fausti, "Debate and Discussion—A Holistic Approach," *The Gavel* 43, 3 (March 1961), pp 49–50.

The application of this phenomenological analysis of the problem-solving process brings an ethical or moral factor into the picture. It must be assumed that the basic character of human need is essentially positive rather than negative; adequacy of the individual is inextricably interwoven with the society of which he is a part. Democracy assumes faith in our fellows—an interdependent society.[11] No member of a society can exist alone. Each must work with, cooperate with, and associate with other members of the society whether he wants to or not. If this frame of reference is continued to its logical conclusion in accord with phenomenological principles, the resultant panacea would be a complete resolution of all the problems of the world.

However, there are some practical implications of phenomenology for the improvement of human relations. If participants in problem-solving situations, in school or on the international level, were to accept the behavior of other participants on a basis of how the others perceive, rather than appying external reasons and logic to behavior, the incidence of emotional conflicts, anger, and possible misunderstandings would be minimized.[12] If each person attempted to understand the frame of reference of the other, instead of applying his own frame of reference to the behavior of the other, an improved relationship would result.

Communication depends on the similarity of perceptual fields of sender and receiver. Exact similarity seldom if ever exists.[13] At best the sender can expect the receiver to extract only a rough approximation of his coded message. The meaning of the sender's symbols do not always convey the same meaning to the receiver, i.e., the graduate students from Thailand who were told this story: "Do you know what Satchmo Armstrong said when he returned from his concert tour of Siam? He said, 'I dig those Siamese cats.' Or the German student who was told that the advertisement for a dachshund dog would read, 'Get along little dogie.'" Effective communication failed, and the self-styled comedian spent some embarrassing moments attempting to clarify a comprehension that somehow continued to evade the foreign students. An aid to insuring communication would be to employ a procedure that requires the receiver to repeat back the sender's message to the satisfaction of the sender before the receiver could reply. Also, the perceptual approach would add humility to the problem-solving process—readiness to admit, "I could be wrong," Proper operation of the phenomenological approach would be a constant concern for the self-adequacy of others.

In teaching discussion, the phenomenological approach must have as goals:

1. Development of students with firm beliefs and convictions resulting from considerations and resolutions of problems in their present frame of perception.

2. Students with an ability and willingness to reexamine continuously their fundamental beliefs and convictions. Students must be allowed to progress toward self-adequacy as dignified persons of integrity and worth,[14] free to develop adequate personalities based on (1) positive self-perception, (2) acceptance of self and others, and (3) close identification of others.

Basic to the learning process is an environment that allows maximum freedom of action. A free atmosphere in discussion presents a minimum of threat and a maximum of enhancement to the student. Freedom to make mistakes is an essential of the learning process.[15] Fear of making mistakes often causes a high degree of rigidity and ultraconservatism. If at all possible, the ever-present threat of grades should be removed. Practically speaking, grades appear "to be here to stay," but the degree to which they affect the learning situation can still be determined by the instructor. Grades should be caused to recede as far from figure into ground as is realistically judicious.

Motivation becomes an individual action on

[11] Combs and Snygg, p. 320.
[12] *Ibid.*, pp. 322–24.
[13] *Ibid.*, p. 372.

[14] *Ibid.*, pp. 378.
[15] *Ibid.*, pp. 378–380.

the part of the student. The teacher merely acts as an agent that will cause the student to become motivated. The student cannot be made to learn discussion. He must be led to want to learn discussion because he sees a personal reason for acquiring the knowledge of discussion and its techniques. Motivation must exist within the student. The teacher's concept of self, perceptual field, and entire personality play a significant part in the motivation process. The instructor is added as an ingredient in the learning situation because his presence acts as a catalyst in the modification of the behavior of the student. The "something" that he contributes to the learning situation is not capable of immediate scientific quantification, or definition. Paradoxical to the existence of a free atmosphere and the indefinable purposes for the existence of an instructor is the fact that the instructor must also establish a relationship with the class that allows an orderly intelligent procedure. Under these circumstances, the instructor proceeds by keeping the student constantly in a state of creative tension through alternation between a state of tension and equilibrium.

The process of instruction necessitates some disequilibrium on the part of the students. The instructor accomplishes this by means of the tasks (problems) that he presents to the students. The procedure is exceedingly delicate, for anxiety must be avoided. Anxiety would cause factors to appear in the student's perceptual field that would impede differentiation. If the anxiety is great enough, "tunnel vision"[16] will insure that there will be little or no learning by the student.

From a Gestalt point of view, disequilibrium is explained thus: "In a problematic situation, the whole is seen as incomplete and a tension is set up toward its completion. The strain to complete is an aid to learning, and to achieve closure is satisfying."[17] The increase in tension is caused by the arousal of a need that exists in the present reality of the individual.

In order for the student to learn—for differentiations in his perceptual field to occur—it is necessary that he return to a state of equilibrium. Should the student remain in a state of disequilibrium, threat and anxiety would result and learning would be stifled. In order to obviate an anxiety state that is deleterious to learning and to encourage creativity, the teacher may employ certain basic techniques of teaching. The student must feel free to make mistakes with impunity. As a leader, the instructor must create a permissive environment in the classroom, rather than the "attack and appease" approach that characterizes much problem solving, especially at the international level.[18] The approach is well known to the average citizen: either the opposition is destroyed (which is good), or some of the demands of the opposition are granted (which is bad).

The problem-solving process must proceed on its quest for solution of the problem. The process must not deteriorate into a game of exercise in which the student looks for the solution that the instructor has previously ordained. The procedure of "fencing-in" or "walling-in" by the instructor choosing the goal forbids creativity. In this improper approach, the instructor runs his charges down a deep channel toward the solution goal. He helps the student who strays from the path by pushing him back into the mainstream of thought. He rewards the student with a grade for running the maze exactly right.

Good leadership results in a feeling of freedom on the part of the student. This free atmosphere rules out "stereotyping" based on the past behavior of the student. Prejudgments based on past behavior must be severely mitigated. People, including students, live their lives forward, not backward. Behavior, although historically a function of what has happened to the student in the past, is an immediate function of his present perceptions. The past plays its part, but present and future behavior should be of primary concern to the instructor. Stereo-

[16]*Ibid.*, p. 167.
[17]Ernest R. Hilgard, *Theories of Learning* (New York: Appleton-Century-Crofts, Inc., 1956), p. 228.

[18]Combs and Snygg, pp. 321–24.

typing presents a formidable barrier to the development of effective human relations.

The process involved in a phenomenological approach to discussion is described in the preface of *Quadrilog*: "The student is introduced to material that mirrors a reflection of attitudes, concepts, beliefs, and ways of doing that can and do exist. The student will subject them to critical thinking at *his* level of understanding in relation to his particular environment as he perceives it. The result of the process, if successful, should be the intellectual growth of the student, and an enlargement, modification, or strengthening of his beliefs and understanding."[19]

[19]G. Erickson, R. Hansen, G. Phillips, and R. Fausti, *Quadrilog*, Dittoed Manuscript (1962), p. 7.

Three
Verbal Communication

How do you think the word "dumb" was used the first time you heard it? Our guess is that it was used either to refer to a stupid person or a stupid action. Do you think we are right? How would you feel if someone called your parents dumb? But what if your parents had lost their ability to speak? How would you then feel if someone called them dumb? It is interesting to note that in our English language we have chosen the same word (dumb) to not only refer to stupid, moronic people but also people who have lost their ability to vocalize words—so preoccupied are we with the use of words.

Part of our effectiveness as communicators is dependent upon our ability to use words. The other part is dependent upon the other person's ability to understand the meaning that we have attached to our words. If we are using specific words to communicate our feelings to another person, the other person needs to share the same meaning for our words in order for understanding to take place.

Sign and Symbol

One of the major obstacles in successful verbal communication is that we use words as symbols but think of them in terms of signs. The word *sign* is derived from the Latin word *signa* which means identifier or label. The unique quality of a sign is that it has a one-to-one relationship. This one-to-one relationship means that the sign carries the same meaning for all people who come in contact with it.

Signs take two forms. First, they may provide direct unintentional meaning.

"HEY JOE! A BEAR'S BEEN HERE!"

If a fisherman were walking along a stream and noticed two huge paw prints along the water's edge, those paw prints would have the same meaning for anyone seeing them. The fisherman would probably think, "A bear was here." (This assumes, of course, that people would recognize the tracks.) However, the fisherman may conclude other things after seeing the paw prints, e.g., "I had better not fish here out of fear," "that bear probably was getting a drink," or "I wonder if the bear is still around." It should be remembered that these other potential conclusions were reached after the sign unintentionally communicated to the fisherman that the bear had been there.

Signs also communicate intentional meanings. Whenever you drive a car and come upon a stop sign, you know that it means that you are supposed to bring your car to a halt. The stop sign has the same meaning for all people who see it. We know that "STOP" means halt, not "spin tires on pavement." In fact, we are now learning single meanings for road signs throughout the world. Do you know what these signs mean?

They have the same meaning for everyone who drives: (1) bicycle crossing, (2) pedestrian crossing, (3) no right turn, (4) no U-turn, and (5) trucks are prohibited on that street.

Too often we think we are communicating to others with signs, while in actuality we are using symbols. The word *symbol* was derived from the Latin *symbolum*, meaning token, and the Greek *sumbolon*, meaning a token for identification. While signs have a single meaning, symbols have many potential meanings.

How do you think you would define the words *time* and *bitch*? Do you think other people would define these words in a similar way? We asked students to define these words and the next page shows what they came up with.

If you think about it, all of our words are symbols. They may mean one thing to you but something very different to someone else. What differences do you notice in the definitions for time and bitch? How do your definitions compare? This is also the difference between denotative and connotative meanings. Usually, denotative meanings are consid-

Time

1. An abstract precious process.

2. A human illusion; paradox

3. A period or span in which all action occurs.

4. Infinity; seconds passing in a day

5. An abstract invention which man has imposed on himself to organize his life around

6. Crutch giving stability to life

7. A measure of life; hours and seconds

Bitch

1. A nagging, ill-tempered characteristic

2. Generally, a selfish, opinionated female

3. A derogatory attitude toward a person or situation.

4. A female dog.

5. Snobbish: slang representing someone who does something which repels you

6. Self-centered female who is hard to get along with

7. A verbal or physical illustration of bad attitudes which is most often tempermental

ered those definitions found within a dictionary—the common definition among different people with respect to a word. The denotative meaning is thus a sign meaning. On the other hand, connotative meanings are symbol meanings, and they have a variety of possible interpretations. We need to constantly keep in mind that while we denote specific things when using words, these words can mean different things to different people.

Meaning

A basic principle of general semantics (the study of the meaning of words) is that meanings are designated by people, not by words. The meaning you assign to different words is based upon the experiences you have had with those words. We began this chapter by asking you to recall your first experience with the word dumb. Most of us could probably not recall when we first discovered what the word meant, but we associated it with the meaning stupid or moronic. Think about the children of speechless parents. Based upon their experiences with the word dumb, would you not think that their meaning for this word would be different?

What are these objects?

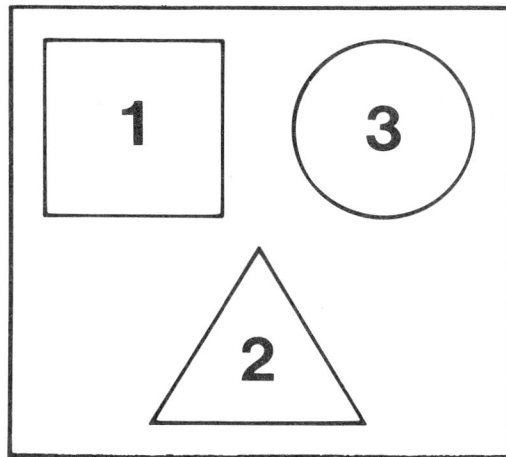

Most of us would say that they are (1) a square, (2) a triangle, and (3) a circle.

How do we know this? The first object is a square because we say a square is a closed object with four equal sides which are at right angles to each other. Why not call this a circle? What reason can you provide for saying this object is a square? We denote it a square, so all of us have a common reference. If we called this kind of object a circle, it would be a circle. Based upon our previous experiences with squares, we know what they are.

What different meanings do you think the term "college professor" might have for the five people listed below? Place a number beside each definition next to one of the persons.

Persons

_____ College professor

_____ Medical doctor

_____ Garbage collector

_____ College student

_____ Unemployed laborer

Definitions

1. "Egghead"
2. Underpaid professional
3. Slave driver
4. Pillars of the community
5. The wrong kind of doctor

It should be noted that it is entirely possible that any one of these definitions could be attributed to any one of the five people. The meaning we assign to words is not based upon a person's stereotyped classification but rather that individual's experience with the word, phrase, or thing it represents. Although many people might assume that the definition "underpaid professional" would probably be attributed to the college professor, it just as easily could be associated with the garbage collector. In summary, our experiences with the words or phrases used in the American language (and in other languages as well) and the objects, places, persons, or things they represent determine the meaning we will assign to them. Since our experiences are always different, our meanings will vary.

Most of us listen to music day in and day out. How many times do you sit down and try to figure out what different songs mean? David Bowie, an English singer and songwriter, sings the song, "Life on Mars," on his album *Hunky Dory* (Bowie, 1971). It may well be a song with which you are familiar. It is an interesting song because it always produces a variety of student interpretations. Here are some excerpts from different analyses.

Student 1: This song is a psychological study of an extremely depressed, lonely, and mentally disturbed young girl. She has a hostile approach toward society, brought on, for the most part, by her obvious paranoiac nature.

The girl views her mother as a symbol of absolute authority who denies her every effort at freedom.... Almost completely opposite of the mother is the girl's father. He is very liberal in his dealings with the girl and exercises very little discipline over her....

The girl is unable to deal with other people and as a result she is without friends. Through her loneliness she displays an animosity for those who refuse to like her. In an effort to escape the responsibility and realities of her own existence, she has developed a "dreamworld" life style where she imagines the world as a generally uninteresting movie with herself as its only viewer....

Student 2: My interpretation centers around a lonely girl who is going through a very frustrating and emotional stage. She's been having an affair with a man that abandons her when she needs him most. Her parents are very upset that she's been seeing this man and have warned her as to what they think his real intentions are. She ends up getting pregnant and her father loses his cool and throws her out of the house. By this time, her lover has vanished and she is left alone with no one to turn to. At this point, she is extremely lonely and depressed.

Out on the street, she is in a daze, wandering aimlessly about trying to piece together her shattered world. Vivid images are racing through her head over and over, reminding her of the dull and monotonous life that she's been leading.

Resentment follows her daydreaming, and she can't understand why all the burden of responsibility should be thrust into her lap. She's saying to herself, "Couldn't it have been someone else instead of me?" It seems the wrong guy ends up losing out. Also, with the lonely deserted feelings, it's like living on a strange planet by yourself with no one to relate to.

Student 3: The writer of this song is trying to get across that television in America influences children now more than ever. . . . Are television viewers left with a decent set of morals after the show is over or are their morals rattled around? Martians would probably wonder if there is life in America, because so many people are glued to their "boob tubes" as though controlled by them.

Television is a means of escape from everyday problems. The girl in "Life on Mars?" is yelled at by her parents; so with her friend gone, she has no one to turn to except her "friend," the television set. The TV may black out her problem for the present, but it will only delay it. When she is faced with the problem or a rerun of it, as an addict she will return to the TV to escape it . . . If there is life on Mars, does television or some similar media influence their lives as much as it does ours in America?

Student 4: At the very beginning of the poem, a young girl has come home and told her parents of her job as a prostitute. She cannot understand their violent reactions because to her, it is only a job. She goes out to find her friend who is supposed to have two customers for her. As she walks along she thinks how her dreams of being a prostitute have diminished, because it is not quite so exciting a job as she had expected.

She goes to the movie theater where she was to have met her friend and chooses the seat with the best view. When the movie begins, she is saddened and bored when she finds out that it is a porno flick which holds nothing entertaining for her because she's lived through everything in the movie at least ten times! This girl is appalled at the film makers for thinking that this type of movie is entertaining to anyone. This movie features sailors, all of whom are on two-day passes away from camp, fighting to get girls in a dance hall. She cannot understand why sailors would act as barbaric as cavemen in trying to get girls when prostitution is legal and also practically priced. It's just too freaky a show for her to even consider realistic. Even the police are doing the wrong thing! They are beating up customers for not paying the bosses of the prostitutes for running such a rip-off operation. She wonders if the police will ever realize that they are also part of this business of prostitution.

The song was exactly the same for each student. The difference lay in the experiences of the students with respect to the words and ideas expressed by Bowie. In fact, there were four totally different interpretations. The first student thought that the song portrayed a girl who was mentally ill. The second student thought that the girl had become pregnant and was abandoned by the father of her child. The third student indicated that the song was a discussion about the impact of television in America. And the last student decided that the girl was a prostitute and the song reflected part of her experiences. Needless to say, these four interpretations were totally different. The meaning was not so much in the song as in the person interpreting it.

Another major principle of general semantics is that the word is not the thing. The word is simply an abstraction of the object, place, event, or quality it represents. The word *dog* is not the four-legged animal which barks when you are trying to sleep; the word *dog* is merely a word which stands for a whole class of canine creatures.

Too often we assume that the word is the thing and react accordingly. We label people as cops, prostitutes, politicians, clergy, doctors, etc., and react to these people on the basis of the label we attach to them rather than the person. Suppose, for example, that you are attending a party where a man, Mr. White, is referred to by a friend as a slumlord. If you were to meet Mr. White, in the course of the evening, how do you think you would react to him? Would labeling him a slumlord affect your interaction to him? Think also how you would react to Mr. White if he were introduced as Lord White.

How many times have you seen people recoil when you mention the name lizard, snake, slimy slugs? People tend to react to different words as if the word itself actually was the thing being discussed. How many words could you think of that would fall into this category? Most obscene words fall directly into this area.

In the English language, we classify words as being nouns, pronouns, adjectives, verbs, adverbs, prepositions, conjunctions, and interjections. We have also been instructed from the time we entered school that words make sentences, sentences make paragraphs, and paragraphs complete papers. We know that words represent things, and we are taught that sentences are the basic units of language, being minimally composed of a subject (noun or pronoun) and a predicate (verb). Supposedly, complete thoughts are communicated in sentences. Apparently, this means that a nonsentence does not contain a complete thought. Have you ever been traveling on an airplane and noticed the little bag placed in the pocket in front of your seat? What do you think is printed on the bag? We have seen the words, "In case of motion sickness." According to the rules of grammar, this is not a complete sentence. It has neither a noun or a pronoun (the *you* is implied) nor a verb (the *use* is also implied). However, we all know what the words printed on the bag mean. The words on the bag serve a specific function. They are informing the traveler to use the bag in case he or she becomes sick.

Functions of Language

Identifies. Language has several functions and the first one is to identify objects, happenings, and qualities. Language helps provide some order to our world. Have you ever been to a restaurant and discovered that the menu contained a list of options, the consistency of which you could not recognize? The purpose of a menu is to provide an orderly list of identifiable foods to choose from. In addition, have you ever noticed the names "Men" and "Women" placed on certain doors at restaurants? Their purpose is to stipulate additional order. Imagine your surprise if you went in your sexually designated room and discovered someone of the opposite sex. Thus, the purpose of language is to transmit information to other people in hopes of providing some order to their lives.

Social Interaction. The human being is a social animal and consequently seeks interaction with other people. Notice how depressed you become when you go for days without ever talking with other people. Worse yet is the case where you wish to engage in communication with other people but are shunned by all. Some people seek such solitude, but most of us relish the idea of interacting with others.

Much of our communication is on the phatic level. Phatic communication is the type that takes place between people when passing each other on a college campus, for example. We're sure that many times you see people walking by and say, "Hi! How are things going?" or some other type of greeting. Actually, you really do not want to know how the other person feels or what effect recent events have had on his or her life. All you really are saying is "Hi! I recognize you!" The interaction is intended to be slight. How do you think you would react if you saw someone and said, while passing, "Hi! How are things going?" and they proceeded to tell you about their marital problems? If you were in a hurry to get to class, you probably would not appreciate the imposition of having to listen to the person, even though you invited the conversation.

Cathartic. Language also serves the purpose of releasing tension. Think about the number of doors, windows, etc., that have been saved from being smashed, because language served the cathartic release of tension. Note that much profanity is saved for cathartic communication. Inventory the types of obscene words and phrases you use. Is there a difference in the way you use some of these words? Do you reserve the use of certain words and phrases for varying degrees of tension-producing situations? Many people have a hierarchy of verbally profane words.

Manipulative. One of the most notable purposes of language is that it is a manipulative device. We use language to prevent action ("No! You cannot use the car tonight."), instruct people to perform old or new behaviors ("Take out a piece of paper and prepare to answer the following questions."), and gain friends ("That is a beautiful skirt you're wearing."). The manipulative function of language is probably the most frequently used and the least talked about. We do not like to think of ourselves as being manipulated by others through the use of language; nevertheless, it happens.

We think that Daniel Webster summed up the importance of language—particularly the type that is uttered by the mouth—when he said, "If all my talents and powers were to be taken from me by some inscrutable Providence, and I had my choice of keeping but one, I would unhesitatingly ask to be allowed to keep the Power of Speaking, for through it, I would quickly recover all the rest" (Webster, 1948).

Articles

We have selected four articles to be read in this chapter on verbal communication. The first article, "Taxonomy of Words: A Study of Meaning," explains that the reason for much of our failure in communication is because we don't "recognize the functional aspect of words." Thus, Schufletowski, the author, sets out to develop a way to look at words. His taxonomy takes up where our dictionaries leave off. Take special note in understanding each of the five word functions. How may such an understanding help you in improving your communication with other people?

Have you ever entered a subculture or different country and noticed how differently they use the English language from the way you do? This is the focus of the second article, "Standard English-Diverse Students." The author argues that (1) we should be taught how people speak, not so much how people *should* speak, (2) we should attempt to understand the social implications surrounding language, (3) we should teach those people who speak with dialects the different functions of language, (4) we should provide the opportunity to learn standard English to those who want to, and (5) we should retrain our teachers. How can you argue against this?

The third article, "Oral Language Activities," picks up where the second one left off. Colquit discusses ways that students should be taught the importance of dialectical differences. How many different dialects are discussed? How many of these dialects have you personally encountered? Have you encountered any additional ones? Have you ever had difficulty understanding the people speaking with these dialects? Hopefully, the article will provide some useful insight.

The final article is an interesting one. It was written by Arthur Schlesinger, Jr., an American political historian, and it discusses the importance of a constantly changing language. What kind of difficulty do you think our founding fathers would have in reading our newspapers today? This article will help you in answering this question.

References

D. Bowie, "Is There Life on Mars?" *Hunky Dory* (New York: Gem Production, RCA, 1971)

D. Webster, "Speaking," in *Leaves of Gold*, C. F. Lytle, ed. (Williamsport, Pa.: Coslett Publishing Co., 1948).

Taxonomy of Words: A Study of Meaning

Frank W. Schufletowski

Man's struggle to communicate precisely and effectively is a problem as old as mankind. Many of our efforts to promote understanding have gone awry because of the ambiguities which pervade language. Frequently, language has failed to convey to the receiver the meaning intended by the communicator. Serious, well-intentioned, and knowledgable people often fail to reach commonality of understanding. Even those experts of the language arts, who may also be dedicated to the procedures of logic, seem to make few serious inroads toward securing meaningful communication for themselves. Because of this language confusion, many have deliberately seized the opportunity to exploit others through advertising and propaganda.

Some of the misconstruation which exists may be attributable to our failure to recognize the functional aspects of words. It was with such a context in mind that I developed a taxonomy for identification and classification of words according to their various uses. It appears that there is some justification for such a system.

A possible taxonomical system of analysis to classify words seems to emerge when language is evaluated in relation to: (1) its image referent, (2) its function as a tool for the user or receiver, and (3) its operational relationship to other words in sentences or paragraphs. Precedence for these three relations has been established in literature of semanticists and linguistically oriented philosophers.

One's familiarity with taxonomies is ordinarily related to experience in the natural sciences. The biological taxonomies which classify animals according to phylum, class, order, family, genus, species, and variety provide a meaningful system of communication. From these taxonomies a biologist is able to differentiate the various aspects of the plant and animal domain and to specify their inter-relationships. Such a system insures the natural scientist that he will be commonly understood by his colleagues, and that they are operating from the same structural framework in discussing the phenomena of their discipline.

If a taxonomy of the functions of words were available, what would be its potential for the teacher of communication skills? Though the dictionary has been a common source book in our understanding of language, its value as a tool for the interpretation of poetry, advertising, propaganda, etc. is limited. The dictionary can

From Frank W. Schufletowski, "Taxonomy of Words: A Study of Meaning," *The Clearing House*, 44 (April 1970), pp 474–78. Reprinted with permission.

61

be helpful in defining how a word is generally used, but it does little to help us identify the particular use to which an individual might put a word. The dictionary fails to provide a sound basis for inferring meaning. We lack a system of analysis for helping students understand poetry, novels, or what they read in the newspaper. Are we content to have a teacher give her interpretation and then expect the students to follow suit? We should think not. Yet, hasn't this been the typical situation in which we have found ourselves?

Several benefits are conceivable from developing a word taxonomy. A taxonomy for word usage would help us to recognize the ways in which a particular word might be used. It would help us in our own selection of words for communication because some words have lost both a specific and a general contextual meaning. Such a system might also help us in establishing curricular goals and in developing lesson plans because of our recognition that certain writings are particularly representative of a certain word function. Finally, if such a taxonomy were found fruitful and became accepted, we would have a common vocabulary for the discussion of the various aspects of language.

Taxonomic Analysis

The closer a word comes to having a single image referent which is widely accepted in a particular area, the more precision of meaning has been attained. When words have several referents or perhaps no referent at all, then ambiguity results. The assessment of meaning becomes more and more nebulous until it reaches the point where a word is a tool only for its user and has lost all meaning to the receiver because he either has no referent for the word, or the receiver's referent is entirely different from the user's.

The relationship of words to their actual referent could be classified as the *semantic* function. This is a very precise function of meaning because a word thus employed has the same referent for both user and receiver. Scientists have been the most consistent in communicating at this level.

Although scientists have attained certain precision in communication, it must be recognized that other disciplines have had similar success, but perhaps not as consistently. Furthermore, one is cautioned against wholesale acceptance that science has no language problems. Linguistic ambiguity is quite as demonstrable in science as in other disciplines. However, science may have fewer difficulties because of its objective orientation and operational definitions (that is, defined in terms of the procedures involved in measuring a particular concept).

When the scientist uses the term "horsepower," he is referring to a standard of measurement which has been conceptually and operationally defined, and which can be communicated to his colleagues because of its direct relationship to a common referent. However, this is usually not true outside of the scientific domain. To the man on the street, horsepower may have so many connotations that its usefulness is quite limited. As we shall see later, the common man's usage of horsepower would be at the level of words which I would classify as "pragmatic."

The second function of words may be classified as the *syntactic* function. The syntactic function involves the relationship of words to other words. Thus the correct parts of speech and the construction of complete sentences and paragraphs are essential to the clarification of the actual intent of words.[1] Philip Phenix acknowledges the importance of such a function when he writes:

In syntax, as in morphology, the primacy of structure in the expression of meaning is evident. Dictionary definitions are by no means the sole clues to meaning. Meanings are also communicated by the grammatical structure. In many cases the meaning of a word can be better understood by reference to the context in which it is used than by

---

[1] Words may involve more than one function of language at a time.

consulting a dictionary. Words have different meanings in different contexts. It follows that the meaning of a whole utterance is not simply the sum of the meanings of its component elements. The meaning is in the complete utterance, and the meanings of the several elements in the composite are dependent on their relation to the whole.[2]

Some of the more flagrant examples of the ambiguity arising from failure to recognize this type of word function are observable in the situation where "a man bought a horse from a stranger with a lame hind leg." or the case of the "woman who borrowed an egg from a neighbor that was rotten." Here we are dealing with misplaced modifiers, but there are many other examples. A simple comma left out or misplaced can alter the meaning of a sentence. (I am referring precisely to the fallacious misuse of words which logicians generally call amphibole.) In the example of the "man who purchased several ties with the following colors: red, black, blue, green and white," regarding the last two colors, we are not sure whether two ties were purchased, one green and the other white, or whether one tie had two colors, both green and white. In written communication, a comma after green would eliminate the confusion if two ties were actually represented.[3]

The relationship of words to their users is representative of the *pragmatic* function of words. Words become tools for the writer or speaker. He may use them in unique ways which are very creative, and the meaning may never be entirely clear to the receiver. Writings of novelists and poets are representative of this function. A British critic, William Empson, contends in his work, *Seven Types of Ambiguity*, that the best poems contain much ambiguity; in

fact, they are the richest when they have several levels of meaning.[4]

Tennyson's "Crossing the Bar" is an excellent example of the pragmatic function of words:

Sunset and evening star,
And one clear call for me,
And may there be no moaning of the bar,
When I put out to sea.

Rephrasing this beautiful verse in the pragmatic vernacular of common folk, it could be stated: "Don't bawl over me when I kick the bucket." Semantically, it would simply be stated: "Don't cry over me when I am dead." A similar analogy can be taken from Henry Fielding's novel *Joseph Andrews*. However, Fielding takes us through several dimensions or functions of words, recognizing that they do exist.

> . . . laying hold on the ground with his left hand, he with his right belaboured the body of Adams till he was weary, and, indeed, till he concluded (to use the language of fighting) "that he had done his business"; or, in the language of poetry, "that he had sent him to the shades below"; in plain English, "that he was dead."

A more mundane analogy would be the case of the used car salesman who refers to a particular car as being a "sweetheart" or a "lemon."[5]

The relationship of words to their receivers or consumers could be designated as the *symbolic* function. Certain words provoke extreme emotional manifestations and therefore are subject to numerous interpretations. Words like "freedom" and "patriotism" have so many connotations that they are of limited value.[6] Though a particular philosopher may have a precise mean-

[2]Philip H. Phenix, *Realms of Meaning*, (New York: McGraw-Hill Book Company, 1964), p.68.

[3]For other examples of difficulties caused by failure to recognize the syntactic function, the reader is referred to W. Ward Fearnside and William B. Holther, *Fallacy: The Counterfeit of Argument*. See specifically p. 158 (ambiguous terms), p. 162 (amphibole), and p. 164 (ambiguous punctuation and word order).

[4]William Empson, *Seven Types of Ambiguity*. (London: Chatto and Windus, 1949), p. 258.

[5]An excellent treatment of language problems related to the pragmatic function is found in Mario Pei's *The Story of English*, pp. 163–84.

[6]Examples representative of the symbolic function may be found in the following: W. W. Fearnside and W. B. Holther, *Fallacy: The Counterfeit of Argument*. p. 81, and S. I. Hayakawa, *Language in Thought and Action*, pp. 87–93.

ing for the word "freedom" within his own philosophical framework, this word is highly ambiguous to the general public—and often to other philosophers! In using such words, one would provide a service to others by defining it in his own terms. Propagandists are particularly adept at taking advantage of this word function.

The essential difference between the pragmatic function of words and the symbolic is that in the former situation the word is a tool for the user, but in the latter situation once the word has been released, it becomes a tool for the consumer, that is, he consciously or not chooses the meaning that best fills his needs.[7] The image referent usually is highly distorted. Words at this level have practically no generic value.

In times of extreme stress, some words acquire connotations which lose meaning on any logical or common experiential basis. Whatever is the source of this anxiety (sometimes it may be war, strife of enemy philosophies from within or without our country, etc.), we tend to project ourselves emotionally into certain words. Such words may relate to our own prejudices and fears as well as to the efforts of propaganda networks to exploit us.

An example of this appeared in Stuart Chase's 1938 book entitled *The Tyranny of Words*.[8] At that time, rulers espousing "fascist" doctrine had become an apparent threat to other members of the world community. Chase showed the results of a poll where various United States citizens were asked the meaning of "fascism." He found very little agreement in their definitions, even though representative occupational and educational levels had been included.

F. H. Sanford in his article, "Speech and Personality," wrote: "There are many indica-

tions that language is a vehicle of personality as well as of thought...."[9] Harold D. Lasswell recognized man's ability to evoke extreme emotional responses by selecting particular words. He said:

> When men want power, they act according to their expectation of how to maximize power. Hence symbols (words and images) affect power as they affect expectations of power."[10]

The relationship of words to their purposes of identification has been designated in this analysis as the *performatic* function. Our names are necessary in performing the everyday affairs of society. We sign checks, wills, and contracts; however, the words in our names though having had etymological origins are still quite meaningless. All proper nouns would be in this category. Names of cities, countries, etc. are representative.

Wittgenstein, writing in his *Philosophical Investigations*, provided an excellent example of what is classified in this analysis as the performatic function.

> The name "Peter" is the name of a person, but this person is not what the name "Peter" means. When Peter dies it is the bearer of the name "Peter" who dies and not the meaning of the name "Peter." Bearers of proper names live and die; meanings can do neither. Proper names are names par excellence, and, in fact, one never asks what proper names mean. We do not ask, "What does Peter mean?" but "Who is Peter?" It would be absurd to say to anyone who did ask what "Peter" means that it meant a person standing by the window. One might, however, answer that "Peter" meant "rock." But there is a difference in this sense of the word "meaning"—the difference between saying that *rouge* means the color at which

---

[7] A number of studies have been made in which personality and verbal behavior were related to language. For an excellent survey of these studies, see John B. Carroll. *The Study of Language*, pp. 79–120.

[8] Stuart Chase, *The Tyranny of Words*, (New York: Harcourt, Brace and Company, 1938), p. 188.

[9] Fillmore Sanford, "Speech and Personality," *Psychological Bulletin*, vol. 39, p. 840.

[10] Harold Lasswell, *Language of Politics: Studies in Quantitative Semantics*, (New York: Stewart, 1949), p. 18.

I am now pointing and saying that *rouge* means "red."[11]

Conclusion

The worth of such a taxonomic analysis as this is in recognizing the various ways in which a word might be used, and that certain functions of words are much more precise in terms of measurement and communication than others. Nevertheless, there are genuine needs in our society for each of the functions of words. The needs of scientists for accurate, precise communications are not the same for poets, novelists, or the man on the street, etc. Their purposes or reasons for communication are not the same, and it is not valid to expect that their functions of words should be similar. Value can-

not be placed on any particular function as to its usefulness in contrast with another function in the word domain.

A study has been completed which demonstrates that this taxonomy can be taught to high school students. The results from this study suggests that students became quite critical of their own word usage and that of their peers. The test given to students after completion of the taxonomy unit indicated that pupils of average ability were capable of correctly identifying many items. Furthermore, an item analysis of the test items confirmed that students who obtained high test scores in relation to their group showed almost consensual agreement on the answers considered to be correct by the instructor.[12]

[11] Justus Hartnack, *Wittgenstein and Modern Philosophy*, (Garden City, N.Y.: Anchor Books, 1965), p. 69.

[12] Gene Liles, *Eleventh Grade Students and a Taxonomical Analysis of the Functions of Words* (Unpublished Master's Research Project, University of Kansas, 1968).

Standard English-Diverse Students

William Proefriedt

When my eleven-year-old son says, "I brang it home" or "I don't got none" I become more enraged than a prurient censor at an Andy Warhol movie. The difference is that I *know* there is no moral dimension to speaking "correctly." I *know* that language usage evolves and that it is not established by any absolute rule-maker. I *know* that different groups within society speak different varieties of the language and that it makes no sense to classify one as superior to the other. But still, I wish my son would stop saying "brang" and "I don't got none."

Why do teachers who ought to know better react with moral outrage to deviations from standard English? The problem is a very complex one, but we ought to at least recognize the fact that we live in a relatively mobile society and that the way in which we speak serves to some extent as both a highly audible indicator of our social status and as a ticket enabling us to move from group to group. Language is used by many as a crucial sorting device in our society. If we wish our own children or our students to be able to operate at certain levels of the society, it is

necessary to equip them with the proper language tools. Emily Post is only read by those moving up—not by those who have no aspirations or by those who arrived a long time ago.

Although that sounds like a particularly sordid role for an English teacher to be playing—a linguistic Emily Post, in fact, it is much more defensible than the role of English teacher as "preserver of standards," or as judge of the right and wrong uses of language. At least it begins to acknowledge the game we are playing. Given the social realities of our society, the moral fervor of the English teacher is partly understandable. Whatever its roots, this fervor too often transmits the message to students that their own use of language is inferior and perhaps even morally objectionable and that there is a standard English, which always was and always will be, towards which all right thinking people should strive. Few contemporary English teachers would consciously subscribe to either of these beliefs, nevertheless they are transmitted. Some English teachers would be willing to make statements like: "I don't want simply to teach my students how language is used. I want to teach them how it ought to be used." What do they mean by such statements? Do they mean that they wish to teach students to speak and write in such a way that their thoughts are effectively communicated? No one could quarrel with that purpose. But, if effective communication is the goal, why do some teachers insist on "It's I" rather than "It's me?" Doesn't each phrase say the same thing? But effective communication has, of course, almost nothing to do with arbitrary rules which do not describe the way in which real people in real situations use language. Learning to communicate well is largely a matter of learning appropriate word and sentence choices within a social context.

Why then am I still angry with my son for his "don't got" and "brang" approach to life? And more importantly who do I question the anger? For the same reason that the English teacher hesitates to accept the role of a linguistic Emily Post. We are not so sure that we want to encourage our children to play somebody else's game. The English teacher may object to the function which society has assigned him: to prepare students to be upwardly mobile. He may further object to society's use of language criteria to determine who shall have access to money and power. He may be in serious conflict with the dominant values of the larger society and not wish to be simply a functionary keeping it running. (It would, of course, be naive to think that all English teachers raise such objections.) But for those who do, the outlook is rather bleak. If the teacher commits all of his energies toward developing language habits which will help his students to climb the social pyramid, he betrays his own best instincts; if on the other hand, he ignores the linguistic and social realities of the society, he may be shortchanging the students in terms of their own goals.

The problems can be seen more starkly in the case of Black, Spanish-speaking and other minority group students. Leaders of these groups see language teaching as a particularly sore point in their relations with white society. For too long, minority group students have been exposed to teacher attitudes which have resulted in poor self-perceptions. Teachers' disdain for a nonstandard dialect or a foreign tongue spoken by a minority group has made no small contribution to a poor self-image. In fact, to be upwardly mobile is often equated by the Black or Spanish-speaking student with turning his back on his own people and destroying the growing solidarity of his own group. Learning different language patterns (like learning new customs in dress, eating, and behavior) raises certain insecurities and doubts about one's present manner of communication. If people are interested in asserting the value of present patterns, then the value of learning another language or pattern of language becomes questionable. In *Black Power: The Politics of Liberation in America* (Random House, 1967), Stokely Carmichael and Charles Hamilton have insisted that "the racial and cultural personality of the black must be preserved and that community must win its freedom while preserving its cultural integrity." That cultural integrity, and the self-acceptance that goes with it, will almost inevitably be challenged in the learning of standard English.

Most English teachers, informed that they are playing the role of cultural imperialists, would react with some degree of surprise. Even though some English teachers are racists and believe in the inherent superiority of their own language and culture, that does not seem to be the major problem, which is that English teachers fail to recognize the nature of power relationships in our society and their own functions within those relationships. The reason that English teachers are teaching standard English to Black and Spanish-speaking students is simply that there are more people with more power and money in our society who speak something close to standard English than there are people who speak Spanish or some non-standard English dialect. What constitutes standard English has nothing to do with morality or aesthetics; it has everything to do with power. Historically, the exercise of that power has been less than gracious.

What then is the English teacher supposed to do when he comes to recognize that his teaching of the language involves him in a whole set of values and structures to which he objects? It seems to me, that there are a number of directions in which he might move and that these directions ought to be chosen on essentially educational rather than political criteria.

First, *students should realistically be taught how people speak*. Students can be encouraged to do rudimentary linguistic field work, and they will quickly learn that different groups in our society speak in quite different ways. An imaginative teacher can construct many field work experiences which would allow students to use their observational skills in an effort to understand how language is used. Such activities necessitate the building of a conceptual framework to aid in the analysis of various language patterns. For example, students can be encouraged to observe how different individuals and groups express the concept of possession in their dialects. What grammatical devices are used? Or, students can pursue the question of how different language groups handle the problem of expressing past, present and future time in their sentence formulations. Such an approach to language places great demands on students, requiring not only the building of a conceptual framework, but also empirical research skills and a rigorous attention to detail. Anyone who sees studying how language is actually spoken as somehow a lowering of standards seems to be using the word "standards" in a rather odd way. Students who engage in this approach would certainly develop more sophistication about language and a greater ability to communicate in various contexts than those who are taught only "proper" English.

Second, building on a scientific approach to the study of language, *teachers can begin to move students into an understanding of all of the social implications which surround language behavior*. Students can be encouraged to carefully examine their own and others' attitudes toward language and to understand the ways in which language is related to the social and economic realities of the society. The important thing is that language be objectified, in the same sense as the anthropologist looks at the particular customs of a group of people. Individual insecurity and fear thrive in a situation in which some mysterious absolute standard is held out to students. Those who fail to behave properly (linguistically or otherwise) are cast aside. The psychological problems generated by an academically disreputable attitude toward language can become a set of objectified problems concerning the relation between language and society.

Third, *those students who speak a dialect other than standard or network English will then be in a position to make a choice, since they have learned the ways in which language functions*. It is a choice that is analogous in all its essentials to decisions about dress. Recognizing that dressing in certain ways will have a given impact on other people in the society, I can choose to act in a number of ways. I can, for example, rebel against the norm and dress in a way that will lead to rejection by some. Another possible stance is to wear whatever clothes will be helpful in achieving one's own purposes. There are all sorts of variations on these attitudes. Such choices are, however, possible only when the clothing issue has been objectified. Believing that there is only one proper way of dressing, almost guarantees insecurity as one attempts to meet that absolute standard.

Fourth, *students who choose to learn standard English for their own purposes ought to be provided with an opportunity to do so*. An understanding of the way in which language functions in the society should, however, precede that choice.

Finally, beyond the steps which might be taken by the individual English teachers, *there is undoubtedly a need for some significant changes in the way in which teachers are trained*. Teachers need to gain a more anthropological view of language. They themselves need to experience the difficulty of learning to speak and read a dialect, other than their native one, with the attendant psychological difficulties. This is an especially important experience for those teaching standard English to a non-standard English speaking group.

Oral Language Activities

Jesse Colquit

If schools really want to recognize cultural diversity and the uniqueness of individuals and divergent groups, they might well begin with an appreciation and understanding of dialect differences. Developing an understanding and appreciation of dialects, one's own as well as others, is a major goal in a pluralistic society. Many students who come to school are rejected by their teachers and classmates, because they are made to feel that their dialect is inferior. It is at school that students expect their identity to be confirmed and validated, not rejected. When we reject the dialect of students, we are rejecting them. However, a study of dialects can be a means of affirming students' sense of their own worth.

Begin by reading aloud to students; introduce them to literature and poetry, music and drama that reflects dialect differences. This promotes an appreciation of dialects rather than teaching the dialects themselves. The oral reading of literature that reflects dialect differences maintains many of the dialect's effective communication devices—variation of rhyme and rhythmic patterns, the exact meaning and mood, or tonal range—which is lost on the printed page.

Of course, in examining dialects as they appear in literature, teachers (and students) need to be conscious of the fact that the material was written by an artist, not a linguist. While writers may be sensitive to dialect differences, their attempts to represent dialect on the printed page are not always entirely accurate or successful. Indeed, as several of the examples which follow show, writers are, on occasion, guilty of presenting dialect stereotypes, but such stereotyping is itself interesting material for class discussion and can help students see the dangers of stereotyping through and in language.

To serve as a springboard in introducing a class to different dialects, the teacher might begin by reading aloud "The Split Cherry Tree" by Jesse Stuart, using examples to illustrate the beauty of its mountain dialect and to help students sense the style, form, and rhythmic pattern reflected in the words of Pa.

"No," says pa, "Jist readin', writin', and cipherin'. We didn't have all this bug larnin', frog larnin', and findin', germs on your teeth and in the middle o'black snakes!

From Jesse Colquit, "Oral Language Activities for Promoting an Understanding and Appreciation of Dialect Differences," *English Journal*, December, 1974. Copyright © 1974 by the National Council of Teachers of English. Reprinted by permission of the publisher and the author.

69

"I aint larned 'em to do that. I aint got much larnin' myself but I do know right from wrong after I see through a thing."[1]

The diversity of dialects often found within a single family reinforces the value of the school's role in fostering an understanding and appreciation of dialect differences. In "The Split Cherry Tree" students can develop awareness and appreciation of dialect differences by examining the speech of Pa in contrast to that of his son Dave and Professor Herbert. Role playing or dramatic readings of a passage like the following can serve usefully:

"I says: Professor Herbert said I could do it some other time. He said for you to go home with me."

"No," says pa. "You are goin. to do as he says . . . I'll help you pay it. I'll ast 'im and see if he want let me help you!"

"I'm going to cancel the debt," says Professor Herbert. "I just wanted you to understand, Luster."

"I understand," says pa, "and since I understand, he must pay his debt fer th' tree and I am goin' to help 'im."[2]

Reading poetry and literature to the class is an excellent way to show how dialects change. Introduce the class to the New England dialect that was used one hundred years ago by reading James Russell Lowell's poem, "The Courtin." Examples from "The Courtin" can help students identify ways in which that New England dialect of a century ago is different from socially acceptable contemporary speech especially in syntax, spelling, pronounciation, and vocabulary:

Zekle crep' up quite unbeknown an' peeked in thru' the winder, an' there sot Hudly all alone, "Ith no one nigh to hender.[3]

To give the class an example of current New England dialect and to reinforce the concept that changes in dialect reflect changes in cultural patterns, introduce Robert Frost's poem, "Mending Wall," to the class after reading "The Courtin." As a follow-up activity, elicit from students the dialect changes in syntax, pronunciation, vocabulary, and spelling found in "Mending Wall." Mark Twain's *Adventures of Huckleberry Finn*, which depicts the dialect of Missouri over one hundred years ago might be used to extend the concept of dialect changes and to show that while written dialect loses much of its effectiveness to the printed page, oral dialect communicates more effectively. They will also become aware that as the intensity of dialect enhances a story it increases its reading difficulty.

"You may well say it Brer Hightower! It is jist as I was a-sayin' to Brer Phelps, his own self. s'e. What do you think of it, Sister Hotchkiss? s'e. Think o' what, Brer Phelps? s'I. Think o' that bed leg sawed off that a way? s'e. Think of it? s'I. I say it never sawed itself off, s'I somebody sawed it, s'I; that's my opinion, take it or leave it, it mayn't be no 'count, s'I, but such as 't is, it's my opinion, s'I, 'n' if anybody k'n start a better one, s'I, let him do it, s'I, that's all. I says to Sister Dunlap, s'I—"[4]

After the students have read the example, silently and reacted to it, ask students who read well to take turns reading it aloud; then elicit their reaction again—leading them to discover that dialect is more difficult to read and is more attuned to the ear than the printed page.

Oral reading of good literature which depicts different dialects helps sutdents learn something new about their country, appreciate people who are different, and recognize cultural diversity and the uniqueness of divergent groups. Students also discover for themselves that while some dialects are not as socially acceptable as others, they can be a much more effective means of communication. For instance, in "The Heifer Hide" (in *The Jake Tales*, a collection of stories

---

[1] J. Kenner Agnew and Agnes L. McCarthy, *Prose and Poetry for Enjoyment* (New York: The L. W. Singer Company, 1955), p. 60.

[2] Agnew, p. 62.

[3] Louis Untermyer, ed. *Library of Great American Writing*, Volume I. (Chicago: Britannica Press, 1960), p. 723.

[4] Mark Twain, *The Adventures of Huckleberry Finn* (New York: New American Library, 1959), p. 271.

by Richard Chase from the Appalachian Mountain folk), while much of the syntax, pronunciation, and vocabulary used is not currently socially acceptable, the effectiveness and clarity of the message is actually *enhanced* by the dialect:

> *"Well, now," she says, "hit's just a little I was a'savin' for my kinfolks comin' tomorrow." "Me and Jack's your kinfolks. Bring it on out here for us."*
>
> *So Jack and him eat a lots of them good rations. Jack was awful hungry, and he knowed she hadn't brought out her best stuff yet, so he rammed his heifer hide again, says, "you blabber-mouthed thing! I done told you to hush. You keep on tellin' lies now and I'll put you out the door."* [5]

Much of the great literature in our heritage is written in a western and southern dialect. To whet the class's appetite for literature in a western dialect, use the ballad, "Whoopee ti yi yo, Get Along Little Doggie," as an example of occupational dialect which has enriched our language:

> *Whoopee ti yi yo, git along, little doggies,*
> *It's your misfortune and none of my own;*
> *Whoopee ti yi yo, git along, little doggies*
> *For you know Wyoming will be your new home.* [6]

For a southern mountain dialect, "Old Fire Dragon," a short story by Richard Chase, can be read aloud and discussed.

While geography has been a major factor in determining diversity in dialect, religious groups, particularly the Quakers, have also contributed special dialects. A major source for introducing students to Quaker dialect is *Friendly Persuasion*, a collection of short stories by Jessamyn West; examples from "The Pacing Goose" might be read aloud to illustrate the dialect contribution of the Quakers, especially in vocabulary:

> *"Eliza," he said, "if Thee wants to go through with it I'll go to Vernon and fee a lawyer for Thee. Thee'll have to go to court. be on the witness stand—and even then I misdoubt thee'll ever get thy goose back. Doe thee still want me to do it?" Yes, Jess I want Thee to do it."* [7]

Like other literary works, music is used to reflect different dialects, and for some children this is the best medium to help them understand and appreciate dialect differences. Make provisions for the class to listen to recordings that represent different dialects. While listening, they can observe the syntax, pronunciation, vocabulary and intonations used. To grasp the flavor of western dialect, the class might listen to "Home on the Range," and for mountain dialect, "You All Come to See Us Now and Then." Elicit from the students dialect differences observed in the two songs. For contemporary dialects, turn to popular music—Bob Dylan, for example.

Some of the major works in literature are written in Black dialect, and efforts should be made to expose students to these literary works. But in selecting literature, avoid the use of material that tends to promote racial stereotypes. In "A Century of Negro Portraiture in American Literature," Sterling Brown noted five major racial stereotypes of Blacks which have been perpetuated by writers: the contented slave, the comic minstrel, the wretched freedman, the brute Negro, and the tragic mulatto. [8] Among the literary works in Black dialect that perpetuate a racial stereotype is, of course, the *Tales of Uncle Remus* by Joel Chandler Harris. Uncle Remus is a hyphenated man with "contentment," a Black man with a childlike mind, the epitome of docility and accommodation; and the wretched freedman noted by Sterling Brown as a racial stereotype was also perpetuated by Harris in his writing of "Free Joe and the Rest of the World."

As an introduction to Black dialect, one might begin with Paul Lawrence Dunbar's poem, "In

[5] Richard Chase, *The Jake Tales* (Boston: Houghton Mifflin, 1943), p. 165.

[6] John A. Lomax and Alan Lomax, *Cowboy Songs and Other Frontier Ballads* (New York: Macmillan Company, 1957), p. 5.

[7] Jessamyn West, *Friendly Persuasion* (New York: Harcourt Brace and Company, 1945), p. 39.

[8] Sterling Brown, "A Century of Negro Portraiture in American Literature," *Massachusetts Review*, VII (1966), pp. 73-96.

the Morning" which was written prior to 1900. By reading the poem aloud, students can identify changes in Black dialect since 1900. In these lines from the poem, note the differences in spelling, grammar, pronunciation, and vocabulary as compared to contemporary black dialect:

Come hyeah; bring me dat ah strap!
Boy, I'll whup you 'twell you drap;
You done felt you' se'f too strong,
An' you sholy got me wrong.
Set down at dat table thaih;
Jes' you whimpah if you daih!
Evah mo'nin' on dis place
Seem lak I mus' lose my grace.[9]

For a contrast in Black verse dialect and to give the class an example of contemporary Black dialect, introduce the class to "The Ballad of the Landlord" by Langston Hughes. A comparison to "In The Morning," shows clear dialect differences.

Landlord, Landlord,
My roof has a sprung leak.
Don't you 'member I told you about it
Way last week?

What? You gonna get eviction orders?
You gonna cut off my heat?
You gonna take my furniture and
Throw it in the streets?[10]

A diversity of rhythms is conspicuous in Black speech and encompasses spirituals, blues, and jazz.[11] Selected poems of Langston Hughes can help students identify the rhythms of Black speech. As an example, these lines from "The Fire" reflect the rhythm of spirituals:

Fire,
Fire, Lord!
Fire gonna burn ma soul!
I mean Fire, Lord!
Fire gonna burn ma soul![12]

Poems from the anthology, *God's Trombones*, by James Weldon Johnson, can be read aloud to the class to extend the concept of the rhythm of spirituals. In "Sylvester's Dying Bed," for example, the rhythm of the blues is reflected in these lines:

But I felt ma time's a-comin',
And I know'd I's dyin' fast.
I seed the River of Jerdent
A-creepin' muddy past-
But I's still Sweet Papa 'Vester,
Yes, Sir! Long as life do last![13]

In these lines from "The Trumpet Player" the rhythm of jazz is reflected:

The music
From the trumpet at his lips
Is honey
Mixed with liquid fire.
The rhythm
From the trumpet at his lips
Is ecstasy
Distilled from old desire-[14]

An effective medium for depicting Black dialect or any other dialect is dialogue or drama. A major source for involving students in drama, as well as poetry and prose, is an anthology, *The Negro Caravan*, by Sterling Brown. Randolph Edmondson's play, "Bad Man," can be dramatized to reinforce the class's understanding of dialect differences in Black English. And, of course, as with other groups, one finds dialect differences within Black families. Have students dramatize "Riding the Goat," a one act play by Willis Richardson, and compare the differences between the speech of Ant Hetty (the grandmother) and that of Ruth (the granddaughter) in the play:

Ant Hetty: *Jes' lef' the minute befo' you come in. He lef' that uniform an' I guess he'll be back.*

Ruth: *Grandma, you should have looked in the sewing room today. You know the Framinghams on Charles Street don't you?*

Ant Hetty: *Now listen, who you'se askin'!*

[9] Stephen E. Anderson, *Understanding the New Black Poetry* (New York: William Morrow and Company, Inc., 1972), p. 93.
[10] Langston Hughes, *Selected Poems* (New York: Knopf, 1959), p. 238-239.
[11] Robert T. Kerlin, *Negro Poets and Their Poems* (Washington, D.C.: Associated Publishers, Inc., 1935), p. 235.
[12] Hughes, p. 20.

[13] Ibid., p. 38.
[14] Ibid., p. 114.

'Course I do; ain't them the folks Mary Riles works fo'? [15]

The question is not whether to use Black dialect, but when? There is a rich store of literary sources in the Black experience in which the use of Black dialect is more appropriate than so-called standard English. But there is also a rich store of literary sources in the Black experience in which standard English has been used. Students might examine the work of a writer like Langston Hughes, who wrote both in dialect and standard English, and discuss the special effectiveness of each.

Since divergent groups and ethnic groups are unique, it follows that their dialect is unique; this concept can be developed by reading aloud examples from *Strawberry Girl* by Lois Lenski. In this example, note the idiom and narrative style, the expressive pattern, the extensive naming and the enumeration of action. Within the paragraph is a complete story encompassing the major ingredients of a story—exposition, problem, rising action, climax, falling action, and conclusion:

"I went amblin' in the scrub," said shoestring in his usual bragging tone, and I came to a little branch, where there was lots bushes grown', and my hound dog baged a rattlesnake. I smelled him first, and in a minute I seed him. I cut me this long bamboo pole and I tied a good strong string 'bout three feet long on the end, with a loop dangling. Ole snake was afeard o' me now and started to run under a thicket. I jest swung my pole, looped the loop right over his head—not tight enough to choke him—pulled it up and dropped him in my sack. And thar he is!" [16]

Helping students understand and appreciate dialect differences is also an excellent way for teachers to see that initial language growth must occur in the student's own culture and dialect. Giving students opportunities for success in their own dialect enhances their self concept and says to them that they are accepted. But it also serves as a basis for extending the student's degree of participation in a variety of language activities, which will, in turn, lead to an extension of dialect into more widely used styles of speech. The prevailing attitude of students concerning their dialect is a reflection of the attitude of teachers; thus a change in the attitude of teachers is a prerequisite for changing the attitudes of students.

Good planning from ample sources, discrimination in the selection of material, followed by guided reading and discussion, can result in an exploration of dialect differences that affirms each student's "identity." This will involve changes in the feeling and attitude of teachers and students concerning dialects and will lead to new awareness and appreciation of cultural diversity.

[15] Willis Richardson, *Plays and Pageants from the Life of the Negro* (Washington, D.C.: The Associated Publishers, Inc., 1930), p. 151.

[16] Lois Lenski, *Strawberry Girls* (Philadelphia and New York: J. B. Lippincott Company, 1945), p. 109.

Politics and the American Language

Arthur Schlesinger, Jr.

> *In our time, political speech and writing are largely the defence of the indefensible.*
> —George Orwell

It takes a certain fortitude to pretend to amend Orwell on this subject. But "Politics and the English Language"—which I herewith incorporate by reference—was written more than a generation ago. In the years since, the process of semantic collapse has gathered speed, verified all of Orwell's expectations and added new apprehensions for a new age. Americans in particular have found this a painful period of self-recognition. In 1946 we comfortably supposed that Orwell was talking about other people—Nazis and Stalinists, bureaucrats and sociologists, Professor Lancelot Hogben and Professor Harold Laski. Now recent history has obliged us to extend his dispiriting analysis to ourselves.

Vietnam and Watergate: these horrors will trouble the rest of our lives. But they are not, I suppose, unmitigated horrors. "Every act rewards itself," said Emerson. As Vietnam instructed us, at terrible cost, in the limit of our wisdom

and power in foreign affairs so Watergate instructed us, at considerably less cost, in the limits of wisdom and power in the presidency. It reminded us of the urgent need to restore the original balance of the Constitution—the balance between presidential power and presidential accountability. In doing this, it has, among other things, brought back into public consciousness the great documents under which the American government was organized.

The Constitution, the debates of the Constitutional Convention, *The Federalist Papers*—how many of us read them with sustained attention in earlier years? A few eccentrics like Justice Black and Senator Ervin pored over them with devotion. The rest of us regarded them, beyond an occasional invocation of the Bill of Rights or the Fourteenth Amendment, as documents of essentially historical interest and left them undisturbed on the shelf. Then, under the goad first of Vietnam and then of Watergate, legislators, editors, columnists, even political scientists and historians—everyone, it would seem, except for presidential lawyers—began turning the dusty pages in order to find out what Madison said in the convention about the war-making power or how Hamilton defined the

From Arthur Schlesinger, Jr., "Politics and the American Language," *The American Scholar*, 43 (1974), pp. 553–62. Reprinted with permission.

74

grounds for impeachment in the sixty-fifth Federalist. Vietnam and Watergate are hardly to be compared. One is high tragedy, the other low, if black, comedy. But between them they have given the American people a spectacular re-education in the fundamentals of our constitutional order.

One cannot doubt that this experience will have abiding political significance. The effect of Vietnam in exorcising our illusions and chastening our ambitions in foreign affairs has long been manifest. Now we begin to see the effect of Watergate in raising the standards of our politics. But I am less concerned initially with the political than with the literary consequences of this return to our constitutional womb. For, in addition to their exceptional qualities of insight and judgment, the historic documents must impress us by the extraordinary distinction of their language.

This was the age of the Enlightenment in America. The cooling breeze of reason tempered the hot work of composition and argument. The result was the language of the Founding Fathers—lucid, measured and felicitous prose, marked by Augustan virtues of harmony, balance and elegance. People not only wrote this noble language. They also read it. The essays in defense of the Constitution signed Publius appeared week after week in the New York press during the winter of 1787–88; and the demand was so great that the first thirty-six Federalist papers were published in book form while the rest were still coming out in the papers. One can only marvel at the sophistication of an audience that consumed and relished pieces so closely reasoned, so thoughtful and analytical. To compare *The Federalist Papers* with their equivalents in the press of our own day—say, with the contributions to the Op Ed page of the *New York Times*—is to annotate the decay of political discourse in America.

No doubt the birth of a nation is a stimulus to lofty utterance, The Founding Fathers had a profound conviction of historical responsibility. "The people of this country, by their conduct and example," Madison wrote in *The Federalist*,"

will decide the important question, whether societies of men are really capable or not of establishing good government from reflection and choice, or whether they are forever destined to depend for their political constitutions on accident and force." The substitution of reflection and choice for accident and force proposed a revolution in the history of government; and the authors of *The Federalist* were passionate exemplars of the politics of reason.

The Founding Fathers lived, moreover, in an age when politicians could say in public more or less what they believed in private. If their view of human nature was realistic rather than sentimental, they were not obliged to pretend otherwise. *The Federalist*, for example, is a work notably free of false notes. It must not be supposed, however, that even this great generation was immune to temptation. When the Founding Fathers turned to speak of and to the largest interest in a primarily agricultural nation, they changed their tone and relaxed their standards. Those who lived on the soil, Jefferson could inanely write, were "the chosen people of God ...whose breasts He has made His peculiar deposit for substantial and genuine virtue." Such lapses from realism defined one of the problems of American political discourse. For, as society grew more diversified, new interests claimed their place in the sun; and each in time had to be courted and flattered as the Jeffersonians had courted and flattered the agriculturists. The desire for success at the polls thus sentimentalized and cheapened the language of politics.

And politics was only an aspect of a deeper problem. Society as a whole was taking forms that warred against clarity of thought and integrity of language. "A man's power to connect his thought with its proper symbol, and so to utter it," said Emerson, "depends on the simplicity of his character, that is, upon his love of truth, and his desire to communicate it without loss. The corruption of man is followed by the corruption of language. When simplicity of character and the sovereignty of ideas is broken up by the prevalence of secondary desires, the desire of riches, of pleasure, of power, and of praise . . . words are perverted to stand for things which are not."

"The prevalence of secondary desires," the desire of riches, pleasure, power and praise—this growing social complexity began to divert the function of words from expression to gratification. No one observed the impact of a mobile and egalitarian society on language more acutely than Tocqueville. Democracy, he argued, inculcated a positive preference for ambiguity and a dangerous addiction to the inflated style. "An abstract term," Tocqueville wrote, "is like a box with a false bottom; you may put in what you please, and take them out again without being observed." So words, divorced from objects, became instruments less of communication than of deception. Unscrupulous orators stood abstractions on their head and transmuted them into their opposites, aiming to please one faction by the sound and the contending faction by the meaning. They did not always succeed. "The word *liberty* in the mouth of Webster," Emerson wrote with contempt after the Compromise of 1850, "sounds like the word *love* in the mouth of a courtezan." Watching Henry Kissinger babbling about his honor at his famous Salzburg press conference, one was irresistibly reminded of another of Emerson's nonchalant observations; "The louder he talked of his honor, the faster we counted our spoons."

Other developments hastened the spreading dissociation of words from meaning, of language from reality. The rise of mass communications, the growth of large organizations and novel technologies, the invention of advertising and public relations, the professionalization of education—all contributed to linguistic pollution, upsetting the ecological balance between words and their environment. In our own time the purity of language is under unrelenting attack from every side—from professors as well as from politicians, from newspapermen as well as from advertising men, from men of the cloth as well as from men of the sword, and not least from those indulgent compilers of modern dictionaries who propound the suicidal thesis that all usages are equal and all correct.

A living language can never be stabilized, but a serious language can never cut words altogether adrift from meanings. The alchemy that changes words into their opposites has never had more adept practitioners than it has today. We used to object when the Communists described dictatorships as "people's democracies" or North Korean aggression as the act of a "peace-loving" nation. But we are no slouches ourselves in the art of verbal metamorphosis. There was often not much that was "free" about many of the states that made up what we used to call, sometimes with capital letters, the Free World; as there is, alas, very often little that is gay about many of those who seek these days to kidnap that sparkling word for specialized use. Social fluidity, moral pretension, political and literary demagoguery, corporate and academic bureaucratization and a false conception of democracy are leading us into semantic chaos. We owe to Vietnam and Watergate a belated recognition of the fact that we are in linguistic as well as political crisis and that the two may be organically connected. As Emerson said, "We infer the spirit of the nation in great measure from the language."

For words are not neutral instruments, pulled indifferently out of a jumbled tool kit. "Language," wrote Coleridge, "is the armoury of the human mind; and at once contains the trophies of its past, and the weapons of its future conquests." Language colors and penetrates the depths of our consciousness. It is the medium that dominates perceptions, organizes categories of thought, shapes the development of ideas and incorporates a philosophy of existence. Every political movement generates its own language-field; every language-field legitimizes one set of motives, values and ideals and banishes the rest. The language-field of the Founding Fathers directed the American consciousness toward one constellation of standards and purposes. The language-field of Vietnam and Watergate has tried to direct the national consciousness toward very different goals. Politics in basic aspects is a symbolic and therefore a linguistic phenomenon. We began to realize this in the days of the

Indochina War. In the middle 1960s Americans found themselves systematically staving off reality by allowing a horrid military-bureaucratic patois to protect our sensibilities from the ghastly things we were doing in Indochina. The official patter about "attrition," "pacification," "defoliation," "body counts," "progressive squeeze-and-talk," sterilized the frightful reality of napalm and My Lai. This was the period when television began to provide a sharper access to reality, and Marshall McLuhan had his day in court.

But the military-bureaucratic jargon could be blamed on generals, who, as General Eisenhower reminded us at every press conference, habitually speak in a dialect of their own. What we had not perhaps fully realized before Watergate was the utter debasement of language in the mouths of our recent civilian leaders. How our leaders really talk is not, of course, easy to discover, since their public appearances are often veiled behind speeches written by others. I know that President Kennedy spoke lucidly, wittily and economically in private. President Johnson spoke with force and often in pungent and inventive frontier idiom. President Nixon's fascinating contribution to oral history suggests, however, a recent and marked decline in the quality of presidential table talk. "A man cannot speak," said Emerson, "but he judges himself."

Groping to describe that degenerate mélange of military, public relations and locker-room jargon spoken in the Nixon White House. Richard N. Goodwin aptly wrote of "the bureaucratization of the criminal class." It was as if the Godfather spoke in the phrases of the secretary of health, education and welfare. When one read of "stroking sessions," of "running out of the bottom line," of "toughing it out," of going down "the hang-out road," or "how do you handle that PR-wise," one felt that there should be one more impeachable offense; and that is verbicide. But what was worse than the massacre of language, which after all displayed a certain low ingenuity, was the manipulation of meaning. The presidential speech preceding the release of the expurgated transcripts was syntacti-

cally correct enough. But it proclaimed in tones of ringing sincerity that the transcripts showed exactly the opposite of what in fact the transcripts did show. "He unveils a swamp," as the *New Yorker* well put it, "and instructs us to see a garden of flowers." In the Nixon White House, language not only fled the reality principle but became the servant of nightmare.

"The use of words," wrote Madison in the thirty-seventh *Federalist*, "is to express ideas. Perspicuity, therefore, requires not only that the ideas should be distinctly formed, but that they should be expressed by words distinctly and exclusively appropriate to them." Madison was under no illusion that this condition of semantic beatitude was easy to attain. "No language is so copious," he continued, "as to supply words and phrases for every complex idea, or so correct as not to include many equivocally denoting different ideas. . . . When the Almighty himself condescends to address mankind in their own language, his meaning, luminous as it must be, is rendered dim and doubtful by the cloudy medium through which it is communicated." Nevertheless, Madison and his generation thought the quest for precision worth the effort. It is an entertaining but morbid speculation to wonder what the Founding Fathers, returning to inspect the Republic on the eve of the two-hundredth anniversary of the independence they fought so hard to achieve, would make of the White House tapes.

The degradation of political discourse in America is bound to raise a disturbing question. May it be, as Tocqueville seemed to think, that such deterioration is inherent in democracy? Does the compulsion to win riches, pleasure, power and praise in a fluid and competitive society make the perversion of meaning and the debasement of language inevitable? One can certainly see specific American and democratic traits that have promoted linguistic decay. But a moment's reflection suggests that the process is by no means confined to the United States nor to democracies. Language degenerates a good deal more rapidly and thoroughly in communist and fascist states. For the control of language is a necessary step toward the control of minds, as Orwell made so brilliantly clear in *1984*. Nowhere is meaning more ruthlessly manipulated, nowhere is language more stereotyped, mechanical, implacably banal and systematically false, nowhere is it more purged of personal nuance and human inflection, than in Russia and China. In democracies the assault on language is piecemeal, sporadic and unorganized. And democracy has above all the decisive advantage that the preservation of intellectual freedom creates the opportunity for counterattack. Democracy always has the chance to redeem its language. This may be an essential step toward the redemption of its politics.

One must add that it is idle to expect perfection in political discourse. The problem of politics in a democracy is to win broad consent for measures of national policy. The winning of consent often requires the bringing together of disparate groups with diverging interests. This inescapably involves a certain oracularity of expression. One remembers de Gaulle before the crowd in Algeria, when the *pieds-noirs* chanted that Algeria belonged to France, replying solemnly, "Je vous comprends, mes camarades"—hardly a forthright expression of his determination to set Algeria free. Besides, oracularity may often be justified since no one can be all that sure about the future. The Founding Fathers understood this, which is why the Constitution is in many respects a document of calculated omission and masterful ambiguity whose "real" meaning—that is, what it would mean in practice—only practice could disclose. Moreover, as Lord Keynes, who wrote even economics in English, once put it, "Words ought to be a little wild, for they are an assault of thought upon the unthinking."

Keynes immediately added, however: "But when the seats of power and authority have been attained, there should be no more poetic license." Madison described the American experiment as the replacement of accident and force by reflection and choice in the process of government. The responsibility of presidents is to define real choices and explain soberly why one course is to be preferred to another—and, in doing so, to make language a means not of deception but of communication, not an enemy but a friend of the reality principle.

Yet presidents cannot easily rise above the society they serve and lead. If we are to restore the relationship between words and meaning, we must begin to clean up the whole linguistic environment. This does not mean a crusade for standard English or a campaign to resurrect the stately rhythms of *The Federalist Papers*. Little could be more quixotic than an attempt to hold a rich and flexible language like American English to the forms and definitions of a specific time, class, or race. But some neologisms are better than others, and here one can demand, particularly in influential places, a modicum of discrimination. More important is that words, whether new or old, regain a relationship to reality. Vietnam and Watergate have given a good many Americans, I believe, a real hatred of double-talk and a hunger for bluntness and candor. Why else the success of the posthumous publication of President Truman's gaudy exercise in plain speaking?

The time is ripe to sweep the language-field of American politics. In this season of semantic malnutrition, who is not grateful for a public voice that appears to blurt out what the speaker honestly believes? A George Wallace begins to win support even among blacks (though ambition is already making Wallace bland, and blandness will do him in too). Here those who live by the word—I mean by the true word, like writers and teachers; not by the phony word, like public relations men, writers and teachers—have their peculiar obligation. Every citizen is free under the First Amendment to use and abuse the words that bob around in the swamp of his mind. But writers and teachers have, if anyone has, the custodianship of the language. Their charge is to protect the words by which they live. Their duty is to expel the cant of the age.

At the same time, they must not forget that in the recent past they have been among the worst offenders. They must take scrupulous care that indignation does not lead them to the same falsity and hyperbole they righteously condemn in others. A compilation of political pronouncements by eminent writers and learned savants over the last generation would make a dismal volume. One has only to recall the renowned, if addled, scholars who signed the full page advertisement in the *New York Times* of October 15, 1972, which read, as the *New Yorker* would say, in its entirety: "Of the two major candidates for the Presidency of the United States, we believe that Richard Nixon has demonstrated the superior capacity for prudent and responsible leadership. Consequently, we intend to vote for President Nixon on November 7th and we urge our fellow citizens to do the same."

The time has come for writers and teachers to meet the standards they would enforce on others and rally to the defense of the word. They must expose the attack on meaning and discrimination in language as an attack on reason in discourse. It is this rejection of reason itself that underlies the indulgence of imprecision, the apotheosis of usage and the infatuation with rhetoric. For once words lose a stable connection with things, we can no longer know what we think or communicate what we believe.

One does not suggest that the restoration of language is all that easy in an age when new issues, complexities and ambiguities stretch old forms to the breaking point.

> *. . . Words strain*
> *Crack and sometimes break, under the burden,*
> *Under the tension, slip, slide, perish,*
> *Decay with imprecision, will not stay in place,*
> *Will not stay still.*

Each venture is therefore the new beginning, the raid on the inarticulate with shabby equipment always deteriorating in the general mess of imprecision of feeling. Yet, as Eliot went on to say, "For us, there is only the trying. The rest is not our business." As we struggle to recover what has been lost ("and found and lost again and again"), as we try our own sense of words against the decay of language, writers and teachers make the best contribution they can to the redemption of politics. Let intellectuals never forget that all they that take the word shall perish with the word. "Wise men pierce this rotten diction," said Emerson, "and fasten words again to visible things; so that picturesque language is at once a commanding certificate that he who employs it, is a man in alliance with truth and God."

*

Four
Nonverbal
Communication

An examination of recent print and electronic media would indicate that the study and discussion of nonverbal communication has grown rapidly in popularity. Writers for the popular book market have produced such books as *Body Language*, *Body Talk*, and *Face Language*, to name a few. Television programming, often centering around societal problems created by ineffective communication, highlights the potential of effective communication. The increased awareness of communication has made course work in the area of nonverbal communication the most rapidly growing area in the field of communication.

Communication seems to be both the source and solution to many of the contemporary problems in society. While the media has focused little or no attention on nonverbal communication, much has been said indirectly about the topic. Prison riots and urban strife have been blamed on a failure in communication or no communication. Family problems and personal adjustments have been based upon the lack of awareness of the communication process, particularly nonverbal communication. The following illustration points out the fact that both status and dress are factors of nonverbal communication. The policeman in our society has a status that affects our communication with him; on the other hand, the other person in the picture transmits a much different nonverbal communication.

The problem described here is only one of many that result from our interpretation and sometimes misinterpretation of nonverbal communication. This section of the book is designed to help you understand the essential elements of nonverbal communication and to determine the relationship of nonverbal communication to the rest of the communication process.

Introduction

Sixty-five percent of all communication is nonverbal. Nevertheless, we spend most of our time in course work, from elementary school on, discussing the verbal aspects of communication. The impact of nonverbal communication is highlighted in various research studies, some of which you will read about in this section. Part of this research suggests that we decide whether we like other people primarily on the basis of the nonverbal communication from that person. We take one look at another person and we decide whether we are interested in knowing that person better. In the previous picture, we probably decided very quickly whether we liked the policeman or the bum. Only seven percent of the total decision of whether or not we like a person is based on the verbal output of that person. Fifty-five percent of our decision to like or dislike is based on facial communication. The vocal quality of pitch, rate, harshness, and volume contribute the remainder of our decision. Given this global approach to other people, we will discuss the nature of nonverbal communication, nonverbal behavior, and the components of nonverbal behavior.

We have already made the distinction between verbal and nonverbal communication. We suggested that they serve hand in hand to facilitate communication. Although we will isolate nonverbal communication to discuss it, conclusions based on one nonverbal characteristic or another are dangerous. The following picture will illustrate this point.

If you were to examine only the facial expression, you might draw the conclusion that the young lady was depressed or angry. If you look at the posture, you may draw the conclusion that she is withdrawn. If you look only at the arm and leg position, you may conclude that she is closed and unwilling to be receptive to communication. On the other hand, if you knew that the environment was cold due to a lack of heat, you might draw a different conclusion. Our point is rather straightforward: you need to look at a cluster of nonverbal cues before you draw conclusions about the nonverbal communication behavior. Another way to check the nonverbal communication is to compare it to the verbal message. If it is congruent with the verbal, you can be certain that you have correctly interpreted the nonverbal communication.

Nonverbal communication is viewed as culture bound. The forms of nonverbal communication that we use in America differ from those of other cultures. Nixon got into trouble using a gesture that meant everything is okay in America, but this gesture was an insult in South America.

There are numerous examples of gestures that mean one thing in one culture and something quite different in another. We stated in the first chapter that we must know the audience with which we communicate. Likewise, we must know the forms of nonverbal communication that are appropriate to the people with which we communicate.

Role of Nonverbal Communication

Nonverbal communication can serve at least three major functions. It can complement the verbal message. For example, the child that tells an adult that he really likes the adult and hugs the person would be complementing the verbal message. If your teacher expresses verbal pleasure in your work, the nonverbal reaction to you should be complementary. However, nonverbal communication can also be contradictory to the verbal message. The child that claims he is not lying, but scratches his head, looks down, and constantly shifts his feet, is displaying a contradictory nonverbal message. In addition, cocktail-party behavior often serves as another example of contradictory nonverbal and verbal communication. How often have you been talking to a person at a party and found the other person looking elsewhere—every nonverbal communication suggesting that that person would rather be with someone else?

Finally, nonverbal communication can serve as a substitute for verbal communication. We mentioned earlier that most of our communication is nonverbal. We often allow nonverbal communication to serve as a substitute for verbal communication. In the last chapter, we included a section on cross-cultural communication. When we are in a foreign country, it is sometimes necessary to rely on nonverbal communication as our only means of communication.

Components of Nonverbal Communication

Since nonverbal communication should not be viewed in isolation, we will examine the six components of nonverbal communication. The most difficult component to discuss in writing is the use of the voice. While words constitute verbal communication, the pitch, rate, quality, and loudness generate nonverbal communication. The expectation when someone whispers is that the conversation is private and not for others to hear. If the person speaks loud and fast, a feeling of excitement fills the air. Have you noticed what happens to your voice when another person is talking loud and fast? Usually, your speed and loudness increase.

We also use our body to communicate nonverbally. In the 1968 Olympics a black athlete raised a clinched fist that shocked the world. Americans were divided over the politicizing of the Games. Nevertheless, this was one nonverbal communication that received widespread publicity. The Nixon gesture was another example. Gestures, posture, facial expression, eye contact, and head movement constitute kinesics or body language.

The use of distance and the environment make up the third component of nonverbal communication. Hall described the zones of distance which relate to Western civilization. The intimate zone is that distance between two people up to 18 inches. From 18 inches to four feet is the personal zone. In this area we hold most of our conversations on a one-to-one basis. When we move to the social zone (four to seven feet), we move to the area where we do most of our business. The personal zone is reserved for our friends; the social zone is used for business, such as the interaction with a sales clerk or the distance between a student and a teacher. Beyond seven feet, we are in the public zone. When an instructor is lecturing, the public zone is the one usually selected. It is much less personal than the other three zones for communication.

What is the best distance for communication? It is the choice of the communicators. Each of us has a preferred distance for communication with one or more people. We select what we feel comfortable with. The difficulty arises when the other person prefers a different distance. For instance, you may spend your time backing a person around a room because you feel more comfortable at a distance of two feet and the listener likes to remain at about four feet.

We do not have the space in this introduction to discuss completely the ramifications of the physical environment on communication. Furniture, room arrangement, lighting, and temperature all influence our communication with others. Some faculty prefer to have students sit on the other side of a desk when meeting during an office hour. Other faculty seek a more comfortable arrangement with a living-room type of seating. Each setting communicates a different attitude toward the student. We are all familiar with the room with the lights low, a fire in the fireplace, and soft music on the stereo.

A component that has received relatively little discussion is touch. Doctors tell us that touch is an important part of parental behavior in early infancy. As we grow older, we rely less and less on touch as a form of nonverbal communication. While we may use touch for intimate nonverbal communication, we generally do not use touch in other communication settings. The decision to touch or not touch is a cultural one. In other societies, touching is not only appropriate, but is expected. Our use of touch for nonverbal communication has been relegated to the formal greeting situation of hello and goodbye. We even accept it when one male grasps the shoulder of another male when shaking hands. Rarely do we allow males to embrace each other as a form of greeting communication.

Time is a very important component of our daily lives as well as an aspect of nonverbal communication. We set aside time for communication and time for no communication. There is a time to speak and a time to listen. We can talk too long or not enough. Our lives are regulated by time. Historically, we have associated time with status. For example, if an instructor was late for class, we would determine academic rank and wait whatever time was appropriate for the rank. Full professors are used to receiving 20 minutes of waiting time.

We usually resort to a series of other nonverbal communication behaviors when we want to indicate that time is of the essence. We look at our watch, shuffle our feet, tap a pencil, or any other behavior to indicate that we are anxious to leave. In class, students think nothing of closing notebooks, putting pencils and pens away, and putting on their coats to communicate nonverbally that time is up and class is over.

Finally, aritfacts serve as a component of nonverbal communication. We define artifacts as those objects that a person uses to communicate. Clothing, cars, and other such objects are used to nonverbally communicate status, power, or competence. Obviously, the same objects could be used to communicate the opposite. Although a breadwinner might be unemployed, one state government office decided that if the family had a television set, it did not belong on the welfare roll. We are not making a value judgment but are suggesting in this case that the tele-

vision set communicates a sign of prosperity rather than poverty.

Uniforms are a very important part of artifactual communication. Police uniforms, badges, and weapons might be thought of as nonverbal communication indicating power and authority, while blue jeans, T-shirts, and tennis shoes communicate something quite different.

Conclusions

It would be very easy to make generalizations about those with whom we communicate, if we stereotyped the various components of nonverbal communication. We would rather that you observe nonverbal communication and use the nonverbal messages in conjunction with the verbal communication. If there are conflicts between the nonverbal and the verbal, seek clarification rather than allow the inconsistency to continue. Communication is a process. As you receive feedback to your communication, you continue to monitor the behavior of your receiver to clarify the communication between you.

Unlike many of the other topics that you will read in this book, you will find more popular books attempting to help you interpret nonverbal communication. We would only caution that the effective interpretation of communication requires a cluster of nonverbal communication cues. The accepting of one specific nonverbal cue can be not only wrong but hazardous.

Articles

Each of the articles in this section explores a facet of nonverbal communication. Hall and Hall provide an overview of nonverbal communication including a discussion of the situation, the place, the use of cultural norms surrounding communication, and the impact of misinterpretation of nonverbal behaviors. The Halls suggest that a person's zone of personal space can be invaded not only physically but indirectly through eye contact, smell, and sound. The article reviews distance as a form of nonverbal communication and concludes with a discussion of a form of communication between members of two cultures. Although we will discuss cross-cultural communication in the last chapter, the Hall example is useful as an illustration of a failure to interpret correctly nonverbal communication.

Mehrabian reviews the role of nonverbal communication in the overall communication process. He talks specifically about variables of the voice including intonation, stress, tone, length, pitch, and speech rate. He ends his article by calling for an application of the principle of nonverbal communication to a variety of settings.

Davis, in her article, describes the role of body language of kinesics in the total picture of nonverbal communication. Her article is filled with examples of the ways we speak body language.

Chiu and Vaughn have interpreted some of the material on space and environment in their article on the effects of crowding and density. They look at the impact of crowding and dense population centers on the individual. Not only do they discuss the problems but they communicate them nonverbally through drawings and pictures. What does the future hold for us?

The Sounds of Silence

Edward and Mildred Hall

Bob leaves his apartment at 8:15 A.M. and stops at the corner drugstore for breakfast. Before he can speak, the counterman says, "The usual?" Bob nods yes. While he savors his Danish, a fat man pushes onto the adjoining stool and overflows into his space. Bob scowls and the man pulls himself in as much as he can. Bob has sent two messages without speaking a syllable.

Henry has an appointment to meet Arthur at 11 o'clock; he arrives at 11:30. Their conversation is friendly, but Arthur retains a lingering hostility. Henry has unconsciously communicated that he doesn't think the appointment is very important or that Arthur is a person who needs to be treated with respect.

George is talking to Charley's wife at a party. Their conversation is entirely trivial, yet Charley glares at them suspiciously. Their physical proximity and the movements of their eyes reveal that they are powerfully attracted to each other.

José Ybarra and Sir Edmund Jones are at the same party and it is important for them to establish a cordial relationship for business reasons. Each is trying to be warm and friendly, yet they will part with mutual distrust and their business transaction will probably fall through.

José, in Latin fashion, moved closer and closer to Sir Edmund as they spoke, and this movement was miscommunicated as pushiness to Sir Edmund, who kept backing away from this intimacy, and this was miscommunicated to José as coldness. The silent languages of Latin and English cultures are more difficult to learn than their spoken languages.

In each of these cases, we see the subtle power of nonverbal communication. The only language used throughout most of the history of humanity (in evolutionary terms, vocal communication is relatively recent), it is the first form of communication you learn. You use this preverbal language, consciously and unconsciously, every day to tell other people how you feel about yourself and them. This language includes your posture, gestures, facial expressions, costume, the way you walk, even your treatment of time and space and material things. All people communicate on several different levels at the same time but are usually aware of only the verbal dialog and don't realize that they respond to nonverbal messages. But when a person says one thing and really believes something else, the discrepancy between the two can usually be sensed. Nonverbal-communication systems are much less subject to the conscious deception that often occurs in verbal systems.

When we find ourselves thinking, "I don't know what it is about him, but he doesn't seem sincere," it's usually this lack of congruity between a person's words and his behavior that makes us anxious and uncomfortable.

Few of us realize how much we all depend on body movement in our conversation or are aware of the hidden rules that govern listening behavior. But we know instantly whether or not the person we're talking to is "tuned in" and we're very sensitive to any breach in listening etiquette. In white middle-class American culture, when someone wants to show he is listening to someone else, he looks either at the other person's face or, specifically, at his eyes, shifting his gaze from one eye to the other.

If you observe a person conversing, you'll notice that he indicates he's listening by nodding his head. He also makes little "Hmm" noises. If he agrees with what's being said, he may give a vigorous nod. To show pleasure or affirmation, he smiles; if he has some reservations, he looks skeptical by raising an eyebrow or pulling down the corners of his mouth. If a participant wants to terminate the conversation, he may start shifting his body position, stretching his legs, crossing or uncrossing them, bobbing his foot or diverting his gaze from the speaker. The more he fidgets, the more the speaker becomes aware that he has lost his audience. As a last measure, the listener may look at his watch to indicate the imminent end of the conversation.

Talking and listening are so intricately intertwined that a person cannot do one without the other. Even when one is alone and talking to oneself, there is part of the brain that speaks while another part listens. In all conversations, the listener is positively or negatively reinforcing the speaker all the time. He may even guide the conversation without knowing it, by laughing or frowning or dismissing the argument with a wave of his hand.

The language of the eyes—another age-old way of exchanging feelings—is both subtle and complex. Not only do men and women use their eyes differently but there are class, generation, regional, ethnic and national cultural differences.

Americans often complain about the way foreigners stare at people or hold a glance too long. Most Americans look away from someone who is using his eyes in an unfamiliar way because it makes them self-conscious. If a man looks at another man's wife in a certain way, he's asking for trouble, as indicated earlier. But he might not be ill mannered or seeking to challenge the husband. He might be a European in this country who hasn't learned our visual mores. Many American women visiting France or Italy are acutely embarrassed because, for the first time in their lives, men really look at them—their eyes, hair, nose, lips, breasts, hips, legs, thighs, knees, ankles, feet, clothes, hairdo, even their walk. These same women, once they have become used to being looked at, often return to the United States and are overcome with the feeling that "No one ever really looks at me anymore."

Analyzing the mass of data on the eyes, it is possible to sort out at least three ways in which the eyes are used to communicate: dominance *vs.* submission, involvement *vs.* detachment and positive *vs.* negative attitude. In addition, there are three levels of consciousness and control, which can be categorized as follows: (1) conscious use of the eyes to communicate, such as the flirting blink and the intimate nose-wrinkling squint; (2) the very extensive category of unconscious but learned behavior governing where the eyes are directed and when (this unwritten set of rules dictates how and under what circumstances the sexes, as well as people of all status categories, look at each other); and (3) the response of the eye itself, which is completely outside both awareness and control—changes in the cast (the sparkle) of the eye and the pupillary reflex.

The eye is unlike any other organ of the body, for it is an extension of the brain. The unconscious pupillary reflex and the cast of the eye have been known by people of Middle Eastern origin for years—although most are unaware of their knowledge. Depending on the context, Arabs and others look either directly at the eyes or deeply *into* the eyes of their interlocutor.

We became aware of this in the Middle East several years ago while looking at jewelry. The merchant suddenly started to push a particular bracelet at a customer and said, "You buy this one." What interested us was that the bracelet was not the one that had been consciously selected by the purchaser. But the merchant, watching the pupils of the eyes, knew what the purchaser really wanted to buy. Whether he specifically knew *how* he knew is debatable.

A psychologist at the University of Chicago, Eckhard Hess, was the first to conduct systematic studies of the pupillary reflex. His wife remarked one evening, while watching him reading in bed, that he must be very interested in the text because his pupils were dilated. Following up on this, Hess slipped some pictures of nudes into a stack of photographs that he gave to his male assistant. Not looking at the photographs but watching his assistant's pupils, Hess was able to tell precisely when the assistant came to the nudes. In further experiments, Hess retouched the eyes in a photograph of a woman. In one print, he made the pupils small, in another, large; nothing else was changed. Subjects who were given the photographs found the woman with the dilated pupils much more attractive. Any man who has had the experience of seeing a woman look at him as her pupils widen with reflex speed knows that she's flashing him a message.

The eye-sparkle phenomenon frequently turns up in our interviews of couples in love. It's apparently one of the first reliable clues in the other person that love is genuine. To date, there is no scientific data to explain eye sparkle; no investigation of the pupil, the cornea or even the white sclera of the eye shows how the sparkle originates. Yet we all know it when we see it.

One common situation for most people involves the use of the eyes in the street and in public. Although eye behavior follows a definite set of rules, the rules vary according to the place, the needs and feelings of the people, and their ethnic background. For urban whites, once they're within definite recognition distance (16-32 feet for people with average eyesight), there is mutual avoidance of eye contact—unless they want something specific: a pickup, a handout or information of some kind. In the West and in small towns generally, however, people are much more likely to look at and greet one another, even if they're strangers.

It's permissible to look at people if they're beyond recognition distance; but once inside this sacred zone, you can only steal a glance at strangers. You *must* greet friends, however; to fail to do so is insulting. Yet, to stare too fixedly even at them is considered rude and hostile. Of course, all of these rules are variable.

A great many blacks, for example, greet each other in public even if they don't know each other. To blacks, most eye behavior of whites has the effect of giving the impression that they aren't there, but this is due to white avoidance of eye contact with *anyone* in the street.

Another very basic difference between people of different ethnic backgrounds is their sense of territoriality and how they handle space. This is the silent communication, or miscommunication, that caused friction between Mr. Ybarra and Sir Edmund Jones in our earlier example. We know from research that everyone has around himself an invisible bubble of space that contracts and expands depending on several factors: his emotional state, the activity he's performing at the time and his cultural background. This bubble is a kind of mobile territory that he will defend against intrusion. If he is accustomed to close personal distance between himself and others, his bubble will be smaller than that of someone who's accustomed to greater personal distance. People of North European heritage—English, Scandinavian, Swiss and German—tend to avoid contact. Those whose heritage is Italian, French, Spanish, Russian, Latin American or Middle Eastern like close personal contact.

People are very sensitive to any intrusion into their spatial bubble. If someone stands too close to you, your first instinct is to back up. If that's not possible, you lean away and pull yourself in, tensing your muscles. If the intruder doesn't respond to these body signals, you may then try to protect yourself, using a briefcase, umbrella or raincoat. Women—especially when traveling alone—often plant their pocketbook in such a way that no one can get very close to them. As a last resort, you may move to another spot and position yourself behind a desk or a chair that provides screening. Everyone tries to adjust the space around himself in a way that's comfortable for him; most often, he does this unconsciously.

Emotions also have a direct effect on the size of a person's territory. When you're angry or under stress, your bubble expands and you require more space. New York psychiatrist Augustus Kinzel found a difference in what he calls Body-Buffer Zones between violent and nonviolent prison inmates. Dr. Kinzel conducted experiments in which each prisoner was placed in the center of a small room and then Dr. Kinzel slowly walked toward him. Nonviolent prisoners allowed him to come quite close, while prisoners with a history of violent behavior couldn't tolerate his proximity and reacted with some vehemence.

Apparently, people under stress experience other people as looming larger and closer than they actually are. Studies of schizophrenic patients have indicated that they sometimes have a distorted perception of space, and several psychiatrists have reported patients who experience their body boundaries as filling up an entire room. For these patients, anyone who comes into the room is actually inside their body, and such an intrusion may trigger a violent outburst.

Unfortunately, there is little detailed information about normal people who live in highly congested urban areas. We do know, of course, that the noise, pollution, dirt, crowding and confusion of our cities induce feelings of stress in most of us, and stress leads to a need for greater space. The man who's packed into a subway, jostled in the street, crowded into an elevator and forced to work all day in a bull pen or in a small office without auditory or visual privacy is going to be very stressed at the end of

his day. He needs places that provide relief from constant overstimulation of his nervous system. Stress from overcrowding is cumulative and people can tolerate more crowding early in the day than later; note the increased bad temper during the evening rush hour as compared with the morning melee. Certainly one factor in people's desire to commute by car is the need for privacy and relief from crowding (except, often, from other cars); it may be the only time of the day when nobody can intrude.

In crowded public places, we tense our muscles and hold ourselves stiff, and thereby communicate to others our desire not to intrude on their space and, above all, not to touch them. We also avoid eye contact, and the total effect is that of someone who has "tuned out." Walking along the street, our bubble expands slightly as we move in a stream of strangers, taking care not to bump into them. In the office, at meetings, in restaurants, our bubble keeps changing as it adjusts to the activity at hand.

Most white middle-class Americans use four main distances in their business and social relations: intimate, personal, social and public. Each of these distances has a near and a far phase and is accompanied by changes in the volume of the voice. Intimate distance varies from direct physical contact with another person to a distance of six to eighteen inches and is used for our most private activities—caressing another person or making love. At this distance, you are overwhelmed by sensory inputs from the other person—heat from the body, tactile stimulation from the skin, the fragrance of perfume, even the sound of breathing—all of which literally envelop you. Even at the far phase, you're still within easy touching distance. In general, the use of intimate distance in public between adults is frowned on. It's also much too close for strangers, except under conditions of extreme crowding.

In the second zone—personal distance—the close phase is one and a half to two and a half feet; it's at this distance that wives usually stand from their husbands in public. If another woman moves into this zone, the wife will most likely be disturbed. The far phase—two and a half to four feet—is the distance used to "keep someone at arm's length" and is the most common spacing used by people in conversation.

The third zone—social distance—is employed during business transactions or exchanges with a clerk or repairman. People who work together tend to use close social distance—four to seven feet. This is also the distance for conversations at social gatherings. To stand at this distance from someone who is seated has a dominating effect (e.g., teacher to pupil, boss to secretary). The far phase of the third zone—seven to twelve feet—is where people stand when someone says, "Stand back so I can look at you." This distance lends a formal tone to business or social discourse. In an executive office, the desk serves to keep people at this distance.

The fourth zone—public distance—is used by teachers in classrooms or speakers at public gatherings. At its farthest phase—25 feet and beyond—it is used for important public figures. Violations of this distance can lead to serious complications. During his 1970 U.S. visit, the president of France, Georges Pompidou, was harassed by pickets in Chicago, who were permitted to get within touching distance. Since pickets in France are kept behind barricades a block or more away, the president was outraged by this insult to his person, and President Nixon was obliged to communicate his concern as well as offer his personal apologies.

It is interesting to note how American pitchmen and panhandlers exploit the unwritten, unspoken conventions of eye and distance. Both take advantage of the fact that once explicit eye contact is established, it is rude to look away, because to do so means to brusquely dismiss the other person and his needs. Once having caught the eye of his mark, the panhandler then locks on, not letting go until he moves through the public zone, the social zone, the personal zone and, finally, into the intimate sphere, where people are most vulnerable.

Touch also is an important part of the constant stream of communication that takes place between people. A light touch, a firm touch, a blow, a caress are all communications. In an effort to break down barriers among people, there's been a recent upsurge in group-encounter activities, in which strangers are encouraged to touch one another. In special situations such as these, the rules for not touching are broken with group approval and people gradually lose some of their inhibitions.

Although most people don't realize it, space is perceived and distances are set not by vision alone but with all the senses. Auditory space is perceived with the ears, thermal space with the skin, kinesthetic space with the muscles of the body, and olfactory space with the nose. And, once again, it's one's culture that determines how his senses are programmed—which sensory information ranks highest and lowest. The important thing to remember is that culture is very persistent. In this country, we've noted the existence of culture patterns that determine distance between people in the third and fourth generations of some families, despite their prolonged contact with people of very different cultural heritages.

Whenever there is great cultural distance between two people, there are bound to be problems arising from differences in behavior and expectations. An example is the American couple who consulted a psychiatrist about their marital problems. The husband was from New England and had been brought up by reserved parents who taught him to control his emotions and to respect the need for privacy. His wife was from an Italian family and had been brought up in close contact with all the members of her large family, who were extremely warm, volatile and demonstrative.

When the husband came home after a hard day at the office, dragging his feet and longing for peace and quiet, his wife would rush to him and smother him. Clasping his hands, rubbing his brow, crooning over his weary head, she never left him alone. But when the wife was upset or anxious about her day, the husband's response was to withdraw completely and leave her alone. No comforting, no affectionate embrace, no attention—just solitude. The woman became convinced her husband didn't love her and, in desperation, she consulted a psychiatrist. Their problem wasn't basically psychological but cultural.

Why has man developed all these different ways of communicating messages without words? One reason is that people don't like to spell out certain kinds of messages. We prefer to find other ways of showing our feelings. This is especially true in relationships as sensitive as courtship. Men don't like to be rejected and most women don't want to turn a man down bluntly. Instead, we work out subtle ways of encouraging or discouraging each other that save face and avoid confrontations.

How a person handles space in dating others is an obvious and very sensitive indicator of how he or she feels about the other person. On a first date, if a woman sits or stands so close to a man that he is acutely conscious of her physical presence—inside the intimate-distance zone—the man usually construes it to mean that she is encouraging him. However, before the man starts moving in on the woman, he should be sure what message she's really sending; otherwise, he risks bruising his ego. What is close to someone of North European background may be neutral or distant to someone of Italian heritage. Also, women sometimes use space as a way of misleading a man and there are few things that put men off more than women who communicate contradictory messages—such as women who cuddle up and then act insulted when a man takes the next step.

How does a woman communicate interest in a man? In addition to such familiar gambits as smiling at him, she may glance shyly at him, blush and then look away. Or she may give him a real come-on look and move in very close when he approaches. She may touch his arm and ask for a light. As she leans forward to light her cigarette, she may brush him lightly, enveloping him in her perfume. She'll probably continue to smile at him and she may use what ethologists call preening gestures—touching the back of her hair, thrusting her breasts forward, tilting her hips as she stands or crossing her legs

if she's seated, perhaps even exposing one thigh or putting a hand on her thigh and stroking it. She may also stroke her wrists as she converses or show the palm of her hand as a way of gaining his attention. Her skin may be unusually flushed or quite pale, her eyes brighter, the pupils larger.

If a man sees a woman whom he wants to attract, he tries to present himself by his posture and stance as someone who is self-assured. He moves briskly and confidently. When he catches the eye of the woman, he may hold her glance a little longer than normal. If he gets an encouraging smile, he'll move in close and engage her in small talk. As they converse, his glance shifts over her face and body. He, too, may make preening gestures—straightening his tie, smoothing his hair or shooting his cuffs.

How do people learn body language? The same way they learn spoken language—by observing and imitating people around them as they're growing up. Little girls imitate their mothers or an older female. Little boys imitate their fathers or a respected uncle or a character on television. In this way, they learn the gender signals appropriate for their sex. Regional, class and ethnic patterns of body behavior are also learned in childhood and persist throughout life.

Such patterns of masculine and feminine body behavior vary widely from one culture to another. In America, for example, women stand with their thighs together. Many walk with their pelvis tipped slightly forward and their upper arms close to their body. When they sit, they cross their legs at the knee or, if they are well past middle age, they may cross their ankles. American men hold their arms away from their body, often swinging them as they walk. They stand with their legs apart (an extreme example is the cowboy, with legs apart and thumbs tucked into his belt). When they sit, they put their feet on the floor with legs apart and, in some parts of the country, they cross their legs by putting one ankle on the other knee.

Leg behavior indicates sex, status and personality. It also indicates whether or not one is at ease or is showing respect or disrespect for the other person. Young Latin-American males avoid crossing their legs. In their world of *machismo*, the preferred position for young males when with one another (if there is no older dominant male present to whom they must show respect) is to sit on the base of their spine with their leg muscles relaxed and their feet wide apart. Their respect position is like our military equivalent; spine straight, heels and ankles together—almost identical to that displayed by properly brought up young women in New England in the early part of this century.

American women who sit with their legs spread apart in the presence of males are *not* normally signaling a come-on—they are simply (and often unconsciously) sitting like men. Middle-class women in the presence of other women to whom they are very close may on occasion throw themselves down on a soft chair or sofa and let themselves go. This is a signal that nothing serious will be taken up. Males, on the other hand, lean back and prop their legs up on the nearest object.

The way we walk, similarly, indicates status, respect, mood and ethnic or cultural affiliation. The many variants of the female walk are too well known to go into here, except to say that a man would have to be blind not to be turned on by the way some women walk—a fact that made Mae West rich before scientists ever studied these matters. To white Americans, some French middle-class males walk in a way that is both humorous and suspect. There is a bounce and looseness to the French walk, as though the parts of the body were somehow unrelated. Jacques Tati, the French movie actor, walks this way; so does the great mime, Marcel Marceau.

Blacks and whites in America—with the exception of middle- and upper-middle-class professionals of both groups—move and walk very differently from each other. To the blacks, whites often seem incredibly stiff, almost mechanical in their movements. Black males, on the other hand, have a looseness and coordination that frequently makes whites a little uneasy; it's too different, too integrated, too alive,

too male. Norman Mailer has said that squares walk from the shoulders, like bears, but blacks and hippies walk from the hips, like cats.

All over the world, people walk not only in their own characteristic way but have walks that communicate the nature of their involvement with whatever it is they're doing. The purposeful walk of North Europeans is an important component of proper behavior on the job. Any male who has been in the military knows how essential it is to walk properly (which makes for a continuing source of tension between blacks and whites in the Service). The quick shuffle of servants in the Far East in the old days was a show of respect. On the island of Truk, when we last visited, the inhabitants even had a name for the respectful walk that one used when in the presence of a chief or when walking past a chief's house. The term was *sufan*, which meant to be humble and respectful.

The notion that people communicate volumes by their gestures, facial expressions, posture and walk is not new; actors, dancers, writers and psychiatrists have long been aware of it. Only in recent years, however, have scientists begun to make systematic observations of body motions. Ray L. Birdwhistell of the University of Pennsylvania is one of the pioneers in body-motion research and coined the term kinesics to describe this field. He developed an elaborate notation system to record both facial and body movements, using an approach similar to that of the linguist, who studies the basic elements of speech. Birdwhistell and other kinesicists such as Albert Sheflen, Adam Kendon and William Condon take movies of people interacting. They run the film over and over again, often at reduced speed for frame-by-frame analysis, so that they can observe even the slightest body movements not perceptible at normal interaction speeds. These movements are then recorded in notebooks for later analysis.

To appreciate the importance of nonverbal-communication systems, consider the unskilled inner-city black looking for a job. His handling of time and space alone is sufficiently different from the white middle-class pattern to create great misunderstandings on both sides. The black is told to appear for a job interview at a certain time. He arrives late. The white interviewer concludes from his tardy arrival that the black is irresponsible and not really interested in the job. What the interviewer doesn't know is that the black time system (often referred to by blacks as C.P.T.—colored people's time) isn't the same as that of whites. In the words of a black student who had been told to make an appointment to see his professor: "Man, you *must* be putting me on. I never had an appointment in my life."

The black job applicant, having arrived late for his interview, may further antagonize the white interviewer by his posture and his eye behavior. Perhaps he slouches and avoids looking at the interviewer; to him, this is playing it cool. To the interviewer, however, he may well look shifty and sound uninterested. The interviewer has failed to notice the actual signs of interest and eagerness in the black's behavior, such as the subtle shift in the quality of the voice—a gentle and tentative excitement—an almost imperceptible change in the cast of the eyes and a relaxing of the jaw muscles.

Moreover, correct reading of black-white behavior is continually complicated by the fact that both groups are comprised of individuals—some of whom try to accommodate and some of whom make it a point of pride *not* to accommodate. At present, this means that many Americans, when thrown into contact with one another, are in the precarious position of not knowing which pattern applies. Once identified and analyzed, nonverbal-communication systems can be taught, like a foreign language. Without this training, we respond to nonverbal communications in terms of our own culture; we read everyone's behavior as if it were our own, and thus we often misunderstand it.

Several years ago in New York City, there was a program for sending children from predominantly black and Puerto Rican low-income neighborhoods to summer school in a white upper-class neighborhood on the East Side. One morning, a group of young black and Puerto Rican boys raced down the street, shouting and screaming and overturning garbage cans on their way to school. A doorman from an apartment building nearby chased them and cornered one of them inside a building. The boy drew a knife and attacked the doorman. This tragedy would not have occurred if the doorman had been familiar with the behavior of boys from low-income neighborhoods, where such antics are routine and socially acceptable and where pursuit would be expected to invite a violent response.

The language of behavior is extremely complex. Most of us are lucky to have under control one subcultural system—the one that reflects our sex, class, generation and geographic region within the United States. Because of its complexity, efforts to isolate bits of nonverbal communication and generalize from them are in vain; you don't become an instant expert on people's behavior by watching them at cocktail parties. Body language isn't something that's independent of the person, something that can be donned and doffed like a suit of clothes.

Our research and that of our colleagues has shown that, far from being a superficial form of communication that can be consciously manipulated, nonverbal-communication systems are interwoven into the fabric of the personality and, as sociologist Erving Goffman has demonstrated, into society itself. They are the warp and woof of daily interactions with others and they influence how one expresses oneself, how one experiences oneself as a man or a woman.

Nonverbal communications signal to members of your own group what kind of person you are, how you feel about others, how you'll fit into and work in a group, whether you're assured or anxious, the degree to which you feel comfortable with the standards of your own culture, as well as deeply significant feelings about the self, including the state of your own psyche. For most of us, it's difficult to accept the reality of another's behavioral system. And, of course, none of us will ever become fully knowledgeable of the importance of every non-verbal signal. But as long as each of us realizes the power of these signals, this society's diversity can be a source of great strength rather than a further—and subtly powerful—source of division.

Communication Without Words

Albert Mehrabian

Suppose you are sitting in my office listening to me describe some research I have done on communication. I tell you that feelings are communicated less by the words a person uses than by certain nonverbal means—that, for example, the verbal part of a spoken message has considerably less effect on whether a listener feels liked or disliked than a speaker's facial expression or tone of voice.

So far so good. But suppose I add, "In fact, we've worked out a formula that shows exactly how much each of these components contributes to the effect of the message as a whole. It goes like this: Total Impact = .07 verbal + .38 vocal + .55 facial."

What would you say to *that*? Perhaps you would smile good-naturedly and say, with some feeling, "Baloney!" Or perhaps you would frown and remark acidly, "Isn't science grand." My own response to the first answer would probably be to smile back: the facial part of your message, at least, was positive (55 per cent of the total). The second answer might make me uncomfortable: only the verbal part was positive (seven per cent).

The point here is not only that my reactions would lend credence to the formula but that most listeners would have mixed feelings about my statement. People like to see science march on, but they tend to resent its intrusion into an "art" like the communication of feelings, just as they find analytical and quantitative approaches to the study of personality cold, mechanistic and unacceptable.

The psychologist himself is sometimes plagued by the feeling that he is trying to put a rainbow into a bottle. Fascinated by a complicated and emotionally rich human situation, he begins to study it, only to find in the course of his research that he has destroyed part of the mystique that originally intrigued and involved him. But despite a certain nostalgia for earlier, more intuitive approaches, one must acknowledge that concrete experimental data have added a great deal to our understanding of how feelings are communicated. In fact, as I hope to show, analytical and intuitive findings do not so much conflict as complement each other.

It is indeed difficult to know what another person really feels. He says one thing and does another; he seems to mean something but we have an uneasy feeling it isn't true. The early psychoanalysts, facing this problem of inconsistencies and ambiguities in a person's communications, attempted to resolve it through the concepts of the conscious and the unconscious. They assumed that contradictory messages meant a conflict between superficial, deceitful, or erroneous feelings on the one hand and true attitudes and feelings on the other. Their role, then, was to help the client separate the wheat from the chaff.

The question was, how could this be done? Some analysts insisted that inferring the client's unconscious wishes was a completely intuitive process. Others thought that some nonverbal behavior, such as posture, position and movement, could be used in a more objective way to discover the client's feelings. A favorite technique of Frieda Fromm-Reichmann, for example, was to imitate a client's posture herself in order to obtain some feeling for what he was experiencing.

Thus began the gradual shift away from the idea that communication is primarily verbal, and that the verbal message includes distortions or ambiguities due to unobservable motives that only experts can discover.

Language, though, can be used to communicate almost anything. By comparison, nonverbal behavior is very limited in range. Usually, it is used to communicate feelings, likings and preferences, and it customarily reinforces or contradicts the feelings that are communicated verbally. Less often, it adds a new dimension of sorts to a verbal message, as when a salesman describes his product to a client and simultaneously conveys, nonverbally, the impression that he likes the client.

A great many forms of nonverbal behavior can communicate feelings: touching, facial expression, tone of voice, spatial distance from the addressee, relaxation of posture, rate of speech, number of errors in speech. Some of these are generally recognized as informative. Untrained adults and children easily infer that they are liked or disliked from certain facial expressions, from whether (and how) someone touches them, and from a speaker's tone of voice. Other behavior, such as posture, has a more subtle effect. A listener may sense how

someone feels about him from the way the person sits while talking to him, but he may have trouble identifying precisely what his impression comes from.

Correct intuitive judgements of the feelings or attitudes of others are especially difficult when different degrees of feeling, or contradictory kinds of feeling, are expressed simultaneously through different forms of behavior. As I have pointed out, there is a distinction between verbal and vocal information (vocal information being what is lost when speech is written down—intonation, tone, stress, length and frequency of pauses, and so on), and the two kinds of information do not always communicate the same feeling. This distinction, which has been recognized for some time, has shed new light on certain types of communication. Sarcasm, for example, can be defined as a message in which the information transmitted vocally contradicts the information verbally. Usually the verbal information is positive and the vocal is negative, as in "Isn't science grand."

Through the use of an electronic filter, it is possible to measure the degree of liking communicated vocally. What the filter does is eliminate the higher frequencies of recorded speech, so that words are unintelligible but most vocal qualities remain. (For women's speech, we eliminate frequencies higher than about 200 cycles per second; for men, frequencies over about 100 cycles per second.) When people are asked to judge the degree of liking conveyed by the filtered speech, they perform the task rather easily and with a significant amount of agreement.

This method allows us to find out, in a given message, just how inconsistent the information communicated in words and the information communicated vocally really are. We ask one group to judge the amount of liking conveyed by a transcription of what was said, the verbal part of the message. A second group judges the vocal component, and a third group judges the impact of the complete recorded message. In one study of this sort we found that, when the verbal and vocal components of a message agree (both positive or both negative), the message as a whole is judged a little more positive or a little more negative than either component by itself. But when vocal information contradicts verbal, If someone calls you "honey" in a nasty tone of voice, you are likely to feel disliked; it is also possible to say "I hate you" in a way that conveys exactly the opposite feeling.

Besides the verbal and vocal characteristics of speech, there are other, more subtle, signals of meaning in a spoken message. For example, everyone makes mistakes when he talks—unnecessary repetitions, stutterings, the omission of parts of words, incomplete sentences, "ums" and "ahs." In a number of studies of speech errors, George Mahl of Yale University has found that errors become more frequent as the speaker's discomfort or anxiety increases. It might be interesting to apply this index in an attempt to detect deceit (though on some occasions it might be risky: confidence men are notoriously smooth talkers).

Timing is also highly informative. How long does a speaker allow silent periods to last, and how long does he wait before he answers his partner? How long do his utterances tend to be? How often does he interrupt his partner, or wait an inappropriately long time before speaking? Joseph Matarazzo and his colleagues at the University of Oregon have found that each of these speech habits is stable from person to person, and each tells something about the speaker's personality and about his feelings toward and status in relation to his partner.

Utterance duration, for example, is a very stable quality in a person's speech; about 30 seconds long on the average. But when someone talks to a partner whose status is higher than his own, the more the high-status person nods his head the longer the speaker's utterances become. If the high-status person changes his own customary speech pattern toward longer or shorter utterances, the lower-status person will change his own speech in the same direction. If the high-status person often interrupts the speaker, or creates long silences, the speaker is likely to become quite uncomfortable. These are things

that can be observed outside the laboratory as well as under experimental conditions. If you have an employee who makes you uneasy and seems not to respect you, watch him the next time you talk to him—perhaps he is failing to follow the customary low-status pattern.

Immediacy or directness is another good source of information about feelings. We use more distant forms of communication when the act of communicating is undesirable or uncomfortable. For example, some people would rather transmit discontent with an employee's work through a third party than do it themselves, and some find it easier to communicate negative feelings in writing than by telephone or face to face.

Distance can show a negative attitude toward the message itself, as well as toward the act of delivering it. Certain forms of speech are more distant than others, and they show fewer positive feelings for the subject referred to. A speaker might say "Those people need help," which is more distant than "These people need help." which is in turn even more distant than "These people need our help." Or he might say "Sam and I have been having dinner," which has less immediacy than "Sam and I are having dinner."

Facial expression, touching, gestures, self-manipulation (such as scratching), changes in body position, and head movements—all these express a person's positive and negative attitudes, both at the moment and in general, and many reflect status relationships as well. Movements of the limbs and head, for example, not only indicate one's attitude toward a specific set of circumstances but relate to how dominant, and how anxious, one generally tends to be in social situations. Gross changes in body position, such as shifting in the chair, may show negative feelings toward the person one is talking to. They may also be cues: "It's your turn to talk," or "I'm about to get out of here, so finish what you're saying."

Posture is used to indicate both liking and status. The more a person leans toward his addressee, the more positively he feels about him.

Relaxation of posture is a good indicator of both attitude and status, and one that we have been able to measure quite precisely. Three categories have been established for relaxation in a seated position: least relaxation is indicated by muscular tension in the hands and rigidity of posture; moderate relaxation is indicated by a forward lean of about 20 degrees and a sideways lean of less than 10 degrees, a curved back, and, for women, an open arm position; and extreme relaxation is indicated by a reclining angle greater than 20 degrees and a sideways lean greater than 10 degrees.

Our findings suggest that a speaker relaxes either very little or a great deal when he dislikes the person he is talking to, and to a moderate degree when he likes his companion. It seems that extreme tension occurs with threatening addressees, and extreme relaxation with non-threatening, disliked addressees. In particular, men tend to become tense when talking to other men whom they dislike; on the other hand, women talking to men *or* women and men talking to women show dislike through extreme relaxation. As for status, people relax most with a low-status addressee, second-most with a peer, and least with someone of higher status than their own. Body orientation also shows status: in both sexes, it is least direct toward women with low status and most direct toward disliked men of high status. In part, body orientation seems to be determined by whether one regards one's partner as threatening.

The more you like a person, the more time you are likely to spend looking into his eyes as you talk to him. Standing close to your partner and facing him directly (which makes eye contact easier) also indicate positive feelings. And you are likely to stand or sit closer to your peers than you do to addressees whose status is either lower or higher than yours.

What I have said so far has been based on research studies performed, for the most part, with college students from the middle and upper-classes. One interesting question about communication, however, concerns young children from lower socioeconomic levels. Are these children, as some have suggested, more responsive to implicit channels of communication than middle- and upper-class children are?

Morton Wiener and his colleagues at Clark University had a group of middle- and lower-class children play learning games in which the reward for learning was praise. The child's responsiveness to the verbal and vocal parts of the praise-reward was measured by how much he learned. Praise came in two forms: the objective words "right" and "correct," and the more effective or evaluative words, "good" and "fine." All four words were spoken sometimes in a positive tone of voice and sometimes neutrally.

Positive intonation proved to have a dramatic effect on the learning rate of the lower-class group. They learned much faster when the vocal part of the message was positive than when it was neutral. Positive intonation affected the middle-class group as well, but not nearly as much.

If children of lower socioeconomic groups are more responsive to facial expression, posture and touch as well as to vocal communication, that fact could have interesting applications to elementary education. For example, teachers could be explicitly trained to be aware of, and to use, the forms of praise (nonverbal or verbal) that would be likely to have the greatest effect on their particular students.

Another application of experimental data on communication is to the interpretation and treatment of schizophrenia. The literature on schizophrenia has for some time emphasized that parents of schizophrenic children give off contradictory signals simultaneously. Perhaps the parent tells the child in words that he loves him, but his posture conveys a negative attitude. According to the "double-bind" theory of schizophrenia, the child who perceives simultaneous contradictory feelings in his parent does not know how to react: should he respond to the positive part of the message, or to the negative? If he is frequently placed in this paralyzing situation, he may learn to respond with contradictory communications of his own. The boy who sends a birthday card to his mother and signs it "Napoleon" says that he likes his mother and yet denies that he is the one who likes her.

In an attempt to determine whether parents of disturbed children really do emit more inconsistent messages about their feelings than other parents do, my colleagues and I have compared what these parents communicate verbally and vocally with what they show through posture. We interviewed parents of moderately and quite severely disturbed children, in the presence of the child, about the child's problem. The interview was video-recorded without the parents' knowledge, so that we could analyze their behavior later on. Our measurements supplied both the amount of inconsistency between the parents' verbal-vocal and postural communications, and the total amount of liking that the parents communicated.

According to the double-bind theory, the parents of the more disturbed children should have behaved more inconsistently than the parents of the less disturbed children. This was not confirmed: there was no significant difference between the two groups. However, the *total amount* of positive feeling communicated by parents of the more disturbed children was less than that communicated by the other group.

This suggests that (1) negative communications toward disturbed children occur because the child is a problem and therefore elicits them, or (2) the negative attitude precedes the child's

disturbance. It may also be that both factors operate together, in a vicious circle.

If so, one way to break the cycle is for the therapist to create situations in which the parent can have better feelings toward the child. A more positive attitude from the parent may make the child more responsive to his directives, and the spiral may begin to move up instead of down. In our own work with distrubed children, this kind of procedure has been used to good effect.

If one puts one's mind to it, one can think of a great many other applications for the findings I have described, though not all of them concern serious problems. Politicians, for example, are careful to maintain eye contact with the television camera when they speak, but they are not always careful about how they sit when they debate another candidate of, presumably, equal status.

Public relations men might find a use for some of the subtler signals of feeling. So might ordinary people, who could try watching other people's signals and changing their own, for fun at a party or in a spirit of experimentation at home. I trust that does not strike you as a cold, manipulative suggestion, indicating dislike for the human race. I assure you that, if you had more than a transcription of words to judge from (seven per cent of total message), it would not.

The Way We Speak 'Body Language'

Flora Davis

A number of the country's top-flight psychiatrists have taken their patients on a trip to Philadelphia in recent years for a visit to a research lab at the Eastern Pennsylvania Psychiatric Institute. There, psychiatrist and patient hold a therapy session while movie cameras purr in the background. Psychotherapy is perhaps the most verbal of all 20-th century experiences. Yet what the film-makers are primarily interested in is nonverbal communication: shifts of posture and muscle tone, gestures, eye movements, and the like. They are looking for recurring patterns, the constellations of body movement which they see as a kind of subliminal language that can be translated by the trained interpreter.

For example, in one particular film the psychiatrist was seeing a family—mother, father, daughter, grandmother—together for the first time. Again and again during the interview, the mother turned flirtatiously to the therapist. She would extend her legs and delicately cross her ankles. Resting one hand on her hip, she would lean forward and talk with great animation for perhaps 20 or 30 seconds. Then, quite suddenly, she would subside, sink back in her

chair, pull in her legs, drop her hands to her sides. The withdrawal was so complete that she looked almost autistic.

So much one can see with the naked eye. But when the film is run through slow motion, a whole constellation of movement suddenly becomes clear. Each time the mother set out to charm the psychiatrist, her husband would begin to jiggle one foot nervously. At this, both daughter and grandmother—who were sitting on either side of the mother—would cross their knees so that their shoe tips almost met and their legs boxed her in. It was after this that she subsided. The sequence occurred 11 times in just 30 minutes of the film.

It is hardly a surprise, then, to learn that the mother's flirtatiousness was a family problem. Experts in kinesics—the study of communication through body motion—cite this fragment of nonverbal drama as a neatly documented example of the way people sometimes use body language to keep others who may be misbehaving in line. Kinesicts believe that all families have similar systems, though they are almost never conscious of having them.

In the past few years, hundreds of researchers across the country have turned to the study of nonverbal language, convinced that

101

what people do with their bodies communicates as importantly as the words they use. No single discipline has a monopoly on this new field, and each researcher brings to it the jargon and biases of his own particular science. The great mass of the new data is being produced by psychologists who are doing classic psych-lab experiments on minute body movements, such as those of the face. There are also psychiatrists working in the field who hope to apply what they learn in psychotherapy, sociologists studying body language in actual social situations and anthropologists doing cross-cultural comparisons.

People speak and move, and you and I respond, and we never stop to think that most of the time words express only the smallest part of our meaning—just 30–35 per cent of it, according to Ray Birdwhistell, who is senior research scientist at the Eastern Pennsylvania Psychiatric Institute and director of the Studies in Human Communication project there. How does a man know when a woman is a possible pickup? How do we know when another person is listening to us or if he really means what he is saying? Sometimes the signs are unmistakable, but often we rely on "intuition." Scientific research is now giving a clearer understanding of what lies behind our institutions. A lot of the work going on merely serves to confirm common sense, but much of it is both subtle and surprising.

Dr. Albert E. Sheflen, a psychiatrist-turned-kinesicist, has demonstrated, for instance, that people in a group often mirror each other's posture. In a large gathering, as many as half a dozen may sit or stand with limbs arranged in an identical—or mirror-imaged way—and if one member of the set then shifts his body, the others quickly do the same. Where two different postures have been adopted by a gathering, those who share a posture usually turn out to share a viewpoint as well. When three people are together, most often one will arrange himself so that his upper body is congruent with one companion and his lower body with the other—making himself into a kind of human link between the two.

Some gestures have a conscious, understood meaning (psychologist Paul Ekman of the Langley Porter Neuropsychiatric Institute in San Francisco calls them "emblems"). The hitchhiker's thumbing is an example that comes easily to mind. Every culture has its own repertoire of these, and they vary from culture to culture. Catching sight of a pretty girl, an Italian will signal his appreciation by pulling one of his ear lobes, an Arab will stroke his beard, but the Englishman will assume an overly casual stance and elaborately look away.

These observations are Birdwhistell's, but he cautions that it is often a mistake to interpret such gestures in isolation. The individual's facial expression or stance—or what he is saying—can give a gesture an ironic twist; as everyone knows, an Army private, when he salutes, can convey everything from blind obedience to complete contempt, depending upon the speed and duration of the gesture and what he does with the rest of his body.

Sociologist Erving Goffman of the University of Pennsylvania speaks of another sort of body language which is not communication but a means of relieving inner tension. "Creature releases," as he calls them, are brief rebellions against the social roles that we are all forced to play ("Fleeting acts slip through the individual's self-control and momentarily assert his 'animal nature'"). Some samples: "At one extreme are the minor releases such as scratching, momentary coughing, rubbing one'e eyes, sighing, yawning, and so forth; at the other extreme are such acts as flatulence, incontinence, and the like; in the middle ranges of the continuum are dozing off, belching, spitting, nose picking or loosening one's belt."

Nonverbal language, when understood, offers psychiatrists valuable clues to their patient's emotions, but most researchers in this new field shun broad theorizing about feelings and motivations. As behavioral scientists, they prefer to isolate, classify and analyze the interaction of *observable* physical acts. Really hardnosed behavioral scientists actually deny that there is any inner-man to study ("According to some psychologists," says Dr. Scheflen, "the head is populated with all sorts of little people —id, ego, superego, They emit communication, transmit messages, cause things to happen. It's a kind of animism, like the primitives who thought trees were alive.")

I talked to four pioneers in the field of body language—Birdwhistell, Scheflen, Goffman and Dr. Adam Kendon, a colleague of Scheflen's at the Bronx State Hospital. Significantly, none of the four refer to it as nonverbal communication. Kendon prefers the term "visible behavior"; his fellow kinesicists, Scheflen and Birdwhistell, who refuse to segregate words from gestures, define their field simply as "communication." (Bristling at the phrase nonverbal communication, Birdwhistell cracked: "That's like saying 'noncardiae physiology.'") Goffman speaks of his specialty as "face-to-face interaction"; he is interested in how the unwritten body codes help people to get along with each other in public.

Writers, artists and psychiatrists have long known that body motions have significance, and the psychologists' first studies of facial expressions were done early in the century. But it was anthropologists such as Franz Boas. Edward Sapir and, in the 1940's, Weston LaBarre and David Efron, who first put forward the notion that body motions are actually a code that can be cracked.

However, sustained, systematic Kinesics research really began with the publication of Ray Birdwhistell's book, "Introduction to Kinesics," in 1952. Tall, 51 years old, with crisp grey hair, Birdwhistell is an anthropologist born and educated in the Midwest. His interest in body language dates back to a field study he did of the Kutenai Indians of western Canada in 1946. While he was living among the Kutenai, he noticed that they looked quite different when speaking English from the way they looked when speaking Kutenai: their gestures their facial expressions changed. It seems that

some people are bilingual in body language as well as in spoken language.*

Birdwhistell's work is elusive. His book is now long out of print, although a new one, "Kinesics and Context," will be published in the fall. His papers, appearing mostly in professional journals, are properly dense and scholarly but short on the mass of documentation that other researchers expect. The man himself is a surprise, then: not at all the dry-voiced scholar, but tweedy, relaxed, with a face that creases easily into a smile and a voice that's resonantly basso profundo.

The day of our interview, Dr. Birdwhistell met my train at North Philadelphia and during the drive over to his lab filled me in on the early history of kinesics research. He started out, he explained with a search for universal gestures, that is, for body language common to all cultures. He now states flatly: "There are no universal gestures. As far as we know, there is no single facial express, stance, or body position which conveys the same meaning in all societies."

This is a controversial statement, hotly disputed by others in the field, including psychologists such as Dr. Ekman of the Langley Porter Neuropsychiatric Institute, who has done cross-cultural research. In one study, armed with photographs of happy faces, sad faces, angry faces, surprised, disgusted and fearful faces, Ekman asked people in half a dozen different parts of the world to name the emotions portrayed in each one. And he concluded that the people in all the places selected, even those in isolated, primitive cultures, associated each photo with the same emotion. If people

*One of the best examples of this was the late Fiorello La Guardia, the popular New York Mayor, who delivered campaign speeches in Italian and Yiddish as well as English—and was a master of the gestures appropriate to each language. His gesturing was so clear, in fact, that Birdwhistell, who has seen films of the speeches, says he could tell what language "The Little Flower" was speaking even with the sound track turned off.

all over the world smile when they are happy, and recognize a happy face, is not the smile, then, a universal expression of emotion—part of our biological heritage (as no less an authority than Darwin said it was)?

Birdwhistell concedes that all humans smile—even blind babies do—for we all have the same face muscles. However, he contends that the *meaning* of the smile is not universal. Even in the United States he has found that there are "high-smile" areas, such as the South, where people do a lot of smiling, and "low-smile" areas, such as western New York State, where they do not (this is not a sign that Southerners are happier). In the South someone who does not often smile may be asked if he is angry, but in the Great Lakes region someone who does smile a lot may be asked what is so funny. It is culture, according to Birdwhistell, that supplies the meaning of the smile, and it cannot be a pleasure reflex.

This is the old nature-nurture argument again, of course: heredity vs. environment. In this case, the two sides are not quite so far apart as they at first sound, since those who believe in universal gestures admit that smiles are culture-modified, and Birdwhistell admits that, anatomically speaking, they *are* universal.

At this point we arrived at the laboratory, which, with its sunny offices and quiet corridors, is actually nothing at all like a lab but more like the premises of some sedate, suburban firm with an interest in the movie-film business. Birdwhistell took me directly to the room where he does kinesic analysis using a slow-motion projector. The film he showed me there was as undramatic as anything you could find: just two people, therapist and patient, sitting opposite each other, talking. The segment he was working on was only a few seconds long, but for each second there were 24 frames of the film, and for each frame he was making a record, using an ingenious shorthand system he has devised, of every body motion of both therapist and patient.

Dr. Birdwhistell approaches the stream of body motion the same way the descriptive linguists approach the stream of speech. The first time you hear a strange language, it makes no sense at all. But if you go on listening, soon you can pick out distinct, recurring units, which may or may not be whole words, and eventually you can hear them combining in regular ways with other "words" into sentences. And if you repeat one of these units to yourself you find it breaks down into smaller units called sound.

In the same manner, Birdwhistell hunts through the stream of body motion for repeated movements. Each position of the head, brows, chin, eyes and other parts of the body has a shorthand symbol: these are the basic units that he calls, "kines," which combine into larger patterns. He records the direction of movement of each "kine" with another set of symbols. Then, he analyzes what happens to the meaning of the message when one kine is removed from the context and everything else stays the same. The meaning, he said is always in the context, never in any particular, isolated body motion. One case in point is Birdwhistell's and Scheflen's assertion that a woman who tightly crosses her arms or legs is relatively inaccessible to any approach. Whether this is correct, both affirm, depends upon such circumstances as what other people are around, what else she does with her body, and so on.

Kinesic stress is one way people reduce verbal ambiguities. As everyone knows, an eyebrow lift often accompanies a question. However, it is also a way to stress a word in the speech stream. There are other ways to signal a question, too, such as an upward tilt of the head or hand, and one can as easily stress something with a nod of the foot or a blink of the eyelids.

Small movements of the head, eyes, hands, fingers or even the shoulders that accompany specific pronouns, verbs or phrases Birdwhistell describes as "markers." With the pronouns "I," "me," "we" and "us" as well as words such as "this" and "how," a hand "marker" would be a motion toward the speaker's body, while the shoulders would be squeezed, or hunched, in the direction of an imaginary vertical line through the center of the body. With future-tense verbs the marker motion is forward; with the past tense, it is backward. All this seems so logical to Americans that it is a surprise to learn that other peoples, for example, some American-Indian cultures, sometimes find these markers confusing or even insulting when combined with their language.

From the projection room we went on to the studio where psychotherapy sessions are filmed, a big, quiet room furnished with a semi-circle of chairs, a closed-circuit TV and one small camera on a tripod that poked its snout unobtrusively through a gap in some curtains. Birdwhistell was interested in filming psychotherapy because it provides an accessible, natural context within which to study body motion. "Natural" is the key word, for he does not believe you can learn much that's valid about communication in the artificial environment provided in psych-lab experiments. "I don't take a fish out of water to learn how it swims," he said.

One of the things Birdwhistell has learned from the psychotherapy project is that even the best therapists usually cannot explain what it is that they do right. In fact, sometimes they do the opposite of what they think they do. A man who believes in being completely non-authoritative, for example, can be seen conducting a group session as firmly as a conductor leads an orchestra, telling one person to speak and another to stop with a glance or a flick of the fingers.

Over lunch that day, Dr. Birdwhistell explained his concept of "gender signals" to me. In every culture he has studied people can distinguish feminine body behaviors from masculine ones. Birdwhistell speculates that because in the human species the secondary sexual characteristics, such as breasts and body hair, are not that dramatically different, body-motion differences function as "tertiary sexual characteristics" to help humans distinguish male from fe-

male. Gender in our society determines such simple matters as who gets up to do the dishes after dinner or who goes through a door first. What is defined as masculine or feminine, furthermore, varies from one culture to the next.

"We think of male Arabs as effeminate and seductive because of the way they close their eyelids—very slowly—in contrast to the speed with which American males do it. We find the way Latin males cross their legs feminine in contrast to the broken-four spread typical of American males." Birdwhistell leaned back in his chair and indicated his own legs: four-shaped, with one ankle propped on the other knee.

When sending gender signals, American women hold their thighs close together, according to Birdwhistell's studies. They walk with upper arms against their bodies and tilt their pelvises forward slightly. In contrast, American men sending gender signals stand with thighs somewhat apart. They hold their arms away from their bodies and swing them as they walk, and they carry their pelvises rolled slightly back.

Birdwhistell denies that these varying walking styles can be attributed to anatomical differences. Otherwise, he argues, they would be the same in all cultures—which they are not. In Eastern European countries, for instance, a man is much less likely to walk with the broad carriage and arm-swinging that we label "masculine," says Birdwhistell.

Inevitably, when Birdwhistell explains gender signals, people leap to the conclusion that what they signal is sexual attraction. Though this is sometimes true, very often it is not. Though gender emphasis may lead to a sexual relationship sometimes, at other times, it is actually a way of preventing one from developing. A woman can protect herself from getting involved by sending inappropriate gender signals. "She sends them so strongly that they exclude all incoming messages. They're an insistence, not a response. That's the difference between a sexy woman and a sexual woman," Dr. Bird-whistell explained.

The belle of the cocktail party, the siren in the low-cut dress who is surrounded by men, is —according to Birdwhistell—surrounded primarily by the men who do not like women or simply do not want to get involved. For them, she is the safest woman in the room to be around, just because she is not in any real sense responsive. Men simply do not turn her on— they cannot, because her volume is already on "high." The sexual woman, on the other hand, may stand on the sidelines looking pretty uninteresting until a man comes along. Then she will respond to him in dozens of subtle, nonverbal ways, perhaps by sending gender signals, perhaps with "courting behavior."

Relegated in the Birdwhistell scheme of things to a category called "parakinesics" are all kinds of fascinating things that he feels are definitely part of the communication system. They include stance and posture; the way skin varies from pale to flushed, dry to oily, flaccid to rigid. Then there are general categories such as beauty and ugliness, gracefulness and awkwardness.

How can being ugly be communicative? Birdwhistell refuses to see ugliness as an inborn characteristic. To begin with, he says, attractiveness may be a very transitory quality, which comes and goes like sunshine on a cloudy day. Everyone recognizes that people sometimes become quite beautiful when they fall in love, or ugly in moments of hate and anger. And on a more long-term basis, looks are one way in which society sorts people out, and being attractive is not necessarily good for a person if it means that too much is expected of him. Some people feel safer being part of the minority group of the unattractive. The point is that culture presents us with certain definitions, and we behave accordingly. If culture says that fat is ugly, then the fat person is saying something with his obesity about how he wants to be treated.

In the presence of Birdwhistell and other kinesicists, for whom every movement has a message, one cannot help being somewhat self-conscious about making dramatic gestures. By the time I interviewed Dr. Albert Scheflen, in fact, I was practically sitting on my hands. He told me that people often react this way: "But their fear is predicated on the idea that body behavior often reveals one's inner dirty work." Again, he reassured me that this is not what kinesicists are looking for.

Scheflen is a towering, white-bearded scientist whose slangy, drawling style of speech sits oddly with his rather formidable qualifications. Born in New Jersey in 1920, he got his M.D. in the nineteen-forties, became a neurologist, then in the nineteen-fifties a psychiatrist. He began private practice and went on to become involved in psychotherapy research. "We weren't getting anywhere with it, though," he recalls, "and then, just as I was looking around for something new to learn, I met Ray [Birdwhistell]. And he had it.

For 10 years, Scheflen shared the trials and triumphs of kinesic research with Birdwhistell. In the division of labor worked out between the two men, Birdwhistell did "microanalysis"— that is he concentrated on mini-movements that are over in a fraction of a second or 10 seconds at the most—while Scheflen tackled the longer stretches of behavior. In 1967, Scheflen moved to New York, where in his own lab, he is now studying day-long and even week-long sequences of body motion. This new Project on Human Communication—Scheflen is project director—is sponsored by the Albert Einstein College of Medicine, the Bronx State Hospital and the Jewish Family Service, and supported by state funds. Lab space is provided by the hospital in an erstwhile nurses' residence.

Scheflen's current project centers on a ghetto neighborhood in the Bronx and involves televising families in their own homes with a camera mounted high on a living room or kitchen wall. The camera is simply left in place for six to ten weeks and family members, self-conscious at first, after about a week seem to forget that it is there. The video signal is recorded in a nearby apartment and researchers work with the tapes of it.

He is not pimarily concerned with the personalities of the people whose daily lives he studies. What he is mainly interested in is territoriality: he studies body behavior by which an individual indicates that he is—or is not—on his own "turf."

I sat with Dr. Scheflen in a room crowded with bulky equipment, while he worked on a videotape of a family. The monitor showed a kitchen. A woman wearing an overcoat drifted into the room, then drifted out again. A moment later she was back and an eddy of small children came with her. It was early morning and she was about to leave for work.

Just then, Scheflen saw something he had been watching for and aimed a Polaroid camera at the screen. He explained that he had spotted an instance of face-to-face confrontation, a phenomenon that he is studying apart from his work on territoriality. So far, he has not found many cases of it in his videotapes. A colleague of Scheflen's, Dr. William Stewart, has a hunch that in poor black families, people look directly at each other less often than people do in middle-class white families. This is a small difference, but it may account for the fact that blacks meeting whites sometimes feel stared at, while whites feel that blacks are avoiding their eyes.

Really documenting such cultural differences, though, can be a lengthy, painstaking process. Dr. Scheflen, for example, will have to do comparison studies of black families and white families before he can back up Dr. Stewart's hunch about face-to-face confrontations with proof, and all that will take one or two years.

(Without new developments in audiovisual equipment, the kind cf research the kinesicists are doing would not be possible—and sometimes their needs has been mother of an invention. Until just about 10 years ago, for example, it was impossible to get a film projector that could be slowed to less than two-thirds normal speed; beyond that point, the image flickered badly. Partly because of the kinesicists needs, some one finally invented a projector that could be run without flicker at any speed down to one frame a minute.)

With Birdwhistell and Kendon, Scheflen has done a lot of research on courting behavior. Everyone knows that when two people are attracted to each other, they show it in sublte ways. Some of the symptoms are well known; others are not. Scheflen has reported that readiness to court is visible first of all as heightened muscle tone. The individual holds himself, or herself, erect; legs have tighter tone and even the face changes—sagging, jowliness and pouches under the eyes all decrease. Eyes seem brighter and skin may become either flushed or pale. And often the person preens. Feminine preening is easy to recognize. Some of the male preening gestures—hair grooming, tie-preening, sock-preening—usually go unrecognized.

Courting couples, of course, exchange long looks. They cock their heads and roll their pelvises. A woman may cross her legs, slightly exposing one thigh, place a hand on her hip, or protrude her breasts. She may slowly stroke her own thigh or wrist or present a palm. Anglo-Saxon. women ordinarily show their palms hardly at all, says Scheflen, but in courting they palm all over the place, even smoking or covering a cough with palm out.

"From that," says Scheflen, "you could perhaps derive a cheap rule: whenever a woman shows you her palm, she's courting you, whether—she knows it or not." But in fact he went on, people show palms in all sorts of relationships. "Showing the palm is an invitation to an encounter, and not necessarily sexual at all. It doesn't mean one person necessarily likes the other, it just means they're coming together in some way, perhaps only on business. The whole thing is the context again."

Scheflen has also discovered a phenomenon he calls quasi-courting, which can occur in practically any situation and need not signal sexual attraction at all. In the American middle class, quasi-courting may happen between parent and child, doctor and patient, at business meetings and at cocktail parties, even between people of the same sex. It is courting with a difference, with subtle qualifiers added that indicate that it is not to be taken seriously. A couple may momentarily seem to be courting. but closer observation will show that their bodies are turned slightly aside from each other, or their voices are a shade too loud for an intimate two-some. One or both may keep glancing about the room, or one person may extend an arm as if to include a third party, or drape the arm across his lap as a kind of barrier. Whatever the signal it changes the whole significance of the be-havior.

Quasi-courting apparently has a social func-tion. In the group therapy films, it appeared regularly as a way to reinvolve someone who was becoming withdrawn. For example, in one film of family therapy, the daughter at first flashed courtship signals at the therapist. When he did not respond, she "decourted," meaning that she lost all that alert muscle tone and began to look uninterested and remote. Soon afterward, the therapist began a quasi-courting sequence: he locked glances with the girl and for a while they dragged on their cigarettes in perfect synchrony. Then, perhaps becoming a little self-conscious about this intimacy, she looked sharply away and placed her arm across her lap as a barrier. Again she began to decourt, and she adopted her mother's posture and smoking rhythm. However, she did not, this time dissociate herself from the group.

These days, while Dr. Scheflen concentrates on his televised families other members of his re-search team are involved in their own projects. For example, there is Dr. Adam Kendon, 36 years old, an Englishman with a luxuriant au-burn beard, who likes to think of kinesics as a branch of zoology, a kind of human ethology. Dr. Kendon's current project, with Dr. Andrew Ferber as a collaborator, is a study of how hu-mans greet one another.

"There are films of chimpanzee greetings," he says, "where you see two chimps approach each other. They shake hands, they embrace, they slap each other on the back. I can show you human greetings that look very similar."

Dr. Kendon's office is dominated by a film projector that has a hand crank added, to make frame-by-frame analysis easier. His greetings film, made at a backyard birthday party, shows a whole series of people crossing the yard to the host, who greets them with open arms.

"Watch now," Dr. Kendon told me, running through a particular sequence with the hand crank. "You'll see that the host moves forward with his neck extended and lifts his arms out and away from his body. Now look at the guest. His trunk is erect, his neck is not ex-tended, and when he puts his arms up for the embrace, they are on the inside, with the host's arms outside. There are several other greetings in the film where you see the same things. These are just some observations we've made lately, but we wonder whether this is a parti-cular greeting posture that you will see in males being greeted on their own territory, a sort of dominant-greeter's posture."

Kendon hopes eventually to do a "typol-ogy" of greetings, describing those that take place at the edges of territories and in public places, between close acquaintances and strang-ers, formal greetings and informal. Then, since animals greet, too, it should be possible to do a comparative analysis—to spot similarities and differences between human and other primate greetings, for example.

The kinesicists are all given to quoting Erving Goffman, as are many of the other re-searchers in the field. In a sense, he supplies the framework and they fill in the behavioral de-tails. I talked to Professor Goffman at his beautiful old Philadelphia town house, in a living room the size of a small ballroom with a ceiling so high that it gradually vanished that day in the late-afternoon dusk. He is a small man, a 47-year-old Canadian with a ruggedly in-telligent face whose interest in nonverbal com-munication dates back to the nineteen forties

Body

Language' **109**

when he took a course taught by Birdwhistell at the University of Toronto.

Goffman does not have a lab. What he has instead is a filing system. When he writes, he puts together things he has read, bits of novels, items from books of etiquette, and what he gleaned from a year he spent studying the social structure of a mental institution. To this he adds his own systematic observation in social situations, from cocktail parties to public meetings, which he has recorded in voluminous detail. (Goffman dislikes being photographed for publication, perhaps, as he jokes, because he will lose anonymity, and thus his ability to do research in social gatherings.)

The results, in cool, precise and measured prose, are his books on face-to-face interaction. He has described, for example, what constitutes proper involvement in a conversation, as opposed to underinvolvement or overinvolvement, and how people accord each other "civil inattention" in public places. By this he means, for example, that a person passing a stranger in the street does not, under the rules, make gestures that indicate too much interest in the other, if he does his behavior is likely to be interpreted as nosy or threatening.

Reading about Goffman's rules of public order, one gets a sense of just how vulnerable human beings really are. We simply assume that when we are out in public no one will attack us or block our way to suddenly start up a conversation; we depend on each other to behave properly. In recent years, though, the free and easy use of public and semipublic places has become subject to question. "What happens in confrontation politics," says Goffman, "is that persons in each other's presence decline intentionally to sustain one or more of the fundamental rules of order. Mental patients use the same strategies for different reasons."

Goffman has written that everything an individual does in the presence of others is made up of tacit threats and promises: indications that he knows his place and will stay in it, that he knows it but will not stay in it, or that he does not and may not. Mental symptoms are

often simply evidence that he is not prepared to keep to his place. "In a hospital setting," he explained, "patients will in a conversation put to you a question much more candid delicate and probing than would anyone but your analyst. They will, when you address them, not answer back. They will be exquisitely slovenly in their dress or withdrawn in their manner or when you're talking will come and lean into the conversation or interrupt it physically. These are all devices aimed at the rules of order."

Young radicals also attack the rules—and signify their refusal to know their place—when they occupy a building, seize the microphone at a public meeting or address a dean by his first name. Goffman cites the story of what happened when during the student demonstrations at Columbia two years ago, Mark Rudd was invited to discuss the issues with some faculty members in a professor's apartment. After coffee was brought in on a silver service, Rudd took off his boots and socks, complaining that his feet were sweating.

This kind of pantomime is not hard to understand—it was an obvious attempt to shock others—but will you and I some day be able to read more obscure motives in a person's body behavior? Certainly some of us will try, though probably with marginal accuracy, since body language is subtle and complex. Most of the time, people simply use the motions prescribed by their culture as suitable in context—which is actually the best way to conceal their true feelings. More important, we may learn to depend more on our intuitions, realizing that they are often based on actual body signals from other people which we perceive on a subliminal level.

As to the future uses of the field, most of the men working in it are not primarily concerned about that. They are doing pure science, not applied science; they study human communication because it is there. But there are, of course, numerous possibilities. Someday language specialists will probably be taught the kinesics of a foreign language along with its grammar and vocabulary. Kinesics should prove a handy tool for the study of child development. And research on intercultural differences could clear up some of the small but alienating misunderstandings between men of different cultures that come about just because they speak different body languages.

Birdwhistell, who has taught his science of kinesics to young psychiatrists in the past, now wants to concentrate on working with educators. He wants to do basic behavioral research on what makes a teacher good, how children learn to be good students, what is an optimum teaching situation.

Individual psychotherapy will not last long, he thinks, because it is too expensive and reaches only a small number of people: "No society in the world has ever been rich enough before so that one person—apart from a king or an emperor—could afford to take up so much of another person's time. A small number of therapists treat a small number of people, but it's a fraction of the population. On the other hand, a very large proportion of the population goes through our school system."

His most ambitious goal, however, is that men—at least some men—will learn to "communicate on purpose," that they will become aware of their own body motions and of what they communicate, and will then exercise the same control over their kinesic behavior that they already do over their words.

But the study of human communication is still in its infancy and it is hard to get a really clear idea of what it might grow up to be. Birdwhistell says that it is only about as far along as microbiology was when the microscope was first invented and people went around wearing face masks to protect themselves from germs. One thing seems certain, though: men will no longer be able to assume that when two people meet, all that is communicated is the words they speak. As Dr. Birdwhistell told me:

"Years ago I started with the question: How do body motions flesh out words? Now I ask instead: When is it appropriate to use words? They're very appropriate to teach or to talk on the telephone, but you and I are communicating on several levels now and on only one or two of them have words any relevance whatsoever. These days I put it another way: Man is a multi-sensorial being. Occasionally, he verbalizes."

Crowding and Density

Tony Chiu and Betty Vaughn

With world population expected to hit seven billion by the year 2000, these dual concepts are important to professional designers. The following three-part report pinpoints problems and uncovers solutions.

... World population growth, expected to hit seven billion by the year 2000, together with the trend toward metropolitization, makes population density—the ratio of people to space—an issue of importance to professional designers. Crowding—the psychological response to density—is of special concern to interior designers, architects and those responsible for the design and management of relatively small spaces.

To deal with the dual concepts of crowding and density, DESIGN & ENVIRONMENT presents a three part report. *Section One, A Primer on Crowding*, is intended to bring interior designers and architects up to date on new psychological and social findings regarding crowding. *Section Two, Density in the Suburbs*, describes the conflict between those who want to preserve green space the the social *status quo* and those who want to increase suburban density, overthrow exclusionary zoning laws, and open the suburbs to blue-collar families. *Section Three, Solutions to Density*, describes new approaches to zoning, taxation and physical design available to professionals concerned with optimum land utilization.[1]

Paradoxically, the United States,with a supply of 1.9 billion acres, has an abundance of land, but its urbanized land has been mis-zoned and misused. Following are but some of the ways.

Land waste—during the early years of this century, zoning, introduced by Edward M. Bassett and other planning pioneers, became a tool for crowding immigrants close together in cities, where they provided a pool of cheap labor. Still essentially an instrument of the middle class, zoning today is used to create wastefully large suburban lot sizes, priced so high as to effectively exclude the poor.

Inflated prices have resulted from the large lots required in many suburbs. For example, the price per square-foot of land purchased with FHA insured mortgages has increased at the rate of nearly 12 percent per year during the last five years.

Mis-zoning is another problem. Recently, Horizon, an Arizona sales company, bought a large tract in the Adirondacks of New York

Reprinted from Design & Environment, Summer, 1972.

[1] Not used in this text.

111

State in order to subdivide it into one-and-a-half and two-acre lots for a resort housing 30,000 people. Such development would irreparably damage a primeval forest and wetland.

Economic segregation has been one of the most harmful effects of large-lot suburban zoning practices. Not only are apartment buildings segregated by district from single-family residences, but families with incomes of $10,000 or less simply cannot afford to buy suburban one-acre lots.

Racial segregation is the other effect of American zoning today. As planning consultant Stephen Sussna remarks, since about 96 percent of those persons in metropolitan areas outside the central city are white, and those who remain in the central cities are increasingly black, two distinct racial societies are confronting the United States. "More than issues of rising public school costs, diminishing tax bases and resources, fears of invading black and poorer residents are at the bottom of suburban large lot practices, says Sussna.

DESIGN & ENVIRONMENT believes that planners, architects and designers will have a vital role to play in curbing suburban sprawl and ameliorating high-density living. But, above all, we believe that physical solutions go hand in hand with social solutions. . . . In looking at density patterns in the suburbs in relation to inner-city problems of housing and jobs, Davidoff has taken the lid off the most crucial civil rights issue of the 1970's. In so doing, he underscores the need for designers to understand and act on social as well as physical problems in the American environment.

Section 1:
A Primer on Crowding

Based on an article by Daniel Stokols
Adapted by Tony Chiu

Psychologists and sociologists are studying crowding in the lab and in the field. Their data suggest that designers can do much to amelio-rate the stress of individuals forced to live in a crowded world. ,

The looming density crisis is of paramount importance to urban planners and architects who have split into two camps while trying to cope with problems of the modern city. The "pro-density" faction points to the attendant excitement and batter of opportunities afforded by large aggregations of people; the "anti-density" faction points to the downtrodden urbanities whose daily lives are a constant hassle. Into this conflict have come recent studies by behavioral scientists that suggest a middle ground. These findings indicate that density is not synonymous with crowding. Instead, crowding is perceived by many researchers as a subjective interpretation of a medley of stresses, of which density is but one. Indeed, it seems possible that someday soon it will be within man's grasp to so arrange his environment that even though density will be high, the dispiriting sensation of crowding will be eliminated.

Frightening glimpses into the consequences of density without environmental safeguards have emerged from laboratory experiments with animal communities. For example, psychologist John Calhoun confined groups of rats in a limited area and allowed them to reproduce. As the rat population exploded, Calhoun observed increasing physiological and social abnormalities among his subjects. Some animals became overly aggressive, while others became extremely passive, withdrawing from all social interaction. The incidence of infant mortality climbed, partly because many females neglected maternal duties. And rats of both sexes showed increased promiscuity, including homosexual behavior. Calhoun linked the disorders to the formation of what he termed "behavioral sinks"—the congregation of several rats at specific points in the cage, where they would remain listlessly over long periods of time.

People tend to act more asocially when there are more of them in a limited space. Researchers investigating census tract data suggest that there is indeed a positive correlation between density and crime and suicide.

Fictional stories of small but well-knit groups of underdogs triumphing over larger opponents seem, according to recent research on the impact of "behavior settings," to be based on psychological truths. R. G. Barker has observed that students at small schools interact more, especially in group activities, while those at larger institutions not only interact less, but tend to derive satisfaction from vicarious rather than first-hand participation.

An efficient board of directors can dispatch its duties as well in a cramped cubbyhole as in a ballroom-sized conference hall, according to studies of group interaction and performance in relation to room size. Through laboratory and field observations, researchers have found that if a group is united in a common cause, its members disregard all but the most extreme environmental conditions. However, the common cause seems to be the prime factor, for study groups without a mission behave differently. Among taskless groups, density appears to be a factor; individuals act more aggressively and more asocially in large groups than in small ones.

Research into human and animal communities suggests that population density is but a contributory condition to the experience of crowding. In order to build upon the results of prior research and channel future studies, the author suggests this model to deal with the social-psychological aspects of crowding. Central to the model is the previously-made distinction between the physical reality of density and the subjective reality of crowding. Crowding stress, according to the model, results from a chronological sequence of events in which physical, social and personal factors interact to limit an individual's allotment of space. That individual, when put in a position of demanding more space, feels crowded.

During phase (1), the individual interacts with his environment. This may lead to (2) stress, or the perception of spatial restriction. The individual responds to (3) this stress,

changing either his environment (4a) or modifying his perceptions (4b). When the sensation of crowding has been alleviated, either the individual or his environment has been adaptively altered (5a, 5b).

The model stresses the fact that an individual's traits and behavioral dispositions contribute to his experience of crowding. But environment also plays a role. And here, architects and designers can make a contribution.

The flexibility of a given space can offset feelings of crowding. . . . Alcoves to relieve montony, ample storage space to hide clutter and mirrors to convey the extension of space make even the smallest studio apartment bearable.

Heat, noise and other physical stressors accentuate one's feeling of crowding. Insulation, which would insure the privacy and security of high-rise residents, must be innovated by engineers. Also, architects can devise interesting details to alleviate the monotony of standardized dwelling units.

Designers have long recognized that the suburbanite demands his square of law, but only recently have planners considered the need of people with urbanized, closely-knit ethnic backgrounds for sidewalks and stoops amenable to social interaction. Within the past year in California, low- and middle-income projects have been built with these features.

Conceptualizing crowding as a subjective experience is but one of several recent theoretical approaches to the relationship between density and crowding. It is my belief that crowding centers around the disparity between an individual's demand for space and the availability of that space.

Others have offered varying hypotheses: psychologist A. Wicker suggests that, within a given space, the ratio of tasks to available executors is a critical index in determining if that space is perceived as crowded; psychologist A. J. Desor proposes that "being crowded" is tantamount to "receiving excessive stimulation from social sources"; City University of N.Y. psychologists Proshansky, Ittelson and Rivlin view that a person will feel crowded if his behavioral options are restricted.

Although these perspectives differ in several respects, they share one common element—an emphasis on the importance of social environment. It has been shown that environment can alleviate—or exacerbate—stress on an individual.

In the context of density, psychological analyses suggest that population concentration, by itself, is not harmful. Rather, it is social interference that is damaging. This interference might result from coordination problems, competition for resources, excessive noise and interpersonal contact or from infringements on privacy and behavioral freedom.

It seems plausible, then, that eliminating sources of social interference through modifications of spatial and nonspatial variables in the environment would reduce crowding stress.

The direction in which density research has moved in the last decade holds several implications for urban designers. Through planning, social interference might be reduced by:

• Improved communication systems that offset information overload.

• Improved transportation facilities that diminish the frictions of moving through space.

• The provision of parks and gardens—green belts—that help neutralize the pressures of high population density.

• Mixed primary functions within city districts that would also alleviate density pressures by increasing the range of activities for residents, attracting non-residents to the district at various times of the day and promoting a more efficient and continuous use of available space.

It must be emphasized that these suggestions are based on crowding hypotheses rather than on validated theories. Most of the research in our field has focused on the reaction of individuals to stress. Certain conceptual problems arise when we try to generalize macrocosmic solutions based on a reading of microcosmic data. Hence, it is conceivable that what may be stressful for individuals in the short run may be advantageous for the general population in the long run.

Thus, more longitudinal studies—assessing the effects of density over a period of time—must be conducted at both the community and sub-group levels. A particularly fruitful approach appears to be the time-series research design, elaborated upon by psycholgist D. Campbell.

Finally, research must be expanded in the field. As worldwide population pressures continue to build, it is essential that we increase our understanding of the relationships between density and crowding.

Field work offers numerous opportunties for collaboration between behavioral scientists and urban designers. Through such collaborations, the utility of psychological perspectives in urban design will eventually be fully realized.

Section 2:
Density in the Suburbs

by Betty Vaughn

Bergen County, New Jersey, is a microcosm of the conflict over density in American suburbs. Bergenites fight to preserve green space and the social status quo. But 80 percent of New Jersey's population can't afford a Bergen County home. These people demand new approaches to zoning, taxation and physical design.

The United States is, for the first time, more suburban than urban, according to 1970 census of population. In the past decade, the nation's population increased by 13.3 percent, *but about 80 percent of the gain took place outside the central cities.* Now planners are beginning to compare inner-city densities with suburban densities for cause and effect relationships. The story of Bergen County, one of the fastest growing suburban areas in the nation, is suggestive of the promise and the problems that new density ratios will bring to suburbs across the nation.

Bergen County with an overall population density of about 6,400 persons per-square-mile, remains a stronghold of the American dream: one man, one house. According to the Bergen County Planning Board, last year there were 35,000 acres of vacant land in the county. Of these, 29,000 were zoned for single-family houses, 690 for commercial use and 5,290 for industrial use, but only 390 for two-family, 67 for garden apartments, and a pitiful 47 for high-rise building.

In short, Bergen County is zoned primarily for single-family housing. Since the cost of building a single-family home plus the cost of a lot would price an average home at over $50,000, moderate and low-income families cannot afford to live in Bergen. Executives in Bergen's .corporate headquarters, computer firms and engineering companies can put down fifty thousand for a home without flinching. But the thousands of blue-collar people, the elderly, newlyweds, college students, college faculty members, policemen and firemen find it either difficult or impossible to locate housing they can afford in Bergen, New Jersey's most expensive county. How did such a situation arise?

Bedroom for New York

Bergen County acquired its reputation as a bedroom of New York when the George Washington Bridge opened in 1931. Residential development came to a stop during World War II, and when the war was over, Bergen was a haphazard patchquilt of old housing, a few new developments started in the 1930s and some industrial development in the southern end of the county. The county population then was about 460,000.

Returning veterans were eager to take advantage of the Housing Law enacted by Congress in 1944 permitting veterans to buy housing with no down payment. At the same time, banks and insurance companies had investment money that had been tied up in World War II in low-yielding government bonds. The combination of desire, builder know-how and enormous amounts of investment capital at low interest rates set the stage for the rapid development of one-family housing and the increase in satellite retail business—supermarkets, shopping centers and other stores. Bergen County grew more citified.

As growth continued in the 1950s, highways began to dissect the area and two superhighways, the Garden State Parkway and the New Jersey Turnpike, led to growth of residential and industrial developments.

It was in this span of time, from 1946–72, that Bergen changed dramatically, reaching a population of nearly one million, with a 15.2 percent increase in population in the last ten years—making it one of the fastest growing and most densely populated counties in the country.

Bergen's Problems and Potential

This Topsy-like growth puts the county in a dichotomous position with both problems and potential. Factors highlighting Bergen's potential are:

• Massive shopping centers, such as Bergen Mall in Paramus, add to the county's $1.7 billion annual retail sales—more than the volume in 12 states.

• Bergen surpasses 12 states in population and in industrial output. Eighty-three of the nation's largest 100 industrial corporations have their corporate headquarters in Bergen.

• The county is slowly but surely becoming autonomous and weened away from Manhattan. A new banking bill has created bank holding companies to handle needs of companies without resorting to New York.

• The coming of the New York Giants to New Jersey's Meadowlands, scheduled for 1975, will be a big drawing card. Said one resident, "We used to go to New York for culture and sports events, but now we seldom do. Everything is here."

So much for Bergen's promise. Its problems are complex, intractable and—for citizens with a sense of social fair play—uncomfortable. Here are some of them.

• Phenomenal growth is severely taxing municipal services. Fort Lee, a two-and-one-half-square-mile southern Bergen County town, has constructed 15 new luxury high-rise residential towers in the past ten years. But residents of these 4,500 new apartment units are overloading sewer systems and schools. Faced with this problem, Fort Lee's planning board, headed by architect Theodore Hanser, has begun to halt high-rise apartment construction until a master plan for Fort Lee's development can be accepted.

• To factory workers in the county, and to other moderate- and low-income families. Bergen's biggest problem is expressed by the term "exclusionary zoning." Especially in its northern region, Bergen's muncipalities use one-, two- and even four-acre zoning ordinances to limit not only the actual number of families that can live there, but also to exclude those without the means to afford a large home.

• More than half-a-million county residents commute daily to New York City to work, while more and more New Yorkers cross the bridge to earn their living in Bergen County. This phenomenon has been called the "cross-over." White suburbanities come to earn their living in Manhattan, while inner-city black males seek blue-collar jobs in Bergen's rapidly expanding industrial plants. Bergen is glad to have the labor supply, but it has, so far, failed to provide housing opportunity.

As pressure mounts, Bergen County will have to provide land on which low- and moderate-income housing can be built. Whether it can do so while retaining the social and environmental amenities that made suburbia attractive in the first place depends on a number of factors. Legislation for a New Jersey state income tax, though defeated in July, must eventually be passed in order to take the burden of paying school costs for new arrivals off the backs of long-time property taxpayers. Also, planned unit development (would provide a physical solution to the problem of rising density in Bergen County. Most important is the outcome of current litigation testing the legality of exclusionary zoning. At the moment Bergen County residents are bitterly resisting every one of these factors. How Mahwah, one Bergen County town, is resisting is described . . . next. . . .

"There are no villains in Mahwah," says the *Bergen County Record* of participants in the nation's most crucial suburban zoning fight. Residents understandably want to keep the town green, upopulated and unpolluted. Mayor Lawrence Nyland and thoughtful city fathers, believing change is sure to come, hope to minimize its impact. Advocate planner Paul David-off insists that Mahwah cannot legally use zoning to prevent Ford assemblyliners from living in the town where they work. He's taking Mahwah and three neighboring towns to court to prove his case.

Mahwah is a gently rolling 25-square-mile township so unpopulated that it appears as it must have looked when the Algonquins roamed its hills. With a density of less than two people per acre, it has 6,000 acres of vacant land suitable for residential development, but virtually all of it is zoned for one- and two-acre lots. This assures that such housing as is inevitable will go on lots large enough to retain the rural flavor of the town. And anyone who has strolled through Mahwah's wooded glens must sympathize with townspeople who want to keep the environment unchanged.

But Mayor Lawrence Nyland knows that changes must come to Mahwah. His strategy appears to be to minimize and postpone change as skillfully as possible. At the moment, Mayor Nyland hopes for adoption of a revised master plan providing for a two-square-mile development between Ramapo College and Route 17. Candeub, Fleissig and Associates, Newark planning consultants who drew up the plan (a mixed PUD) envision single-family homes plus 1,000 garden apartments, townhouses and senior citizen units for about 300 acres. This would bring in some 3,000 residents, increasing Mahwah's population by 30 percent. The plan recommends that townhouses be sold for $40,000 and garden apartments for $20,000.

Using the rule of thumb that a man should not pay more than double his annual salary for his house, the Candeub, Fleissig plan assures that few earning less than $10,000 will move into Mahwah. A 385-acre parcel of the area proposed for rezoning has already been sold to developer George Lethbridge for development as an office park.

While Mayor Nyland's proposed zoning revision may suit Mahwah residents (by providing $98.2 million worth of tax ratables) and their wish for home rule and maintaining the rural quality of the town, it doesn't meet the housing needs of Ford's blue collar workers who want to live near their jobs. Of the 4–5,000 workers at Ford, only 88 management-level people have been able to buy homes in Mahwah. The blue collar workers, 40 percent black and Spanish-speaking from inner-city ghettoes, are zoned out. To remedy this situation, the United Auto Workers, on behalf of Ford's workers, approached Ford nearly three years ago with a proposal that they jointly develop moderate-priced housing near the Ford plant. Such a solution would alleviate Ford's problem of employee turnover and absenteeism during bad weather, and Ford workers' commuting four hours per day at an annual cost of $1,200–1,500 per worker.

Since Ford already owned the land, the UAW's proposal, according to UAW administrator Richard DiPalma, was that 1,000 acres of land near Ringwood, N.J. five minutes from the Ford plant, be used for a moderate-income community (average Ford wages are $10,000 per year). According to UAW's lawyer Paul Giblin, Ford first denied owning the land. Later it announced that it did own the land, and, although not interested in a joint housing venture, was willing to sell it under a 90-day option. The UAW couldn't raise the money and the land now supports a truck terminal and a rock quarry.

According to Ford regional public relations manager, Mel Mutcher, Ford would like to see a change in zoning in Mahwah that would permit lower-cost housing than is presently avail-

able. But the history of Ford's relationship with the UAW suggests that Ford is unwilling to jeopardize its presence in Mahwah by cooperating with the UAW in developing moderate-priced housing.

Because its efforts to buy land around Mahwah had become stymied, the UAW, along with the National Committee against Discrimination in Housing, decided to fight Mahwah's exclusionary zoning practices in the courts. The first court battle was initiated on January 28, 1971. And on June 12 of this year a three-judge appellate panel of the New Jersey State Supreme Court released their decision that the court's Division on Civil Rights does not have jurisdiction over this case. The UAW and the NCDH have now asked the State Supreme Court to hear an appeal on this jurisdictional decision.

In February of this year a second complaint was filed in the Superior Court of the State of New Jersey against Mahwah and three neighboring towns for exclusionary zoning practices. The Urban League of Essex County and the North Jersey Community Union, as plaintiffs, are preparing a case that will ask the court to order Mahwah and the other three towns to repeal their master plans, building codes and zoning ordinances and submit new plans and laws allowing vacant land to be developed for low- and moderate-income homes for workers in the area. Headed by advocate planner Paul Davidoff, the Suburban Action Institute, which is dedicated to opening the suburbs to racially and economically integrated housing, is providing legal assistance in this suit. SAI has also countered the Candeub Fleissig development plan favored by Mayor Nyland with a plan to build 6,000 units of low- and moderate-income housing to accommodate 20,000. SAI presented its plan on the morning before the public hearing of the Candeub, Fleissig proposed plan for rezoning 1,234 acres. The SAI proposal caused so much commotion that the Candeub, Fleissig proposal could only be considered in relation to the SAI proposal, and rezoning in Mahwah came to a standstill.

Whether Mahwah ends up contributing to the solution or to the problem, New Jersey must begin to meet its housing needs. These needs include accommodation of workers within reasonable distance from employment opportunities, provision of reasonably-priced housing for blue-collar families and preservation of open land around housing for ecological and psychological well-being.

Mahwah's latest response to these needs suggests that preserving Mahwah, as is, comes before providing moderately-priced housing for Ford workers. Last year, Mahwah refused to act on re-zoning that would have allowed a PUD on 8,000 acres of wooded land west of the Ramapo River. In May of this year, Mahwah announced plans to spend more than $100,000 for constitutional law specialists to launch a counterattack against those who would change its zoning practices.

Five
Listening

"To listen perceptively requires that we fasten our whole attention upon the sounds as they come floating through the air; that we observe the patterns they form, and respond to the wellsprings of thought and feelings out of which those patterns have emerged" (Machlis, 1963, p. 3). The author of this passage was talking about listening to music, but he just as easily could have been talking about any form of perceptive listening. When people talk to us, how often do we seriously listen to them? Some words seem to merely go in one ear and out the other. That's because listening is not an easy job.

What is listening? We like to think of it as the process whereby we receive information through our ears. It is merely one way we receive information. We listen to people speak (various forms of verbal communication) as well as listen to millions of different sounds within our environment (various forms of nonverbal communication). Unlike communication which is constantly changing, listening is a straightforward process where you first hear a sound (perceive it), identify and recognize it, and act upon it. The process moves through time from one stage to another; it is a linear process. You do not identify sounds before you hear them. The following cartoon represents this process.

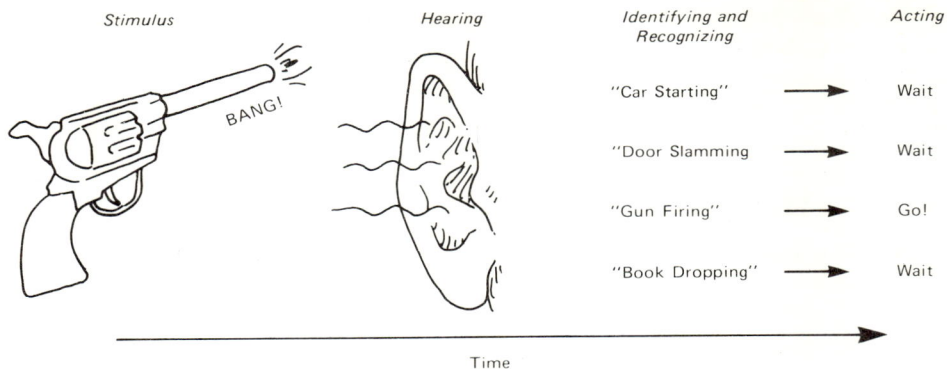

It should be apparent that a specific period of time elapsed from the time the starting gun was fired until the time the runner jetted off the starting blocks. First, the official had to fire the gun. Second, the sound waves had to be sent and picked up by the runner. Third, the runner had to identify the sound (hopefully, in a rather short period of time). Finally, he had to act upon his perception of the sound and begin running. Thus, four separate stages can be easily identified.

Hearing

Hearing the sound is the second stage in the listening process. Sounds in our environment are produced. They reach all parts of our body, but our ears are designed to receive and transform them, sending them to the brain for the third stage to begin.

The ear consists of three distinct regions of which each has its own special part to play in hearing. These regions are the outer, middle, and inner ear. The sound waves are caught by the semicircular shell of skin and cartilage protruding from the side of your ear (called the pinna) and directed down your ear.

There the sound waves strike your eardrum membrane setting up tremendous vibrations. This is where the outer ear stops and the middle ear begins.

The middle ear is a chamber hollowed out of bone. Attached to the eardrum membrane is a small bone commonly called the hammer. The vibrations cause the hammer to move and strike a second bone, the anvil (so called because of its shape). In turn, the sound is transmitted from the anvil to the third bone in the middle ear called the stirrup. Its name also resembles its shape. The bottom of the stirrup fits snugly into a small oval window which opens into the inner ear. The inner ear consists of a complicated group of interconnected canals and sacs appropriately called the labyrinth. The oval window opens into the vestibular canal which is filled with fluid. The vibrations are passed on through another canal (tympanic canal) striking another membrane. These vibrations within the inner ear cause minute hair cells to rub against the organ of corti which is covered by a thin membrane. This movement of hair cells against the thin membrane produces nerve impulses which are transmitted by the auditory nerve to the brain.

Outer ear

Inner ear

Anvil

Hammer

Sound waves

To brain

Auditory nerve

Middle ear

Stirrup

Oval window

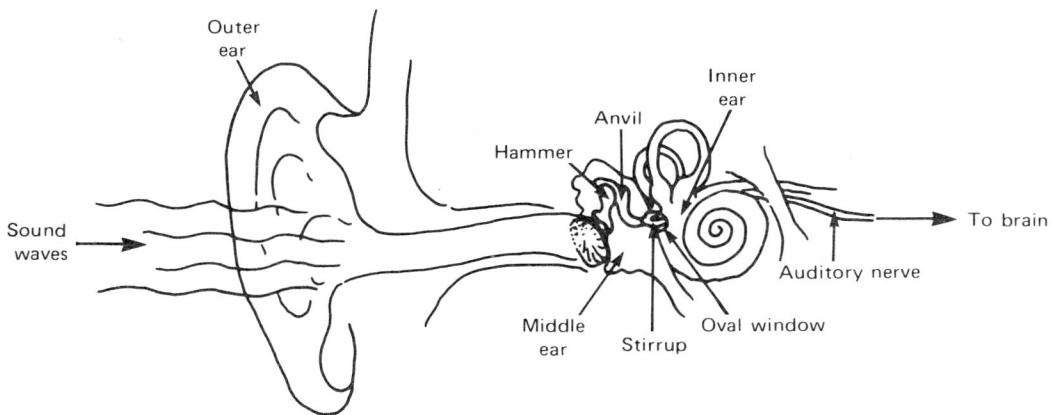

Identifying and Recognizing

Identifying and recognizing the nerve impulses is the third major step in the listening process. The individual listener must sift through all of his or her past experiences in order to classify the sound. In the previous diagram that showed the four stages of the listening process, the listeners (runners) heard the gunshot and then had to identify and recognize it. While there are sounds similar to gunshots (starting pistols indicating the beginning of a race, policemen shooting criminals, etc.), the runners assign meaning to that particular sound based upon previous experience with gunshots. If the runners had never heard a gunshot nor had any experience with starting pistols beginning races, there probably would have been some other meaning attached to the sound. All of us have seen on a television program where native Africans were frightened by gunshots fired by an expedition lead by white hunters. The natives probably did not have the sound of gunshots within

their field of experience. How many sounds within your environment can you identify and recognize without seeing what produces the sound? Try closing your eyes and see how many different sounds you can first hear and then identify and recognize. Open your eyes and check your accuracy.

Acting

What happens after you hear something and assign meaning to it? Some form of action takes places, and this action can take the form of overt behavior. When the official fired the starting pistol, the runners will immediately begin running around the track. Other forms of action may be much more subtle. When talking with another person in order to show that you are listening, you may occasionally nod your head.

Storing of information may be another avenue people take. If you happen to enjoy snow skiing and listen to a travelogue on skiing in Switzerland, you may act on this information by merely thinking to yourself, "That sure seems like fun." Although this action does not express itself in terms of overt behavior, it is nevertheless the manner in which the listener utilizes the information.

Purposes of Listening

Listening takes up a large amount of our time. How often do you turn on your television, radio, or stereo for background noise? Even though you may be a passive listener, you nevertheless are spending many hours listening. Bird (1955) studied female college students and discovered that they spent 42 percent of their time listening, 25 percent talking, 15 percent reading, and 18 percent writing. How do you think those female college students compare with you?

Why do you listen? The four most important reasons we listen are (1) to listen for pleasure (2) to listen for information (3) to listen for evaluation and (4) to listen for understanding.

Listening for Pleasure. People usually spend most of their time listening to things for pleasure. Recent studies (Chaffee and Petrick, 1975) have indicated that our television sets are turned on an average of six hours and 18 minutes each day. While people listen to their televisions for reasons other than merely a source of pleasure, enjoyment is a big reason why the television set stays on. However, television sets are not the only sources of listening pleasure. Some 62 million American homes (98.6 percent of them) have at least one radio (Chaffee and Petrick, 1975). How many cars nowadays are sold without radios? In addition, think about how many cars

have been fitted with stereo tape players and stereo FM radios, all sources of listening pleasure.

It was mentioned at the beginning of this chapter on listening that perceptive listening requires pleasurable concentration. When you go to music concerts as students, the purpose of your listening is for pleasure. In fact, you will find this kind of listening the easiest; it does not require much thought. Listening for pleasure is a means of escape. It lets you get carried away.

Listening for Information. Not all listening is for pleasure. Much of your time is spent listening for information. When you sit down in a classroom and begin taking notes on a prepared lecture, you are listening for information. Since many teachers realize that you will probably forget about 50 percent of what you hear, they often repeat material in hopes you will be caught listening at one time or another. When listening to things, identify the purpose. Note that it is more difficult to listen for information than for pleasure.

Listen for Evaluation. The most difficult listening purpose is listening for evaluation. It not only requires us to become actively involved in the listening process but also to critically examine the material being thrown at our ears. Since people do not pause after every sentence for us to evaluate it, it is difficult to keep up with the amount of information we hear. Toffler's article supports this idea.

Sound judgements are not easily reached. We must identify what is really being said and determine whether or not it is an adequate statement. If you are listening to a speaker talk about legalizing the use and possession of hard drugs, you need to evaluate the speaker's reasoning and evidence used to support the vocalized thoughts. This evaluation action is the least frequent use of listening. How often do you avoid it?

Listening for Understanding. One of the most important reasons for listening, to other people is to understand that other person and how they feel. While this may appear to be a relatively easy thing to do, let us assure you that it is not. To engage in empathic listening (listening for understanding) requires that you see the other person's world from his or her viewpoint, without making any value judgements. Empathic listening becomes an important factor in the development and maintenance of good interpersonal relationships.

The results of empathic listening are numerous. Here are some of the more important ones.

1. *Willingness of expression:* When you engage in empathic listening with other people, they feel more secure in what they are saying and have a tendency to more freely express their opinions. How often have you felt like not talking to a person who immediately begins judging the value of your comments?

2. *Development of trust:* Empathic listening promotes the development of trust between people, which leads to stronger and longer lasting interpersonal relationships. When you attempt to view something from another person's point of view, it communicates to that person that you respect his or her ideas and opinions. This promotes trust and additional self-disclosure.

3. *Promotes knowledge:* If people feel confident and secure in a conversation

with you, they will reveal more information about themselves. You will more readily find out things about people in nonthreatening situations.

While we have broken down the purposes of listening into four areas for the purposes of discussion, it should be realized that they do not necessarily exist independently from one another. Much of our listening time is spent listening to things for many reasons at the same time. When we listen to the CBS "60 Minutes" program on television, we may be listening for pleasure and information at the same time, while also critically evaluating certain aspects of the program.

Articles

The articles selected for inclusion within the listening section were chosen for their insight into the listening process. They also provide three different views on when to listen and how to improve your listening ability.

The first article is called "Learn the Useful Art of Listening." It was originally published in *Changing Times.* The article begins by discussing the importance of listening. Did you know that as college students you probably spend around 80 percent of your time listening? How many courses have you taken in listening?

What are the problems of listening? "Learn the Useful Art of Listening" focuses on some of these problems, but there are additional ones not mentioned in the article. For instance, how often do you avoid listening to something because you know it will not be interesting? Many times we tell ourselves at the outset not to listen to something because we know it will be boring. Did you know that this is a self-fulfilling prophecy? When you tell yourself something will be dull, it usually is. Similarly, when you tell yourself not to listen, you usually won't. Try to hold off on these premature judgments.

Another problem in listening relates to something at which you are undoubtedly an expert—faking attention. How many times have you sat in class smiling at the teacher, leaning forward, and generally appearing to be totally engrossed in what the teacher is saying, while you are actually miles away in thoughts not pertaining to class? You are faking attention. You are also trusting that the teacher will not call upon you for an answer. Hopefully, the teacher will call upon those not demonstrating interest. The problem is that you do not know anything that is being said. In short, you are not listening.

The second article, "Listen To What You Can't Hear," was principally written for the businessman. It also provides some useful suggestions for anyone wanting to improve his or her listening habits. Sigband explains that there are three ways in which we can improve our listening. These three ways are (1) concentrate upon what is being said, (2) listen for the facts, so you can identify the basic ideas, and (3) listen for the feelings of the communicator, so you will know what is behind the words being said. It should be noted that there are no simple ways to improve your listening. It is absolutely necessary that you avoid passive listening and engage in active listening. This means that you have to concentrate on what is being said and make a conscious effort to remember it. Take careful note of this information and attempt to apply it. You will soon discover that not only are you improving your listening habits but others will also appreciate the time and effort you pay to them.

The final article discusses empathic listening. Kelly explains the value of critical empathic listening. Note that he does not argue that critical listening does not have any value. Rather, it should not be used in all situations.

References

D. E. Bird, "Teaching Listening Comprehension," *Journal of Communication,* 3 (1953).

J. Machlis, *The Enjoyment of Music, An Introduction to Perspective Listening* (New York: W. W. Norton & Co., 1963).

Learn the Useful Art of Listening

At work, at school or just chatting with friends, much of life is spent in listening. But unless you are very unusual, you miss or misunderstand most of what you hear. Really good listeners usually strike people as being bright, clear-headed, keen. And it's not just because they pay attention. It's because they tend to be on course while most others are zigzagging around a subject.

Isn't listening just a natural thing that you do when somebody else talks? Not any more. Doing what comes naturally isn't enough in these days of self-improvement. More and more activities, it develops, can be *learned* methodically. Left to themselves, kids brush their teeth in the wrong direction, readers backtrack and waste time, bosses manage badly.

It should be no surprise, then to discover that listening also can be cultivated and developed. At least 125 scholars have written Ph.D. dissertations on listening comprehension. And a lot of major companies are convinced of its importance. They claim to be delighted with the results after sending hundreds of supervisory

Reprinted by permission from *Changing Times*, The Kiplinger Magazine, (December 1967 issue). Copyright 1967 by The Kiplinger Washington Editors, Inc., 1729 H. St., NW, Washington, D.C. 20006.

personnel to special courses in the art of listening.

"Most white-collar workers spend at least 40% of their workday listening—so nearly half their pay is earned in that way," says C. Howard Watts, head of a Los Angeles firm of consultants in management communications. "Yet tests show that most of them have only 25% efficiency at this task."

Among students the situation is even more acute. In grade school the teacher spends over half the class time talking. The percentage is greater in high school. And by the time a student gets to college, over 80% of his time in class is spent listening to lectures—because this is considered the most effective and cheapest method of spreading one man's knowledge to many learners at once.

But the method isn't efficient unless the listening is as good as the lecturing. What's going on at the other end? Research studies show that college students who hear a ten-minute talk can recall only half of it immediately after and no more than a fourth of the message two weeks later.

Even in simple, two-person conversation, few of us can really listen without tuning out while we decide whether our own pet ideas are being hurt or what we should say in response.

The worst part is that the more important the person you're talking with, the likelier you are to stop hearing properly; your worry about having a good comment ready is likely to devour an even larger part of your attention.

All these troubles, according to Dr. Ralph G. Nichols, head of the University of Minnesota's Department of Rhetoric and a top authority in this field, stem from these three main causes:

- A mistaken belief that you can relax and listen at the same time.
- A desire to break into the act with your own thoughts or words.
- An emotional reaction to certain words or ideas that blots out the rest of the message.

Now Hear This

There are ways to overcome these human frailties, though, and feel fully with it in a social conversation or a serious one. Key men from General Motor, Ford, AT&T, Western Electric, Minnesota Mining and other big corporations who have studied under Dr. Nichols swear by his methods. Here are some of the main pointers that you would get if you attended one of his seminars on listening:

First, make up your mind that listening is hard work. If you relax, slump and let your eyes wander, you end up with the nagging frustration of having missed the point. Good listening is signaled by faster heart action and blood circulation, even a slight rise in temperature. Sitting up and looking the speaker in the eye is not just a courtesy to him; it is the best way for you to take in what he's saying. Relaxing is for later, when you can enjoy the feeling that your half of the communication job was well done.

Next, learn to overpower distraction. Nothing is so important as practice. Create artifical distractions, if necessary, and try to overcome them. For example, try listening to a serious talk on the radio while a nearby TV set chatters and flickers. Practice is more meaningful if you have certain definite tools for keeping your mind tuned in. Here are some useful ones:

- Try to guess what the speaker's next point is likely to be. If you are wrong, the surprise will impress his real point on your mind. If you are right, the point hits your mind twice and reinforces the memory.
- Listen for evidence that the speaker uses to support his point.
- Mentally summarize as he comes to the close of each part of his presentation. But be sure the summary is of *his* thoughts, not your own reactions to them.

As you listen, study the structure of the person's remarks. Speakers generally lay out their ideas according to certain stock patterns. One of the commonest is the "time sequence." A person says, "Let me tell you what happened to me today . . ." and then relates it chronologically. Another frequent pattern is the "space sequence." For example, "Here is what I think about LBJ's chances on the West Coast. . . . But in the East. . . . And in the South. . . ."

There are also much subtler types of structure. The speaker may use a metaphor: "This subject is a broad river with many tributaries." Or he may not mention the metaphor, yet make points that *you* can visualize in symbolic form—thinking to yourself, "These arguments add up to a big pyramid with a broad base built up to support one dominant point." Or maybe less favorably, "He's just putting a lot of wispy clouds up there with no formation or relationship."

Analyzing the remarks in this way also helps you to identify the central ideas, to separate the important from the unimportant. Only the main and enduring points will fit into the pattern. Bear this in mind especially if you take notes. The shorter and more condensed the notes, the greater their value. Voluminous notetaking can be a terrible distraction, but a brief record of the most meaningful points is definite help in learning and remembering.

Finally, learn to control your own emotions as you listen. This is the hardest step to master, but simple awareness will take you a good part of the way.

Consciously watch for the times when you

tend to tune out a speaker because you don't like his personality or his ideas. Even if your goal is to argue him down, you owe it to yourself to listen fully.

Notice the words or thoughts that make you develop deaf spots. Dr. Nichols has found that some of the standard ones are computerize, fellow-travelers, pervert, square, fink, mother-in-law. Today some people develop static on hearing words like mod, cool, beat, hippie, Black Power. And there are special terms that jab persons involved in certain fields and distort their listening judgment. A man who has been having trouble with a newly purchased house may go "deaf" at the mention of leaks, termites or contractor; his interest perks up, but he hears mainly his own jangled thoughts. One who has been speculating in the stock market may tune out anyone who says losses, sharp drop or selloff.

Think about any word that seems to invade a sensitive area of your mind. Reflect that the word is neither good nor bad in itself. Try to neutralize its effect on you by realizing it's a symbol that affects different people in different ways, depending on the experiences they have had. You can't make yourself into an automation. But if certain words are that painful to you, the subject is probably important. So it is doubly useful to hear what's said correctly when it comes up.

Think Quick!

"When am I going to do all this thinking if I'm supposed to be listening?" you may wonder. The answer is easy: You can think about four times faster than you can talk. While someone is talking at about 125 words a minute, you can easily be thinking about 500 words worth of thoughts. Most people use the spare time to make brief excursions away from the subject, then dart back to listen. They sometimes stay away too long and lose a key point. But by applying the spare thinking time to analysis of what's being said, along the lines suggested above, you'll be able to get the most out of your listening.

Another benefit not mentioned by the listening experts can result from this new approach. It's a mind-expanding experience, a normal and healthy way of stretching the mind that beats all the artificial devices being tried these days.

Professional writers often say their secret for getting into high gear before approaching the typewriter is to read the work of some other fine writer. Without borrowing his ideas, they soak up the rhythm and richness that is waiting to be tapped. A good listener can do the same thing with thought patterns. By becoming conscious of the ways that others structure their ideas, he can add variety to his own thoughts and ways of presenting them.

Listen to What You Can't Hear

Norman B. Sigband

Today's executive spends roughly 40 per cent of his work day just listening. The higher he rises in the management hierarchy, the greater that percentage is apt to be, thanks to more meetings, as well as to interviewing, counselling, exchanging of information and decision making.

To the manager, it is vital to listen as the effective salesman must listen—to determine what the "prospect" will buy.

The manager must "sell" his ideas to his superiors; he must persuade his subordinates; he must inform his associates. But in every case he will not be aware of what to sell, how best to persuade, and in what areas to inform, if he first does not listen to those around him.

He must not only listen, he must try to hear what is not said.

Take the case of Supervisor Galvin. Joe has just approached him to report:

"Well, Mr. Galvin, I finally locked up the Bahr Co. order. Boy, was it a mess! But you said it was an emergency job, and I saw to it that it went out today—right on the button. You know, I've been here every night this week

and almost all last weekend to tie that darned thing up. Bahr's specifications are ridiculous, but the order is on its way, even though my wife may throw me out. And let me tell you, if I never see another job as tough as that, I'll be plenty happy. It really required blood, sweat and tears."

If Mr. Galvin should answer, "Great Joe. Now let's get to work on the Sunnyvale order," he hasn't really been listening.

What was Joe really saying? We'll never be sure but he was not simply saying the Bahr order was difficult. He probably was saying, "How about giving me a pat on the back, Mr. Gavin?" or "Why do you give me all the problem jobs?" or "I hate to work nights."

The sensitive, effective manager will hear what the other fellow often is inhibited from stating directly, due to ego, emotions, position held, or what have you.

Let's tune in on Supervisor Jackson's interview with extremely conscientious Jim Cantonelli, who has just been offered a promotion to section chief.

"I sure appreciate the offer, boss, but I don't think I can handle it. You know I only been in the States seven years, I murder the language, I don't write well. What am I goin' to do about the weekly reports? And I'm not too hot on the reading angle; wow, all those instructions that come down. And the guys laugh now when I try to talk; how can I hold meetings? And you know yourself that all I know about switching systems, I picked up around here."

If Supervisor Jackson continues to press, and points out the increased salary, new title, and other ego satisfying factors, Cantonelli may accept. This, however, may place a hard-working production man in a position over his head and result in failure for him, decreased morale in the department, and financial loss to the firm.

What should Jackson have perceived from Cantonelli's reaction to the offer? He probably should have heard him saying, "I'm not ready for the job, I'm afraid to take it on, I don't think the men will be with me."

Obviously a supervisor can't back away from every worker who appears reluctant to accept promotion. Many such promotions work out very well. But when a manager hears a Cantonelli say what he said, that is the time to perceive correctly.

You Have to Concentrate

One basic barrier to effective listening is simply inability to concentrate, which causes facts and ideas to be lost.

Lack of concentration may have several roots. Most of us speak about 140 words per minute, but we can comprehend at a much faster rate. This permits us to take mental excursions into other areas as we listen.

For a few seconds, the listener thinks about that faulty car transmission; then he returns to the speaker's topic; then he is off again. This time he wonders about the football game: Will it be worth $5.50 per ticket? And again back to the speaker. But what about vacation? Two weeks in September should be O.K. And back to the speaker.

But now the speaker is too far ahead; the listener has missed something vital on one of his excursions. Besides, the topic seems very com-

plex. Oh, well, not concentrating is easier than trying to concentrate. And another listener now is just hearing.

Opinions and prejudices can also cause poor concentration. When a statement the listener doesn't like is made, he may figuratively reach up into his brain and turn the communicator off. Or he may concentrate on a statement with which he disagrees, allowing other statements to go unheard.

The style of the speaker's clothes, the look on his face, his posture, his accent, the color of his skin, his mannerisms, or past experiences with him may also cause the listener to react emotionally and tune him out.

Try to put aside your preconceived ideas or prejudices. The man who is speaking may have a new concept that is worth putting into practice.

And if you want to concentrate, don't try to do something unrelated to the discussion while the man you wish to listen to is talking.

Also, by the way, make him realize, you are concentrating. Look directly at him, and sit up straight. Don't protest that you listen best when you are relaxed, hands clasped behind your head and feet propped on the desk. This may be true, but the speaker may see lack of interest and perhaps discourtesy on your part. The result would be a barrier to clear communication.

Listening for Facts

The good listener makes a definite attempt to listen to every statement for facts and for feelings.

In listening for facts, you should first attempt to perceive the theme or the thesis of the presentation. In a speech, this may be stated in the first few minutes. It probably will be noted in different words several times during the talk, and may well serve as a concluding statement.

The basic ideas should then be recognized. What are the four key points in the entire talk? The alert listener will be able to perceive them, even if the speaker doesn't label each specifically. Facts to support the ideas should be assimilated. But once the ideas are firmly fixed in your mind, they will help you recall specific facts.

If you listen analytically, you can recognize major ideas and separate them from minor ones. Of course this requires your full effort. Effective listening is hard work.

Sometimes, you find yourself listening to someone who hasn't organized his ideas too well. He seems to be going in circles. He repeats himself. He barely mentions a key fact. It's up to you to organize his presentation in your mind, as he talks.

Taking notes during the talk will help you retain ideas and facts. But you should never become so absorbed in the task of taking notes that you lose the ideas being transmitted. And if the talk goes on for any length of time, the good listener occasionally will hastily review in his mind the ideas and facts which have already been cited.

All in all, to perceive the facts that are stated, you need to be attentive and analytical, and to develop an ability to be retentive.

Listening for Feelings

Listening for feelings is more difficult.

Here you must try to perceive what is really behind a seemingly obvious statement. You must give, insofar as you are able, the same connotations to words that the other fellow gives. You must also try to recognize his biases and his frame of reference. You must try to remember his salary level and his desires.

When a slow, easygoing man says, "We must get on this job right away," you interpret "right away" as "in a week or two." When an employee you know to be conscientious and slow to give praise calls another a "hard worker," your connotation probably will be very similar to his.

You must constantly "listen" to the other person's nonverbal communications. His inflections, his gestures, his finger tapping, the look in his eyes, and the changing lines in his brow.

If his words say, "Well, it really isn't very important to me anyway," but his posture is stiff, his knuckles white, his eyes hopeful and his forehead glistening with perspiration, you had better hear the nonverbal message. If you don't, communication will not be effective.

Here is a situation similar to one which may have occurred to you or one of your salesmen just yesterday. Mr. Big, President of the Acme Co., is very proud of the newly completed offices for his five immediate subordinates. They had been scattered in different sections of the plant; now they all will be on the same floor with him.

You are trying to sell him office furniture and you tell him you have an especially good buy for his company on five beautiful executive walnut desks. Mr. Big is unimpressed.

"They don't seem quite right," he says. "They're very modern and they look terribly short of drawer space. Of course they are beautiful, but they don't have file drawers. And holy smokes, why does our controller or purchasing head need so much surface area? Why, these desks must be twice as big as mine!"

Now, if you know Mr. Big at all, you should be able to tell what he is really saying.

There is no point in pressing him about how inexpensive, or beautiful or functional the five desks are. For what he is telling you is, "I don't want my subordinates to have bigger, more beautiful desks than mine. It hurts my ego."

Of course, he can't say that. Nevertheless, you must hear what he does not say and respond tactfully to it. If you don't—no sale.

The Results

Effective listening on your part produces many salutary results.

First, there will be more effective listening on the other person's part. When he notes that you are sincerely and carefully listening, and not merely waiting for him to pause and inhale so you can jump in, he does not feel threatened. Thus, after he has had his complete say, he is ready to listen carefully to you.

Second, the speaker presents more information which may benefit you. Your careful listening usually will motivate him to cite as many facts as he can. Then you are in a better position to make correct decisions.

Third, your relationship with the speaker often is improved, and you understand him better. He has an opportunity to get facts, ideas and hostilities off his chest. And you may recognize that one man requires frequent praise, while another does not; that one responds favorably to counselling, while another resents it; that he is an extrovert, while she is an introvert.

Everyone wants understanding—with or with-out agreement—and there is no better way of giving it than through sensitive listening.

A fourth product of careful listening often will be unexpectedly easy solutions to problems. When the other person is permitted to speak in an unthreatening environment, and feels he has the listener's complete attention and respect, he may hear himself more clearly. As a result, solutions may come through to him or you more clearly.

All in all, effective listening, both to what is said and what isn't said, can bring major benefits to a businessman. Too often, the business manager says, "I don't have time to listen carefully." The only reply to that is, "You don't have time NOT to listen carefully."

Empathic Listening

Charles M. Kelly

In a research project exploring listening behavior, industrial supervisors gave the following reasons for communication problems in large mangement-level meetings and conferences: "things discussed here are often side issues that don't interest everyone," "I think about my job upstairs," "they get off the subject," and "a lot of people like to hear themselves talk." A content analysis was made of these and other responses dealing with the perceived deficiencies of meetings and discussions. Results indicated that most of the dissatisfaction centered around the general feeling that many different issues were discussed at a typical meeting, and that usually some of these issues were not directly related to all of the participants.[1]

Complaints such as the above are not unusual, and frequently are justified. Every text of discussion and conference methodology deals with the problems of keeping the discussion on relevant and significant issues, and of motivating the participants. However, most of the emphasis in the past has dealt with the obligations of the discussants (both leaders and participants) as *speakers*, rather than as *listeners*. This unbalanced emphasis, especially as it actually affects persons in real discussions, could be an important *cause* of the problems that speaking is supposed to cure: e.g., the reason a discussion leader may have difficulty clarifying the comments of another, may be that he did not listen carefully to begin with; when one is overly concerned about what *he* is *going* to say, he really can't devote his full attention to what *is* being said by others. If a person in a group preoccupies himself by privately bemoaning the irrelevancies that inevitably occur in discussion, he may be less able to get the group back on the track; he misses opportunities for constructive action because he lacks an *accurate* analysis of the flow of ideas, even the irrelevant ones.

Of course, listening is a multi-faceted activity and it can be considered from different viewpoints, but at least two ways of categorizing listening seem especially fruitful for theoretical analysis: *deliberative listening* and *empathic listening*. Most recent writers have treated listening as a unitary skill, i.e., as a rather definite and "deliberative" ability to hear information, to analyze it, to recall it at a later time, and to

---

Charles M. Kelly, "Empathic Listening," in *Small Group Communication: A Reader*, Robert S. Cathcart and Larry A. Samovar (Dubuque, Iowa: William C. Brown, 1970), pp 251–59.

[1]Charles M. Kelly, "Actual Listening Behavior of Industrial Supervisors as Related to Listening Ability, General Mental Ability, Selected Personality Factors and Supervisory Effectiveness," Unpublished Ph.D. Dissertation, Purdue University, 1962, 129.

draw conclusions from it. Commerically-published listening tests and most listening training programs are based on this, the deliberative listening, viewpoint. On the other hand, empathic listening occurs when the person participates in the spirit or feeling of his environment as a communicative *receiver*. This does not suggest that the listener is uncritical or always in agreement with what is communicated, but rather, that his primary interest is to become fully and accurately aware of what is going on. (See Figure 1.)

It should be observed that the terms "deliberative listening" and "empathic listening" are not mutually exclusive or exhaustive. Their main purpose is to differentiate between two basic ways of viewing the same listening activity. The desired result of both deliberative and empathic listening is identical: accurate, understanding of oral communication. However, this understanding is achieved by different routes. The deliberative listener *first* has the desire to critically analyze what a speaker has said, and secondarily tries to understand the speaker (this can be the result of personal inclination or of training which emphasizes procedure at the expense of listening). The empathic listener has the desire to understand the speaker first, and, as a result, tries to take the appropriate action.

The former kind of listening is characteristic

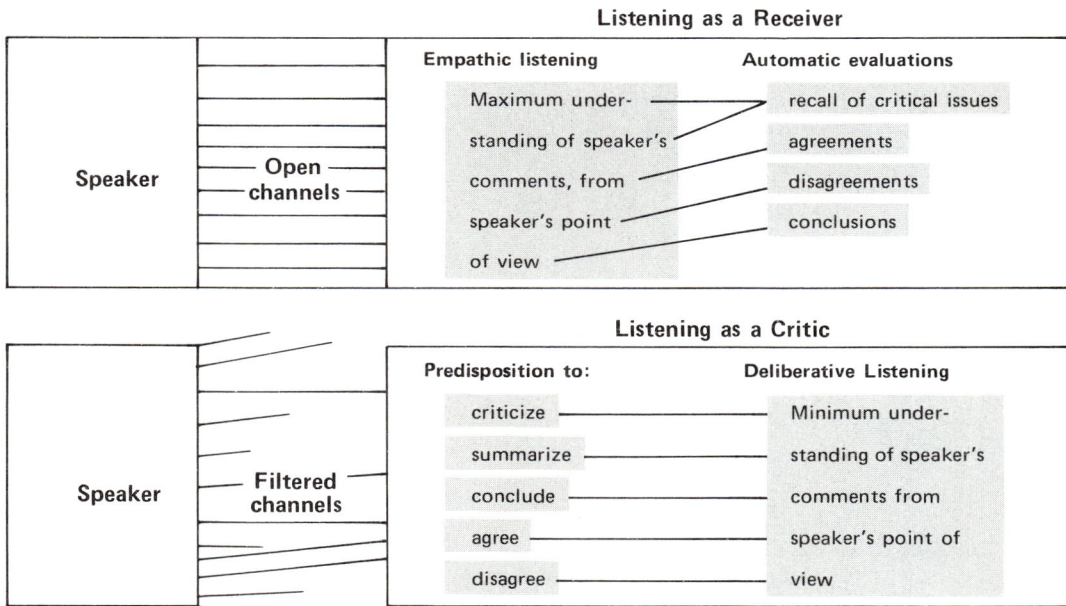

Listening as a Receiver

Speaker	Open channels	Empathic listening	Automatic evaluations
		Maximum under-	recall of critical issues
		standing of speaker's	agreements
		comments, from	disagreements
		speaker's point	conclusions
		of view	

Listening as a Critic

Speaker	Filtered channels	Predisposition to:	Deliberative Listening
		criticize	Minimum under-
		summarize	standing of speaker's
		conclude	comments from
		agree	speaker's point of
		disagree	view

Figure 1. The differences between empathic listening and deliberative listening are primarily motivational. Both listeners seek the same objective: accurate understanding of the communication from another. The model suggests that the motivation to receive information is superior to the motivation to use critical skills. The empathic listener lets his understanding of the speaker determine his modes of evaluation, which are automatic; the deliberative listener's understanding of the speaker is filtered through his predetermined modes of selective listening, and actually spends less time as a communication receiver. The empathic listener is more apt to be a consistent listener, and is less prone to his own or other distractions. This theory is correct, only if the assumption is true that persons can and do think critically without deliberate effort—*while listening*. (Of course, if persons do not make the effort to listen *per se*, little or no understanding will occur.)

of the discussant who is predisposed to be disagreeable, or to summarize, or to clarify—even when there is little that is significant to disagree with, when there is no need to summarize, or when further clarification is a waste of the group's time. The latter kind of listening is characteristic of the person who is able to adapt quickly to the real needs of a situation because he has a presence of mind and a greater confidence in the accuracy of his awareness—he does not handicap himself by deciding in advance that he does not have to listen to a particular person who is poorly dressed, or that he must be sure to expose all faulty reasoning if he is to demonstrate his competence.

This is not to say that various skills in critical thinking are less important than empathic listening. Without critical analysis, listening in a problem-solving discussion would be useless. The point is, however, that a person uses quite naturally whatever critical skills he has already acquired, as long as he is interested and actively listening; to the extent that he is not listening, critical skills will be of little value. Actually, a case can be made that "deliberative listening" is a self-contradiction and a misnomer—and that "empathic listening" is a redundancy. To the extent that one is deliberating (mentally criticizing, summarizing, concluding, preparing reports, etc.) he is *not listening*, but formulating his own ideas. And listening, by its very nature, *has* to be empathic; a person understands what he has heard, only to the extent that he can share in the meaning, spirit, or feeling of what the communicator has said.

There is some evidence that this line of reasoning is correct. In one experiment,[2] a researcher presented a 30-minute talk dealing with "The Supervisor and Communication" to 28 supervisors at a regularly scheduled business meeting. The supervisors were in no way led to believe that they were in an experiment or that their listening performance would be tested. Following the presentation, they were given a 30-item multiple-choice "surprise" listening test. During the following two weeks, the supervisors were given the Brown-Carlsen Listening Comprehension Test, the STEP Listening Test, the Otis Quick-Scoring Mental Ability Test, and the Cattell 16 Personality Factor Questionnaire. (Because of the nature of the Brown-Carlsen and Step listening tests, subjects have to know in advance that their listening ability is being tested.)

[2] This study is reported in detail: Charles M. Kelly, "Mental Ability and Personality Factors in Listening," *Quarterly Journal of Speech*, XLIX, (April, 1963), 152–56.

Table 1

Correlations (Pearson r) Among the "Surprise" Listening Test, the Brown-Carlsen Listening Test, the Step Listening Test, and the Otis Test of General Mental Ability[a]

	Brown-Carlsen	STEP	Otis
Surprise Listening test	.79	.78	.70[bc]
Brown-Carlsen		.82	.85[b]
STEP			.85[c]

[a] All correlations are significant at the .01 level.

[b] The difference between the two correlations so designated is significant at the .05 level, t = 2.205.

[c] The difference between the two correlations so designated is significant at the .05 level, t = 2.162.

The results (Table 1) indicated that the supervisors' "listening ability" (as measured by the Brown-Carlsen and the STEP) was indistinguishable from general mental ability (as measured by Otis) when they knew in advance that their listening was being tested. In fact, the listening tests correlated *lower* with each other, than each did with the test of mental ability. In other words, when the supervisors had the extra motivation of a test, or were constantly listening, they made full use of their general mental ability, and the listening tests became orally-presented tests of general mental ability, rather than of "listening." On the other hand, when the supervisors did not know their listening was being tested, their listening performance was significantly less related to general mental ability.

Further insight can be gained by analyzing the results in terms of personality variables

Table 2

Statistical Significance of Differences (Chi Squares with Yates' Correction) Between "High" and "Low" Criterion Groups (as Determined by Scores on Each of Four Tests) on the Cattell 16 PF Scales

Cattell Scale Low Score vs. High Scores	Surprise Listening Test[bcd]	Brown- Carlsen[b]	STEP[c]	Otis[d]
Aloof vs. Outgoing	.14	.00**	.14	.00
Dull vs. Bright (intelligence factor)	.57	5.16	2.29	2.29
Emotional vs. Mature	3.57***	1.28	3.57***	1.28
Submissive vs. Dominant	.14	.00	.00	.15
Glum vs. Dominant	.14	.00	.00	.00
Casual vs. Conscientious	.00	.00	.00	.00
Timid vs. Adventurous	9.19*	.57	2.29	.57
Tough vs. Sensitive	.00	.00	.00	.57[a]
Trustful vs. Suspecting	.57[a]	.00	.00	.00
Conventional vs. Eccentric	.00	.00	.00	.00
Simple vs. Sophisticated	3.65***	1.31	1.31	1.31
Confident vs. Insecure	.00	.57[a]	.00	.00
Conservative vs. Experimenting	.00	.59[a]	.00	.00
Dependent vs. Self-sufficient	.00	.00	.00	.00
Lax vs. Controlled	2.29	.00	.00	.00
Stable vs. Tense	7.00*[a]	.14[a]	1.31[a]	2.29[a]

*X^2 of 6.64 = 1% level.

**X^2 of 3.85 = 5% level.

***X^2 of 2.71 = 10% level.

[a] High scorers on the test scored low on the Cattell personality scale.

Using the sign test for statistical significance, the following differences were observed between tests, on the basis of personality scales (intelligence scale, "Dull vs. Bright," was not included:

[b] difference between tests so designated was significant at p = .03

[c] p = .008

[d] p = .055

(Table 2). Again, the Brown-Carlsen and STEP listening tests are indistinguishable from the Otis, when compared on the basis of personality variables; the same personality factors appear about equally important (as expressed in chi square values) in the test of general mental ability as in the tests of listening ability. However, the "surprise" listening test showed significantly more substantial personality differences between good and poor listeners than did the other three tests.

The most significant differences between good and poor listeners, when they had no unusual motivation to listen because of test awareness, were that good listeners were more adventurous (receptive to new ideas), (emotionally) stable, mature, and sophisticated. Although the other six differences in Table 2 (under "surprise listening test") were not statistically significant, it is interesting to note that all were in the same direction, with the good listeners being more emotionally mature: outgoing, bright, dominant, enthusiastic, trustful and controlled (will control). The opposite ends of the personality scales, describing the poor listeners in the surprise listening test, were: aloof, dull, emotional, submissive, glum, timid, suspecting, simple, lax, and tense.

This and other studies[3] strongly indicate that when persons know that their listening comprehension is being tested, differences between individuals are primarily matters of general mental ability; when they do not know their listening performance is being tested, differences are due to personality differences (including motivation to listen), as well as general ability. Of these two kinds of research situations, the latter is more representative of realistic listening events.

It is likely that most communication problems arise either because of participant inattention (poor motivation), or because of a lack of general mental ability—not because of anything

that can be called "listening ability." Do teachers in a faculty meeting miss the details of registration because of a lack of listening ability, or because of a lack of motivation? Does an engineer fail to understand an explanation of a new process because he lacks listening ability, or because he simply has not yet been able to visualize unfamiliar relationships? In the rare cases when a discussion is vitally important to everyone and motiviation is high (as in a listening test), there is little chance of an important point (or its significance) being missed, unless the listener simply lacked the mental ability to understand or appreciate it to begin with. But in most of the everyday discussions that deal with the nagging problems of industrial production, proposed new school construction, traffic safety, curriculum changes, etc., motivation to participate (and, hence, listen) is moderate at best and is not evenly distributed among the discussants—and with some persons, inattention seems to be habitual.

In terms of *listening* theory, it is far more important to stress empathic, rather than deliberative, listening in discussion. This observation in no way depreciates the need for education and practical experience in critical analysis, debate, general semantics—or in any of the various mental skills brought into play *while* listening. But it is a mistake to consider these skills *as* listening, since this viewpoint suggests that the listener's analysis is part of the receiving process.

The degree to which one is able to listen, and to perform other mental acts at the same time is an open question; research into the exact nature of listening, as it relates to other general mental abilities, is unclear at best. However, because of the obvious difficulties that occur in discussion when listener motivation is poor or nonexistent, and in view of the probability that problems in discussion are due to factors other than listening *ability* when participant motivation is high, the following suggestions seem warranted:

Remember the characteristics of the poor listener. It is easy to sit back in your chair and complain to yourself that the discussion is bor-

[3] For a detailed analysis of this issue, see: Charles M. Kelly, "Listening: Complex of Activities—and a Unitary Skill?" *Speech Monographs*, XXXIV, (November, 1967), 455–66.

ing or unimportant. However, the description of the kind of person who habitually does this is not very flattering, and should serve as an incentive to better listening; research suggests that the poor listener is less intelligent, and less emotionally mature than the good listener. Obviously, there are times when a person may be just as well off *not* listening, but the poor listener tends to make this a crutch for the easy way out of difficult listening events.

Make a firm initial commitment to listen. Listening is hard work and it takes energy. If you have had difficulty listening in the past, and now decide merely to *try* to listen and to participate in the spirit of the discussion as long as you can, you will soon fall into old habits. Above all, don't make an initial decision *not* to listen; if discussions in the past have proved deficient, according to your standards, accurate listening will better enable you to correct them in the future.

Get physically and mentally ready to listen. Sit up, and get rid of distractions; put away paper you were reading, books, pencils, papers, etc., unless you plan to use them. Try to dismiss personal worries, fears, or pleasant reverie until a later time. Will these kinds of thoughts be more productive of personal gain than your participation in this discussion?

Concentrate on the other person as a communicator. View the others in a discussion as sources of ideas and information, not as personalties. If you are reacting to another as being dishonest, unethical, stupid, tedious—or as a college professor, or Republican, or student rioter, or disgruntled parent—it will be difficult for you to accurately perceive what he is trying to say. There is little fear in such an open approach. Shoddy thinking or speaking needs no label to be recognized, and fewer good ideas will be discarded because they were never really listened to. Of course, it goes without saying that persons communicate with gestures as well as with their voices, and the listener is concerned with perceiving the total communication environment as accurately as possible.

Give the other person a full hearing. Avoid interrupting another person unless you are sure you understand him fully, and that it is necessary. If you feel that you aren't sure you understand him, a well phrased question is usually more appropriate than an attempt by you to clarify his position. Impatience with others can lead to false understanding or agreement, and eventually leads to greater difficulties.

Use analytical skills as supplements to, not instead of, listening. To the degree that successful participation in discussion requires your understanding of others, rather than your speaking contributions. it is important not to be distracted by our own note taking, mental review of main points, critical analysis, or preparation for argumentative "comeback." An especially dubious recommendation frequently found in articles on listening is that, since listeners can listen faster than speakers can talk, the extra time should be used to review main points, "read between the lines," etc. Whether this conscious effort is exerted between words, sentences, or major ideas is never made clear. However, interviews with subjects following "surprise" listening tests have indicated that one of the major causes of listener distraction was a speaker's previous point: "I suddenly realized that I didn't know what he was talking about, because I was still thinking about what he had said before."

Omitted from this list are the many sound suggestions that have been made by other writers about: analyzing the speaker's intent, figuring out what he is going to say or what he has not said, note-taking, mental organization of a speaker's comments, etc. These, and others, are perfectly valid tools to be used in an oral communication setting, but their success is due to factors other than listening. For example, a discussion leader may wisely decide to mentally review the progress of a discussion while "listening" to a certain person unnecessarily repeating himself—but the wisdom of his action is due to his prior analysis, not to "listening ability." While listening to a specific individual, he may briefly jot down the person's main ideas for future reference; if he has developed an efficient note-taking skill, he may not miss anything significant—but he is effective because he is able to take notes with very little or no conscious effort, not because note-taking is a *listening* activity. Other less talented persons may never be able to take notes without distracting them from what is truly listening.

Conclusion

Many factors make up a discussion, and listening is only one of them; however, it is an extremely important factor, and it has been diluted in the past by a shift of its meaning from one of reception to one of critical analysis.

Empathic listening cannot of itself make a good speaker out of a poor one, a clear thinker out of a dull thinker, or a good discussion out of a bad discussion. But to the extent that problems result from a lack of participant reception and understanding of the discussion interaction, empathic listening appears to be the best answer.

2

Communication Settings

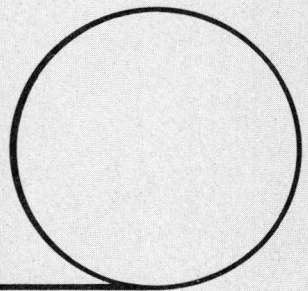

Six
Interpersonal
Communication

Interpersonal communication literally means communication between people. We wish to narrow the focus of interpersonal communication in this chapter to refer to those special qualities that exist when one person interacts with a single other. While these qualities are important in all communication settings (as will be noted throughout), they are heightened in the one-to-one dyadic communication situation. This is because two people are interacting directly with each other. Interpersonal communication refers to the quality of honesty, trust, disclosure, empathy, and openness shared between two people when they are interacting with each other.

Distinguishing Characteristics

Direct Interaction. Direct interaction is the first aspect which distinguishes dyadic communication from other forms of communication. Most of the time dyadic communication involves a situation where two people are facing and interacting with each other. Here, it is pos-

sible to use almost all your senses to check for potential meaning. Not only can you hear the other person talk but you can see the nonverbal cues being emitted, e.g., the smell of perfume or cologne. Depending upon the degree of the relationship, you may want to touch the other person. You have a greater chance of understanding what is being communicated because of your "cross-senses" checking.

Sometimes dyads are separated because of electronic equipment—principally the telephone. However, based upon a previously experienced relationship with that person, interpersonnal communication takes place. The focus is on the directed interaction, not the face-to-face contact.

If people have interacted before in a face-to-face situation so that they have an understanding of the other person and the type of nonverbal cues emitted by that person, they are interpersonally interacting. For example, my mother and aunt constantly talk to each other over the telephone. It is interesting to

try and trace their conversation backward to determine how they got from one subject to another and to see the amount of visual nonverbal communication which transpired, unseen but perceived. Because of previous face-to-face interaction, they know what kinds of nonverbal information are being communicated.

Do you do the same thing with close personal friends over the telephone? Next time you are talking on the telephone to someone you know extremely well, see if you use your hands to gesture. Does this happen when talking to other people you do not know so well?

Reciprocal Interaction. Genuine interpersonal communication involves an exchange between people whereby they build upon the information provided by the other person. However, this reciprocal interaction is not where two people talk *at* each other but *with* each other. Buber (1965) pointed out that genuine dialogue is rarely seen among people. The type of interaction most prevalent in our society (especially among debaters) is a situation where there are two monologues disguised as a dialogue. The individuals are more concerned with what they have to say than with increased understanding which is derived from the exchange of human thoughts and experience. The most common two-monologue status is exemplified in the following diagram.

The information exchanged between two communicators needs to be reciprocal. The total interaction should be the result of a dialogue built upon genuine concern for what the other person said.

Attraction

Interpersonal attraction refers to the reasons why we are drawn to another person. These reasons may be because we like the way the other person looks, the knowledge he or she possesses, the capabilities he or she has for performing some task or his or her ability to entertain us in social situations and make us feel at home. What do you like in other people? List the ten things you think are the most important things a good friend of yours should possess.

1. _____
2. _____
3. _____
4. _____
5. _____
6. _____
7. _____
8. _____
9. _____
10. _____

Do all your friends possess all these qualities? Why? Have you ever been attracted to anyone who did not have these qualities? Why? All of us become attracted to other people. Since we are social animals, we need to relate to others.

Remember that old saying, "opposites attract." It is not always true. When it comes to interpersonal attraction, most of us look for sameness rather than op-

posites. Do most of your close friends think like you do or are they totally different? Indicate in the space provided whether your closest friend shares your views or differs on the same subjects. This does not mean that your friend necessarily does the same things as you (although this might reflect similarity), but rather that he or she expresses attitudes similar to yours on the subjects listed.

	Same	Different
1. College football	_____	_____
2. Cheating on exams	_____	_____
3. Fraternities	_____	_____
4. Classical music	_____	_____
5. Marijuana	_____	_____

Heider (1958) proposed a model of attitudes which indicated that we tend to seek balance. In his model he included three major components and the attitudes between them.

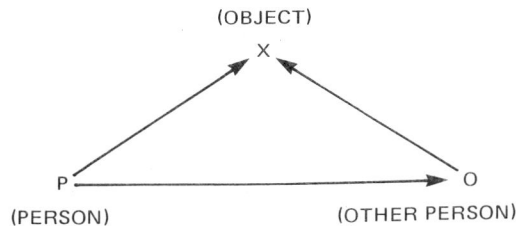

(OBJECT)
X
P → O
(PERSON)   (OTHER PERSON)

Imagine that you are "P" and your closest friend is "O". Place each of the five subjects into the "X" slot one at a time. Heider indicated that we are always trying to maintain a state of balance. If you have a positive attitude toward school and your closest friend has a positive attitude toward school, everything will be balanced because you will also have a positive attitude toward your friend. The model looks like this.

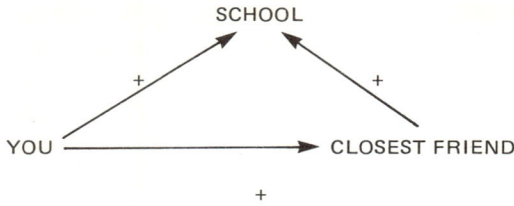

Similarly, if both you and your closest friend disliked school, the model is still balanced. Mathematically, Heider said that if the signs were multiplied by each other and the derived product was positive, ($[+] \times [+] \times [+] = +$ and $[-] \times [-] \times [+] = +$) the model would be in a state of balance—the condition that we seek. On the other hand, if you and your friend do not have a completely negative attitude toward school and your friend even holds a positive attitude, a state of imbalance takes place ($[-] \times [+] \times [+] = +$). Heider argued that either you or your close friend will change your attitude toward school or you will change your attitude toward your close friend.

While Heider's model helps call attention to the fact that we share common attitudes with our friends and different attitudes toward our nonfriends, there are some important weaknesses to his model. First, it does not consider O's attitude toward P. Second, it does not explain which attitude will change (the attitude toward the object or the person). Third, it assumes that attitudes are either positive or negative and not degrees of the latter. And fourth, there is no allowance for the amount of importance that either P or O attaches to the attitude. Two people may have a different attitude, but one might be more willing to change his or her opinion if either has less ego involvement attached to the attitude. These limitations need to be rec-

ognized and incorporated in your own model of interpersonal attraction. Nevertheless, we are usually attracted to people who share common attitudes about things which are important to us.

Proximity (remember the discussion of space in the chapter on nonverbal communication) is another factor which affects our attractions to others. Research by other scholars has generally shown that, assuming other things are equal, people will be attracted to people living closer to them than those living many miles away. Festinger, Schachter, and Black (1950) discovered that people living near the stairway in apartment complexes were thought to be more popular than those living elsewhere. With respect to houses, they found that people in houses facing into a court of other houses were also thought to be more popular among their neighbors.

Have you ever lived in a college dormitory or group house? Who were your friends? Were you more attracted to people in the same dorm than to people living in other dorms? Was it more likely that your friends were those people living close to you within the same dorm or house? Priest and Sawyer (1967) conducted a study to answer these very questions. They found that with respect to college students living in a male dormitory, there was a greater likelihood that friendships would develop between (1) roommates than two people living on the same floor, (2) people living on the same floor than different floors, (3) people living in the same dorms than other dorms, and (4) when people became attracted to each other, they would move closer to one another. How did their results compare with yours?

The old saying that beauty is in the eye of the beholder also applies to the concept of interpersonal attraction. Each year we spend millions of dollars in an attempt to look more attractive. Do blonds really have more fun? Will Maybelline actually make our eyes blossom? Why is it that he can never forget you when you use Wind Song perfume? However, we do not want you to think that we are taking a chauvinistic attitude with respect to beauty aids. Men are just as susceptible to this kind of advertising. Did you know that Givenchy Gentlmen *eau de toilette* is an "investment in spending," that "Winston makes the difference," and that Sear's menswear makes it look "like you're out to win"?

In the nonverbal chapter, you learned that artifacts are used to make our bodies look more attractive. The purpose of this is simply to make contact with new people. Numerous studies have shown that we usually tend to maintain relationships with people we find physically attractive and terminate relationships with those we find unattractive. Nevertheless, it should be kept in mind that what may be attractive to one person may prove to be unattractive to others. Thus, one person's treasure may be another's ugly elephant.

Risk Taking

A key ingredient in interpersonal communication is risk taking. This means that people are willing to expose their innermost feelings to people by risking disclosure to others. Interpersonal relations rarely begin with the most secret feelings being revealed first. Should this happen, you would probably smile and terminate the relationship. Risking is tied to trust. You have to expose (risk) yourself little by little to other people, trusting that not only will they keep the communication confidential but begin disclosing themselves to you. In short, a healthy spiral is developed through this trusting type of relationship.

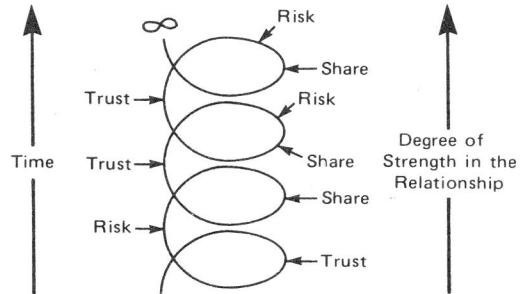

Articles

The first article by Joseph Zima relates to taking inventory on yourself. "Know thyself" is a comment to which Zima addresses himself. What strengths and weaknesses do you have as a communicator? How satisfied are you with your relationships? Since you are your own best critic, take some time not only to think about answering Zima's questions but also what the questions and your answers mean to the types of relationships you have with others.

What makes a good conversation? McGhee wrote a short guest editorial in *Saturday Review* discussing what constitutes good conversation. It closely approximates our discussion of the geniune dialogue. What additional information do you gain from this? Let's hope that after reading this article your conversations, if not more purposeful, are at least more pleasurable.

The third article, principally written for women, discusses what happens to marriages when husbands refuse to reveal their feelings to their wives. We suspect that after reading this article you could develop a less sexist example of self-disclosure through interpersonal communication in interpersonal relations.
tions.

Finally, we have chosen an article by John Stewart, "An Interpersonal Approach to the Basic Course." He explains the important aspects of interpersonal communication as they relate to the beginning communication course at his university. In one sense, this is a good article because it highlights some important factors (what interpersonal communica-

tion is not, understanding transactional communication, meaning of personal involvement, etc.). In another sense, it allows you to note how many similarities there are between the course you are now taking and the suggestions offered by Stewart.

References

M. Buber, *Between Man and Man: The Realms* (New York: Macmillan, 1965).

D. Fabun, *Communications* (New York: Kaiser Aluminum & Chemical Corporation, 1965).

L. Festinger, S. Schachter, and K. Back, *Social Pressures in Groups* (New York: Harper and Brothers, 1950).

F. Heider, *The Psychology of Interpersonal Relations* (New York: John Wiley & Sons, 1958).

R. F. Priest and J. Sawyer, "Proximity and Peership: Bases of Balance in Interpersonal Attraction," *The American Journal of Sociology*, 72 (1967), 633-49.

Self-Analysis Inventory: An Interpersonal Communication Exercise

Joseph P. Zima

Recent articles in speech journals have emphasized the need for more effective assignments in undergraduate speech-communication courses. McNally[1] has proposed the creative use of antiquity as a stimulating opening exercise. King[2] has suggested an inductive opening exercise, and Hootman and Ochs[3] have tested an audience analysis approach. Patterson[4] has proposed an activities approach, and Gorden[5] has recently explored the place of games in speech-communication curriculums. The interest in greater use of experience-based learning in speech-communication has been long overdue.

From Joseph P. Zima, "Self-Analysis Inventory: An Interpersonal Communication Exercise," *Speech Teacher*, 20 (March 1971), pp 108–114. Reprinted with permission.

[1] James R. McNally, "Hermognes in the Modern Classroom," *The Speech Teacher* XVIII, 1 (January 1969), 18–20.

[2] Thomas R. King, "An Inductive Opening Exercise, *The Speech Teacher*, XVIII, 1 (January 1969), 21–2.

[3] Richard Hooton and Donovan J. Ochs, "Audience Analysis: An Exordium for the Basic Course," *The Speech Teacher*, XVIII, 1 (January 1969), 23–5.

[4] J. W. Patterson, "The Activities Approach in the First Course," *The Speech Teacher*, XVIII, 3 (September 1969), 223–29.

[5] William I. Gorden, "Academic Games in the Speech Curriculum," *Central States Speech Journal*, XX, 4 (Winter 1969), 269–79.

However, the greatest emphasis still appears to be primarily directed toward public address courses. How many students in your speech-communication courses will be in a large number of public speaking situations? This is not to say public address training should be eliminated; it should be a part of every student's experience. Rather I am suggesting that students need more training and classroom experiences in developing their interpersonal communication skills. One of the most essential factors in achieving better relationships among people is "interpersonal feedback." How much emphasis is presently being given in speech-communication courses to learning to give and receive feedback?

Although the articles cited above do imply some interpersonal feedback experiences, more exercises should be designed to directly involve the student in giving and receiving feedback. Interpersonal feedback is the communication of an individual's own feelings or reactions to the behavior (verbal, nonverbal, intentional or unintentional) of the person to whom it is directed. Through interpersonal feedback, students gain an idea of the impact they have on other students. By comparing that impact with their assumptions and intentions, they can see the range of different perceptions of any given act.

In addition, they can discover common qualities as well as the unique differences of other individuals, and, if they wish, try out new ways of interacting. Much of my thinking has been influenced by sensitivity training and the currently popularized variations including names like encounter groups, T-groups, personal growth groups, group dynamics, communication workshops, and marathons. The idea that most of these experiences are completely unstructured is a false one. A number of "structured" exercises have been generated and are being assimilated into the repertoire of human relations workers.[6] A "structured" experience could be defined as a game, exercise, or activity with built-in controls and goals to be completed within a specific time period. Participants need not always go through the initial high tesions of the structureless verbal groups.

This paper deals with my effort to develop a structured experience for use in the speech-communication classroom. The exercise is called "Self-Analysis Inventory." This exercise has been used in courses of public speaking (undergraduate and adult), discussion, honors courses in communication, graduate seminars in human communication, and communication for engineering students. Gauged by student reactions and my own learning, the results have been very favorable. The Inventory is designed to help students structure thinking about themselves, and then to test their self-perceptions against reality—others' perceptions. It can be

used as an opening exercise to get students thinking about communication, or can be used after students have learned some communication theory and have become "acquainted" with one another.

Rationale for Self-Analysis Inventory

One model that I have found particularly useful in providing a rationale for the Self-Analysis Inventory is the Johari Window.[7] The model describes the dynamics of interpersonal interactions and describes the changes in individuals as group communication matures. Changes in the window reflect the extent to which defensiveness and anxiety are diminished and more satisfying relationship developed.

The four quadrants of the Johari Window represent the whole person in his relationships with others. Quadrants are divided on the basis of awareness of behavior, feelings, and motivation.

Area 1 is behavior and motivation known to self *and* known to others. This is the region of free exchange between individuals. The larger the area, the more an individual is able to use his personal resources for effective and satisfying living, and the more available are his needs and abilities to himself and others.

Area 2 is the blind area and represents behavior and motivation *not* known to self but apparent to others. Examples would include speech mannerisms or gestures of which the

---

[6] J. William Pfeiffer and John E. Jones, *A Handbook of Structured Experiences for Human Relations Training*, vols. I and II (Iowa City, Iowa, 1969).

[7] Joseph Luft, *Of Human Interaction* (Palo Alto, California, 1969); also described in *Group Processes: An Introduction to Group Dynamics* by Joseph Luft (Palo Alto, California, 1963).

The Johari Window

	Known to Self		Not Known to Self	
Known to Others	Area of Free Activity	1	Blind Area (Bad Breath Area)	2
Not Known to Others	Hidden or Avoided Area	3	Area of Unknown Potential	4

person is unaware—but which are quite obvious to everyone else.

Area 3 refers to behavior, feelings, and motivation open to self but hidden from others. In new groups, this region is large because we do not know much about each other and each of us feels the need to be cautious regarding our self-revelations. For example, sometimes a person knows he resents a particular remark but keeps it to himself.

Area 4 refers to unknown activity (or "region of potential") where behavior, feelings, and motivation are neither known to self nor others. Occasionally, we can become aware of some aspects of ourselves which neither we nor the group had known before. These unknowns frequently represent resources and capabilities, which when recognized can initiate movement from Area 4 into other areas.

Hopefully, through structured interpersonal experiences, the window should come to look more like the one at the bottom of the page. In this picture growth has occurred in the sense that more of the individual is available to himself and others for effective, realistic, and satisfying interrelating.

Preparation for Self-Analysis Inventory

Before the instructor asks students to "open up" or begin to reveal themselves, a more natural and satisfying interaction will follow if students perceive the instructor as being willing to open up. An exercise that I have found effective at the first meeting (or even later meetings), is simply to ask students to react on paper to a series of questions or statements. I usually preface this exercise with a statement such as, "You have already made some decisions about me the minute I walked into the room. Now I'd like to give you a chance to discover the accuracy of your perceptions by making some judgments about me."

1. Estimate my age.
2. In what part of the country did I grow up?
3. What do you think is the color of my wife's hair?
4. How many children do I have?
5. What kind of car (or cars) do I drive?
   Year _____ Make _____
6. Was I in a fraternity (or sorority) or not?
7. Briefly write a paragraph describing your initial impressions of me.

Students enjoy making guesses about the instructor, particularly when the responses are read back to them verbatim. Besides demonstrating your willingness to be evaluated, this brief exercise sets the stage for the introduction of the Self-Analysis Inventory. Now that students have had a chance to evaluate the instructor, they should be more willing to evaluate themselves by completing (in writing) the Inventory. They should be told that the next two class meetings (at least two one-hour meetings should be allowed to properly process the important data generated) will be laboratory sessions in which students will be divided into groups and asked to discuss their responses to the Inventory. About five members per group is optimum size. In the discussion it may help to tell students to assume the role of interviewers, while at the same time each person sets his own limits regarding how much to tell about himself. The instructor should act as "facilitator." In other words, he assumes the responsibility for activity, insuring that data which are generated are appropriately and adequately processed by the participants.

	Known to Self	Not Known to Self
Known to Others	Free Exchange 1	Blind 2
Not Known to Others	Hidden or Avoided 3	Unknown 4

The Self-Analysis Inventory

The Inventory consists of eight questions in addition to some sub-questions or probes. The following discussion of the Inventory will include an analysis of the objectives of each question and some of the data that the questions have generated.

1. *Define "communication" in your own words*

This is a non-threatening question designed to get students to explore the various meanings assigned to the term "communication." The group can start by each member reading his definition followed by discussion of similarities and differences. A number of questions could be used here to facilitate discussion: When can it be said that one has communicated? What is effective communication? Is communication the process of transferring a message or meaning? Do words mean or do people mean? Awareness of different kinds of communication should be brought out here. For example, communication could be classified as verbal, nonverbal, intentional, or unintentional. Perhaps the idea of intrapersonal communication should be introduced. Students should start thinking of themselves as self-contained communication units. The feedback variable could also be discussed. If students can begin to explore the various meanings attributed to the term communication, they will have fulfilled the objectives of this question.

2. *How effective am I as an interpersonal (face-to-face) communicator?*
   a. *List communication strengths:*
   b. *List communication weaknesses:*
   c. *List specific measures that can be taken to overcome weaknesses:*

Each group member is asked to tell the group the communication strengths he has listed. Typical examples include: "good voice," "friendliness," "I support what I believe in," "outgoing personality." This may take some prodding at first, but most participants enjoy a chance to talk about themselves. Other group members are also asked to comment on communication strengths they perceived in other members which were not mentioned. After the strengths are explored, each student mentions some weaknesses. Weaknesses usually include items such as poor vocabulary, bad grammar, faulty logic, poor pronunciation, unclear meanings, inability to take criticism, nervousness or "stage fright." One student commented that "I have a full set of dental braces and these impair my speech somewhat." One weakness most frequently mentioned concerns nervousness. This is a good place to ask other group members how they feel about talking in front of a group. By sharing their experiences, they usually find that they all share a common problem and are much less self-conscious about it. In one experience, a student revealed that he had a great deal of anxiety about taking a speech course because he was a stutterer and had put off the course until it got to the point that he couldn't graduate without it. He revealed to the group that he felt much better because he had a chance to talk about it.

After communication weaknesses have been explored, students are asked to list a number of specific behaviors or activities they can do to overcome a particular weakness. For example, if a student has commented that he has a barrier toward initiating interpersonal communication, he may indicate that he will make at least one attempt a day to initiate communication. Engineering students frequently listed impatience as a weakness. That weakness could be overcome by a conscious effort to listen and to be more responsive to others. If a group member has trouble trying to think of ways of overcoming weaknesses, the group should be called upon to suggest or volunteer different methods.

3. *Describe situations in which you have the most difficulty communicating with others. (Why?)*

By listing specific situations and discussing them, group members often find that many of them share the same reservations. Some typical answers to this question included the following: "When I first meet someone that I don't know." "When the conversation turns to a topic I have limited knowledge about." "I have the most difficulty communicating with others when I am confronted with a large audience. The reason is because of my lack of exposure to this type of communication." A male student may have problems in asking a girl for a date. He may find that other guys in the group have the same problem and together they can explore some ways of overcoming it. If the group includes some girls, perhaps the girls can offer some advice on male dating behavior and explain how they feel. In other words, a number of "normal neuroses" may be brought out and explored.

4. *How satisfied am I with my progress in the following areas? (Why or Why not?)*

    a. *Educational:*
    b. *Occupational or career choice:*
    c. *Social:*
       Other:

This question gives group members a chance to talk about their degree of satisfaction in at least three important areas of their life. In discussing educational success with an engineering class, several students revealed that they had strong reservations regarding a career in engineering. Others admitted to similar reservations, but thought that an engineering background was invaluable for training as a manager. Still others were quite content with their career choices. The most healthy experience learned was that it is very normal to have reservations about educational choices.

In the area of social successes, students talked about dating, opportunities to meet new people, to participate in various activities, and suggested means of improving certain conditions. Regarding occupational success, such things as job satisfaction and career goals can very profitably be discussed.

Under the "Other" category some typical

examples included: "I would like to have more time to develop myself physically." "I spend too much time doing nothing, I'd like to develop some hobbies." "Religion—I have strong views but inadequate knowledge."

5. *What are my most outstanding "hangups," both positive and negative (attitudes, prejudices, values)? Describe them below:*

    a. *Ones with which I am satisfied. (Why?)*
    b. *Ones with which I am dissatisfied. (Why)?*

The purpose of this question is to get students to thoughtfully examine some of their particular "hangups" including attitudes, prejudices, and value and belief systems. The problem of psychological barriers and stereotyping often emerge here, particularly regarding the black-white problem. In a predominantly white undergraduate discussion class, a black girl came to class the first day wearing an Afro hairdo. When the class was divided into groups, I asked the group with this particular girl as a member what they associated with the Afro hairdo. They commented that their immediate reaction was that the girl was a militant black and had it not been for this encounter, would probably not have associated with her. Actually, they found the girl was rather quiet and conservative. Some students who had never interacted with blacks found this a particularly rewarding experience. Other problems usually include attitudes toward smoking marijuana, moral values, abortion, overpopulation, Viet Nam, etc.

6. *How do each of these "hangups" affect my interpersonal communication?*

This question is an extended probe of number 5 above. Here specific "hangups" can be discussed in relation to interpersonal communication. One student commented that "I sometimes don't want to listen to others because they oppose my ideas. I also contradict myself because my ideas are mixed and sometimes I don't think." Another student said "I try to determine a person's attitude toward Negroes before I make my opinions known." Other people correctly perceive me to be aloof and disinterested in many cases and this affects my relationship with them." By verbalizing these particular barriers, students become aware of the effect of these barriers on their communication behavior.

7. What kind of initial impression do I leave with others? (Why do you think so?)

Students should be very willing to talk about initial impressions. They are particularly interested in knowing the kinds of impressions they make, but most have never really tested them against reality—other's perceptions. After each student talks about the initial impression he thinks he usually makes, other students are asked to express their initial impressions of each other. By this time there is usually a great deal of openness and fun in sharing impressions. More importantly participants are learning to give and receive feedback. They might also learn that self-disclosure is not so devastating as they may have imagined.

8. Write a paragraph describing your personality as you see it, and comment on how your perceptions of "you" compare with others' perceptions of you.

Participants are usually asked to describe the personality of each group member. After the different perceptions are discussed the student reads the prepared description of his personality and compares it with the group's perceptions. By this time students are enjoying the interaction and are anxious to compare their perceptions of themselves against others.

Summary and Conclusions

One of the most essential factors in achieving better relationships among people is the ability to give and receive "interpersonal feedback." Since giving interpersonal feedback is a difficult skill and requires a good deal of experimen-

tation and practice to do well, speech-communication courses should provide students with the necessary experiences. To give good feedback requires that the "giver" be in good contact with his own feelings and judgments and have adequate language skills for communicating them. On the receiving side, one needs the ability to receive feedback without feeling attacked or threatened. On both sides of the communicational exchange, good feedback should lead to greater mutual trust and increased communication awareness. The Self-Analysis Inventory is one exercise that begins to provide this kind of experience. Some of the advantages include the following:

1. Helps students start thinking about their own communication behavior (Intrapersonal).
2. Gives students insights into other students behavior.
3. Helps students learn how they are perceived by others.
4. Helps students learn to give and receive feedback.
5. Helps students overcome feelings of strangeness and unfamiliarity.
6. Helps students discover that they share common problems or "hangups" and can share solutions.
7. Shows students that communication problems can be reduced by sharing and cooperating in constructive criticism.
8. Helps interpersonal learning take place—working with others facilitates greater openness and free exchange.
9. Gives the instructor an opportunity to learn about himself and his students.
10. Establishes a receptive and favorable attitude toward instructor and course.

With an understanding of the importance of interpersonal feedback, the possibilities for developing exercises that focus on interpersonal feedback are only limited by the effort and imagination of speech-communication instructors.

The Lost Art of Conversation

George C. McGhee

What has happened to the lost art of conversation? By *conversation* I am not thinking merely of word exchanges between individuals. I am thinking of one of the highest manifestations of the use of human intelligence—the ability to transform abstractions into language; the ability to convey images from one mind to another; the ability to build a mutual edifice of ideas. In short, the ability to engage in a civilizing experience.

When the word *art* is applied to conversation, one conjures up an image of Dr. Johnson uttering words of wisdom, with a devoted Boswell taking them all down on paper. Boswell quoted Mrs. Thrale as having remarked about Johnson that his "conversation was much too strong for a person accustomed to obsequiousness and flattery; it was mustard in a young child's mouth."

But where does one find good conversation these days? Certainly not in the presence of the television set, which consumes half of the average American's non-sleeping, non-working hours. Much of the remaining free time is given to games. No matter how rewarding "bridge-

From George C. McGhee, "The Lost Art of Conversation," *Saturday Review*, 2 (June 28, 1975), pp 6–7. Reprinted with permission.

talk" may be, it is not conversation. Neither is chatter.

What makes good conversation? In the first place, it is essentially a mutual search for the essence of things. It is a zestful transaction, not a briefing or a lecture. Pushkin correctly identified the willingness to listen as one of the vital ingredients of any exchange. When two people are talking at the same time, the result is not conversation but a collision of decibels,

Nothing is more destructive of good talk than for one participant to hold the ball too long, like an over-zealous basketball dribbler playing to the gallery and keeping it away from everyone else. Pity the husband or wife with a garrulous mate who insists on talking long past the point where he or she has anything to say.

To be meaningful, a conversation should head in a general direction. It need not be artfully plotted to arrive at a predetermined point, but it should be gracefully kept on course—guided by many unforeseen ideas.

It has been said that if speech is silver, silence is golden. Certainly silence is preferable, under most circumstances, to inconsequential chitchat. Why is it then that so many people, when they are with others, are discomfited by the absence of human sound waves? Why are they not willing merely to sit with each other, silently enjoying the unheard but real linkages of congeniality and understanding? Why aren't people content to contemplate a lovely scene or read together in silence? "Made conversation" should not be a necessity among intimates. They know whether the weather is good or bad; both are as well or poorly informed about current events. If there is nothing to say—don't say it.

It is true that strangers meeting for the first time seem to feel uncomfortable if they do not engage in small talk to relieve their mutual awkwardness. This is the scourge of the cocktail party, but it is necessary if strangers are to size each other up. Usually, however, this is harmless. In desperation one seeks an artificial gambit. I remember one from an English girl: "Oh, say, are you frightfully keen on cats and dogs?" Unfortunately, I wasn't.

There is a disease shared by many, particularly with new acquaintances, that leads to "dropping names" or "colleges." This is often a useful device, since a common friend or university experience can be a helpful point of departure for conversation leading to better understanding. It is, however, more often woefully abused as a means of showing off. The references are usually to the influential rather than to one's less distinguished friends: "Of course I know Ina Gottrocks. She is a very dear friend. Such a nice person [actually an awful bore]. We had lunch only yesterday [on an airplane, sitting in different class sections]." One is less inclined to refer to one's alma mater if it is Oshkosh U.

Genealogical topics should also be avoided. The danger of boring one's conversation partner and of becoming self-serving is far too great. In the first place, others don't really care about your ancestors. They know, as you should, that everyone has quite a variety ranging all the way from bums to princes. If one goes back eight generations, one has 256 forebears. How easy to pick out the one who glitters most as your claim to fame. Even the one who gave you your name is still only one in 256.

Cocktail-party necessities aside, however,

some elementary rules for conversation are well worth our consideration. In the first place, certain subjects should be taboo in any general conversation. Kitchen topics—the best cleansers, recipes, and troubles with servants—should certainly be limited to interested women. Straight man-talk, such as business, golf, and hunting exploits, may be permissible in board or locker rooms but should be taboo in general discussion, along with bus schedules and all other dull or specialized things. One does not mention precise figures descriptive of one's wealth or income—not even an artful "The deal netted me something in six figures." The first digit was probably 1.

People even forget, I'm afraid, that their illnesses and operations should be outlawed as conversational topics. Only if some relative asks you on a need-to-know basis, or a doctor is interested from a professional standpoint, should you ever volunteer anything about your ailments. Everyone understands this; yet it never seems to apply to you. Remember, even if it's the most dramatic operation ever performed, it is not something to be offered gratuitously to friends at conversation time. They really don't want to hear about it.

There is also the conversationalist who must under every circumstance be right—who always has to win the game. There are those of us who want to moralize. There is the intruder into emotional subjects like religion or personalities, the malicious gossip. All should be inadmissible by any rules of good conversation. Vulgar words, even the four-letter words, can sometimes be effective—as in the English use of *bloody*. More often, however, they are in bad taste—particularly when they conjure up a revolting image at mealtime. Shouldn't there be some law against pollution?

An intriguing conversational gambit was disclosed by H. Allen Smith, which could, if you got by with it, amaze your dinner partners. In preparation he boned up on traditional Chinese uses of funereal jade in the body orifices. It is best to choose a subject that would appear alien to your normal interests. A lawyer, after consulting the art histories, might break into the Pre-Raphaelite painters. A hostess at a country weekend might try: "Yes, the country is lovely here. The lower Catoctin greensand, Upper Jurassic, you know, underlies much of the Austin chalk of the valley." Stephen Potter's books on gamesmanship and one-upmanship are of course treasure-houses of this sort of off-putting play.

If conversation need not always be purposeful, it must at least be for pleasure. It should be congenial to good society—to better knowing one's conversation partner. Above all, it should be joyful and amiable, for as Addison put it: "Good nature is more agreeable in conversation than wit, and gives a certain air to the countenance which is more amiable than beauty." I do not object to enforced conversation—say, by the hostess who interrupts an after-dinner group with, "Come, we must all hear John tell us about his trip to Africa." I am less tolerant, however, of those who would arbitrarily stop a good conversation which has exciting possibilities with a flat "Come, now, let's stop all this serious talk." A good conversation is a fragile thing that must be nurtured carefully.

And, finally, I want to encourage the pixie of the conversation who can add zest and interest. Our talk too often reflects the dull things we do all day. Conversation does not always have to be in earnest. Provocation, whimsy, laughter, mockery, and flirtation all have their place in the art of good conversation, of which it has been said. "Be prompt without being stubborn, refute without argument, clothe weighty matters in a motley garb."

Why Husbands Can't Say, "I Love You"

Jack O. Balswick and James Lincoln Collier

American men are raised to be undemonstrative, to keep their feelings bottled up no matter how much it hurts their wives, their children and themselves. But such men can be changed into open, giving husbands and fathers.

In the United States we have long admired what I call the "John Wayne" type—the man who kisses his horse instead of his girl—as a symbol of masculinity. He likes girls, of course, but he finds it easier to conquer a new frontier than to talk with a woman. His way of expressing affection for a brother or an old friend is to punch him on the shoulder or slap him on the back. Strong and capable in the world of men, he's shy in his dealings with the people he loves.

Back when marriages were judged on how well the partners produced—the husband as provider, the wife as manager and mother—the John Wayne type was an ideal to strive for. But today we have a different ideal. We believe that partners in a marriage—all members of a family, in fact—ought to be companions and friends. We no longer have houses full of relatives—aunts,

Reprinted by permission of *Woman's Day* Magazine, a Fawcett publication, and John Cushman Associates, Inc. Copyright © by Jack O. Balswick and James Lincoln Collier.

uncles, cousins, grandparents—to fill the gap if one member of the family is uncommunicative.

Today's families are not only smaller than in the past, they move frequently, leaving friends and relatives behind. We have become increasingly dependent on members of the family for affection, communication, friendship. Husbands and wives often have nobody else with whom to share their joys and sorrows—a situation that magnifies the tragedy of the man who is unable to express his feelings.

Some things have not changed, however. Despite a growing effort by the women's movement to eliminate the old-fashioned stereotypes in child-rearing, most boys growing up in America still learn very early that a "real man" doesn't vent his feelings. When his sister cries, she is comforted; when he cries, he is told, "Big boys don't cry." If he talks about his feelings—about being unhappy or worried or scared—his friends look at him askance. If he gives up his baseball game to take his little sister to the beach, they taunt him; if he cries, they jeer. In the movies and on television he sees male heroes brawling and shooting each other; rarely does he find a hero who is tender toward a friend or loved one.

The most difficult influential hero in a boy's life, however, is his father. If he never hears his father say "I love you," if he never feels his father's arm around his shoulder hugging him, if he never sees his father cry, it confirms his impression that these are things men don't do. Inevitably, by the time he reaches manhood, he has learned not to show his feelings—regardless of how deeply he may (and often does) care about his family and friends.

This male inexpressiveness is no laughing matter; it's a real tragedy for the man's wife, his children, and most especially for himself. Think of the wife who, year after year, never hears the words "I love you." Consider the child who is never told, "Fine work, I'm proud of you." And think of the tragedy of the man himself, crippled by an inability to let out the best part of a human being—his warm and tender feelings for other people.

I know what this is all about because I grew up as a typical inexpressive male myself. Fortunately I happened to meet and marry a warm responsive woman who was willing to draw me out. She began pointing out that I wasn't very expressive. "Why don't you talk about your feelings more?" she asked. "Everybody has them, but you don't ever admit yours to anybody." It finally began to dawn on me that I was missing a lot by keeping my feelings bottled up. And being a sociologist, I was better prepared than most men to understand how I got that way.

My personal experience has convinced me that men who have trouble expressing their deeper feelings *can* change—if they really want to. I see more and more evidence of it every day—particularly among the younger generation that participates in sensitivity training and encounter groups. As part of their rebellion against exaggerated distinctions between the sexes, they are becoming more in touch with their emotions and more comfortable in expressing them.

While the inexpressive males contribute to the rising number of divorces, those who manage to break out of the pattern often develop very strong marriages. Although some are able to show their emotions only within the con-

fines of marriage, they do learn to express their feelings toward their wives and this can lead to stronger emotional bonds and greater fidelity.

Obviously, then, it behooves women to recognize the problem and try to help their husband overcome it. To begin with, a concerned wife can help her husband understand that while he sees himself as the standard American male, his family sees him as silent, shy, reserved, distant, untalkative, even cold. He should understand how painful and frustrating this can be for the people to whom he means so much. He should realize, for example, that his wife can be hurt when he reaches for her sexually after hardly speaking to her all evening. He should understand that his children are pained when he fails to be enthusiastic about their triumphs.

A woman can help a man realize how much he has shut off his feelings by saying, "I'd really be interested to know what's going on at work —you never tell me anything about it." Or she can say, "Sometimes I really wonder how it was when you were a kid." or "I wish I knew what it is about that workshop that appeals to you so much."

Once a man begins to talk, it becomes easier to lead him into more revealing conversations. The trick is to open up an area he is relatively comfortable with—his youth, his work, his hobby—and then ask him how he feels about it. While it may be comparatively easy to explain what he does at work, it is much harder to say that he enjoys, despises or is bored with his job—and that's what is crucial to communication between spouses. Similarly, he may find it a lot easier to talk about how he used to play football every afternoon after school than to explain how miserable he felt when he wasn't very good at it.

I suggest, then, that a wife try her husband on such straightforward topics from time to time. If he shrugs her off with a noncommittal answer ("I don't mind my work"), she might push on with, "But would you rather have some other kind of job?" If he remains noncommittal, it's probably wise not to press him, to be patient and try again some other time.

Once a man begins to open up a little, his wife must be encouraging and supportive. This isn't always easy. If she asks him about his job and he suddenly blurts out that he hates it and wants to quit, she may well begin to panic and say "Oh, you can't do that; think of the children!" or some such. It is far better to say something like, "From what you tell me, I don't blame you. I'd hate it, too." Few men will simply quit their jobs and leave their families in the lurch. But the man who has aired his discontent and received encouragement from his wife is better able to move to a more satisfactory career.

The key point is for a wife to open her heart to her husband whenever he offers to share some of his feelings. She may think he is wrong sometimes—that he shouldn't have felt so angry when his boss criticized his work or when his father gave his brother the old car—but if she wants him to communicate with her, she must show compassion. And it's possible to be sympathetic even when you don't agree.

Suppose for example that your husband has a disagreement with his father. He says angrily, "I can't get anything through his thick head." Even if you secretly side with your father-in-law you can support your husband by saying something like "I'm glad to know how you feel about it; what do you think is the problem?" Once he's ventilated his feelings on the subject you might say, "I don't completely agree with you, but I'm pleased you wanted to discuss it with me."

This is what psychologists call "positive reinforcement." By showing your appreciation whenever he does open up, you encourage him to open up some more. You can also use positive reinforcement to help your husband be more demonstrative to his children. If he tells a child, "I'm very proud of you for getting such good grades," you might say to him afterwards, "I could tell it meant a lot to Johnny when you complimented him on his report card." It's more difficult to be supportive when he expresses troublesome feelings about his job or family, of

course, but it's important to encourage him to go on talking. If you attack him when he's feeling vulnerable, he may never trust you with his feelings again.

It's also helpful for a wife to assure her husband that she is secure in his masculinity—that she has no doubts about his "maleness." She can do this quite simply by telling him occasionally what a good man he is. The more confidence a man has that his wife sees him as solidly male, the more he can allow himself the "weakness" of revealing his feelings to her.

A wife should also try to develop lines of communication between her husband and the children. In many cases, mothers have the habit of answering a child who's upset about a friend's behavior, has a problem with a teacher, or simply wants somebody to talk to. But if she directs the child to his father, she can force him to open up a little. She might say, "Why don't you ask your father; he knows a lot about that." Or she can say to her husband, "You probably had the same thing happen to you—why don't you tell Johnny how you felt about it.

Finally, a wife can help her husband by being more expressive herself. It may not be easy—especially when she doesn't get much response—but giving something of her own spirit, revealing her own feelings, is a good way to encourage her husband to respond in kind.

The expressive woman also provides important examples for her husband. Sometimes a man fails to express himself simply because he doesn't know how. He literally doesn't know what words to use. Thus when a wife says "Thanks for backing me up last night when I needed it," or "I really feel close to you today." or just "I love you," she gives her husband a lesson in the expressive forms of the English language.

I don't mean to suggest that it's a wife's job to change her husband. She can only make it easier for him; any changes must still come from within the man. I know from personal experience that it isn't easy. I found it very hard at first to tell my wife and children that I loved them, to say how proud I was of their achievements, to talk about my own fears, joys and disappointments.

But I did it—and the rewards have been enormous. Not only has my marriage been enriched and my relationships with my children deepened, but the change has spread throughout my whole life. Being willing to let people see who I am in my strengths and my weaknesses makes me a better teacher, a better friend, even a better scholar.

An Interpersonal Approach to the Basic Course

John Stewart

The recent, unusually successful introduction of at least three basic speech texts that approach the first course from an "interpersonal" perspective suggests that "interpersonal communication" might become as common to college freshmen and sophomores of the seventies as "public speaking" has been to undergraduate students of the fifties and sixties.[1] Contributors to recent issues of speech communication journals are also exploring such interpersonal variables as self-perception,[2] role anticipation and performance,[3] interpersonal trust,[4] social alienation,[5] and communication as dialogue.[6] However, when a faculty considers either moving toward an interpersonal approach to the basic course or adding an interpersonal course to the curriculum, legitimate questions arise: How does this approach differ from what's been done before? Is interpersonal communication just another term for dynamic public speaking? Does interpersonal communication designate the primarily behavioral study of such variables as "Propinquity and Prestige as Determinants of

From John Stewart, "An Interpersonal Approach to the Basic Course," *Speech Teacher*, 21 (1972), pp 7–14. Reprinted with permission.

[1] John Keltner, *Interpersonal Speech-Communication* (Belmont, Calif., 1970); Kim Giffin and Bobby R. Patton, *Fundamentals of Interpersonal Communication* (New York, 1971); James C. McCroskey, Carl E. Larson, and Mark L. Knapp, *An Introduction to Interpersonal Communication* (Englewood Cliffs, N.J., 1971). At this writing adoption figures are available only for the Keltner and Griffin-Patton books. Keltner's text was used during its first year of publication (1970–1971) by over 150 schools. Less than six months after publication, Griffin-Patton had been adopted by about 125 schools. Examples of other recent books that indicate the growing popularity of "the interpersonal approach" in speech include: William D. Brooks, *Speech Communication* (Dubuque, Iowa, 1971); Arthur Solomon, *Interpersonal Communication: A Cross-Disciplinary Approach* (Springfield, Ill., 1970); George A. Borden, Richard B. Gregg, and Theodore Grove, *Speech Behavior and Human Interaction* (Englewood Cliffs, N.J., 1969), part II; and Giffin and Patton, *Basic Readings in Interpersonal Communication* (New York, 1971).

[2] E.g., Joseph P. Zima, "Self Analysis Inventory: An Interpersonal Communication Exercise," *Speech Teacher*, XX (March 1971), 108-114; and H. Bedford Furr, "Influences of a Course in Speech Communication on Certain Aspects of the Self Concept of College Freshmen," *Speech Teacher*, XIX (January 1970), 26–31.

[3] E.g., Thomas J. Burneau, "Utilizing Role Playing in the Basic College Speech Course," *Speech Teacher*, XX (January 1971). 53–8.

[4] E.g., Dale G. Leathers, "The Process Effects of Trust-Destroying Behavior in the Small Group," *Speech Monographs*, XXXVII (August 1970). 180–87.

[5] E.g., Kim Giffin, "Social Alienation by Communication Denial," *Quarterly Journal of Speech*, LVI (December 1970), 347–57.

[6] Richard L. Johannesen, "The Emerging Concept of Communication as Dialogue," *Quarterly Journal of Speech*, in press.

Communication Networks," and "The Spatial Ecology of Groups"?[7] Is it a principally humanistic study of such difficult-to-quantify concepts as existence risk, dialogue, and empathy? Or is interpersonal communication actually an innocuous substitute for less academically-palatable but more accurate terms like "encounter group," "T-group," or "sensitivity training"?[8]

Each characterization is accurate for some groups. I would like to respond to these questions, however, from the perspective of an interpersonal approach to the basic course developed over the last twelve quarters at the University of Washington.[9] This essay outlines both the theoretical foundations and some practical implications of this approach by (1) noting what our interpersonal communication classes are *not*, and (2) developing three concepts that distinguish what we call interpersonal comunication from other orientations to the basic course.

Interpersonal communication is not simply a form of public speaking. The public speaking approach has been undeniably popular; a 1967–1968 survey of the basic course indicated that public speaking was emphasized at that time by the majority of colleges, universities, and junior colleges.[10] Public speaking courses are typically grounded in a combination of neo-Aristotelian rhetorical theory and recent social-psychological and speech communication research, and emphasize topics like delivery, supporting material, outlining, and audience analysis.[11] There are

three public speaking courses in our undergraduate curriculum, and they all deal with creating an effective, i.e., appropriate, organized, and substantive, message and presenting it effectively in a speaker/audience situation. As the explanation below should clarify, however, this is not the focus of the basic, interpersonal course.

Interpersonal communication is also not simply a "skills" approach. In our course each student is expected to read most of what is presently a 410-page text, all of a 170-page supplementary paperback, and, depending on the class section, from five to seven additional articles or chapters on other books. Students also write analyses of communication breakdown, evaluations of classroom experiences, and examinations.

On the other hand, interpersonal communication is also not simply a "content" or "theory" approach, because it emphasizes the need for the student to *experience* the application of concepts. We operate on the assumption that Carl Rogers is at least partly right when he says that any learning of consequence must be self-discovered, self-appropriated learning.[12] We are convinced that students often manage to avoid genuine learning by intellectualizing about concepts *instead* of experiencing what it is like, for instance, to try a new style of interpersonal relating. In short, oral assignments and exercises are vitally important. We do not believe each student must give ten speeches—or even five. But each student does have the opportunity to participate in a wide variety of exercises in which he can validate what he has read and discussed by experiencing it.

Finally, the argument that interpersonal communication courses are disguised encounter groups is based on a pervasive assumption that I believe is fundamentally unwarranted and inaccurate; namely, that concern with spontaneous, open, honest human relationships is only appropriate in a context of combat, therapy, or sex. Like sensitivity training, interpersonal communi-

[7]Dean C. Barnlund, *Interpersonal Communication: Survey and Studies* (Boston, 1968).

[8]Larry A. Samovar, "Equal Time," *Western Speech*, XXXV (Spring 1971), 135–36.

[9]We offer two versions of the basic course, a five-hour one that fulfills the General Education requirement and a three-hour version required for the Provisional Teaching Certificate. However, since both are similar in the respects mentioned here, I will refer to "the course" rather than "the courses."

[10]James W. Gibson, Charles R. Gruner, William D. Brooks, and Charles R. Petrie, Jr., "The First Course in Speech: A Survey of U.S. Colleges and Universities." *Speech Teacher*, XIX (January 1970), 15.

[11]*Ibid.*

[12]"Personal Thoughts on Teaching and Learning," *On Becoming a Person* (Boston, 1961), p. 276.

cation borrows from humanistic psychology, but the approach does not demand 24-hour therapeutic marathons or nude body language exercises. We are concerned with concepts and skills that will enable students to deal with ordinary communication problems that occur in family and work groups, between parent and child, husband and wife, employer and employee, student and teacher, and so on. But we are neither qualified nor inclined to take the place of trained counselors. In short, *the approach does require the teacher to commit himself as a human being to his students, but it does not require him to be a clinical psychologist.*

There are two reasons why it is somewhat easier to describe what interpersonal communication is not than to explain what it is. First, as the variety of textbooks indicates, the term "interpersonal" is used in a number of ways. Sometimes it designates a communication setting;[13] sometimes it identifies an essential psychological element;[14] and sometimes it denotes a quality of communication.[15] In addition, the concepts and skills studied in an interpersonal course are often difficult to define and almost always unavoidably overlap.

In the approach we have developed. "interpersonal" is a *quality* term. The quality it identifies is somewhat awkwardly called "non-interchangability." When one objectifies another, i.e., approaches him as just "a student," "another teacher," "a parent," "a black," or "a hippie," interpersonal communication is impossible. This quality of communication can only occur when each participant recognizes his uniqueness as a communicating person *and* acknowledges the unique, idiosyncratic personhood of each other. Only when one assumes that he *is not* an interchangable part of the communication situation, i.e., that his relationship with the other communicators would be radically different if different individual persons were involved, can he approach interpersonal communication. We attempt to develop this quality by emphasizing three dimensions of human communication which are not usually stressed in the basic course.

The first is the view that human communication is not simply an act or even an interaction by a *transaction*. It is possible to approach communicating as primarily a job of message-creating and message-presenting. In this case one might emphasize inventional processes, organization of ideas, and effective and stylistic delivery. If that is one's primary focus, it might be said that he is viewing communication primarily as an *act* that a communicator prepares for and performs. On the other hand, one might approach communication as an *interaction* of "mutual or reciprocal influence between two or more systems . . . that relation between animals in which the behavior of either one is stimulus to the behavior of the other."[16] He might then see the participants in a communication event as units or organisms which enter a situation and mutually affect each other's behavior.

The interpersonal approach we have developed stresses the idea that human communication is a *transaction*. In contrast to an interaction, a transaction is defined as "a psychological event in which all parts or aspects of the concrete event derive their existence and nature

---

[13] E.g., face-to-face; see Borden Gregg, and Gove, p. 75.

[14] E.g., "perceptual engagement;" see Barnlund, p. 8. Or "reciprocal bond;" see Keltner, p. 10.

[15] E.g., "congruence," "empathy," "unconditional positive regard;" see Carl R. Rogers, "The Interpersonal Relationship: The Core of Guidance," *Harvard Educational Review*, XXXII (Fall 1962), 416–29. For Martin Buber, "dialogue" is a quality term. See his "Elements of the Interhuman," *The Knowledge of Man*, ed. Maurice Friedman, trans. Maurice Friedman and Ronald Gregor Smith (New York, 1965), especially pp. 85–9.

[16] Horace B. English and Ava Champney English, *A Comprehensive Dictionary of Psychoanalytical Terms* (New York, 1958), p. 270. David Berlo offers a relatively complex discussion of this view in *The Process of Communication* (New York, 1960), pp. 106–131. The interactive view is also currently influential; see Donald K. Darnell, "Toward a Reconceptualization of Communication," *Journal of Communication*, XXI (March 1970), 5–16.

from active participation in the event."[17] This transactional perspective is important, because if one sees human communication simply as an action or interaction, he is liable to overlook the fact that we construct the persons with whom we communicate. That is, humans do not perceive the world by simply reacting in a mechanistic, causal way to their environment. As the psychologist George Kelly explains, each man erects for himself a representational model of the world which allows him to make some sense out of it and which enables him to chart a course of behavior in relation to it.[18] The model Kelly discusses is a system of what he calls "constructs." Each individual "construes" the events he experiences in his own way. Human communication is thus transactional in the sense that each communicator "construes" the persons who are active participants in the communication event with him.

Richard Dettering contrasts an interaction and a transaction this way:

> In an *interaction* A and B, although related, keep their identities unaffected; for example, two drivers passing on a highway, two patrons seated in the same theater, two gamblers playing in the same casino. In such cases the presence or behavior of the one person is not important for the other to be or to be doing what he is.
>
> If, however, A and B are in a *transaction* their intimate identities and functions are at stake. One cannot be a husband without a wife, a teacher without a student, a business partner without a business partner.[19]

From a transactional point of view we construe—or construct—the other with whom we communicate, in the sense that we choose from the infinite number of cues he "gives off" and organize our chosen perceptions into a configuration that is "our him."

Dean Barnlund suggests that in a dyadic communication situation the communicators construct six "persons," each of whom is involved in the transaction.[20] For example, in Sam's communication with Sally, Sam's image of himself is one "person." In addition, there are Sam's image of Sally, Sam's impression of the way Sally sees him, Sally's image of herself, Sally's view of Sam, and Sally's concept of how Sam sees her.[21] In short, according to the transactional view, human communication is not a matter of the action-reaction patterns of static beings. Each of us constructs the other and is constructed by him in each communicative interchange.

There are at least three important implications of the transactional orientation. First, we are reminded of the impossibility of not communicating.[22] Since each of us contructs the messages he receives, every person in our perceptual field can communicate with us, and we communicate continually with everyone who perceives us. Thus a transactional orientation encourages increased awareness of the myriad of communicative cues available in every interpersonal situation; the scope of speech communication study is consequently significantly broadened. The importance of the here-and-now is another implication of the transactional

---

[17]*Ibid*, p. 561. Cf. *Exploration in Transactional Psychology*, ed. Franklin P. Kilpatrick (New York, 1961), pp. 1–5; and Neil Postman and Charles Weingartner, *Teaching as a Subversive Activity* (New York, 1969), especially pp. 87–98.

[18]George A. Kelly, *A Theory of Personality: The Psychology of Personal Constructs* (New York 1955 and 1963), pp. 8 ff. Cf. D. Bannister and J. M. M. Mair, *The Evaluation of Personal Constructs* (London and New York, 1968), p. 6. Kenneth Boulding discusses a similar process in *The Image* (Ann Arbor, 1966).

[19]"The Syntax of Personality," *ETC: A Review of General Semantics*, XXVI (June 1969), 141. Cf. Dean

C. Barnlund, "A Transactional Model of Communication," *Foundations of Communication Theory*, ed. Kenneth K. Sereno and C. David Mortensen (New York, 1970), p. 88.

[20]Dean C. Barnlund, "Toward a Meaning-Centered Philosophy of Communication," *Journal of Communication*, XI (1962), 203.

[21]Keltner identifies four "persons" which he calls "my me," my you," "your me," and "your you." See *Interpersonal Speech-Communication*, chapter 3.

[22]Paul Watzlawick, Janet Helmick Beavin, and Don D. Jackson, *The Pragmatics of Human Communication* (New York, 1967) pp. 48–51.

view. The most notable communication event often becomes the one that is happening at a given moment. Students are sometimes a little hesitant to try to cope with what is actually going on in their own classroom—as are some teachers. In addition, too much contemporaneous analysis can become the kind of navel-gazing that is neither comfortable nor productive. But a sensitive, judicious discussion of, for example, the student's general unwillingness to disagree with the instructor or the teacher's tendency not to give verbal feedback can both improve the cohesiveness of the class and introduce and develop important concepts.

Probably the most important implication of this transactional orientation is that interpersonal communication classes are meaning-centered as opposed to message-centered. This approach emphasizes the insidiousness of the "myth of idea transmission,"[23] that is, the notion that human communication consists essentially of passing back and forth "ideas," "thoughts," "messages," etc. Communicating is viewed as a process of meaning-creating rather than message-sending-and-receiving, an ubiquitous, circular, complex, irreversible, unrepeatable process involving the totality of each person concerned. This approach admits that "the words of the messages are important, but regards as most critical the state of mind, the assumptive world and the needs of the listener or observer."[24] A "good" message-centered communicator carefully creates a well-ordered, stylistically appropriate, factually supported unit of discourse and displays or performs it before "his" "audience." A meaning-centered communicator, on the other hand, concentrates as I will discuss below, on becoming personally involved in the communication event, staying in as close and constant perceptual contact with the other persons present as he can, and trying to evoke meanings consonant with his intent

and his perceptions of himself, of others and of his situation.

To the degree that it is useful to discuss the "location" of meaning, one could also say that, according to the interpersonal approach, meanings are not in words, but they are also not simply "in people." Instead, meaning is "located," as Martin Buber suggests, *between* persons. Buber writes,

> The fundamental fact of human existence is neither the individual as such nor the aggregate as such. Each, considered by itself, is a mighty abstraction.... The fundamental fact of human existence is man with man. What is peculiarly characteristic of the human world is above all that something takes place between one being and another the like of which can be found nonwhere in nature. Language is only a sign and a means for it; all achievement of the spirit has been incited by it. Man is made man by it.... It is rooted in one being turning to another as another, as this particular other being, in order to communicate with it in a sphere ... *the sphere of "between."* Though being realized in very different degrees, *it is a primal category of human reality.*[25]

The second distinguishing characteristic of our interpersonal approach is its emphasis on personal involvement. We stress the idea that personal involvement does not mean frantically hurling oneself into every event or at everybody. In a communication situation involvement can be achieved by the appropriate application of the skills of non-evaluative listening and self-disclosure.

Carl Rogers emphasizes the importance of nonevaluative listening when he asserts that "the major barrier to mutual interpersonal communication is our very natural tendency to judge, to evaluate, to approve (or disapprove) the statement of the other person or the other group."[26] Constant evaluation often prevents

[23] Francis Cartier, "Three Misconceptions of Communication," *ETC: A Review of General Semantics,* XX (July 1963), 135–44.

[24] Barnlund, "Toward a Meaning-Centered Philosophy," 201.

[25] Martin Buber, *Between Man and Man,* trans. Ronald Gregor Smith (New York, 1965), pp. 202-3.

[26] Carl R. Rogers and F. J. Roethsliberger, "Barriers and Gateways to Communication," *Harvard Business Review,* XX (July-August 1952), 19.

complete understanding; in fact, "to the extent that one is deliberating (mentally criticizing, summarizing, concluding, preparing reports, etc.) he is *not listening* but formulating his own ideas."[27] The goal of nonevaluative or empathic listening is "to see the expressed idea and attitude from the other person's point of view, to sense how it feels for him, to achieve his frame of reference in regard to the things he is talking about."[28] Sometimes the skill is described as listening *with* as opposed to listening *to* a person, or trying to think *with* him instead of "thinking ahead, mentally jumping forward to get the story over with before the other person is halfway there."[29]

Several authors, including Rogers, Abraham Maslow, and Sidney Jourard, underscore the importance of appropriate self-disclosure to interpersonal communication. They note that self-disclosure does not mean baring one's most intimate secrets; such complete disclosure is probably appropriate only in therapeutic situations. However, they emphasize the importance and value of transcending the typical role-to-role relationships that characterize many human transactions. As Jourard explains, in an interpersonal relationship,

> each experiences the other as a person, as the origin and source of his intentional acts. Each participant aims to show his being to the other *as it is for him*. Transparency not mystification is one of the goals. It matters little whether the dialogue is nonverbal or verbal; whether it occurs between a philosopher and his pupil, a therapist and his patient, a parent and child, or two friends. The aim is to show oneself in willful honesty before the other and to respond to the other with an expression of one's experiences as the other has affected it.[30]

Jourard has also identified and experimented with what he calls the "dyadic effect," i.e., the hypothesis that self-disclosure begets self-disclosure. He suggests that increased self-disclosure alone can materially enhance an interpersonal relationship.[31] In addition Jourard and others have explored the corollary benefits of self-disclosure, including clarified self-concept and increased ability both to empathize and to evaluate accurately.[32]

Both self-disclosure and empathic listening clearly involve risk. Regardless of whether one chooses to disclose an affection for bananas or a profound fear of communicating with members of the opposite sex, he cannot be sure how his disclosure will be accepted. Similarly, if one becomes able to listen with genuine understanding and thus to enter part of another's private world and see the way life appears to him, without evaluating what he sees, he runs the risk of being changed himself. It is the often unspoken assumption of interpersonal communication, however, that the risk is worth the candle. The argument is, roughly, that you get out of something what you put into it. Superficial relationships are easy to achieve but seldom fulfilling. Authentic communication, on the other hand, is unquestionably difficult; however, it is at least rewarding and at most, if Martin Buber is right, necessary to become a fully human being: "I require a You to become.... All actual life is encounter ... Human life and humanity come into being in genuine meetings."[33]

The third characteristic of this interpersonal approach is an emphasis on *relationship* communication. Both Jurgen Ruesch[34] and Watzla-

[27]Charles M. Kelley, "Empathic Listening," *Small Group Communication: A Reader*, ed. Robert S. Cathcart and Larry A. Samovar (Dubuque, Iowa, 1970), p. 253.

[28]Rogers and Roethsliberger, 19.

[29]Allen Katcher, "Self-Fulfilling Prophecies and Active Listening," *Experiences in Being*, ed. Bernice Marshall (Belmont, Calif., 1971), p. 136.

[30]*Disclosing Man to Himself* (New York, 1968), p. 21.

[31]*Ibid.*, pp. 23–5.

[32]See, e.g., Terry O'Banion and April O'Connell, *The Shared Journey: An Introduction to Encounter* (Englewood Cliffs, N.J., 1970), pp. 41–6; John Powell, J. J., *Why Am I Afraid To Tell you Who I Am?* (Chicago, 1969), pp. 50–85.

[33]*I and Thou*, trans, Walter Kaufmann (New York, 1970), p. 62; "Distance and Relation," *The Knowledge of Man*, p. 69.

[34]"Communication and Human Relations: An Interdisciplinary Approach," Jurgen Ruesch and Gregory Bateson, *Communication: The Social Matrix of Psychiatry* (New York, 1968), p. 21.

wick, Beavin, and Jackson[35] make the point that every communication includes both content or information messages and messages that define the relationship between the persons communicating. For example, "Please stand up," "All rise," and "Git up, dammit!" have almost identical content, but their relationship aspects differ markedly. In other words, relationship communication specifies how the content is to be taken by indicating the way the communicating persons relate to each other. No two things can be related, however, until one has some idea of what they are. How is a socket related to a ratchet? How is a bobbin related to a zipper foot? Both answers require some knowledge of what each of those things is. Similarly, if two persons are to establish a relationship, each must also have some notion of who he is and who the other person is. Watzlawick, Beavin, and Jackson put it this way: "On the relationship level people do not communicate about facts outside their relationship, but offer each other definitions of that relationship and, by implication, *of themselves.*"[36] Consequently, person perception, i.e., perception of one's self and of others, is also emphasized in the interpersonal communication class. Each student is encouraged to become more familiar with what Kenneth Boulding calls his "Image," his individual, subjective way of perceiving himself, objects, and, perhaps most importantly, other persons.[37]

Self perception is emphasized because, as Keltner puts it, "no one really talks or communicates with the total other or even with the real other person. What we actually do as we speak with and to each other is talk to ourselves."[38] Hence accurate self perception can facilitate accurate perception of the other. Or, as a student laboriously but correctly put it, "You can only see others in terms of your own sets, so in order to see them at all as they are,

and thus to be able to communicate with them, you need to know who *you* are so you can know what *your* self does to your perception of them."

It is also important to study the way one perceives others. For example, Hastorf, Schneider and Polefka explain how "we perceive other people as causal agents, we infer intentions, we infer emotional states, and we go further to infer enduring dispositions or personality traits."[39] The conclusions we draw from our perception of others determine our definitions of them and materially affect our definitions of ourselves, and hence of the transactional relationship.

Finally, although relationship communication can be verbal or nonverbal, the most significant relationship messages are usually communicated nonverbally. Tone of voice, facial gestures, physical proximity, and placement of the desk in one's office often clearly communicate how one sees himself, how he sees others, and how he sees them seeing him. As a result, the use of and sensitivity to nonverbal communicative cues is much more important in interpersonal communication classes than in most classes taught following the more traditional approaches.

Recent publications make it easier to deal with nonverbal communication in the basic course. Useful information is available for both the teacher[40] and the student,[41] stressing the

[39] Albert H. Hastorf, David J. Schneider, and Judith Polefka, *Person Perception* (Reading, Mass., 1970), p. 17.
[40] E.g., Ray L. Birdwhistell, *Kinesics and Context: Essays on Body Motion Communication* (Philadelphia, 1970); J. R. Davitz, *The Communication of Emotional Meaning* (New York, 1964); Weston La Barre, "Paralinguistics, Kinesics, and Cultural Anthropology," *Approaches to Semiotics*, T. A. Sebeok, A. S. Hayes, and M. C. Bateson, eds. (The Hague, 1964), pp. 191–220; and Jurgen Reusch and Weldon Kees, *Nonverbal Communication* (Berkeley, 1966).
[41] E.g., Haig A. Bosmajian, ed., *The Rhetoric of Nonverbal Communication* (Glenview, Ill., 1971); Kelner, chapter 6; McCroskey, Larson, and Knapp, chapter 6; Joseph A. DeVito, *Communication: Concepts and Processes* (Englewood Cliffs, N.J., 1971), pp. 88–140; and Brooks, chapter 6.

[35] *The Fragmatics of Human Communication*, pp. 51–4 and 80–93.
[36] *Ibid.*, p. 84. Italics added.
[37] *The Image*, pp. 3–18.
[38] Keltner, p. 52.

interpersonal effects of such variables as verbal-nonverbal consistency, types of nonverbal support and rejection, ambiguity in nonverbal messages, nonverbal cues and person perception, translating verbal messages into nonverbal ones and vice-versa, etc. Some discussion of and experiences with personal space and interpersonal communication can also be beneficial. The overriding goal, however, is a clear realization of the fundamental importance of nonverbal cues to relationship communication. That is, the nature of every interpersonal relationship is ultimately defined nonverbally.

In sum, the fundamental elements of our interpersonal approach to the basic course are a transactional view of human communication, an affirmation of the importance of personal involvement, and an extensive treatment of the nature and function of relationship communi-cation. Assignments and exercises deal with topics like meaning-centered communicating, non-evaluative listening, appropriate self-disclosure, self-perception, perceiving others, and nonverbal codes. Interpersonal communication is not simply dynamic public speaking. It does not deal only with experimentally testable variables, but draws from social psychology, humanistic psychology, and dialogical philosophy. And the interpersonal communication class does not have to be an encounter group.

Our experience with this approach indicates that it is not always successful, and it is sometimes frustrating. The approach requires many changes on the part of both students and teachers. But our classes are often what it seems to me all classes ought to be: personally challenging and personally rewarding; rigorous and relevant; intellectually stimulating and fun.

Seven
Small Group
Communication

Introduction

If you have any awareness at all of the communication process, you are probably breathing a sigh of relief because you feel it is easier to relate to people in a group rather than on a one-to-one basis or as a very large audience. Students do view small group communication as being more comfortable than many other forms of communication. While you may feel more at ease in it, there are many things you need to know in order to make small group communication effective for you. In this introductory section, we hope to clarify the role of small group communication and consider its many uses.

If you were to stop and think for a moment of the number of groups in which you participate, you would be amazed at both the number and the variety. Informally, you probably have a small group of friends with whom you prefer to interact rather frequently. You may also participate, on a more formal basis, with a fraternity, sorority, or social organization. You might be part of an athletic team or some other extracurricular activity which constitutes a small group. By now, we are sure that you have used the small group setting for discussion of various activities in your communication class. You can't escape using the small group environment.

We must underscore the use and importance of the small group. Almost every activity in which you become involved reflects the small group setting. Your job, social contact, the family structure, and religious experience are likely to be reflected in a small group approach. You may recall that we suggested that most forms of communication are in the nonverbal mode. We want to point out at this time that most interaction with other people occurs in the small group setting. Therefore, we hope the material provided here will be useful to you as you interact with others.

We define a small group as three or more individuals who come together for some common or observable purpose. Cartwright and Zander (1964) believe a group characterizes itself in one or more of the following ways:

1. Individuals engage in frequent inter- action.
2. They define themselves as members.
3. They are defined by others as belong- ing to the group.
4. They share norms concerning mat- ters of common interest.
5. They participate in a system of inter- locking roles.
6. They identify with one another as a result of having set up the same ideal in their superego.
7. They find the group to be rewarding.
8. They pursue intricate attendant goals.
9. They have a collective perception of their unity.
10. They tend to act in a unitary manner toward their environment.

While we have mentioned that three or more people can constitute a group, we also suggest the upper limit to be somewhere around 15 to 20. There is certainly no real agreement in the litera- ture on small groups as to what consti- tutes the largest small group that can in- teract effectively. We suspect that a group much beyond 15 or 16 would be too large to allow people to interact ef- fectively in the small group study. Any larger group would consider to be public communication.

In the 10 characteristics of the group, it can be seen that individuals who par- ticipate in a group must have a sense of being a part of the group in order for it to exist. There needs to be interaction, and individuals must share some com- mon interest. Obviously, without this in- terest there would be little reason for the group to exist. Most sororities and frater- nities are formed because individuals share a common goal or interest. Groups and organizations like the Chess Club, Choral Club, Foreign Language Club, and Debating Society are formed by in- dividuals having a common interest in or are working toward common goals. In- dividuals lose interest in their groups and groups are dissolved when the group ex- perience is not rewarding or does not promote a common goal.

Why do individuals participate in groups? We believe the fundamental reason for joining and participating in a group is the satisfaction of individual needs. If you recall the discussion in the first chapter of this book, you will re- call our concept of self-interest. Com- bining that discussion with the reasons for joining a group, we find that one participates in a group to satisfy one's own self-interest.

There are several things about a group that can satisfy the self-interest of the individual. First, you can be attracted to the members of the group and thus want to be a part of the group. You may join a fraternity or sorority because many of your friends are already members. Peo- ple join groups because the "right" peo- ple are members.

A second reason for joining a group is that you may like the activities in which the group engages. You may select a group because its members party all of the time. You may join because they take interesting trips. You have probably seen the television advertisement for apartments which suggests their members have more fun than members of another housing complex. Finally, you may want to join a group because you agree with the goals of the group. You may join a political organization because you think it represents what is best for the country. Many people join service organizations because they like the goals of the group. We can select churches because we believe in the intentions of the organization.

You may select a group for any or all of the above reasons. The more reasons you have for joining a group, the more likely you are to want to remain a member of that group. You are indeed fortunate if you belong to a group which has people you like, activities you enjoy, and goals to which you aspire.

Group Function

Groups are generally formed to serve two functions. The first function a group can perform is that of decision making or problem solving. Hall, in his article on decisions, states that if a group were to define a horse, it might come out looking something like a camel. On the other hand, when we want decisions made and we want participation, we generally refer the decision-making process to some kind of committee or small group. The President of the United States has several groups serving in an advisory capacity which aid in the decisions that he must ultimately make. University departments are generally run by the chairperson acting with a group selected from the department or, in some cases if the department is small, with a group or committee of the whole. In some communication classes, the instructor may ask the class to discuss and decide how the class might be graded or what types of assignments might be made. In each case, the group's purpose is to serve in a *problem-solving capacity* in order to reach some kind of

a decision. We are saying then that the group has a task function to perform. Perhaps the best example of this kind of group is the jury in the courtroom Several movies and television programs have been produced which highlight drama of small group behavior. The jury has a specific task to perform in reaching a verdict. (See the last article in the last chapter on legal communication.)

The second function for a small group is that of providing for the social-emotional needs of the individual participants. The group aids in and supports the formation of attitudes and values. The function of the social-emotional group is not so much the collective decision-making process but the act of participating in and being part of the group.

Needless to say, the separation of the two functions can be made only on a theoretical level. Within each group you will find both the social-emotional function and the task orientation. Although a fraternity may exist to satisfy social-emotional needs, the group must perform certain task functions in order to survive. In fact, we can look at a group on the following continuum:

```
├──────────────────────────┤
```
Social-Emotional   Task Function
    Function

If you were to place groups on the continuum, your fraternity or sorority might be closer to the social emotional side, while a choral society might be viewed as a task-oriented group. Try to label some of the groups you belong to.

Leadership

No discussion of small group communication would be complete without talking about leadership within a group. What makes an effective leader? It is obvious that when we use democratic principles and elect one to serve as a leader, we make certain assumptions about the leader's ability and effectiveness. We said earlier that a group basically has two functions to serve. Leadership must also serve these two functions. A leader must serve the social-emotional function and the task function. In fact, we can say categorically that no group can exist effectively without a leader providing both of these functions.

In performing the task function, a leader must see that the group follows a given agenda, discusses the topic thoroughly, makes sure everyone participates, and ultimately—if it is a problem-solving group—find a solution to the problem. An effective group cannot function without someone in the group undertaking these task-oriented leadership functions.

On a social-emotional basis, a leader must make certain that the individuals in the group are cooperative, satisfied with their experience, and generally having their needs met by the group. Such behavior is commonly referred to as the social-emotional function of a group leader.

What is interesting about small group communication is that these functions are performed by one or more people in a group. Even if a group appoints a leader, a different person may serve as the task and/or social-emotional head of the group. There are numerous examples of groups that had leaders who failed to perform one or both of the functions and required others in the group to assume the leadership. Our point is that re-

gardless of the group, someone will assume these functions. Every group will have an individual to serve as the social-emotional leader and as the task leader.

There are two other observations that we want to make about small group leadership. A group can only be led when it wants to be. If a group decides to go in a direction different from that of the leader, the group will turn to another member for leadership. We are reminded of a group discussion in which the members elected a leader and made up an agenda of things they wanted to discuss before the rest of the class. During the discussion, the group (but not the leader) got interested in a different aspect of the topic, verbally removed the leader, and appointed someone else to continue the discussion. The leader can only lead a group that wants to be led.

Leadership is generally shared among all of the group members. Although it may be necessary to appoint or elect a person to get the group started, most effective groups work best when all members of the group know about leadership functions and can take over when necessary. This is not to imply that an effective group is a leaderless group. Rather, the effective group is the one where many members know the requirements of leadership and can assume this role whenever the group needs it.

We cannot leave a discussion of leadership without talking about the unique skills a leader should possess. A leader should possess all of the qualities that a good Boy Scout possesses, i.e., trustworthiness, loyalty, helpfulness, courteousness, kindness, etc. Research literature has not been very clear as to what qualities make a good leader, and most of the results have been inconsistent regarding leadership qualities. Nevertheless, we believe a good leader is sensitive to the members of the group and possesses skills in communication. These two qualities can help a person function effectively as a group leader.

Group Membership

Rather than discuss all types of members that any one group can have, we are going to summarize a number of the types of participants you can find in a group.

1. *Harmonizer*: Agrees with the rest of the group; brings together opposite points of view; accepts whatever the group decides to do; is not agressive toward others

2. *Encourager*: Friendly; responsive to others in the group; diplomatic; makes others feel good in the group; helps others make significant contributions

3. *Clarifier*: Restates the problem or solution in order to make it clearer to others; summarizes points after a discussion; introduces new or late members to the group by bringing them up to date on what has happened.

4. *Initiator*: Suggests possible procedures or problems or discussion topics when needed by the group; proposes alternate solutions; is the "idea person" for the group.

5. *Energizer*: Urges the group to make decisions; insists on covering proposed agenda; prods the group to take action and nail down decisions

6. *Questioner*: Asks questions; request clarification or repetition of idea or decisions for self or others; is constructive critic of the group o its members

7. *Listener*: Looks interested in what i going on even though he may b talking little or not at all; is in volved in what the group is doin and shows his interest by facia and bodily expressions

8. *Tension Reducer*: Helps the grou by joking or clowning at appropri ate times in meeting, thus makin other members feel more relaxed

9. *Opinion Giver*: States own belief o opinion about a certain point o problem or issue and gives own ex perience to illustrate the point

10. *Dominator*: Interrupts others; launch es on long monologues; is ove positive and over dogmatic; trie to lead the group and assert hi authority

11. *Negativist*: Rejects ideas suggested by others; takes a negative atti tude on issues; argues frequentl and unnecessarily; is pessimistic refuses to cooperate

12. *Deserter*: Withdraws from the group and its activities by being indif ferent, aloof, excessively formal daydreaming, doodling, whisper ing to others, wandering from the subject or talking about own ex perience when it is unrelated to the group discussion

13. *Aggressor*: Tries to achieve impor tance in the group; boasts, criti cizes or blames others; tries to get attention; shows anger or irrita tion against the group or individ-

uals; deflates importance or position of others in the group

How many of these types can you pick out from one of your class discussions? Do you have any of these types in other groups to which you belong? Which ones serve a useful function for the group and which ones are counterproductive to the group's goal? While the person who constantly questions the group and its goals is annoying, that same person can serve the role of the devil's advocate. Such a person can get the group to think about a problem in a different light. Even the devil's advocate can facilitate an effective group interaction.

Conclusions

We cannot conclude our discussion of small group communication without pointing out some of the similarities and differences of small group communication and interpersonal communication. The principles of attraction and risk taking, which were discussed in the last chapter, apply to small group communication and can occur in the small group setting. On the other hand, you have to deal with more than one person in the small group setting. If it is difficult to know the attitudes and values of one person, it becomes more complex to know the members of a group. While you have direct interaction with one person, you must be able to interpret the feedback of another person to you and the feedback of the rest of the group to your interaction with the other person. In interpersonal communication, the responsibility for communication is shared between two people. In small group communication, the responsibility can be spread out among all of the individ-

uals so that the burden (if you view it that way) is borne by all of the group members. While you can concentrate on one other person in interpersonal communication, such behavior would be viewed as monopolizing the conversation if it happened in a small group setting. If you and several of your friends are discussing the relative merits of going out for a pizza, you may have to suggest to one friend that you go out because you're hungry, say to a second that you go out for the friendship, and mention to a third that you want to get a beer. Each of these would be messages designed for specific members of the small group.

This observation leads to another difference between interpersonal and small group communication. While the amount of adapting you need to do in small group communication increases with the size of the group, the potential for feedback also increases. However, as the potential for more feedback from many people increases, the chances for them to voice the feedback may be less. Have you noticed when you're talking with friends how impossible it is for you to ease your thoughts into the conversation because everyone else is talking? This is what we mean when we say that the opportunity for the listener to present some kind of response to the speaker decreases as this listener moves into a small group setting. As we move into larger communication relationships, we'll find that the opportunity for feedback decreases even more.

Articles

The first article by Hall discusses one of the outcomes of small group communication. He describes situations in which decisions have been made by small groups. To test his concepts, he includes an exercise requiring small group decision making.

Shepherd discusses the features of a successful group. His article augments the material we have presented in this introductory section.

Finally, we have included a set of guidelines, developed by Hanson, of what to look for in groups. His questions can help you diagnose small group communication of others and your own. The thirty-four questions touch all of the topics we have described in this introduction and in the other articles in this section.

References

D. Cartwright and A. Zander, eds. *Group Dynamics: Research and Theory*, 2nd ed. (New York: Harper & Row, 1964).

Decisions, Decisions, Decisions

Jay Hall

A disgruntled group member once defined a camel as a horse put together by a committee. Group decisions often are frustrating and inadequate. All members want agreement, but they also want to make their own points heard. So they bargain, they compromise and the final product is often a potpourri that no group member really believes in. And when group members expect their decisions to be inadequate, they usually are—a self-fulfilling prophecy.

But the group process need not be so ineffective. I have found that when a group's final decision is compared to the independent points of view that the members held before entering the group, the group's effort is almost always an improvement over its average individual resource, and often it is better than even the best individual contribution.

A decision exercise that I developed to illustrate this potential is *Lost On The Moon*. Astronauts have crashlanded on the moon, and their mission is to reach the mother ship 200 miles away. The task is to rank 15 items according to how useful each would be to the lunar mission.

I got experts at National Aeronautics and Space Administration's Crew Equipment Re-

search Department to rank the 15 items for me, with the help of Matthew Radnofsky of NASA's Manned Spacecraft Center in Houston. So there is a correct solution to the *Lost On The Moon* task, or at least a *best* solution.

When individuals take the *Lost On The Moon* test on their own and then meet with three to seven other persons to produce a consensus on the test, the groups's decision may be better—closer to NASA's expert opinion—than any of the individual decisions had been.

Whether or not this happens depends on the ground rules that the group operates by. I have discovered several rules for group effectiveness in studying the behavior of thousands of small groups.

Movie. As a social-psychological consultant to industry I have conducted many seminars on group effectiveness for management executives. A favorite exercise in these seminars, developed by Robert R. Blake and a group of his graduate students, involves the movie *12 Angry Men*, a juryroom drama that is itself an excellent study of group behavior. It is a feature-length movie, released by United Artists, with superb verteran actors, including Henry Fonda, Lee J. Cobb and E. G. Marshall, and it allows viewers to go through a unique group-decision experience of their own.

The movie opens as 12 weary jurymen receive instructions from the judge in a murder trial, then file into the juryroom. It appears that their deliberations will be brief. They are eager for a quick verdict—it's a hot day, they are tired and close to agreement. They have heard overpowering testimony that the teen-aged defendant had killed his father with a knife.

They take an informal poll, and all are willing to vote "guilty" except one man—played by Henry Fonda. They continue to deliberate, and each man explains how he feels about the case. Many try to persuade the maverick juror to go along, E. G. Marshall, as a superobjective stockbroker, tallies all the facts in the case and concludes that it is obvious the boy is guilty. Still, says Fonda, there is a reasonable doubt.

After 38 minutes of movie time they take a second vote—this time by secret ballot, with Fonda abstaining. When the foreman (played by Martin Balsam) counts the slips of paper, there are 10 votes for "guilty" and one for "not guilty."

At this point I stop the movie.

Guess. "As you can see," I tell the audience, "one of the jurors has switched his vote to 'not guilty.' On the basis of what you have seen of the men—their occupations, their backgrounds, their apparent biases and personalities—I want you to guess which juror it was. By the end of the movie all of the jurors, one by one, have changed to 'not guilty.' Your task is to predict the order in which they will change their votes."

The viewers, already assigned to groups of five to eight members, have a seating chart of the jury to familiarize themselves with the film's characters. They rank Henry Fonda as juror number one, because he was the first to vote "not guilty." I instruct the subjects to rank each of the other jurors in the order in which he will change his vote.

The task is of course subjective and imprecise. But it is reasonable, because in the first 38 minutes of the film, scriptwriter Reginald Rose foreshadows the outcome by supplying insights into each juror. Jack Klugman, for example, reveals that he was raised in a slum environment similar to the defendant's. Ed Begley, as an overtly bigoted old garage-owner, is incredulous that anyone could fail to see guilt in the dark-skinned defendant. And Jack Warden implies that he will go along with any decision that will speed up the deliberations—he wants to go to a baseball game across town.

I tell the seminar subjects that they can have as much time as they want to make their individual rankings. They usually take 10 to 15 minutes. I then ask the subject to make the same judgments in their small groups—they must reach agreement and produce a group decision on the sequence in which the jurors will shift their votes.

Grist. In their small groups the subjects realize that they have developed different impressions of the 12 angry men. For example, Lee J. Cobb has revealed in the movie that his son, about the same age as the defendant, is cowardly, ungrateful and disrespectful. Some take this to mean that Cobb will therefore be one of the last to change because he is prejudiced against all young people. Others think that Cobb is brooding over his lost son and will atone for his own mistreatment of and lack of understanding for his son by giving the defendant a symbolic last chance. Still others argue, from a different perspective, that Cobb will be the last to change his vote because Hollywood filmmakers would want to save a famous star for a last dramatic hold-out of the movie. These arguments are grist for the decision mill. I give the groups as much time as they need to reach a decision. Most take about an hour. When every group has reached its final ranking the subjects reassemble and see the rest of the movie.

I score the individuals and group predictions for accuracy by error-points. For example, a subject who predicted that the baseball fan would be the ninth juror to switch would be off by two error-points, because the baseball fan was actually seventh. Another subject who said the baseball fan would be fifth would also be off by two points. The total score is the sum of all the error-points. The best possible score is zero, the worst is 60. The average individual score is about 22.

Continuity. The *12 Angry Men* task is an excellent research tool for investigating the group-decision process. In one of my experiments with this task I wanted to find whether groups assembled just for the experiment would be as effective as already-established groups in which the members knew each other's strengths and weaknesses. Martha Williams and I studied several established groups of business managers that had spent at least 50 hours together. Seven men who had worked together for several years in an office made up one group, for example, and five men who had served on a research committee made up another. We studied 20 such groups, and 20 ad-hoc groups made up of similar businessmen who had not worked together prior to the experiment.

The established and ad-hoc groups started with comparable resources—their average individual scores were about 23 error-points in each case. After discussions the ad-hoc groups improved their scores to 16.6 points, on the average, but the established groups improved significantly more, to 13.15.

There was also a clear difference in the ways the groups handled conflict. For example, one group might have members with individual scores ranging from 20 to 26, with an average of 23. Another might have the same average, with scores ranging from 10 to 40. The two groups would obviously have different levels of initial conflict.

We measured the degree of conflict within each of the 20 ad-hoc groups, and found that the 10 with the lowest internal conflict did slightly better than the 10 that had started with a wide range of opinions. In established groups, however, the amount of initial agreement was critical—the groups that started with great internal conflict did much better than groups with less conflict. A wide variety of opinions is beneficial to an established group, but disruptive to an ad-hoc group.

The reason, I believe, lies in the different ways people perceive and respond to conflict. Differences of opinion are not likely to be seen as particularly threatening to a group that is already well-established. Disagreements are seen as natural; they indicate a need for further discussion and offer a variety of alternative solutions, but they don't imply interpersonal hostility or threaten the integrity of the group.

But in a group of semistrangers the situation is different. Here there is no group commitment, and the cohesion is tenuous and temporary. Conflict threatens the group's already flimsy interpersonal structure, thus members try to smooth conflicts over rather than resolve them. When disagreement arises, the members of an ad-hoc group make quick compromises to get along with each other, or they resort to neutral, automatic solutions, such as majority rule. (It is possible, of course, for even cohesive groups to find it more important to get along than to find the best solution to a problem. When that happens, they are practicing what Irving Janis calls groupthink.)

Dealing. We analyzed the group data to see whether the groups actually had different ways of dealing with conflict. We found that groups faced with high internal conflicts tended to abandon the existing resources in the group and come up with *unique solutions*—choices that none of the members had originally held. For example if individual members of a group ranked the stockbroker as number two, number nine and number 11, the group might decide on a unique solution for the stockbroker and rank him number four. When we studied the unique solutions that our group came up with, we found that in established groups the unique solutions tended to be good ones—on the whole better than the average individual ratings. The unique solutions that ad-hoc groups produced, however, did not improve upon the resources already available in the group. The tendency to produce wildly inaccurate solutions was most pronounced in the ad-hoc groups that had great internal conflict.

In other words, unique solutions in the established groups tended to be *creative*; while in the ad-hoc groups the unique solutions were *compromises*.

As group members experience each other more and more, they seem to develop more effective ways to deal with conflict, and the group becomes more and more effective in making decisions. Established groups do not necessarily make quicker decisions (established groups and ad-hoc groups took about the same amount of time to reach agreement and the groups that finished quickly did no better or worse than groups that took a long time) but established groups make better, more accurate decisions. Still, the established groups were not as effective as they might have been.

Knowing this, I wondered whether it would be possible to train groups to be more effective. Martha Williams and I took advantage of several two-week laboratory programs in group dynamics designed to teach people the attitudes toward group action that we had observed in established groups. The programs taught the critical elements of group life with several exercises that allowed participants to confront and solve dilemmas in actual group practice.

To see whether these programs actually produced effective group members, we studied 51 college-student trainees. After the training sessions we let some of these subjects work in the same groups they had been in throughout training. We divided the other trainees into new ad-hoc groups just for the *12 Angry Men* task. We also tested 45 similar college students—some in established school groups and some in ad-hoc groups—who had not gone through the training programs

To find whether our results could be generalized to other populations, we also ran identical studies on 141 management executives—ranking from foreman to company president—and on 140 neuro-psychiatric patients who had been in hospitals for periods from several months to several years.

Synergy. In these studies we found that the ad-hoc or established nature of a group made little difference. More important was whether group members had undergone training in group effectiveness. Trained groups did significantly better than untrained groups. And although the three populations started out at different levels on the *12 Angry Men* task (the college students did better than the businessmen, and the businessmen did better than patients), group-effectiveness training was a leveler: trained

---

A Test—*Lost on the Moon*

Your spaceship has just crash-landed on the moon. You were scheduled to rendezvous with a mother ship 200 miles away on the lighted surface of the moon, but the rough landing has ruined your ship and destroyed all the equipment on board, except for the 15 items listed below.

Your crew's survival depends on reaching the mother ship, so you must choose the most critical items available for the 200-mile trip. Your task is to rank the 15 items in terms of importance for survival. Place number one by the most important item, number two by the second most important, and so on through number 15, the least important.

_____ Box of matches
_____ Food concentrate
_____ Fifty feet of nylon rope
_____ Parachute silk
_____ Solar-powered portable heating unit
_____ Two .45-caliber pistols
_____ One case of dehydrated milk
_____ Two 100-pound tanks of oxygen
_____ Stellar map (of the moon's constellation)
_____ Self-inflating life raft
_____ Magnetic compass
_____ Five gallons of water
_____ Signal flares
_____ First-aid kit containing injection needles
_____ Solar-powered FM receiver-transmitter

You and four to seven other persons should take this test individually, without knowing each other's answers, then take the test as a group. Share your individual solutions and reach a consensus—one ranking for each of the 15 items that best satisfies all group members. You should read the article, particularly the group-decision instructions on page 180 before taking the test as a group.

NASA experts have determined the best solution to this task. Their answers and reasoning are on page 181.

mental patients actually did better in groups than untrained business executives did.

We were especailly pleased to find that many trained groups did better than even their best individual members. We called this happy event *synergy*: the ability of a group to out perform even its own best individual resource. The ad-hoc groups achieved synergy about as often as the established groups did, but the lab-training program was more important—half of the trained groups achieved synergy, but only 13 per cent of the untrained groups did. Needless to say, we were encouraged by these results, but I wondered whether a full two-week lab program was necessary. Perhaps the lessons of the lab training could be learned more quickly.

I carefully studied several hundred groups to see whether there were typical behaviors that the most effective groups had in common and whether there were interfering strategies that characterized groups that did poorly.

I found that groups that had improved the most and scored the best consistently tried to get every member involved. They actively sought out the points of disagreement, and thus promoted conflicts, especially in the early stages. The most ineffective groups on the other hand, tended to use simple decision techniques, such as majority rule, averaging and bargaining. They seemed to feel a strain toward convergence, as if it were more important to complete the task than to come up with a decision they could all agree on. As one subject in a particularly inept group put it, "the members seemed more committed to reaching a decision than to committing themselves to the decision they reached."

Rules. When I summarized the behaviors of the most effective groups I found I could list all of the apparent decision rules in the form of instructions for group consensus on one typewritten page essentially as follows:

GROUP-DECISION INSTRUCTIONS

Consensus is a decision process for making full use of available resources and for resolving conflicts creatively. Consensus is difficult to reach, so not every ranking will meet with everyone's *complete* approval. Complete unanimity is not the goal—it is rarely achieved. But each individual should be able to accept the group rankings on the basis of logic and feasibility. When all group members feel this way, you have reached consensus as defined here, and the judgment may be entered as a group decision. This means, in effect, that a single person can block the group if he thinks it necessary; at the same time, he should use this option in the best sense of reciprocity. Here are some guidelines to use in achieving consensus:

1. Avoid arguing for your own rankings. Present your position as lucidly and logically as possible, but listen to the other members' reactions and consider them carefully before you press your point.
2. Do not assume that someone must win and someone must lose when discussion reaches a stalemate. Instead, look for the next-most-acceptable alternative for all parties.
3. Do not change your mind simply to avoid conflict and to reach agreement and harmony. When agreement seems to come too quickly and easily, be suspicious. Explore the reasons and be sure everyone accepts the solution for basically similar or complementary reasons. Yield only to positions that have objective and logically sound foundations.
4. Avoid conflict-reducing techniques such as majority vote, averages, coin-flips and bargaining. When a dissenting member finally agrees, don't feel that he must be rewarded by having his own way on some later point.
5. Differences of opinion are natural and expected. Seek them out and try to involve everyone in the decision process. Disagreements can help the group's decision because with a wide range of information and opinions, there is a greater chance that the group will hit upon more adequate solutions.

Test. These instructions seem to encapsulate the lessons that the trainees had learned in the two-week lab programs. I wondered whether untrained persons could become effective group members by simply reading the list of rules instead of going through the full training program. Fred Watson and I answered this question, using the *Lost On The Moon* exercise with 148 upper-management personnel from several business organizations. We separated the subjects randomly into 32 discussion groups of four to six members each. They worked on other group activities for about six hours before taking the *Lost On The Moon* test, so in terms of previous

ANSWERS TO TEST ON PAGE 179

Items	NASA's Reasoning	NASA's Ranks	Your Ranks	Error Points	Group Ranks	Error Points
Box of matches	No oxygen on moon to sustain flame virtually worthless	15				
Food concentrate	Efficient means of supplying energy requirements	4				
Fifty feet of nylon rope	Useful in scaling cliffs, tying injured together	6				
Parachute silk	Protection from sun's rays	8				
Solar-powered portable heating unit	Not needed unless on dark side	13				
Two 45-caliber pistols	Possible means of self-propulsion	11				
One case of dehydrated Pet milk	Bulkier duplication of food concentrate	12				
Two 100-pound tanks of oxygen	Most pressing survival need	1				
Stellar map (of the moon's constellation)	Primary means of navigation	3				
Self-inflating life raft	CO_2 bottle in military raft may be used for propulsion	9				
Magnetic compass	Magnetic field on moon is not polarized worthless for navigation	14				
Five gallons of water	Replacement for tremendous liquid loss on lighted side	2				
Signal flares	Distress signal when mother ship is sighted	10				
First-aid kit containing injection needles	Needles for vitamins, medicines, etc., will fit special aperture in NASA space suits	7				
Solar-powered FM receiver-transmitter	For communication with mother ship but FM requires line-of-sight transmission and short ranges	5				

Total _____

Scoring for Individuals

0–25 – excellent	56–70 – poor
26–32 – good	71–112 – very poor
33–45 – average	suggests possible faking or use
45–55 – fair	of earth-bound logic

Error points are the absolute difference between your ranks and NASA's (disregard plus or minus signs).

experience with each other, the groups were somewhere between the ad-hoc and established groups of our previous studies.

After all subjects had taken the test individually we had 16 of the groups go to their respective group meeting rooms to reach the best decisions they could. We gave the remaining 16 groups the simple instruction sheet and went over it briefly before they went to their meeting rooms.

The instructions were effective. The uninstructed groups, which started with average individual resources of 47.5 error points, produced final decisions averaging about 34 points. But the instructed groups improved significantly more—from 45 points as individuals to 26 points as groups.

Success. The most important factor that determined how well a group performed was the success of its unique judgments—those instances in which the group abandoned existing resources in favor of a new solution that they created for themselves. Both types of groups produced unique judgments on 27 per cent of their decisions. But the instructed groups created qualitatively better solutions than the uninstructed groups did. Thus, the uninstructed groups responded to internal conflict with compromises, which may have eased group tensions, but did not improve the group's decisions. Instructed groups, on the other hand, used conflict to their advantage as an opportunity for creativity.

Most of the instructed groups achieved synergy—75 per cent produced group decisions that surpassed even the best individual decisions. Only 25 per cent of the uninstructed groups did this.

Up. We reached two major conclusions from these studies; 1) that groups function as their members make them function, and 2) that conflict, effectively managed, is a necessary precondition for creativity. Thus, when they follow a few brief instructions, decision-making groups can be expected to do better than even their best members, at least on multiple-judgment tasks of the sort we have studied. There is nothing in the group process that makes committees, boards and panels inherently inept.

Ludicrous, ineffective solutions to problems are the product of groups that are pessimistic about their own potential, and have imperfect ways of dealing with conflict.

The horse that is put together by a committee that understands group dynamics won't turn out to be a camel; it may be a thoroughbred filly fit for the Triple Crown.

Features of the Successful Group

Clovis R. Shepherd

The following portrait of a successful group is provided in order to give the reader a model against which to assess his personal experiences and to indicate what the author feels is consistent with small group theory and research. It is a descriptive (as opposed to analytic) model and embodies discussion of some of the problems which confront groups.

The model includes five features of groups. These five features do not exhaust all descriptive categories but they do serve the purpose here reasonably well. These features are objectives, role differentiation, values and norms, membership, and communication. The meaning of these terms will become clearer as they are discussed.

Objectives refers to the goals of a group, its purposes, its reasons for existence, the ends it seeks, or whatever other term one may wish to use. Generally a successful group has clear objectives, not vague ones, and the members of the group have personal objectives which are identical or compatible with the group's objec-

tives. If the group's objectives are vague the members will probably be working at cross purposes since they are unlikely to have the same or compatible personal objectives. Consequently, the more time a group spends in developing agreement on clear objectives the less time it need spend in achieving them and the more likely the members' contributions will converge toward a solution.

Role differentiation refers to the clarity of the roles played by and expected of the members of the group, including whatever leadership roles exist. A successful group is one in which each member's role is clear and known to himself and to others in the group. It is also important that the official and unofficial leaders be known and that they function in ways to facilitate communication so that no member hesitates to contribute his ideas and feelings, and so that some degree of shared influence is present. The confusion when roles are unknown or unclear is obvious, but it is less obvious that the successful group is one in which role differentiation is clear and graded in terms of status and prestige. The popular notion that the democratic ideal is a group in which all members exert an equal amount of leadership may be a desirable ideology, but it has little support in research.

Clovis R. Shepherd, "Features of the Successful Group," in *Small Groups: Some Social Perspectives.* Copyright © 1964 by Chandler Publishing Company. Reprinted by permission of Thomas Y. Crowell Company.

Values and norms deal, respectively, with the desirable and with the expected. A value is something desired or wanted by a person, something believed in. In everyday life a value is usually signified by one or more of the following verbs: believe, desire, wish, want, value, or prefer. A norm is a rule governing behavior, established and enforced by a group (or by some collectivity). Some of the verbs used in everyday life to denote a norm are: ought, should, must, or better.

Values, although an individual phenomenon and, hence, apt to differ among any collection of persons, are similar in at least some ways in a successful group. Having similar values may not (and probably does not) stem from members influencing each other, but from members discovering that they already hold some values in common. A group in which members do not share at least some relevant values is likely to be successful only for limited and short-run objectives. Though some differences in values may be present in a successful group, very little difference in norms can be tolerated. To be sure, some varaiation in general social norms is possible (people have different backgrounds and group affiliations), but the norms that develop in the group to govern the behavior of its members must be agreed upon. These group norms refer to procedure, including how decisions are to be made and implemented, as well as to the roles of the members. In a successful group these norms of various types are clear and agreed upon, and the group takes action through consensus, not through majority vote or minority railroading. Values and norms, though different, shade into each other at some point, especially when people try to justify a norm, since their justification often turns out to be that the norm is consistent with or contributes to some shared value.

Membership in a successful group is clearcut and members are heterogeneous. Clarity in membership criteria helps continuity, commitment, and the development of group structure and process. Membership criteria, when made explicit, also involve attention to other features

of the group, since at least some membership criteria will be relevant to the nature of the group's objectives, its values and norms, and its role differentiation. Heterogencity in the group refers to diverse skills, experience, and interest, factors which will encourage role differentiation and flexibility in functioning. Few things destroy or incapacitate a group more than discontinuity or homogeneity in membership. Too much heterogencity, however, may make it impossible to agree on shared values, much less accept norms. Of course, a successful group can absorb some discontinuity—it will likely have to weather the loss of a member or two and the admittance of a newcomer or two.

Communication in a successful group is open and full. No one withholds relevant information, whether it be ideas or feelings, and each member provides that information when appropriate. In addition, at least some biographical information becomes shared, since open and full communication includes nonverbal as well as verbal responses. It is possible, of course, that some relevant information will be withheld, especially when disruptive consequences may occur. No husband tells his wife everything, nor do members of a successful group act solely on impluse. On the other hand, in a successful group no member withholds information because he is frightened, anxious, disgusted, or curious to see what will happen when he finally drops his bomb or quietly provides crucial information after the rest of the group has gone down some divergent path.

These five features, of course, do not exhaust relevant characteristics of groups. No mention has been made of cohesion, an admittedly important feature, nor of productivity, equally important. Cohesion and productivity are, in a sense, outcomes of a group. Cohesion is an internal product which, in a successful group, is likely to be high. Productivity is partly an external product, the contribution or output of a group, which is also likely to be high in a successful group. So, in effect, the above five features of a successful group are features of a group with high cohesion and high productivity. Or, to put it another way, the definition of a successful group is a group with high cohesion and high productivity, in which objectives, role differentiation, values and norms, and membership criteria are clear and agreed upon, and in which communication is open and full.

Finally, some mention must be made of another feature of groups, their autonomy—their degree of freedom from control or influence by other groups or persons. A group of high autonomy is apt to be a fairly successful group since there are few if any external forces maintaining it. If members do not have to be in the group, or the group need not exist, its very existence is some testimony to the presence of shared objectives and shared values and norms. Also, since no forces external to the group have organized it, whatever organization exists is likely to be a spontaneous, evolved product. This kind of origin means that the developing character of the group is considered desirable by the members if it continues to exist. On the other hand, a group of low autonomy is confronted at first with an organization—with objectives, roles, values and norms, membership criteria, and communication styles already established. But merely because they are established does not mean that they are understood or accepted by the group. Having them, a group of low autonomy can appear to be successful when, in fact, it is not.

What to Look for in Groups

Philip G. Hanson

In all human interactions there are two major ingredients: content and process. The first deals with subject matter of the task upon which the group is working. In most interactions, the focus of attention of all persons is on the content. The second ingredient, process, is concerned with what is happening between and to group members while the group is working. Group process or dynamics deals with such items as morale, feeling tone, atmosphere, influences, participation, styles of leadership, leadership struggles, conflict, competition, cooperation, etc. In most interactions, very little attention is paid to process, even when it is the major cause of ineffective group action. Sensitivity to group process will better enable one to diagnose group problems early and deal with them more effectively. Since these processes are present in all groups, awareness of them will enhance a person's worth to a group and make him a more effective group participant.

. . . Some observation guidelines to help one process analyze group behavior (follow).

Reprinted from J. William Pfeiffer and John E. Jones (eds.), *The 1972 Annual Handbook for Group Facilitators*. La Jolla, Calif.: University Associates, 1972. Used with permission.

Participation

One indication of involvement is verbal participation. Look for differences in the amount of participation among members.

1. Who are the high participators?
2. Who are the low participators?
3. Do you see any shift in participation, e.g., highs become quiet; lows suddenly become talkative? Do you see any possible reason for this in the group's interaction?
4. How are the silent people treated? How is their silence interpreted? Consent? Disagreement? Disinterest? Fear? etc.
5. Who talks to whom? Do you see any reason for this in the group's interactions?
6. Who keeps the ball rolling? Why? Do you see any reason for this in the group's interactions?

Influence

Influence and participation are not the same. Some people may speak very little yet they capture the attention of the whole group. Others may talk a lot but are generally not listened to by other members. What to look for in groups.

7. Which members are high in influence?

186

That is, when they talk, others seem to listen.

8. Which members are low in influence? Others do not listen to or follow them. Is there any shifting in influence? Who shifts?

9. Do you see any rivalry in the group? Is there a struggle for leadership? What effect does it have on other group members?

Many kinds of decisions are made in groups without considering the effects of these decisions on other members. Some people try to impose their own decisions on the group, while others want all members to participate or share in the decisions that are made.

10. Does anyone make a decision and carry it out without checking with other group members? (Self authorized) For example, he decides on the topic to be discussed and starts right in to talk about it. What effect does this have on other group members?

11. Does the group drift from topic to topic? Who's topic jumps? Do you see any reason for this in the group's interactions?

12. Who supports other members suggestions or decisions? Does this support result in the two members deciding the topic or activity for the group? (Handclasp) How does this affect other group member?

13. Is there any evidence of a majority pushing a decision through over other members objections? Do they call for a vote? (Majority decision)

14. Is there any attempt to get all members participating in a decision (Consensus)? What effect does this seem to have on the group?

15. Does anyone make any contributions which do not receive any kind of response or recognition (Plop)? What effect does this have on the member?

Task Functions

These functions illustrate behaviors that are concerned with getting the job done, or accomplishing the task that the group has before them.

16. Does anyone ask for or make suggestions as to the best way to proceed or to tackle a problem?

17. Does anyone attempt to summarize what has been covered or what has been going on in the group?

What to look for in groups:

18. Is there any giving or asking for facts, ideas, opinions, feeling, feedback, or searching for alternatives?

19. Who keeps the group on target? Prevents topic jumping or going off on tangents?

Maintenance Functions

These functions are important to the morale of the group. They maintain good and harmonious working relationships among the members and create a good atmosphere which enables each member to contribute maximally. They insure smooth and effective team work within the group.

20. Who helps others get into the discussion (gate openers)?

21. Who cuts off others or interrupts them (gate closers)?

22. How well are members getting their ideas across? Are some members preoccupied and not listening? Are there any attempts by group members to help others clarify their ideas?

23. How are ideas rejected? How do members react when their ideas are not accepted? Do members attempt to support others when they reject their ideas?

Group Atmosphere

Something about the way a group works creates an atmosphere which in turn is revealed in a general impression. In addition, people may differ in the kind of atmosphere they like in a group. Insight can be gained into the atmosphere characteristic of a group by finding words which describe the general impressions held by group members.

24. Who seems to prefer a friendly congenial atmosphere? Is there any attempt to suppress conflict or unpleasant feelings?
25. Who seems to prefer an atmosphere of conflict and disagreement? Do any members provoke or annoy others?
26. Do people seem involved and interested? Is the atmosphere one of work, play, satisfaction, taking flight, sluggish, etc.?

Membership

A major concern for group members is the degree of acceptance or inclusion in the group. Different patterns of interaction may develop in the group which give clues to the degree and kind of membership?

27. Is there any sub-grouping? Sometimes two or three members may consistently agree and support each other or consistently disagree and oppose one another.

What to look for in groups:

28. Do some people seem to be "outside" the group? Do some members seem to be most "in"? How are those "outside" treated?
29. Do some members move in and out of the group? Under what conditions do they come in or move out?

Feelings

During any group discussion feelings are frequently generated by the interactions between members. These feelings, however, are seldom talked about. Observers may have to make guesses on tone of voice, facial expressions, gestures, and many other forms of nonverbal cues.

30. What signs of feelings do you observe in group members? Anger, irritation, frustration, warmth, affection, excitement, boredom, defensiveness, competitiveness, etc.
31. Do you see any attempts by group members to block the expression of feelings, particularly negative feelings; How is this done? Does anyone do this consistently?

Norm

Standards or ground rules may develop in a group that control the behavior of its members. Norms usually express the beliefs or desires of the majority of the group members as to what behaviors *should* or *should not* take place in the group. These norms may be clear to all members (explicit), known or sensed by only a few (implicit), or operating completely below the level of awareness of any group members. Some norms help group progress and some hinder it.

32. Are certain areas avoided in the group (e.g., sex, religion, talk about present feelings in the group, discussing leader's behavior, etc.)? Who seems to reinforce this avoidance? How do they do it?
33. Are group members overly nice to each other? Are only positive feelings expressed? Do members agree with each other too readily? What happens when members disagree?
34. Do you see norms operating about participation or the kinds of questions that are allowed? (e.g., "If I talk you must talk," "If I tell my problems you have to tell your problems.") Do members feel free to probe each other about their feelings? Do questions tend to be restricted to intellectual topics or events outside of the group?

Eight
Public Communication

Formerly, the common term for the event of public speaking was oratory. King (1948) summarized much of the feeling surrounding oratory.

> Oratory is the greatest art known to man and embraces a number of great arts. In music tradition furnishes the ideas. The poet clothes them in words. The composer sets these to music, and the singer renders them into song. The orator must be able to do all these things. He must furnish the ideas, he must clothe them in words, he must give these a rhythmic arrangement, and he must deliver them with all the care with which a singer sings a song. Each of these elements is of supreme importance. The ideas must be right and seem alive. The language must be chaste and expressive. The arrangement must be logical, natural and effective. There must be a natural unfolding of the subject matter.

A few years ago research indicated that most basic courses in communication were taught from the public speaking format (Gibson, et al. 1970). Students were taught that there were five kinds of speeches (to inform, persuade, stimulate, convince, and entertain) and practiced preparing and delivering them.

It did not take much longer for the cry to run throughout the university, "What's the relevance of public speaking?" Many argued that attention should be devoted more to everyday interactions between people than to public speaking. Public speaking was something of the past. In modern times the likelihood of students giving speeches was very slight. This approach gained considerable support, and today throughout the nation many colleges and universities no longer teach public speaking in their basic course.

The defenders of public speaking argue from many fronts. Some pointed out that the field of speech was traditionally based upon public address, and we need to study the foundations of good speech making for good citizenship. This argument was grounded in the assumption that citizen participation in government is partly founded upon the citizen's ability to communicate effectively in public. Others argue that the training one receives from sound speech preparation and presentation carries over to other forms of discourse. The one-to-one small group and mass communication situations are mini- and macro-representations of public speaking. The principles of invention (coming up with ideas); arrangements (the organization of the ideas into a clear, concise manner); style (the language chosen to express the ideas); delivery (the manner and gestures used by the speaker when presenting the message); and memory (the ability of the speaker to recall not only the entire speech without aid or with minimal aid but also previous experiences which relate to material contained within the speech) prove to be useful in all walks of life as well as other communication situations. Still others contested that public speaking is not fading into the past. They pointed out that many students are called upon later in life to speak (1) in behalf of their business interests, (2) to parent-teacher organizations in support of their children's education, (3) to county councilmen, and (4) to a whole host of other people and organizations. Thus, there is still relevancy for public speaking in the twentieth century.

We think that there is room for both perspectives. However, there is more to public communication than the preparation and presentation of speeches. Communication implies the interaction of at least two people. Public communication is the interaction between a speaker who has prepared a formal message and the audience. The interaction is usually referred to as feedback. Audience analysis means more than determining prior knowledge about your audience and designing a message for them. It also implies that throughout the entire speech presentation the speaker will analyze the nonverbal communication from the lis-

teners and adapt the message accordingly.

Public communication also suggests that the listeners assume some responsibility in the acceptance of a public message. Good listeners need to constantly evaluate what public speakers are saying. If you avoid active participation as listeners, too often you will become duped into believing untruths. Through the process of evaluation, listeners improve their ability to detect fraud. Perhaps former President Nixon might not have stayed in office as long as he did if more people had listened more closely to what he did and did not say.

Stephen Toulmin (1968), a British philosopher, developed a method of reasoning which can be used in everyday communication. With some modifications it looks like this.

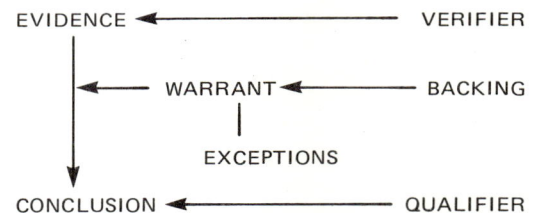

Evidence: Statements which are used to support conclusions
Verifier: Statements which support the probable truth or soundness of the items of evidence
Warrant: An influence license which allows one to move from evidence to a conclusion
Backing: Statements which support the probable truth or soundness of the warrant
Exceptions: Indicates the times in the situation discussed when the warrant is not true
Conclusion: Statements the speaker wants the audience to accept
Qualifier: Words or phrases which reflect the degree of confidence of the conclusion

The purpose of speaking before an audience is to have them accept what you are saying. Those things you want them to accept are your conclusions. If you said that "most of the time bicycle riders avoid using the bike paths," the qualifier to this conclusion is "most." The conclusion is limited because there are times, implied within the statement, when the bicycle riders use the bike paths. Using the subject of bicycle paths, it is also possible to demonstrate what a warrant is. As defined, a warrant is an inference license. This means it is the reasoning which permits one to move from some form of evidence to a conclusion. For example, suppose a speaker was arguing that "bicycle riders are dangerous when riding on the malls." The speaker might cite some campus police statistics of the number of serious accidents that result from bicycle riders journeying across the campus on the malls. The inference license permitting the speaker to draw his conclusion is: "whenever people are injured by bicyclists, the bicyclists prove to be a danger." However, an exception to this warrant might be: "unless the person injured causes the injury by not looking where he or she is walking."

Verifiers and backings are statements that support the probable truth or soundness of the evidence and warrant. Many times a list of a person's qualifications acts as the verifier of evidence. Additionally, citing previous times the warrant proved to be reasonable serves as backing.

One thing we have to carefully evaluate is the evidence provided in a speech. Sometimes speakers avoid support for their conclusions. We should be cautious in accepting these types of conclusions. Evidence is found in the form of (1) statistics, (2) factual examples, (3) testimony of lay witnesses, (4) opinions of au-

thorities, and (5) documents and legal papers. Evidence is that material which the speaker brings to the speech to support the conclusions and those items the speaker wants the listener to accept. When evaluating a speech, listen for each of these items. If they are not present or are unacceptable, be cautious in endorsing the speaker's conclusions.

It should be realized that speakers usually start off with their evidence and lead their audience to their conclusion. This is most often done with audiences who might oppose the speaker's point of view. However, it is easier for a listener to evaluate things in reverse. This way the listener knows what the speaker wants the listener to accept and can trace back the qualifiers, warrants, evidence, etc. Unfortunately, it is difficult to do when the speaking is ongoing. Thus, the listener should hold in check any judgment of the evidence and warrant until the conclusion is heard.

See if you can now identify the elements within the Toulmin method in the following examples. Take care to note that not all seven elements are always present.

1. "Yesterday I saw a moving truck pick up the Harris' furniture. Since the truck had an inscription on the side, "A. B. C. Moving," I assumed that Mr. Harris had obtained a new job. How was I to know that it was a group of burglars?"

2. "You won't believe this, Jane. Last night I was at the drive-in theatre with Pete and I saw Betty with some strange guy. I guess Betty and Tom must have had a fight."

3. "This morning I was reading my local newspaper and noticed that the F.B.I. Crime Report said that crime in our city had risen over 25 percent in the past

three months. You know, it simply is not safe to venture out of your house anymore."

See how often people avoid mentioning their warrants.

Critical listeners also become more knowledgeable about the world in which they live. Public speaking is usually centered around some information that the speaker has and wants to share with an audience. In order to be successful in persuading an audience toward a particular point of view, the speaker needs to marshall his or her support to prove all the points. The perceptive listener can learn from this information.

The sound audience member can gain some new ideas about what are and are not effective communication techniques. Although former President John Kennedy was president more than fifteen years ago and many of us can't remember what he did, few of us can ever forget his phrase, "Ask not what your country can do for you, ask what you can do for your country." This is a persuasive technique where the speaker tells you what not to think or do and follows with the positive thought or course of action.

There is a whole host of other things you can learn from public speeches, but it is also important to know what bad habits to avoid. If, by chance, you encounter a speaker who paces back and forth throughout his or her entire speech and you notice how distracting it is, you have learned a behavior to avoid while speaking yourself. Chances are that if something proves distracting to you, it will also distract other audience members. There is absolutely nothing wrong with learning from others. It is the principle way we are taught new things.

When listening to a speaker about whom you have previously drawn conclusions, be aware that your evaluation of this speech will be affected. This is called the Halo Effect. It recognizes that if you think a person is either good or bad outside the speech, your evaluation of their speaking and speech will be biased by this feeling. While we realize it is difficult for you to hold your feelings in check, you have to make some attempt. Think about the speeches you may hear in your class or other classes. Do you judge the better-liked students to be better speakers? Do you like the better-known students? This also applies to oral performances in terms of oral reports. These are things that usually happen.

Articles

We have devoted much of our discussion to the evaluation by the listener in public discourse. The focus of the articles is designed more for the benefit of the speaker. The first article by Bramer dwells on the principle intent of public speaking: the seeking of truth and harmony in the world in which we live. Notice the different rhetorical theories discussed. Perhaps it would be valuable to point out that the classical definition of *rhetoric* was the art of persuasion—beautiful and just.

The next three articles give other helpful hints to the speaker. After reading and assimilating them, create your own summary listing. Do you have any new ideas for preparing and delivering a speech? While this information will not guarantee that you will be able to give a dynamite speech, it nevertheless should provide more insight into what needs to be done and what other people attempt to do.

References

J. W. Gibson, C. R. Gruner, W. D. Brooks, and C. R. Petrie, Jr., "The First Course in Speech: A Survey of U.S. Colleges and Universities," *Speech Teacher*, 19 (1970).

M. P. King, "Oratory," in *Leaves of Gold*, C. F. Lytle, ed. (Williamsport, Pa.: Coslet Publishing Co., 1948).

S. Toulmin, *The Use of Argument* (Cambridge, England: Cambridge University Press, 1958).

Truth and Harmony as Rhetorical Goals

George R. Bramer

In the revival of rhetoric that has been going on in American schools during the past several years, perhaps too little attention has been given to the ultimate purposes or goals of rhetoric. Certainly we cannot talk about adapting discourse to its ends, or about the relevance of rhetoric for the schools, unless we identify those purposes or goals. I want to suggest that the best purposes of rhetoric are to communicate truth and to achieve harmony, and that it is precisely those goals which give rhetoric its greatest relevance in the schools. If teachers can agree with that suggestion, they can begin to show students how to adapt their writing to those ends.

Aristotle, and the main rhetorical tradition after him, have conceived of the purpose of rhetoric as persuasion. Cicero mentioned other purposes—to teach and delight. George Campbell in the eighteenth century, in a position reminiscent of Cicero's, suggested that rhetoric could have purposes besides persuasion, and helped prepare the way for nineteenth- and twentieth-century four-forms-of-discourse rhet-orics—those which define the functions of rhetoric as description, narration, and exposition in addition to persuasion.[1] In our time I. A. Richards has insisted on the expository function, considering rhetoric the "study of misunderstanding and its remedies."[2] And Kenneth Burke has seen the end of rhetoric as "identification," "cooperation," or even "consubstantiality."[3]

A combination of the views of Richards and Burke, I think, might be more adequate than either view alone. Richards stresses grasp of the truth (understanding), while Burke stresses harmony, as the goal of rhetoric. A merger of their two emphases would produce a rhetoric of truth and harmony.

If we assume that the two basic ideals of humans in their interrelationships are love and truth (corresponding roughly to will and intellect), we can posit a theory of rhetorical goals, and a set of rhetorical modes, related to the

[1] *The Philosophy of Rhetoric*, as partially reprinted in James L. Golden and Edward P. J. Corbett, eds., *The Rhetoric of Blair, Campbell, and Whately* (New York: Holt, Rinehart and Winston, Inc., 1968), p. 145.

[2] *The Philosophy of Rhetoric* (New York: A Galaxy Book, Oxford University Press, 1965), pp. 24 and 3.

[3] *A Rhetoric of Motives* (New York: Prentice-Hall, Inc., 1950), pp. 20-27.

ideals. We can conceive of rhetorics of love and truth, and others of pseudo-love and psuedo-truth. I will call them rhetoric of harmony and rhetoric of dissent, sentimental rhetoric and rhetoric of abuse.

Sentimental rhetoric expresses enthusiasm not warranted by the facts. It may affirm a condition of harmony where actually there is conflict. It often prefers the unexamined spontaneous "consensus" to methodical polling, and glories in "unanimous" decisions. Frequent in its vocabulary are *we* and *ours* and other expressions which can intimidate dissenters. Given an adequately chauvinstic audience, any honorific generalization might work. It could be *American, Christian, intellectual, VW owner.* This rhetoric can also protect wayward members of the group before outsiders; it often says there is "no trouble here." When the president of a middle-caliber university says, "We defer to no one in the quality of our education," when student protesters claim their food strikes and dormitory raids are expressions of "school spirit," when politicians and athletes say, "We're going to win," the audience is being given one kind or another of sentimental rhetoric.

Just as sentimental rhetoric can appear to work for harmony and love, rhetoric of abuse can appear to work for truth. Actually it emphasizes conflicts unnecessarily and creates them unjustly. It can employ pejorative generalizations: *troublemaker, sellout, radical, establishment, militant, up-tight.* Frequently it indulges in reckless imputation of ulterior motives. An SDS leaflet distributed last summer at a blues festival in Ann Arbor, Michigan, called Chicago "Pig City" and a "festering American wound," and referred to "our 'government' of vampire rules." Often language of the New Left is even stronger, but rhetoric of abuse is not limited to dissident groups. What else is a phrase like "effete corps of imprudent snobs"? And what else is much of Max Rafferty's language? He has referred to the SDS membership as "slovenly and slobbish" and as "bully-boys,"

and he has suggested that movie houses in this country currently are not fit to enter for people who are not "satyrs, nymphomaniacs, homosexuals, or saddist."[4] Dissent and rebuttal are important in a free society, but they should embody fact and logic rather than negative feeling.

Rhetoric of dissent makes distinctions and defines differences. If it creates conflict, it is only because of irrational response to it. It can occur as an abstaining vote, a dissenting vote, a sober minority report, or a rational public protest or censure. When inadequate procedures or means seem destructive of common purposes or ends, it focuses on the inadequacies. It might point out discrepancies between policy statements and performance. It could ask if a university's national advertisement claiming an atmosphere of free expression and boasting of efforts by its faculty and students against tryanny was consistent with the lack of grievance committees for students and faculty members.

Perhaps less factual and logical than rhetoric of dissent is rhetoric of harmony. It affirms likenesses and strengthens common bonds. It can transcend differences and conflict, define honorable compromise, and disregard irrelevant flaws. When the actual is divisive, it can ascend a ladder of abstraction to the cohesive ideal. At a time of national crisis it might call for a united, nonpartisan stand. It might rise above squabbling in a social agency by referring to the common altruistic aim of its employees.

Obviously the sentimental and abuse rhetorics would conflict with those of harmoy and dissent, since the spurious always conflicts with the genuine. No less insignificant, however, is the apparent conflict between the rhetorics of harmony and dissent, of love and truth. Truth sometimes is compromised in the effort to establish or preserve harmony, and harmony sometimes is disturbed by unpleasant truths. Adults sometimes urge children to abuse truth for the sake of harmony. "Tell Tommy you're

4"New Teen a Mr. Clean," *The Omaha World-Herald* (June 22, 1969) 13-B.

sorry you hit him." "Tell him we're not at home." Tell her you enjoyed the party." Children sometimes disrupt harmony by their candor. They refer to others' physical defects, ask the neighbors how much money they make, and tell relatives what has been said about them in their absence. Gradually young people learn that truth is often considered offensive, while untruth is often accepted as a means of making or maintaining peace or love. They may learn to implement a double standard, glorifying disruptive disagreement with adult authorities but suppressing or punishing dissent within their own circles.

The association of truth with dissent, and the suggestion that love and harmony are something separate from truth, may seem unacceptable. It might be asked if truth cannot produce agreement or harmony as well as disagreement or division. The answer should be yes. In spelling out degrees of love in Plato's *Symposium*, Socrates suggests that the highest is contemplation of Beauty, that is, knowledge or understanding. In the ideal world harmony could result automatically from general contemplation of the truth. In a sense, truth and love could be the same thing.

In our real, imperfect world, however, love or harmony does not flow automatically from truth. In fact, virtually every truth seems at least potentially divisive in a pluralistic society. Abuse and sentimental rhetorics are both untrue rhetorics, of course, and are destructive. But it seems possible, and even necessary, to conceive of a constructive rhetoric of harmony which might do some violence to truth. The line between harmony and sentimental rhetorics could easily become blurred, then, and could be kept clear and sharp only by the closest vigilance and the most sensitive application of situation ethics. Even then, any legitimate violation of truth done in the interest of harmony should ultimately yield to a challenge issued in the quest for truth. Granting that truth and harmony are both important goals of rhetoric, then, the effort to adapt discourse to its ends can become very complex and difficult.

The theory of rhetorical modes being posited, liked the theories of Richards and Burke to which it is related, has its basis in semantics. The implementation of it in the classroom would emphasize word meanings and word choices. Thus, the theory and the pedagogical practice would run counter to some of the main forces in the current revival of rhetoric. If we think of three dimensions in language study—formal, functional, and semantic—we can see that the emphases in the revival of rhetoric have been on the functional and the formal. The revivers of classical rhetoric stress such functional concepts as the topics of invention (definition, comparison, exemplification and the like), and the functional parts of classical arrangement (proem or introduction, *confirmatio* and *refutatio* or body, *peroratio* or conclusion). In 1959 Daniel Fogarty developed the thesis that roots for a new rhetoric lay in Richards, Burke, and General Semantics.[5] But most of those who have sought new rhetorics in the revival of the discipline, have concentrated on formal or structural matters, often showing the influence of structural linguistics and modern grammar. Francis Christensen explores paragraph structures according to the principles he discovered in his study of contemporary sentence structures; the tagmemists take the key concept in their slot-and-filler grammer, the tagmeme, and build a theory of paragraph structures on it. W. Ross Winterowd has focused on the concept of form in prose discourse, asserting that a contemporary rhetorician must grasp generative grammar, and leaving "semantics to the semanticists." Richard Ohmann has looked to transformational grammar for new enlightenment in the study of style.[6] None of those inquiries or ideas seems ultimately as important as S. I.

[5] *Roots for a New Rhetoric* (New York: Teachers College, Columbia University, 1959).

[6] Christensen, "A Generative Rhetoric of the Paragraph," *CCC*, 16 (1965) 144–56; A. L. Becker, "A Tagmemic Approach to Paragraph Analysis," *CCC* 16 (1965) 237–42; Winterowd, *Rhetoric: A Synthesis* (New York: Holt, Rinehart and Winston, Inc., 1968), pp. 103 and 88; Ohmann, "Generative Grammars and the Concept of Literary Style," *Word*, 20 (1964) 423–39, reprinted in Martin Steinmann, Jr., ed., *New*

Hayakawa's identification of words that snarl and words that purr, or Richard Weaver's study of god terms and devil terms.[7]

Charlton Laird wrote in a recent article, "I question whether organizations like the NCTE and the CCCC should have spent so much time talking about grammar and structure and so little talking about vocabulary and meaning."[8] The structures of sentences, paragraphs, and larger units are fascinating and important concerns for the teacher and student of writing. But I think most people know instinctively that the qualities of words are humanly more significant than the structures of all those larger units of discourse. If you call someone a hoodlum, a fool, a bastard, or a pud (I learned the last one from my eighth-grader son), it doesn't matter how you manage your consolidation or embedding of kernel sentences, whether you do it in a T-R-I or a P-S paragraph, or whether your essay has a proem or not. You're using a devil term, and the other person will assume you're snarling at him.

The offensive term has pejorative connotations. The distinction between denotation and connotation is surely one of the semanticist's most important concepts. Another is the distinction between abstract and concrete. Those two distinctions can be the basis of an approach to rhetoric which would be both relevant in the classroom and useful to the teacher.

Leo Rockas has built a theory of rhetorical modes on the distinction between abstract and concrete.[9] It has been more or less neglected in the revival of rhetoric. You will not find it represented, for example, in prominent efforts to select and list representative writings on rhetoric.[10] But the system deserves more attention, if only because it seems to have grown out of some fascinating classroom experiences Rockas has had, and suggests a way to bring some life and interest into composition teaching. However, Rockas has not explored the implications for truth and harmony of the abstract and the concrete. Moreover, I think the other fundamental distinction of the semanticists, that between denotation and connotation, is more promising as the chief basis of a vital rhetoric theory, pedagogy, and practice.

Without trying to cover all the theoretical ground involved, it is fair to say that the denotation of a word has some relation to something existing in the "extensional" order, or in the objective world, while the connotation has some relation to something in the "intensional" order, or within one's subjective self. One could distinguish relatively objective from relatively subjective uses of language, then, and emphasize that distinction in his teaching and writing. He would not overlook what is to be learned from the distinction between abstract and concrete, certainly, or for that matter what is to be learned from studying prose structures and functional resources. But I think he would find that the goals of truth and harmony could best be served by exploration of the semantic dimension of discourse, especially the distinction between objective and subjective.

A study of the semantic dimension does not limit one to a study of isolated words. In the effort to identify the characteristics of objective and subjective writing, one would make distinctions between kinds of sentences and larger units as well as kinds of words. Objective sentences

Rhetorics (New York: Charles Scribner's Sons, 1967), pp. 134–60.

[7]Hayakawa, *Language in Thought and Action* (New York: Harcourt, Brace and Company, 1949), pp. 44–46; Weaver, *The Ethics of Rhetoric* (Chicago: Henry Regnery Company, 1953), pp. 212 and 222.

[8]"A Simpleminded Look at Language and Grammar," *CCC*, 20 (October 1969) 184.

[9]*Modes of Rhetoric* (New York: St. Martin's Press, 1964), esp. pp. 1–13.

[10]It does not appear in Dudley Bailey, ed., *Essays on Rhetoric* (New York: Oxford University Press, 1965); Eugene H. Smith, ed., *Rhetoric and School Programs* (Champaign, Illinois, 1966); Robert M. Gorrell, ed., *Rhetoric: Theories for Application* (Champaign, Illinois, 1967); Steinmann, ed., *New Rhetorics*; Richard Larson, ed., *Rhetoric* (New York: The Bobbs-Merrill Company, Inc., 1968); or Edward P. J. Corbett, "A Basic Bibliography on Rhetoric Prepared for the NCTE/ERIC Clearinghouse on the Teaching of English" (n.d.).

would be factual (verified or verifiable), subjective sentences unfactual (demonstrably false or unverifiable). Objective larger units would be logical, and subjective larger units illogical or perhaps alogical.

The contrast between objective and subjective language has not been overlooked by teachers and authors of textbooks, of course. But often it is not given much attention except in an isolated unit on fact and opinion, and many students seem not to have grasped the unit. Possibily a program which made that distinction central, both in rhetoric theory and instructional effort, would produce writers more able, and even more determined to implement it.

It seems that the ideas of denotation and connotation may be more valuable than those of abstract and concrete (or general and specific) in teaching a rhetroic of truth, since denotation is almost synonymous with factualness or objectivity. However, the more specific or concrete our utterances, the closer to objective fact, also. And many ambiguities destructive or suppresive of truth are set in abstract terms. For example, in the recent October 15 Moratorium to protest this country's role in Vietnam, many persons "participated" because they "want peace." Whether or not many of them were protesting this country's role was left indefinite.

Often those ambiguous abstractions permitted people in difficult situations to maintain at least short-term harmony, where candid specificity would probably have caused polarization or fragmentation in their groups. College presidents, high school principals, and teachers were prominent among those eager to remain vague about their convictions. Probably many of them were guilty of sentimental rhetoric on that occasion. Nevertheless, in teaching rhetoric of love or harmony, the idea of the abstract, or abstraction, may be the most valuable semantic concept, Kenneth Burke has discussed the rhetorical device of "spiritualization," which resolves or transcends conflicts and differences by using relatively abstract (or spiritual) language in dealing with them. "Are things disunited in

'body'?" he asks. And he answers, "Then unite them in 'spirit.'" And "Is an organization in disarray?" Then, "Talk of its common *purpose*."[11] However, abstract words can also be divisively evaluative, so in some situations harmony can be preserved by sticking to concrete, factual, non-evaluative terms. Rather than tell someone his violin playing is poor, it might do more for harmony to point out that he is grasping his instrument in a manner different from most violinists, including almost all the professionals.

That factual statement, like most truthful utterances, would be at least potentially divisive, of course, and if harmony were one's goal it might be more readily achieved by telling the violinist he has an interesting technique, or by borrowing an abstract expression of approval from the younger generation: "All *right*!" Regardless of which of those responses might be best for interpersonal harmony, you can speculate which of them would contribute most to improvement of the violinist's playing. The difficulty of answering such a question, along with other considerations, can persuade one to rely heavily on forthright, factual, denotative communication, and to prefer rhetoric of truth over any rhetoric of harmony which seems careless of the truth.

We should ask if there can be genuine or long-range harmony not founded on truth. And even if the answer is yes, we should ask if harmony cannot be destructive, where there is no vigilance for truth. The rhetoric being proposed would have truth not as its only goal, but as a constant and very important goal. And it would concentrate on the difference between objective and subjective language, since surely some important truths are beyond the grasp and utterance of those who have failed to master that distinction.

Contemporary public media—print, aural, and

---

[11] "Rhetoric—Old and New," in Steinmann, ed., *New Rhetorics*, p. 76. Burke's essay originally appeared in *Journal of General Education*, 5 (1951), 203–9.

visual—would be useful in the classroom presentation of the proposed semantics-based rhetoric. And I think they should be integral to it. If rhetoric must be made relevant in the classroom, it must be relevant for the student in his life beyond the classroom. The dominant communications in that life are those of public media. He should learn to respond critically to those communications, and he should be able to find among them his best models for imitation.

Newspapers provide the most obvious examples of relatively objective treatment (in news stories) and relatively subjective treatment (in editorials) of vital human concerns, especially those of the marketplace and the political forum. English teachers often express contempt for journalistic writing, preferring the poets and the novelists, I suppose. But the minds of the voters in our culture continue to be formed primarily by journalism, so its language should be given constant study, both for its strengths and its weaknesses.

If models, or specimens, from newspapers and other media can deepen the student's understanding of truth rhetoric, others from the same sources can sharpen his awareness of the language of harmony. The inaugural addresses, testimonial speeches, and eulogies reported there are rather obvious examples of that genre. Some of the editorials are further examples. Much of this is ceremonial rhetoric (Aristotle called it epideictic), celebrating shared ideals, faiths, and dreams. Often it is neither concerned with or limited by literal truth. Sports and glamor writing are conspicuously given to exaggeration, meant to elevate well-coordinated young men and attractive young women to transcendent positions. Celebration of the hero or queen and identification with him or her and the group values they embody, contribute to cohesiveness or harmony. Therefore this writing often functions as rhetoric of harmony. More serious news is, or should be rhetoric of truth, and is potentially much more divisive. I think students could grasp and appreciate the difference.

The proposed rhetoric should have certain obvious pedagogical effects. Students would learn important things about the qualities of words, and would develop discrimination in their choice and use of words. They would become more logical. Beyond those results, however, the students could be expected to refine their moral consciousness. They should have increased awareness of the difference between understanding and feeling, fact and opinion, reality and fantasy, truth and falsehood. Some may object that the schools are not churches, that it is not their business to deal so directly in values, and that in any event rhetoric should be an art and not an ethic. The truth, however, is that the schools do deal directly in values which are widely or almost universally acceptable, for example interracial brotherhood. The values of truth and harmony should be equally acceptable. Actually, the matter of ethics has been inseparable from rhetoric since its beginning in ancient Greece. Plato's grievance against the Sophists were ethical. Aristotle tried to concentrate on art rather than ethics, but he included some questionable advocacies of so-called ethical appeals and emotional appeals, and his disciples ever since have been urging a morally questionable program on their students. If Aristotelian rhetoric is acceptable in the schools, Platonic rhetoric should also be.

Teachers do transmit values. When I see a keynote speaker at a national political convention acknowledge the help of a rhetoric teacher, I wonder if what she taught him and what won him success was skill in being honest or dishonest. We must ask if it is wholesome, in school debate programs, to train students to take either side of a question with determination and the desire to win? I doubt that it is. A young man selling magazines (as I was soon to learn) greeted me at my door and asked, "You don't recognize me, do you?" That was sentimental or pseudo-harmony rhetoric, I believe. He wanted me to think he was the son of nearby neighbors—possibly some who had purchased our daughter's Girl Scout cookies. But he wasn't. It is painful but important to reflect that he may have learned to invent such strategies in his speech or English class. He was trying for an effective ethical appeal, or persona. He was role playing.

It would be theoretically possible simply to expose students to rhetorics of truth and love as well as their opposites, teach them the characteristics of the various types, and leave it to them to decide what kinds they wanted to use. Ultimately, the teacher must do that. But it is difficult to conceive of teachers constantly dealing with those classes of language and never disclosing ones they favor.

If we are to consider the relevance of truth and harmony rhetorics, we must reflect that dishonesty language is a form of violence. Language which substitutes emotion for thought, language that is subjective rather than objective, can be dishonest and it can be violent. The writer of a *Time* magazine essay wondered, quite legitimately I believe, if the assassinations of President Kennedy, Doctor King, and Senator Kennedy had occurred in a climate of political violence created in part by verbal violence.[12] I believe I have demonstrated that there is a verbal violence in our political and public life.

Young people who are disaffected from American society today often say the society is hypocritical, without truthfulness. Often the young themselves can be caught using sentimental or abuse rhetoric rather than rhetoric truth, but I think it is more from lack of instruction and example than from lack of idealism.

I do not know at what ages children should be brought into conscious contact with the ideas of harmony and truth as goals of rhetoric, or when the exposure of abuse and sentimentality

in language should begin. But I think that, in teaching writing and other communication skills, we should begin to think of adapting discourse to the ends of genuine truth and substantial harmony rather than those of tenuous sentimentality and divisive abuse. I think we should infuse our teaching with the idealism of Weller Embler. He recalls that Winston Smith in Orwell's *1984* insists there is "some spirit, some principle" in the universe "that the power-mad will never overcome." And Embler writes, "That spirit, that principle, is the indifferent, innocent truth, indifferent, that is, to parties and politics, by nature incapable of self-corruption. It is that which we are a part of and is a part of us, that which is ours as well as everyone's; it is individualistic as well as communal, the possession of all people...."[13] Embler's words justify the hope that truth can be the basis and source of harmony. Truth is our ultimate common ground, our universal unifying principle. It seems that rhetoric teachers have an excellent opportunity and a serious obligation to instill in our students some of the devotion to that principle expressed by Embler. He writes, "For human thought searches out the closest possible correspondence between things in the outside world and our inner understanding of them, it seeks (with a hopefulness which if it were naive would be intolerable mockery) the near-perfect adaptation of a sane intellect to a sane world. And that is why the human perversion of even the smallest truths strikes us as so perilous and why the perversion of the massive truths becomes so unforgivable."[14]

[12] "Politics and Assassination," *Time*, 91 (June 14, 1968) 21.

[13] "Language and Truth," in S. I. Hayakawa, ed., *The Use and Misuse of Language* (Greenwich, Connecticut: A Premier Book, Fawcett Publications, Inc., 1962), p. 233.

[14] *Ibid.*, pp. 233-34.

Characteristics and Organization of the Oral Technical Report

Roger P. Wilcox

The use of the oral technical report is increasing as a means of communicating information within industry. An engineer may be called on to investigate and report on such things as a production problem, a new manufacturing method, a new material, new equipment, or a new layout. He may make only an oral report on his findings, or he may present the oral report along with a written report. It may be a progress report or a final report and it may or may not contain recommendations.

But what is an oral technical report? How does it differ from a written technical report? How does it differ from a speech for any other occasion?

The oral technical report has characteristics which distinguish it from other forms of communication. There is, however, one essential feature it shares with all forms of communication—namely, to be effective the communication must "get through" to the listener or reader. Any communication must be prepared with the thought as to what background must be provided, what terms must be defined, and how the thoughts should be arranged. If the reader

From Roger P. Wilcox, "Characteristics and Organization of the Oral Technical Report," *General Motor Engineering Journal*, 6 (October-December, 1959), pp 8–12. Reprinted with permission.

or listener cannot follow a communication with at least a reasonable degree of understanding, it makes little difference how thorough the investigation, how clear the language, or how polished the presentation—the report is a failure. This is true as if it were a product designed for the market. No matter how ingenious, well made, or attractive it might be, if it does not sell, it has failed to fulfill its purpose.

Oral Report Differs From Written Report

It is easy to form misconceptions when comparing the oral report to the written report and to believe that the oral report consists merely of the written report read aloud, that it is a "boiled down" version of the written report, or that the oral report is somehow better than the written report, or vice versa. The fact is that the two are not identical, nor is either better than the other. Each is prepared for a different situation and each has its advantages and disadvantages.

Four basic characteristics of the oral report distinguish it from the written report.

Special Audience

The written report, once in print, may be read by any number of individuals. The writer, therefore, must try to adapt his writing to a broad level of reader understanding and interests. The oral report, however, is usually prepared for a special audience—for example, a project committee, a safety committee, a design staff—and the speaker must prepare his report specifically to the particular interests and level of understanding of this audience.

Limited Scope

The reader of a written report may read the entire report or only certain parts. The amount of material included in a written report, therefore, may be comparatively unlimited but should include, of course, all pertinent data, either in the body of the report or in an appendix.

The oral report, however, is usually prepared with a specified time limit in mind and the speaker must adapt the scope of his material to fit the time limit, which may include a question and answer period.

Keeping in mind a definite time limit, the speaker must prepare his report to include a clear explanation of the problem and the main sub-conclusions and general conclusions reached. Most of the detailed substantiating data may be omitted, with perhaps a brief description of the general methods used to arrive at the conclusions being retained. If the speaker has also prepared a written report on the same subject, he may limit his talk to only or or two phases covered by the report. As a guiding principle, it is better to cover less, but cover it thoroughly, than to try to cover too much and do only a superficial job.

Personal Presentation

The medium of the written report is the printed page, but the medium of the oral report is the speaker. Therefore, the delivery of the speaker becomes of critical importance. His posture, gestures, eye contact, and facial expression, as well as his general appearance, are bound to affect the attitude of the audience. So are such factors as his voice projection, enunciation, pronunciation, and the degree to which his speaking style seems relaxed, conversational, and expressive.

A question may arise as to what method of preparation gives the most effective style of delivery. Of the four methods available—impromptu, extemporaneous, manuscript, or memorized—the extemporaneous is usually preferred. In this method the outline of the speech is carefully prepared, but the speech is neither written nor committed to memory. The impromptu method is obviously inappropriate, while the manuscript and memorized methods tend to be inflexible and sound artificial.

Another implication arising from the oral presentation concerns the language. In the written report the language is properly impersonal and formal. Only in the letter of transmittal does the writer use such personal pronouns as "I" or "you" and no time does he use colloquialisms or slang. But since the oral report is delivered in a setting more informal and personal, the language may also be more informal and personal. The speaker may say "I" or "he" or "they didn't" freely, and even such colloquialisms as "we had a terrible time getting the thing to work," provided he maintains an attitude that is essentially objective and businesslike, and is careful to be specific and accurate where he needs to be.

The opportunity for questions from the audience is another characteristic of the oral report. Sometimes, the questions may be asked as they arise during the presentation, or they may be deferred to a question and answer period following the formal presentation. While each method has its advantages, it is usually more satisfactory to defer any extensive questioning until the formal presentation has been completed.

An appropriate physical setting for the oral report also is important. The location normally is in a conference room comfortable in size for the number attending. Ideally, it should be equipped with a lectern, chart stand, and blackboard, and should be capable of being darkened for possible screen projections. The room should be reasonably free from noise distractions. The general atmosphere, as in the conference situation, is informal.

Instant Understanding

If some portion of a written report is not immediately clear, the reader may reread it, refer back or ahead, or even consult other sources. But the oral report disappears into thin air the moment it is presented. This means that the speaker must be exceedingly careful to be as clear as possible.

Three ways to faciliatate instant understanding are:

(a) *Use of Voice*: the speaker can help the listener if he uses his voice properly. First, he must project adequately and enunciate distinctly so that even those seated farthest away will have no difficulty hearing him. Second, he should use pauses freely to break up his flow of ideas into meaningful thought units and give an opportunity for his ideas to "soak in." Finally, he should speak with sufficient forcefulness and use a variety of voice inflection, not only to avoid monotony, but also to give life and meaning to his words.

(b) *Use of Language:* the speaker can help his listeners by using language that is easy to understand. If the reader of a written report encounters an unfamiliar term he can refer to a dictionary. But in an oral report, the speaker must define the term for the listener. Obviously, the problem will vary from one situation to another, but the speaker should be sure the listeners understand his terminology since he may be using special terms or else familiar terms with special meanings. This problem of terminology can be a major one in writing as well as in speaking. Different branches of engineering have become so specialized in their jargon that engineers in different departments often have difficulty in understanding each other. Not only must the terminology be clear, but the language must not be too abstract or involved.

(c) *Use of Transitions and Summaries*: the third way for easier listener comprehension is in the use of transitions and summaries. It is not enough that the speaker understand his pattern of development. He also must make it constantly clear to his listeners. Having developed a section of his report, he should summarize it briefly before moving to the next section and should show the relationship between the various sections. The main preview of his report will occur, of course, in the introduction, and the main summary in the conclusion.

Instant understanding is absolutely vital in the oral report. It is difficult to emphasize enough the importance of the speaker being constantly solicitious of the listener's need to "keep with" the report as it is presented.

Basically, the oral technical report is a different medium of communication from the written technical report and is designed for a different kind of communication situation. It also differs from non-technical speaking.

Main Purpose of Oral Technical Report: to Inform

A speaker may attempt to secure any one of three basic responses from his audience. He may want them to be entertained or interested (as in the case of the after-dinner speaker); to believe or act differently (as in the case of a safety talk); or to understand (as in the case of directions on how to operate a machine). Basically, the oral technical report is expository or informational. The speaker should strive for all three basic responses, but his main purpose is to advance the audience's understanding of the topic under discussion.

If the main pupose of the oral technical report is to inform, the speaker must be objective and impartial towards his material. Even though he may present strong advantages in favor of some recommendation, he scrupulously presents

EVALUATION OF THE ORAL REPORT

YES | NO

Introduction

Did the speaker effectively capture the interest and attention of his review group right from the start?

Did the speaker give the necessary explanation of the background from which the problem derived?

Did the speaker clearly state and explain his problem?

Did the speaker indicate the method(s) used to solve the problem?

Did the speaker suggest the order in which he would report?

Organization

Was the plan of organization recognizable through the use of:
  (a) Sufficient introductory information
  (b) Successful use of transitions from one main part to the next and between points of the speech
  (c) Appropriate use of summary statements and restatements?
Were the main ideas of the report clearly distinguishable from one another?
Was there a recognizable progression of ideas that naturally led to the conclusion?

Content

Did the speaker have adequate supporting data to substantiate what he said?
Was all the content meaningful in terms of the problem and its solution? (Avoidance of extraneous material.)
Did the speaker present his supporting data understandably in terms of the ideas or concepts he was trying to communicate?
Were the methods of the investigation clearly presented?

Visual Aid Supports

Did the speaker effectively use charts, graphs, or diagrams to present his statistical data?
Did the speaker use clear drawings, charts, diagrams or blackboard aids to make his facts or explanations vivid to the review group?
Did the visual aids fit naturally into the presentation?
Did the speaker give evidence of complete familiarity with each visual aid used?
Did the speaker clutter his report with too many visual aids?

Conclusion

Did the speaker conclude his report with finality in terms of one or more of the following:
  (a) The conclusions reached
  (b) The problem solved
  (c) The results obtained
  (d) The value of such findings to the corporation or industry at large
  (e) Recommendations offered?

The Question Period

Did the speaker give evidence of intelligent listening in interpreting the questions?
Were the speaker's answers organized in terms of a summary statement, explanation, and supporting example?
Did the speaker show freedom in adapting or improvising visual aids in answering questions?

Delivery

Did the speaker use a natural, communicative delivery?
Did the speaker use adequate eye contact in maintaining a natural, communicative delivery?
Did the speaker use sufficient movement and gestures?
Did the speaker use good clear diction to express himself?
Could the speaker be heard easily by everyone?
Was the speaker confident and convincing?
Did the speaker display enthusiasm when communicating his ideas?

Table I—This checklist for the evaluation of an oral technical report was developed at General Motors Institute. It gives a concise view of the qualities demanded in the oral report.

its disadvantages as well. The speaker stops short of playing the role of the advocate arguing for the adoption of a special point of view. He is more like a scientist reporting his latest findings to a group of fellow scientists.

In keeping with the objective point of view, the development of the oral technical report is primarily factual. Although an occasional anecdote may be valuable for illustration or enlivenment, the body of the report should consist of such objective data as explanations, descriptions, definitions, statistics, and expert opinion. Any conclusions offered should be based strictly on the facts available.

Yet, the speaker must take care that emphasis on the data does not obscure understanding of what the data support. An example of this is the speaker who is so preoccupied with explaining certain equations employed in his study that he never makes clear what his equations were intended to prove, nor what results they produced.

Although an oral technical report does not necessarily need the use of visual aids, they are usually recommended. Graphs, diagrams, models, and samples are employed freely for such purposes as explaining mechanisms and processes, presenting statistics, and stating objectives or listing main points. Because it is so easy to use visual aids ineptly, a few suggestions are:

- Charts and diagrams should normally be prepared before instead of during the presentation, when valuable time may be needlessly consumed
- Aids should be kept simple, focusing only on what is most pertinent
- Each drawing or chart should be adequately titled and labeled
- Diagrams and labels should be large enough to be fully legible to those seated farthest away
- Charts should have a professional look. Drawings and lettering not neat in appearance detract from the report.
- Normally, materials should not be distributed during the presentation since they divert attention from the speaker

- Aids should not be revealed until they become pertinent in the presentation.

Proper Organization Important for Effective Report

As in any form of communication, the pattern of development is very important. The organization of the oral technical report can be most conveniently discussed in terms of the three major divisions of the report: body, introduction, and conclusion.

The *body* is normally organized in terms of the steps involved in the problem-solution sequence. They include:

(a) An analysis of the problem to show what is wrong (the evidences of effects of the problem); the conditions which brought about the problem (the causes); and a statement of what is desired (the criteria or expectations)

(b) An explanation and analysis of one or more solutions in terms of their advantages and disadvantages in solving the problem and meeting the criteria.

The report need not always follow the entire sequence. Sometimes it may only analyze the causes of a problem or explain and evaluate a solution to a problem.

The discussion of each phase of the analysis should close with a statement showing the subconclusions arrived at during that phase.

The *introduction* prepares the audience for the body of the report. This is done by motivating the listener to want to hear what the speaker has to say and orienting the listener as to what the report contains.

Motivating the audience depends on two steps. First, the speaker should dwell briefly on the importance of the problem so the listener will have the feeling, "Here's something I want to find out about." Second, the speaker should establish the distinct impression that he has something worthwhile to offer on this subject. This can be done indirectly by referring to the speaker's interest and background concerning the problem and particularly to the amount of time spent and methods used in his investigation. Another way is to create an impression of competence, both in the introduction and throughout the report.

Orienting the listener is accomplished by:

(a) Identifying and defining the problem by showing its relationship to the area from which it was taken, making clear what phases of the problem will be included in the report, and being explicit as to the exact purpose of the report

(b) Providing whatever background is necessary concerning how the problem arose

(c) Giving a preview of what the main divisions of the report will contain.

When the introduction is completed, the listener should be motivated to want to listen to the report and should know what it will cover and in what order.

The *conclusion* normally fulfills three main functions. First, the various sub-conclusions presented during the report at the close of each unit are summarized. Second, general conclusions, in the form of generalizations drawn from the sub-conclusions, are presented. And finally, any recommendations, arising from the general conclusions are offered. The conclusion normally will provide a transition to the question-and-answer period.

At General Motors Institute, many of the points discussed have been summarized in a checklist to help obtain a uniform evaluation of oral reports presented by students (Table I). These oral reports, in many cases, are required in addition to regular written reports which are a part of the Fifth-Year Program at the Institute. In this fifth year, graduates of the four-year cooperative engineering program are assigned, and must complete satisfactorily, an extensive plant project to qualify for the degree of bachelor of mechanical engineering or bachelor of industrial engineering.

Summary

The oral technical report is becoming more popular as a means of communication. Any engineer may be required at some time to prepare one on a variety of subjects. Although it has many characteristics found in other forms of communication, the oral technical report differs from both the written report and non-technical speech in several aspects. Properly used, it can be a useful tool in industry.

A Few Words About Speeches

Charles A. Boyle

When I first went into business, my goal was to simply write speeches for other people and let it go at that. However, I found out rather quickly that many of my clients were not taking advantage of all the opportunities that giving a speech can generate . . . such as press coverage and printed copies distributed to various people and publications. And so I began offering advice in these allied areas.

As a result, when I had my new brochures and business cards printed, I changed them from Confidential Speech Service to Charles A. Boyle, Writer/Consultant. But, I'm not as impressed by the term consultant as much anymore as I once was.

Lately, when I see the word consultant on a title or letterhead, I'm amused because it reminds me of the two old maids who live in my neighborhood. They have a big, black tomcat and they call him Sylvester.

It used to be that every night about ten o'clock, Sylvester would raise a fuss to get out of the house. And when they couldn't stand it anymore, the ladies would turn him loose to roam the neighborhood.

From Charles A. Boyle, "A Few Words About Speeches," *Vital Speeches of the Day,* 41 (September 1, 1975), pp 682–85. Reprinted with permission.

Of course, they wouldn't see him again until the next morning when he'd get hungry.

Well, it bothered those two old maids to realize that Sylvester was having all that fun . . . so they decided to do something about it and took him down to the veterinarian where they had Sylvester fixed, figuring that would solve their problem.

The net result is that Sylvester still makes his evening calls . . . but now he goes around as a consultant.

I stole that story from Mick Delaney . . . a friend of mine who is a professional speaker. But I'm not a professional speaker . . . I never get paid for giving a talk. I'm a professional writer and get paid for writing talks for other people to give. And everything I write is stolen from somebody. I want you to understand however, that it's not plagiarism.

Plagiarism is when you take stuff from *one* writer . . . when you take it from a lot of writers, it's called research. In the course of my research for this talk I stumbled across some of the history of Johann Von Goethe.

I always thought of Goethe (if I ever thought of him at all) simply the author of Faust and one of history's greatest writers.

But Goethe was more than a writer . . . he

207

was a politician and, in a friendly meaning of the word, a bureaucrat. Early in his career he held many civil offices and, with his extraordinary intelligence, was able to develop a keen understanding and deep insight of the people known as the general public.

Goethe believed . . . and said . . . "The public wishes itself to be managed like a woman: One must say nothing to it except what it likes to hear."

This could be done in Goethe's day, but if we use the popular ways of reaching the public in 1975 it's nearly impossible. To paraphrase Lincoln, we can tell some of the public what it wants to hear all of the time, but not all of the public what it wants to hear even some of the time.

The reason for this inability to please everybody with our words is that we try to reach the public simultaneously, instantly and indiscriminately through the mass media. And since we are aware of the vast range of differing opinions in the radio, television and newspaper audience, we begin thinking in defensive terms before we open our mouths rather than aggressive advocacy of our cause.

For we know that a large percentage of those listening will be in sharp disagreement with us . . . no matter what we say.

Consequently, in an effort not to be too offensive to a large portion of that audience in a TV commercial, or when we speak in the presence of reporters, whenever we say black is black or white is white, we most likely qualify it by acknowledging every shade of gray.

Goethe didn't have this problem . . . there was no mass media in his day.

When he spoke to the people of Frankfurt gathered in small audiences, he didn't have to dilute his remarks in fear of offending the people of Berlin or Munich. He knew the desires and needs of his audience in Frankfurt and spoke to them alone . . . not to them and the people of Berlin at the same time.

A leading public relations counsel and author, Phillip Lesley of Chicago, put it this way . . . "the more closely a communication is beamed to a specific audience, the more likely it is to be received and accepted . . . each communication activity must reach SPECIFIC publics in ways that can gain THEIR interest and motivate THEIR support."

It's pretty hard to motivate the public while vacillating and apologizing.

But that's what's done too often by business and political leaders trying to tell their story through the mass media *alone*, because they KNOW they are not reaching a specific public . . . they're hitting the whole spectrum of thought and opinion and pull their punches accordingly.

Whether deserved or not, business and government are under massive attack with no holds barred. And their defense, through the mass media, is soft-sell.

It's about all they can do in a 30 second radio or TV pop whether that 30 seconds is in the form of news or a commercial.

Lately, some industries began to realize that those 30 second announcements . . . *alone* . . . are not enough. More of the story has to be told and it takes longer than 30 seconds to do it.

Here's an example—

In the April 11, 1974 edition of the Wall Street Journal, the headline read . . .

"BIG OIL COMPANIES HIT LUNCHEON TRAIL TO BATTLE BAD IMAGE."

According to the journal story, many oil companies are creating speakers bureaus or are expanding the ones they already have.

A. D. Gill, who heads Gulf Oil Corporation's Vital Source speaker's bureau, says their program has been expanded from 200 speech-giving employees to 350. Gill says Gulf reached about 400 audiences in 1973 and one thousand audiences in 1974.

In the past year or so, the oil companies have probably been the most visible target of the "anti's." But the power companies, lumber industry and phone companies are ships in the same convoy coming under attack. To some degree, most of the industries realize that a pretty ad alone cannot tell their story effectively and gain support from the general public. And the general public, incidentally, really isn't totally committed to one side or the other—but it does lack information from both sides of an issue.

As I mentioned, the oil companies . . . and some others . . . have discovered that speaking to live audiences, where there is time to say more than what can be said in a minute or less and where there is an opportunity for face-to-face questions and answers, can be a very effective way of getting a message across.

There is a rub, however. Too many speeches are done badly.

And, with typical American free enterprise initiative . . . or what's left of it . . . a number of firms have cropped up recently to teach the fundamentals of speech-making to company executives.

One of these firms is Carl Terzian Associates of Los Angeles.

Terzian personally receives two thousand requests a year to give speeches and responds to about 200–250 of them.

Just to give you an example of how much money or trouble some executives will pay for coaching, Terzian had one client . . . a vice-president of a firm in Portland . . . who had Terzian meet him once a month. Terzian would fly to Portland, meet his client at the airport where they had lunch, coach him for an hour in a conference room, get back on a plane and return to Los Angeles.

Terzian told me . . . and it's been published in California Business magazine . . . that on an average day in Los Angles there are 25 thousand audiences meeting. In New York, it's 40 thousand a day ranging all the way from PTA's and high school assemblies to conventions, garden clubs and service clubs. And they all want a speaker.

When I first decided to go into my own business about 2 years ago, I wondered how many speeches were being given in the Seattle area. Using the Rotary Club as a barometer . . . 20 clubs in the Seattle area meeting 52 weeks a year for about one thousand speeches at Rotary clubs alone . . . I figured that at least 5 or 6

thousand speeches were being given in Seattle each year. It's probably more like 1 or 2 thousand a day. Or more.

The audiences are there and always have been.

Speeches are a great way to reach the public . . . and the best way to reach and tell a story to specific publics.

But only if the speeches are done effectively.

The trouble is, too many speeches are deadly.

How many times have you heard the phrase . . . "I have to go and listen to a speech?"

What a negative reaction to speeches that is!

And yet, almost every great thought of mankind was first expressed in a speech.

Aristotle, Socrates and Cicero gave speeches that were taken down in shorthand by slaves and then written in longhand and—in the case of Cicero—sold to the public.

Shakespeare wrote plays which were mostly speeches.

Or even today, how many people can remember the words John Kennedy wrote in his book, "Profiles in Courage?"

How many people can forget what he said in his inauguration speech . . . "Ask not what your country can do for you, but what you can do for your country."

Which, incidentally, was first said in a speech about 300 years ago by Frederick the Great of Prussia.

I ask you . . . can you quote from the books of Winston Churchill? Can you forget his phrase . . . "the iron curtain" . . . given in a speech at Columbia, Missouri?

Newton Minow may be a name the public cannot remember. But the public remembers what he called television in a speech . . . a vast wasteland.

From Washington's farewell to Lincoln's Gettysburg Address . . . to Roosevelt's "we have nothing to fear" to Churchill's blood, sweat and tears, the list of memorable speeches is endless.

Good speeches are *printed* and *quoted* and *remembered*.

The audiences can be far greater than those present at the time they are given.

But none of those great speeches was given spontaneously.

None of those great men got up before an audience, hemming and hawing, stumbling and searching for words . . . trying to put thoughts into continuity at the same time they were speaking.

They put their thoughts in order on paper *BEFORE* they spoke.

Whether you agree with their words or not, good speakers . . . while on the platform . . . never give you the uncomfortable feeling that you have to help them out. You won't see them groping around for words while you squirm and say to yourself . . . "come on, I know the word you're looking for . . . say it."

Mark Twain said . . . "it usually takes more than 3 weeks to prepare a *good, impromptu* speech."

But the sin of most people called on to give a speech is that they direct their efforts in proportion to the size of the audience.

For instance, if a businessman was given the opportunity to speak to the 500-member downtown Rotary Club, he would probably be willing to pay for help in coming up with a good speech.

But if that same businessman was asked to speak to a small Rotary Club in some suburb, he might not be too anxious to go to any expense over it.

Yet, with one good speech he could give it to 15 small Rotary Clubs, not only reaching a bigger audience than the downtown club, but some of the people doing make-ups at the smaller clubs.

I had one client last year who gave the same speech 30 times to 30 different groups in a period of one month. He was giving the speech every day or evening . . . sometimes twice a day. He not only reached two thousand people in person, but parts of his speech were quoted in the two big daily papers the first time he gave it and in the neighborhood weeklies the rest of the month.

I'm happy to say he was promoting a certain cause and it was successful.

Giving a speech is sort of like being on the stage. I suppose there's a little bit of the ham in all of us and, if we perform well, favorable attention will be directed our way.

I'm sure you've all heard of movie actors who want to be in Broadway plays . . . they want to see and feel the reaction of the audience.

Even Lloyd Cooney, who's on television every day, still likes to give speeches where he can be in touch with his audience.

And he always reads his speeches.

But speakers and potential speakers are told time and time again that they should never . . . never, use a script or read a speech.

That's ridiculous . . . unless you happen to be a professional speaker. And you'd be amazed at how many professional speakers use scripts . . . it just looks like they aren't.

When's the last time you ever saw a president or a governor give a speech without a script? And, if it was on television and they didn't have a script in front of them . . . you can bet it was on the teleprompter.

Even Lincoln wrote the Gettysburg Address . . . not once, but five times. Parts of it were used in other speeches for years before he spoke those immortal words in Pennsylvania. And when he gave it, he had the script in his hand, in spite of the fact that it was only about two minutes long.

Businessmen and political leaders should always use a script. After all, once they utter the words . . . they can't be erased. And by talking from the top of your head, even if you've mentally outlined your talk or are using notes, the wrong words have a way of slipping out inadvertently and the right word is too often forgotten at the moment. This can't happen if a script is followed faithfully.

The trouble with most speech writers, however, is that they write material that's great to read at your leisure. That's a written speech . . . pretty to the eye of the silent reader. But someone has to stand up and SPEAK that speech. The good speech writer knows that and writes for an oral presentation . . . for the EAR.

There's a great deal of difference between material that is written to be read and material written to be heard.

Another, anti-script argument is that some people think it's an insult to an audience to read a speech. I think it's a compliment . . . by putting your thoughts down in the form of a script, you are, in effect, saying that you care enough for your audience's time to spend hours . . . not talking and rambling . . . but researching and writing. And people who are experts in their field usually have enough knowledge and information about their field to talk for hours. The trick is to boil it down to the time frame allotted and still make the essential points.

Winston Churchill was asked on at least one occasion how much he would charge to give a half-hour speech. He said . . . $2,500 dollars. The people who asked him thought that was kind of high, so they asked how much it would cost for a 15 minute speech. Churchill replied . . . $5,000. Twice as much for half the time. He . . . as most of us . . . found it harder to say something in fewer words.

As for the person who hires a professional to put his knowledge into a concise presentation; if the audience should guess or know that someone else wrote the speech, the person that hired the writer is telling the audience that . . . he cares enough about them to spend some money to give them the best talk he can.

One of the things I always try to do myself, and depending on the type of audience, advise my clients to do, is never to the bitter end of the allotted time with a prepared talk, but leave some time for questions and answers. That's what I'm about to do now. But I can't resist slipping in at least one bit of philosophy which may be appropriate to our times.

In recent years the word rhetoric has been demeaned. Perphaps you've heard people say, in effect, no more rhetoric . . . let's have some action.

Well—rhetoric *is* action. Plato said, "Rhetoric is the art of ruling men's minds." And, of course, once you've ruled their minds, you rule all of them. I think it's time businesmen . . . who are men of action . . . start sharpening their skills of rhetoric. Lord knows, the people tearing down business have been using it.

I think businessmen should be blowing their own horn more often, for—as W. S. Gilbert put it—"If you wish in the world to advance—your merits you're bound to enhance; you must stir it and stump it, and blow your own trumpet, or trust me, you haven't a chance."

How to Be A Better Speaker

Vincent Vinci

Here are some tips about the art of getting your message across to an audience.

Whenever Cornelius Warmerdam, the former world pole-vaulting record-holder, missed a jump, he said he could trace it back to some mistake he had made in his approach or take-off.

It is much the same with a speech or a sales presentation. An unprepared speaker will stand out like an unseasoned juggler.

A solid presentation is founded on three elements:

Preparation.

More preparation.

Still more preparation.

The flaws that show up during a presentation are the fault of a lack of preparation. Here is how you can avoid that pitfall.

● *Beware of the short notice.* No doubt there are speakers who can fill in on short notice and give an excellent speech. Unfortunately, most of us are not professional speakers. And even many speakers renowned for giving extemporaneous talks actually spend much time in preparation.

Allow yourself plenty of time to get ready. If you are asked to give a talk on short notice, decline gracefully.

It is better to turn down an invitation to speak than to speak poorly. An ineffective speech leaves the audience with the impression that you didn't care enough to do your best or that you can't speak effectively.

● *Avoid presenting a paper.* Too often, a speech or presentation is a carbon copy of a technical or scientific paper. This is particularly true at conferences, symposia, and conventions. If you present a paper instead of a speech, you are doing the audience and yourself an injustice. A speech is written for the ear, while a paper is written for the eye.

Aristotle, in his "Rhetoric," distinguished between the language of writing and language of speech. A speech is transitory. Therefore, you should unfold only the highlights of your research.

The background, tests, equations, and other detailed data should remain in the technical paper. With a paper, the reader—unlike the listener—can study and absorb every idea at his own pace. The listener, however, has only an instant to understand a thought before the speaker moves to the next phrase or idea.

Remember, as a speaker, you are carrying

your purpose and words to others mainly through voice. Keep in mind, when you write your talk, that you must appeal to the auditory sense as the gateway to your listeners' minds.

• *Consider audience makeup.* Recently, an executive couldn't understand why a speech he made failed to elicit a favorable reaction from his audience. His topic was lively and up to date, but the audience seemed listless and uninterested.

After some questioning, it was clear that the executive knew very little about the composition of the group. He did not know the average age, or the occupations, convictions, loyalties, level of understanding, and interests of his audience.

What you say must be related to your audience's interests. For example, a discussion of the gross national product would probably have very little appeal to members of a ski club. Unless, of course, the speaker can show how the GNP will affect their everyday lives—and maybe even skiing.

A timely topic may automatically receive some attention, but you still must slant it in the direction of your listeners' areas of interest, desire, and understanding.

• *Get help.* "I've given presentations before, and I've written my own talks before, so why should I depart from my normal procedure?" Fine. You don't feel you need help in preparing your talk. However, very often managers who are capable of researching, planning, and writing their material let time slip away.

Then they realize too late that only a short time remains before the engagement. What results, in most cases, is a poor talk. The weakness sometimes appears in the visual aids used by the speaker. Too often, a speaker rushes into the graphics department at the last moment and asks for a dozen visuals. Quality slides, charts, or film strips, like a well-prepared speech, are not created overnight.

Getting help from a speechwriter or an audiovisual expert does not indicate weakness, but strength. A good manager has an agency prepare advertising, industrial relations personnel

write letters to employees, and designers develop packaging.

If you employ a writer, be sure to give him all the information you have about the speaking engagement so he can do the proper research. Also, give the writer your ideas about what you would like to say and how you would like to say it. The more he knows about your views, the closer the speech will reflect them.

• *Have only one objective.* Is the speaker for or against the proposition? What does he want us to do or believe?

I am sure you have sat through a talk wondering what a speaker was leading to and never finding out. The speech suffered from poor organization, perhaps the result of having too many objectives.

This is the bane of novice speakers.

To make a good speech, you must have a specific objective—a goal you can state in one sentence. For instance: To prove that the gold standard won't work in today's world economy.

This objective, and the way you phrase it, will help you focus your arguments and supporting data.

• *Keep it simple.* One of the best ways to lose an audience is to inundate it with facts and figures. Many managers assume that is the way to show themselves as experts.

Don't believe it.

That approach proves only that the speaker is insensitive to his audience or doesn't care whether his speech sinks in.

You are already an expert in your field, otherwise you would not have been invited to speak. You needn't prove what your audience takes for granted.

Remember, the burden of communication is on you. It is up to you to be on the audience's wavelength, if you want your message to be received.

This means you must not talk over the heads of your listeners by using technical jargon, acronyms, or other unfamiliar terms. Analyze who your audience is, and begin at the audience's level of comprehension.

• *Use visuals judiciously.* A university professor, lecturing in a film series on rocketry, used 35 slides. Each contained the same information plotted in a different way. The message was the same, never varying from slide to slide. The result was an exhibition of chartmanship, but very little information was imparted to the audience.

Visual aids should be used judiciously. They should not form an outline for you, but should augment, support, or clarify a point.

That means audience consideration comes first. Use visuals only if they help the audience understand. If not, visuals are unnecessary and a distraction.

• *Check it out*. The speaker who arrives at the meeting room at the last minute, and finds there is no lectern or microphone for him, may start off quite upset. Plan ahead. Get to a meeting early enough so there is time to check out the lectern and mike and any other equipment or props that are necessary to your talk. There is more than the lectern and audio system to check. For example, screen placement—if you occasionally want to look up and note whether you are on the right slide—projectors, remote cords, and reading light.

By arriving well ahead of time, you can better sense the mood of the audience, and perhaps you can pick up some timely information or local color which you can integrate into your speech. In addition, if there is another speaker preceeding you who is an absolute dynamo or a bore, you can adjust your own delivery to obtain the best audience response.

Maybe you don't need another chicken dinner, but you owe it to the audience and yourself to be at your best.

That means leaving little to chance.

• *Don't be yourself*. Some speech experts say that the key to public speaking is to be yourself. This is followed by advice to speak in a conversational manner, because speechmaking is very similar to conversing and you'll sound more sincere.

Don't fall for that advice.

First of all public speaking is not like conversing. A conversation is a two-way affair; a a speech or presentation is basically one-way communication. The audience comes to listen, not converse.

During a conversation, a participant can repeat, explain, and ask questions. This does not happen during a speech.

Secondly, when making an address, you are the whole show. Therefore, you should be more animated than when simply conversing. Perhaps the proper advice is: Be yourself—and a little more.

• *Be humorous—but apropos*. Everybody enjoys a humorous story in a speech. Right?

Right and wrong.

Many speakers succumb to the temptation to tell the latest story they've heard. They tell themselves this establishes a rapport with their audience. Well, humor does establish rapport, if it makes a point and is relevant to your topic. Otherwise, your listeners' minds will wander as the audience tries to establish a connection between your joke and your talk.

A story that interrupts the audience's train of thought does not build rapport and should be avoided.

• *Rehearse, rehearse*. An East Coast company has a "murder board" composed of knowledgeable and experienced managers who listen to—and tear apart, constructively—presentations fellow managers will make to outside groups. Indirectly, the board provides another service—forcing the speaker to rehearse.

Even if you have given the same talk very recently, it pays to rehearse before you deliver it again. Rehearsing once isn't enough. You need to rehearse and rehearse.

The secret of success in speaking, as well as in life, is preparation.

Nine
Mass Communication

As you read the material in this book, you are engaged in a form of mass communication. Mass communication includes television, radio, film, newspapers, and other printed material. In fact, we are bombarded by the many different forms of mass communication.

As an overview, the mass communicator, unlike a person engaging in interpersonal communication, must direct the message to a mass or large audience. The speaker can no longer be uniquely concerned with the self-interest of each and every listener. Assumptions must be made about the collective self-interests of the large group of viewers or listeners. When television station managers plan to air a program, they attempt to determine the appeal of that program to a large segment of the population. We know from studies of viewing habits that news specials, documentaries, classical music programs, and theatrical productions fall outside the range of the self-interest for the vast majority of the viewing public. (In fact, only two percent have an interest in attending fine-arts-type activities.)

You should be able to immediately see the differences between mass communication and other forms of communication we have discussed. As a listener, the only response you can make to a television or radio program is to write or call the producer or stop buying the sponsor's product. In either case, a great deal of time has elapsed between the communication and your response to that communication. Your feedback has been greatly delayed. It is the apparent inaccessibility of the listener to respond to the communicator that prevents many people from providing feedback to mass media communication. While letters to the editor, calls to producers, and letters to sponsors are useful feedback, the communicator must turn to indices of listener response or to some form of public polling. You may have seen the Nielsen ratings about listener response to various television programs. Each week the top twenty programs are usually listed in the television section of the local newspaper. These limited samples of response are used as indices for the entire viewing public. On the basis of as few as 1,200 responses to a potential viewing public of fifty million, television shows are cancelled or retained.

The average American watches approximately six hours of television per week and has listened to approximately 17.5 hours of radio during the same period.

Each household has an average of 2.2 television sets and 98.6 percent of all homes in America have a radio. There are approximately 63,000,000 copies of newspapers sold daily. We buy magazines, records, tapes, photographs, and (perhaps in the very near future) video tapes as other forms of mass communication.

Table I
Amount of Household Viewing
(hours per home per day—yearly average)

1960	5 hours 3 minutes
1962	5 hours 6 minutes
1964	5 hours 25 minutes
1966	5 hours 32 minutes
1968	5 hours 46 minutes
1970	5 hours 56 minutes

Table II
Growth in the Televison Industry

	1960	1970
Number of Stations and Systems in Operation		
Commercial TV		
UHF	75	183
VHF	440	508
Educational TV		
UHF	10	106
VHF	34	78
CATV Systems	640	2350
Television Household Data		
Number of sets in use	53 million	88 million
Percent of all households with TV	87.5	95.5
Percent of all households with color TV	*	40**
Percent of TV households with two or more sets	12.5	30.5
Percent of TV sets equipped with UHF	8	52
Percent of households subscribing to CATV	*	7.5

*Less than one percent.
**Based on estimates from *Electronic Market Data Book*, Nielsen data, and 1970 survey findings.

Table III

"Now, I would like to get your opinions about how radio, newspapers, television, and magazines compare. Generally speaking, which of these would you say . . .?"

IN PERCENTAGES

Which of the Media:	Television		Magazines		Newspapers		Radio		None/NA	
	1960	1970	1960	1970	1960	1970	1960	1970	1960	1970
Is the most entertaining?	68	72	9	5	13	9	9	14	1	0
Gives the most complete news coverage?	19	41	3	4	59	39	18	14	1	2
Presents things most intelligently?	27	38	27	18	33	28	8	9	5	8
Is the most educational?	32	46	31	20	31	26	3	4	3	5
Brings you the latest news most quickly?	36	54	0	0	5	6	57	39	2	1
Does the most for the public?	34	48	3	2	44	28	11	13	8	10
Seems to be getting worse all the time?	24	41	17	18	10	14	14	5	35	22
Presents the fairest, most unbiased news?	29	33	9	9	31	23	22	19	9	16
Is the least important to you?	15	13	49	53	7	9	15	20	7	5
Creates the most interest in new things going on?	56	61	18	16	18	14	4	5	4	5
Does the least for the public?	13	10	47	50	5	7	12	13	23	20
Seems to be getting better all the time?	49	38	11	8	11	11	10	15	19	28
Gives you the clearest understanding of the candidates and issues in national election?	42	59	10	8	36	21	5	3	7	9

1960 base: 100 percent = 2427
1970 base: 100 percent = 1900

From Television and the Public by Robert T. Bower. Copyright © 1973 by Holt Rinehart and Winston, Inc. Reprinted by permission of Holt, Rinehart and Winston.

Movies are better than ever. Our environment is inundated with a variety of mass communication, and there is little disagreement that the mass media plays an important part in our daily lives.

It is generally agreed that television has become the dominant medium for conveying information to the public. The preceding tables illustrate the acceptance we have had for the television media.

There is no question that advertising and politicking have moved to take advantage of the role that the mass media, particularly television, can play in the dissemination of information about a product or candidate. (It is sometimes hard to tell the difference.)

Although we know that television is used as a source of information, the effect of television is less clear. Much research has been conducted on the effects upon children of violence on television, with the conclusions unclear and unqualified. More research must be conducted on the effects of television and the rest of the mass media.

Functional Analysis of Mass Communication

The following table describes the four functions of the mass media, including the possible dysfunction of each.

It is obvious that we rely upon the mass media to perform these functions. Periodically, however, we question the effectiveness of the media in each of the categories. When the media releases government information which has been labeled classified, we suggest that it is time to provide restraints on the media.

The more the discussion of restraints on the media, the more the public is reminded of the events of Watergate and the role of the media in performing a surveillance function. (You will note some of the pictures which are included in an article later in this section. The editor of the respective publication engaged in correlation and selection of what he or she thought was appropriate at the time.) Wright's table suggests the latent dysfunction of editorial selection, interpretation, and prescription. In the field of entertainment, citizens raise objections to the types of programming to which families are exposed. Each new television season can be labeled as the year of _____ . (Please fill in the blank with (1) cops and robbers, (2) doctor's dilemma, (3) sitcoms, (4) other.)

Gatekeeper

Although we have discussed the function of the mass media, we must include a dimension that does not appear in interpersonal, group, or public communication. Mass communication, of necessity, must have a person who performs the function of the gatekeeper. The next example should illustrate our point. Suppose that you have just written the following for the campus newspaper:

> On Saturday evening, the local chapter of the Chi Chi Chi sorority had a beer party that resulted in six members of the organization being incarcerated. The president and five other officers were jailed for creating a disturbance and for providing liquor to a minor. Sally Johnson, President, whose parents are the well-known leaders of the X church, told arresting officers to get lost . . .

Table IV
Partial Functional Inventory for Mass Communications

	System under Consideration			
	Society	Individual	Specific Subgroups (e.g., Political Elite)	Culture
1. MASS-COMMUNICATED ACTIVITY: SURVEILLANCE (NEWS)				
Functions (manifest and latent)	Warning: Natural dangers Attack: war Instrumental: News essential to the economy and other institutions Ethicizing	Warning Instrumental Adds prestige Opinion leadership Status conferral	Instrumental Information useful to power Detects: Knowledge of subversive and deviant behavior Manages public opinion Monitors Controls Legitimizes power Status conferral	Aids cultural contact Aids cultural growth
Dysfunctions (manifest and latent)	Threatens stability: News of "better" societies Fosters panic	Anxiety Privatization Apathy Narcotization	Threatens power: News of reality "Enemy" propaganda Exposés	Permits cultural invasion
2. MASS-COMMUNICATED ACTIVITY: CORRELATION (EDITORIAL SELECTION, INTERPRETATION, AND PRESCRIPTION)				
Functions (manifest and latent)	Aids mobilization Impedes threats to social stability Impedes panic	Provides efficiency: Assimilating news Impedes: Overstimulation Anxiety Apathy Privatization	Helps preserve power	Impedes cultural invasion Maintains cultural consensus

(Continued on page 220)

(Continued from page 219)

Dysfunction (manifest and latent)	Increases social conformism: Impedes social change if social criticism is avoided	Weakens critical faculties, Increases passivity	Increases responsibility	Impedes cultural growth

3. MASS-COMMUNICATED ACTIVITY: CULTURAL TRANSMISSION

Functions (manifest and latent)	Increases social cohesion: Widens base of common norms, experiences, etc. Reduces anomie. Continues socialization: Reaches adults even after they have left such institutions as school	Aids integration: Exposure to common norms, Reduces idiosyncrasy, Reduces anomie	Extends power: Another agency for socialization	Standardizes, Maintains cultural consensus
Dysfunctions (manifest and latent)	Augments "mass" society	Depersonalizes acts of socialization		Reduces variety of subcultures

4. MASS-COMMUNICATED ACTIVITY: ENTERTAINMENT

Functions (manifest and latent)	Respite for masses	Respite	Extends power: Control over another area of life	
Dysfunctions (manifest and latent)	Diverts public: Avoids social action	Increases passivity, Lowers "tastes", Permits escapism		Weakens aesthetics "Popular culture"

From Charles R. Wright, "Functional Analysis and Mass Communication," *Public Opinion Quarterly* (1960), pp. 605–20.

A gatekeeper, the editor of the newspaper, might elect to print the following story:

> On Saturday night, six members of a local social organization were arrested as the result of a party which got out of hand. The president and five other members were arrested.

The gatekeeper selected those events which he or she thought were appropriate for the newspaper. Every mass media has individuals who perform the function of gatekeeper. Just as the reporter selects from all of the available events for a report, the editor selects from those events to report through the mass media. The following model illustrates this point.

EVENT	REPORTER	EDITOR	LISTENER
a			
b	a		
c	c	c	
d	d	d	d
e	e	e	e
f	f		
g			

In our model even the listener selects from the variety of events reported through the mass media. The listener selects those events which tend to satisfy the self-interest we discussed in the first section. If the listener is not satisfied with the reporting or editing of the events, he or she can call the station, write the producer or station, or stop buying the sponsor's product. As suggested earlier, the feedback to mass media sources tends to be delayed.

Conclusions

Since mass media is such a ubiquitous phenomenon, it is important that you know something about its functioning. It is here to stay and can only increase in its use. With the advent of two-way cable, greater use will be made of the media for educational purposes. Since travel is becoming more expensive, we may rely on mass media rather than interpersonal contact with family and friends. Sarnoff describes the home communication center of the future.

> Today's console and table model furniture may be displaced by an all-purpose television screen mounted on the wall. It would be coupled to a sound system and a high-speed electronic printer for recording any information the viewer wishes to retain.
>
> This means that the major channel of news, information and entertainment in the home will be a single integrated system that combines all of the separate electronic instruments and printed means of communication today—television set, radio, newspaper, magazine and book.
>
> The home will thus be joined to a new, all-embracing information medium with a global reach. This medium will serve a vast public of differing nationalities, languages, and customs, and its impact will be profound.

Articles

The article by Chesbro and Hamsher describes the role of television series and our values. They conclude that television series have an effect on our value system. Rabinowitz follows this with her article on watching the sitcoms. She takes a look at the heroes of some of the more popular series such as "All in the Family," "The Jeffersons," "The Mary Tyler Moore Show," and "The Bob Newhart Show."

A short piece is included which describes the credibility of television among the American public. While the results are not that surprising, they may provide some cause for alarm.

Morgan explores the role of the mass media in the world of advertising. Although he is specific in his discussion of individuals who have participated in the advertising world, you might enjoy a behind-the-scenes look at what is occurring in television advertising. He also explores the changes that have happened in advertising over the past years.

Day describes the growth of the media in the international realm. While some of his figures may appear astounding, the laser and other developments in communication technology will allow for tremendous growth and development in communication.

The final article by Mallette gives a vivid description of the role of the gatekeeper in the selection of news pictures that could have been printed. In addition to the correlation function discussed earlier, this article raises ethical considerations which must be faced by the mass media. While the pictures may not appeal to your senses, they do vividly make a point on gatekeeping and ethics.

Communication, Values, and Popular Television Series

James W. Chesebro and Caroline D. Hamsher

Communicating is inherently a selective process. Faced with an ever changing and ongoing set of human transactions, both the source and the receiver are forced to make choices about what they say and hear. Consciously and unconsciously, these choices are typically controlled by the needs and motives of those communicating. Try as one may to be "objective," the very decision to communicate reveals particular and personal needs, fears, and commitments. In this sense, all communicative acts selectively highlight one set of human values rather than another set. We are ultimately left with the conclusion, aptly expressed by Gerald R. Miller, that "every communicative act involves, of necessity, a value judgment." [1]

Popular television series are communicative acts. A source (producers, directors, and writers) conveys an identifiable message enacted through a plot played out by characters who ultimately cast certain behaviors as better than others. Consequently, these plots and characters —whether intentionally or accidentally—reflect, convey, and reinforce certain values about what is "good" and what is "bad." In this context, Richard D. Heffner recently argued that television series may appropriately be viewed as "subtle persuaders," He observed,

> There is much more to television than meets the eye. Understanding the medium requires not only a familiarity with the series plots that continue from week to week, but also an awareness of TV's less explicit levels; its off-handed comments; its modes of thought and action that we have come to take for granted. It is, you see, this *less-than-conscious* level of television's content that educates us, subtly, without our even realizing it.... Television, the newest and far more prevalent form of fiction, is even more profoundly influential in our lives—not in terms of the stories it tells, but more importantly, the values it portrays. [2]

While we may wish to ignore the issue, it now appears essential to view television series as persuasive efforts. Consider the case. First, the producers of television series seem overtly aware of their decision to persuade through their se-

From James W. Chesebro and Caroline D. Hamsher, "Communication, Values, and Popular Television Series," *Journal of Popular Culture*, vol. 8, pp. 589–603. Reprinted by permission of the editor.

[1] Gerald R. Miller, *An Introduction to Speech Communication*, 2nd ed. (Indianapolis: Bobbs-Merrill, 1972), p. 10.

[2] Richard D. Heffner, "Television: The Subtle Persuader," *TV Guide* (September 15, 1973), pp. 25–26.

ries. Grant Tinker, producer of "The Mary Tyler Moore" and "Bob Newhart" shows, initially argues that the "qualities in our shows . . . are not important. . . . These are comedies, after all—and if the themes were too serious, we'd lose the comedic element." Tinker does note upon reflection, however, that Mary "does come close, in her 1970s version, to the good old-fashioned virtues we find in the Waltons. In fact, now that I think of it," he notes, "in its own way, the show is projecting all the different values we have been talking about. The show appears to be rather hip on TV, but in fact she and all the characters in that show—forgetting their comedic eccentricities—are all four-square people."[3] (More overtly, Quinn Martin, producer of "Streets of San Francisco," "Cannon," and "The F.B.I." observes: "I am a patriot. In the police stories that I do, I show the police in an idealized way. Without respect for the police, I think we'd have a breakdown in our society."[4] Similarly, Lee Rich, producer of "The Waltons," notes that "the success of this series is because of what is going on in the country today, the loss of values. Many people see ethical qualities in this family that they hope that they can get back to."[5] Producers appear overtly aware, then, of the value-orientation controlling their series. Second, viewers perceive the series predominantly as entertainment rather than persuasive acts. We may repeatedly observe that entertainment may be persuasive; persuasion may be entertaining. Yet viewers act as if the series offered an opportunity "to get away from all the pressures." Third, millions watch the shows. Fourth, these persuasive efforts rely, not upon one presentation of a value, but some twenty or so reinforcements depending upon the number of shows within the series (not to mention reruns). As Heffner puts it, television "combines the traditional two steps of impactful communications: statement

and reinforcement. . . . TV is so highly integrated in our lives that its characters create their own effective credibility, influencing us more than we realize with the life styles they portray."[6] The intentions of the producers, perspective of the viewers, size of the audience, and reinforcement process obligate us to view popular televison series as persuasive acts, for as Andersen and Andersen argue, such values "influence social perception by providing us with a set of basic rules by which we judge the behavior and beliefs of others."[7] In addition, Nielsen observes that if we ignore "the fundamental values" of communicative efforts, we ignore "vital information needed by the listeners if they are to make intelligent decisions."[8]

However, doesn't something more need to be said? We might reasonably ask: *What values are conveyed by popular television series? How do those values gain credibility before television viewers? How desirable are the values conveyed by television series?* Such questions are significant; answering them requires a critical assessment of particular television series. The answers provided here stem from critical methods generated by communication theorists. Particularly, the form and the content of television series are treated in this analysis as the factors which transform and convey the values into more subtle and thereby acceptable messages for the viewers.[9]

While many methods exist for describing the

[3] Quoted in Bill Davidson, "Forecast for Fall: Warm and Human," *TV Guide* (February 16, 1974).
[4] *Ibid.*
[5] *Ibid.*

[6] Heffner.
[7] Kenneth E. Andersen and Mary Andersen, "Ethics and Persuasion," *Persuasion: Theory and Practice* by Kenneth E. Andersen (Boston: Allyn and Bacon, 1971), p. 313, See also Ronald L. Applebaum, Karl W. E. Anatol, Ellis R. Hays, Owen O. Jenson, Richard E. Porter, and Jerry E. Mandel, *Fundamentals in Human Communication* (San Francisco: Canfield Press, 1973), p. 91.
[8] Thomas R. Nilsen, *Ethics of Speech Communication*, 2nd ed. (Indianapolis: Bobbs-Merrill, 1974). p. 76.
[9] We have sought, in an earlier essay, to justify and explain how such an approach may be used to examine persuasive messages. See James W. Chesebro and Caroline D. Hamsher, "Rhetorical Criticism: A Message-Centered Procedure," *The Speech Teacher*, 22 (November 1973), 282–90.

formal characterisitcs of persuasive messages and thus for distinguishing major types of persuasive messages, Northrop Frye[10] provides a critical framework we find relevant and useful for an analysis of television series. In Frye's view, two variables generate and distinguish the major persuasive forms: (1) the central agent's or hero's apparent relationship to the audience, and (2) the hero's ability to control circumstances. These two variables produce five particular persuasive forms. In *irony*, a hero is inferior in intelligence and power to others and unable to control environmental factors. In *mime*, the hero is one of us and able to control circumstances with the same skill we possess. In *leader* centered forms, the hero is superior to others in degree but again able to manipulate the environment with the same degree of control possessed by others. In *romance*, the hero is superior in degree to others and the environment. In *myth*, the hero is superior to others and the environment in kind. These five persuasive forms constitute the formal framework we shall use to assess popular television shows.

The content or substantive dimension of popular television series may certainly vary from show to show. As we shall employ a concern for content in this analysis, however, the focus is upon those ideas, notions, or principles, which repeat themselves from show to show during the series. Attention is thereby given to the persistent or enduring principles continually advocated throughout the series.

The range of methods used to describe the central· symbols or principles of persuasive messages varies. However, Kenneth Burke's "dramatistic process" may be employed to describe the stages of communicative progressions ordering popular television series. As we use the dramatistic process to identify central principles of television series, four questions function as a critical framework: (1) *Pollution*—What norms are violated and cast as disruptive to the social system involved? (2) *Guilt*—Who or what is generally held responsible for the pollution? (3) *Purification*—What kinds of acts are generally initiated to eliminate the pollution and guilt? (4) *Redemption*—What social system or order is created as a result of passing through the pollution, guilt, and purification stages? By way of example, the Christian conception of salvation may be revealed by way of the dramatistic process: man sins by violating God's law (pollution); man is held responsible for the sins although Christ accepts the responsibility because of His great love (guilt); Christ is crucified to eliminate man's sin and responsibility (purification); and all men are thereby allowed to enter Heaven after death (redemption). While our example may not be as detailed here as a reader may wish, the central point is that the dramatistic process may be used to reveal systematically the central symbols or principles controlling a drama.

Our concern for the form and content of popular television series generates a five by four critical matrix which is used here to identify systematically and comprehensively major television series' persuasive appeals. Figure I depicts this matrix. While providing the foundation for a systematic and comprehensive identification of persuasive appeals in popular television series, the matrix also offers a method for contrasting types of television series as well as for grouping those series which employ essentially the same persuasive appeals.

Some forty-one popular television series constitute the data base for this analysis. All forty-one series have been classified into the matrix. Five of the series are highlighted and examined

[10] Northrop Frye, *Anatomy of Criticism* (Princeton, New Jersey: Princeton University Press, 1957), especially pp. 33–4. We are obviously adapting Frye's analysis to our particular interests. The adaptation may distort Frye's particular objectives.

[11] While some differences emerge between our treatment of the dramatistic process and the perspective offered by Bernard L. Brock, Brock offers one of the most convenient summaries of a rhetorician's view of the dramatistic process; see: Bernard L. Brock, "Rhetorical Criticism: A Burkeian Approach," *Methods of Rhetorical Criticism: A Twentieth Century Perspective*, ed. Robert L. Scott and Bernard L. Brock (New York: Harper and Row, 1972), pp. 315–27.

SUBSTANTIVE CHARACTERISTICS	FORMAL CHARACTERISTICS				
	Irony	Mime	Leader	Romance	Myth
Pollution					
Guilt					
Purification					
Redemption					

Figure I. The Critical Matrix

in detail as representative of each of the formal characteristics identified in the matrix: Irony—"All in the Family"; Mime—"The Mary Tyler Moore Show"; Leader centered—"Maude"; Romance—"Marcus Welby, M.D."; Myth—"The Six Million Dollar Man." Four of these series were selected because they were the top ten according to the 1973–74 Nielsen ratings; "The Six Million Dollar Man," while not in the top ten, was most highly rated among the series categorized as myth. Two shows from each series were randomly selected, videotaped, and analyzed to illustrate and establish the claims made about each of the series.

"All in the Family" conveys a range of identifiable messages. The series implies, initially, that *bigots only hurt themselves*, that their attack on human frailties ultimately destroys their own esteem and individuality and reveals them to others as insensitive. In the particular shows examined here, Archie Bunker verbally assaults George (a mentally retarded person) and Joe Tucker (an uemployed man seeking psychiatric aid), only to gain the scorn of his family for the attacks.

A second message of this series is that *bigots can be laughed at instead of hated*. Such a message implies that bigots only reveal their own limits as people and that their assertions are shallow and therefore formal; the family provides a comic dimension to bigotry. In the shows

we considered, Archie's behaviors make him a source of bewildering amusement (typified by his son-in-law Michael's reactions) rather than an agent of evil.

The series posits yet a third message: *the WASP is dying as a national norm and ideal*. Archie is a white Ango-Saxon Protestant who asserts the WASP position: that being white is better than being nonwhite; that the Anglo-Saxon heritage is better than the Eastern European, Asian, or African heritage; that being Protestant is better than being Catholic or Jewish. For Archie, the non-WASP's quest for equality is a sign of his or her being "uppity." The series denies Archie's ideal; cultural differences are presented as equally valid life styles. People often need help, thereby rejecting the WASP ideal of rugged individualism and independence. Thus, both George and Joe Tucker seek assistance from others; the impact of both shows is that requesting and receiving help allows individuals to develop more fully.

Finally, "All in the Family" suggests that *change is good as long as it is moderate and liberal*. Extreme responses, whether conservative or radical, are cast as unreasonable. Archie's rejection of the retarded and those seeking psychological help is viewed as too conservative. Correspondingly, blacks who hate whites are cast as too extreme; Archie's black neighbor, Mr. Jefferson, is presented as Archie's equally misguided counterpart. The argument of the series is that the best change is that which is thoughtful and evolving, respecting individualism.

These messages, even when explicitly stated, as we have done here, are by no means automatically acceptable. The messages are conveyed in ways which disarm the viewer and make the viewer more susceptible to accepting them. In particular, Archie's drama (like that of "Sanford and Son") is ironic to the audience. Archie lacks intelligence and power; he cannot control his environment; his pride is a reflection of his stupidity. Archie's flaw is placed in a social context which makes him incapable of success; Archie becomes, therefore, a pathetic figure to be pitied rather than hated. The ironic form of the series sets bigotry in a formal setting which denies its power as a social force.

As the ironic drama is played out in show after show, the bigot becomes even less of an object to be treated seriously. The hero, Archie, causes the pollution in each show and thereby creates the irony. Repeatedly, Archie is assigned the guilt; the irony is extended because the hero is responsible. Purifying acts as initiated by others to minimize the hero's pollution and guilt. As a final touch, redemption is a return to the old order as Archie re-establishes himself as ready to engage in additional ventures in exactly the same manner.

Certainly such messages, when cast in the form of an ironic drama, deserve critical response. At first the series may disarm us and make us forget the power of bigotry. But bigots are not always ironic and we should not assume that bigotry only emerges ironically. The bigot may be presented in mythical, romantic, leader centered, or mimetic drama. Men such as Hitler, Spiro Agnew, and George Wallace have utilized forms which add power to the claims of bigots. The ironic form is seldom selected by the bigot as a vehicle for persuasion. "All in the Family" should not encourage us to look for bigotry only in ironic guise.

Moreover, we need to realize that even ironic bigotry may reinforce racial and religious intolerance. From a random sampling of viewers in the United States and Canada, Neil Vidmar and Milton Rokeach demonstrated that to the unprejudiced persons Archie was a "dumb, bigoted 'hard-hat'" but that to the prejudiced, Michael is the object of scorn and cast as a "long-haired, lazy 'meathead Polack' who spouts liberal slogans."[12] Thus, rather than dissuading bigots, the series creates an opportunity for bigots to perceive a new enemy selectively without disrupting their belief structures. On a weekly basis, the irony of bigotry may reinforce rather than eliminate bigotry.

Consequently, we may wish to be more cautious in believing that liberals always possess the power to disarm bigots. The liberal wish to see bigots as ironic does not guarantee that bigots are therefore devoid of power. Groups such as the John Birch Society and the Christian Anti-Communist League have members whose educational, economic, and political activism exceed the national norms. There are things to fear in this world; some problems must be taken seriously. Liberalism may not have taken the most positive step in casting bigots as ironic; clearly the labeling process does not diminish the power of bigotry.

"The Mary Tyler Moore Show" embodies and conveys a different set of messages to the audiences. The series initially suggests that *Puritan morality is a viable philosophic system.* The world is perceived in moral terms in which good works promise salvation. In particular, honesty, simplicity, cooperation, self-discipline, orderliness, personal responsibility, and humility are cast as desirable values. Mary is honest; she may not always want to be, but she worries about complete honesty and, if forced, she must tell the truth. One of the shows, in fact, is based on the premise that Mary once lied and all of the evils of the "white lie" are revealed; Mary suffers for the lie. Mary is, moreover, a prototype of contemporary simplicity and orderliness. Her

[12] Neil Vidmar and Milton Rokeach, "Archie Bunker's Bigotry: A Study in Selective Perception and Exposure," *Journal of Communication*, 24 (Winter 1974), 38.

dress and hair are uncomplicated and efficient. Her apartment is itself an "efficiency," and she lives in the Midwest, the core of simple American purity. Mary is cooperative; she is part of a "team" and tries to make all members of the team feel good. She will, for the team, even agree to do tasks when they inconvenience or hurt her. In one show, Mary lends Rhoda money for a flower shop when she, Mary, needs it for a car. Mary is self-disciplined and personally responsible. In one show, she works all night on obituaries, and fatigue leads her to write humorous death notices; she is suspended for two weeks when one of these obituaries is read on the air. Mary says she wants "no special treatment," for she was responsible and lacked discipline. Mr. Grant responds, "You have to be punished." After realizing the impact of the suspension, Mary observes, "I'm usually so in control of myself." She even reflects that when she was a child her mother put her in the room that needed the most cleaning for Mary released anxiety by tidying up. Another Puritan virtue is Mary's humility. She admits she needs others, wants to be with her office mates: "I feel lousy without my friends." Whatever success Mary achieves, she finds it ultimately linked to the efforts of others; she is humble.

Achievement and success are important values; this is a second message of the series. Upward social mobility is held to be especially important, particularly in business, so Mary is delighted with her title of Associate Producer even though the job is often secretarial. In one show, Mary is nominated for a "Best Documentary" award; she is pleased to be recognized for such success. In another show, Ted Knight, the extreme manifestation of the values, feels sorry about the likelihood of Mary's losing her job but is reluctant to defend her, noting that, "There's no percentage in everyone's head being cut off." To Ted, Walter Cronkite is "top dog"—Cronkite occupies the most esteemed position in his field and for his achievement warrants great respect if not awe. Achievement and success are thus seen as powerful values to be sought and secured by all.

This series also promotes a third message: *Effort and optimism are always rewarded*. Mary tries. Ted tries. Murray tries. Lou tries. The whole team tries. And while the team may not have produced a top rated news program, the implicit communication of the series is that one day the effort and optimism could be rewarded. If nothing else, trying hard and thinking postively make everyone feel happier and more fulfilled.

A fourth message of "The Mary Tyler Moore Show" is that *sociability, external conformity, generosity, and consideration for others are appropriate modes of social interaction*. If one serves others, they will appreciate one. Getting along, being loved, being worthy of love—these are particularly important social values. Mary prepares coffee for all; she holds parties at her apartment and suggests surprise birthday parties even when these gatherings offer her no opportunity for personal growth. After an argument with Rhoda, Mary clearly expresses the value: "I hate being on the outs with someone I like," even though Mary has every reason to be cross. As Mary puts it, "It's lonely being right."

Finally, the series suggest that *patriotism is an essential spiritual value*. Patriotism is cast as loyalty to tradition, both occupationally and socially. Thus when Mary, having been suspended from her job, has an opportunity to get another position, she asserts, "I want to come back. I don't like it out there. I like it here." Likewise, on the job, everyone refers to the head of the newsroom as "Lou" except for Mary, who has for years perceived him as "Mr. Grant." Socially, Mary retains traditional commitment, and she "feel[s] lousy without my friends." Patriotism functions, as a result, as a pattern of identification. If the pattern is broken, the life is destroyed. Mary is, correspondingly, destroyed when her job or her friends are destroyed.

These messages become credible within the framework of the mimetic drama, which employs the common, the familiar, as its central mode of action. The values conveyed in "The Mary Tyler Moore Show" appear realistic and relevant because the values are cast as operative within social and circumstantial relationships shared by all of us. As the mimetic drama unfolds, pollution may be generated by Mary, by others, by circumstances or accidents, but customarily the pollution occurs when the best of intentions are operating. Correspondingly, guilt may be assigned to Mary or to her close friends, but the guilt must always be qualified because of the force of circumstances, accidents, and good intentions. As a result of the development of the pollution and guilt frames, purification is seldom a decisive moment; it results from someone's admitting or accepting the responsibility for wrongdoing or recognizing the force of external causation. Self-victimization or mortification strategies possess a genteel quality in the purifying stage of mimetic drama. No one is ever really "evil" and so the punishment itself is never severe. Redemption, consequently, requires only a return to the old social system with "greater wisdom" about the nature of this system. Life goes on, but one is a bit wiser for the experience. It would seem to us that a host of popular television series employ the mimetic drama to espouse essentially the same values found in "The Mary Tyler Moore Show"; these would include "Rhoda," "Friends and Lovers," "The Bob Newhart Show," "Happy Days," "Good Times," "The Little House on the Prairie," "That's My Mama," "Movin' On," and "Chico and the Man."

The mimetic drama and the cluster of values it casts as credible require a critical response. The form assumes that conflicts are really only "differences of opinion" rather than profound confrontations. All people are viewed as basically decent and wholesome. The perspective is conservative, offering a limited view of actual experience, and it may thereby preclude a realistic approach to the wide range of human relationships. Also, the form presents the "establishment" or "status quo" as the most viable mode of organization. The mimetic framework highlights *means* (hard work, optimism, achievement, effort, and the like), seldom questioning the *ends* toward which those means are directed. As we face "real" confrontations, we may be so

"drugged" by such shows that we assume our means can satisfy all demands made upon our society when, in fact, new systems may have to be devised. We must continually assess our social objectives as well as the means employed to secure those ends. The failure to question the evolution of the entire social system—even if we do not change the direction or the rate of change—ought not to be the result of popular televison series which function as societal narcotics.

"Maude" is a vehicle for yet another set of messages conveyed to television viewers. The series suggests first that *individuals, especially women, can be strong and powerful.* None of the characters in the shows—husband, wife, daughter, grandson, housekeeper—lacks "backbone." The women in particular are more than weak or passive. Depending on one's perspective, Maude is either a powerful symbol of independence and autonomy for women or she is, in the vernacular, a "ball buster." Carol, Maude's daughter, is involved with women's liberation. Both these women avoid housework and the values typically associated with femininty. Maude, in fact, does a predictable slow burn which erupts into a violent attack when women as a class are cast as "housewives" or viewed as passive and obedient servants of males. Maude would determine her own fate; four marriages and three divorces suggest that Maude's quest for self-determination is to be taken seriously.

A second message is conveyed by the series: *the nuclear family is not sacred or private.* Traditionally, the family has been considered stable, permanent, and closed to outsiders. But Maude's four marriages contravene such a traditional conception of the nuclear family, although Maude obviously tries to make the system work. Sex is openly discussed, and "private" interpersonal issues become public among friends.

The series also implies that *liberals have more fun.* Liberals traditionally tend to hold individual rights and individual development as primary values for the society; the responsibility of the liberal (and of society, therefore,) is to provide equal opportunities to secure those rights and therefore attain happiness. In "Maude," liberals have more experience, more action in their lives. They are wittier, happier, more interesting. Liberals can afford face lifts, housekeepers, and cocktail parties. Liberals are middle class; their conflicts are predominantly differences resolved by and for the liberal.

The series also suggests, however, that *liberals may be right but liberalism may be a rocky road*. Maude's contests are often rugged; tensions and voices are raised. Yet liberals remain strong and powerful; they prevail.

These messages gain credibility and subtly affect viewers because Maude is a leader. The leader centered drama provides a context supportive of a strong, if not dominant, personality. Leaders do dominate others, mobilizing intended responses from their followers. We anticipate that the followers may often feel overpowered, lack comparative power, or even experience jealousy. Leaders do, by definition, introduce and formulate goals, tasks, and procedures. They are centers of action, often delegating and directing action. They integrate and pull individual efforts together; they often summarize group efforts and offer transitions between acts. Thus, we expect those cast as leaders to appear confident of their values, to use those values to interpret events and create issues, and to label forces as "right" and "wrong." Correspondingly, those cast as followers use the leader's values for perceptual and interpretative categories.

With respect to Maude's leadership, pollution occurs when the liberal ethic is somehow challenged: individual rights are violated, or individual opportunities are not provided because of race, religion, sex, or nationality. Maude views the Puritan ethic as often overpowering people at the expense of the liberal ethic. In one of the particular shows examined here, Maude requires that her domestic must have faced racial, religious, sexual, or ethnic discrimination. Maude's black housekeeper (who is leaving) is ultimately replaced by a Puerto Rican woman. As Florida (the black woman) puts it, "Maude is a bleeding heart liberal."

Guilt, in the leader center drama, may be as-

signed by victimization or by self-mortification. Self-mortification is the commonly used liberal approach: Maude tends to assume guilt for societal injustice. In the liberal framework, it is the way in which individuals use or do not use the system which creates circumstances producing minority problems; minority group members are seldom perceived as having caused their own plight, whatever it may be. As Florida aptly puts it, "Maude feels guilt"; so any servant of Maude's must be a representative of a minority group. In another show, Maude feels that she must first get her friends Arthur and Vivian to talk; then she must ultimately get them married. If Maude touches their lives, she feels she must assume responsibility.

As might be expected, in a leader centered drama the leader generates purification. At this particular stage, Maude is the source of change and improvement. She mobilizes others; she introduces and formulates goals, tasks, and procedures; she delegates and directs. Maude is, after all, described as a "Betsy Ross" and a "bra-burner" in the series' theme song. Thus, she initiates those actions necessary to get Vivian and Arthur married. Maude hires the housekeeper while Carol, Arthur, and Florida make bets about whom she'll hire. Maude is verbally labeled, in the show, as "the big bad wolf," "the slugger," "the tail end of the batting order," "anything but tranquil," and a "prizefighter."

The drama concludes, reaches redemption, when Maude's values and goals control and dominate; individualism is thus secure. Because Maude accepts guilt, carries out those acts necessary to eliminate the pollution, her set of values prevails in a final moment of redemption. Conflict is thus eliminated and happiness returns.

A host of televison series employ the leader drama as the vehicle to justify the messages generated; included would be "Get Christie Love," "McMillan and Wife," "Mannix," "Police Surgeon," "Cannon," "The Rookies," "Gunsmoke," "Adam-12," "M*A*S*H," "Barnaby Jones," "Lucas Tanner," "Petrocelli," "Ironside," "Streets of San Francisco," "Harry O," "The Rockford Files," "Columbo," and "Mc-

Cloud." Virtually all of these series cast the hero as leader; these leaders act out much the same kinds of dramas. Critic-observers can readily discern a liberal bias permeating these series as well.   .

These shows offer a reasonable set of messages in an entertaining manner. However, a critical examination of the leader centered form raises noteworthy issues. During periods of cultural transformation when interpersonal relationships and institutions are often in flux, a stress on "rugged individualism" may diminish attention to the development of needed social and community relationships and systems. Moreover, messages emphasizing hierarchies (leaders-followers) in interpersonal relationships as exciting and viable approaches would appear to detract from the growing and reasonable trend toward interpersonal equality. Finally, the liberal vision tends to conceive of cooperation rather than conflict as the most desirable base for human interactions. While we would not advocate fighting, certainly conflict is a dimension of human conduct which may often be essential to growth and development. Perhaps we need to prepare people for both cooperation and conflict rather than encouraging them to accept uncritically those messages which promise cooperative redemption as the most desirable outcome of human interaction.

"Marcus Welby, M.D." communicates a fourth set of messages to television viewers. As the series evolves during a season, audiences are left with several specific conclusions. First, they are advised that *wiser counsel and more thoughtful planning than we are capable of emanates from a select few*. On one of the shows considered here, Gary is slowly losing his voice, essential for his continued functioning as an airport flight controller. Gary is unable to detect or handle the physical, circumstantial, and psychological implications of this change in his life. Welby, although a family practitioner, possesses the perceptual framework and critical facilities Gary does not have. Welby recognizes his power; Gary is, in Welby's words, "a very insecure young man," "headstrong," "ignoring what must be done." Welby knows, moreover, that

Gary's wife "has the psychological strength" to understand and help Gary "if only she will." Besides possessing this grasp of complex psychological variables, Welby observes that some "6,000 people get hit by carcinoma each year" and that a laryngectomy, in Gary's case, indicates the use of one of the newly developed vocal resonators. While Welby certainly consults with experts on particular medical questions, he generally recognizes the symptoms, severity of the case, and nature of treatment well before the specialists articulate the issues. If we are to believe what Welby's face suggests before the formal diagnosis and if we have listened carefully to Welby's previous "hunches," we know what Welby knows before his patients or his colleagues do. Beyond his control of such psychological and physiological issues, Welby handles the circumstantial variables as well. Extremely expensive medical treatment can, Welby affirms, be "worked out." While Gary may be unable to continue in his immediate job, Welby makes all of the arrangements necessary to obtain an equivalent job for him. Thus, while Gary believes he'd rather "die" than go through the entire transition, Welby offers superior advice and planning to reconstruct Gary's life.

The series also suggests that *agents possessing special vocational skills warrant unique social respect*. As each show evolves, Welby's professional skills control emerging circumstances; it is only a matter of time until the other characters in the show recognize that Welby's skills stem from a depth of sensitivity, human understanding, and compassion more profound than theirs. Welby's medical rank, expertise, and success are direct indicators of the social respect he deserves.

The notion that *the external or objective perspective can recognize and resolve human dilemmas* pervades the series. Welby's patients exist in relatively closed social, psychological, and physical systems; Welby enters those ongoing systems essentially as an outsider. His external or objective point of view generates new views and insights. Welby knows, for instance, that Gary's wife is "the biggest influence in his life." Gary does not know; Gary's wife believes simply that "he had to be goal oriented" to raise himself above his background. Welby goes on to predict, as circumstances begin to affect Gary, that "he doesn't realize what an unexpected blow this will have on him." Welby's sense is uncommon; his insights appear reasonable only if we assume that the role of "external, objective agent" functions as a perspective essential to recognizing and resolving human dilemmas.

These messages appear credible when cast as part of a romantic drama. The romantic hero is part of a legend and possesses a chivalric love for others. There is a supernatural aura essential to romance, and correspondingly the romantic hero appears adventurous, mysterious, and all knowing. As a romantic hero, Welby does not create but rather identifies and describes pollution. Other agents or circumstances create the pollution; Welby identifies the nature and extent of problems of the mind, body, and environment. Likewise, the romantic hero assigns blame to those agents or circumstances generating the pollution. Blame is assigned so that the romantic hero can grapple with or purify the social system; the hero, employing the special skills he possesses, slowly but decisively corrects the problems of the mind, body, and environment. The redemption stage of the romantic drama is essentially a recognition of the skill and sensitivity of the romantic hero in recognizing and resolving the pollution and guilt through a particularly wise set of purifying actions. The other characters in the show overtly acknowledge the constructive role of the hero at this stage in the drama as well as explicitly admitting that the hero has profoundly altered their lives. This kind of romantic drama is a framework for several other popular television series including "The Waltons," "Kojak," Medical Center," "Hawaii Five-O," "Kung Fu," and "Apple's Way." In each of these series, the hero possesses a unique set of special skills, and each series likewise conveys essentially the same kinds of messages found in "Marcus Welby, M.D."

These series provide confidence and security for the viewers through the concept that exter-

nal agents will resolve human dilemmas; however, viewers are thereby encouraged to perceive themselves as more passive, less responsible for themselves, and more dependent upon the efforts of mystical figures for solutions to extremely real problems. Some of the same dangers that were discussed with respect to mimetic and leader centered dramas reappear in this construct. Such reliance on the romantic illusion, the "happily ever after" ending, tends to stifle critical thought and realistic efforts at human problem solving.

"The Six Million Dollar Man" conveys a set of predominantly inspirational messages to viewers. A central message is that *human imagination and creativity have no limits*. The premise of the series is grounded in a kind of ultimate faith in the human ability to overcome all limitations. Steve Austin, hero of the series was a relatively successful astronaut until a nearly fatal accident forced him to lose an eye, an arm, and both legs. The government intervened; Steve was transformed into a bionic man at a cost of six million dollars. He can run 60 miles an hour, he has X-ray and infrared vision, he can leap thirty feet into the air, and he has superhuman strength in his bionic legs and arm. An experiment in human imagination and technology has transformed Austin from a helpless cripple into a quasi-mechanical superman. Only human choice, we are led to believe, can preclude us from employing technology in more creative and imaginative ways.

The series further suggests that *technology aids and may also be complementary to the human condition*. As a bionic man, Steve is a perfectly balanced biological and engineering construct. Human creativity is retained and transformed into a more viable and usable structure. Technology is thus cast as a more constructive means for carrying out the human intent. Implicitly, a promise of immortality and physical perfection is associated with technology in the series.

Humans may ultimately exercise absolute control of their environment, we are told by the series. Steve's bionic system promises profound and thorough-going control of complex environmental forces. Not only can he see; he can see through physical objects with X-ray precision. His speed on the ground enables him to cover territory efficiently without the aid of a vehicle. Moreover, Steve has a superhuman sense, the ability to view and detect heat without the use of touch. Violent or forceful environmental factors are negated by virture of his superhuman strength. While Steve cannot fly unassisted, his leaps are of such size that flying seems but one "step" away in the evolution of human technology. The series implies, then, that control of the environment is not far away.

Such messages, while initially incredible assertions, gain force when placed in the context of a dramatic myth. Mythical drama involves universal struggles such as the quest for absolute truth or beauty, or for a permanent peace, or the conflict between good and evil. Both sacred and timeless issues are at stake; the mythical drama possesses, as a result, ritualistic and dreamlike qualities. In the classical myth, the source of the form, the hero possesses skill or knowledge which others do not have; the hero has supporters who also may have special powers; the hero engages in a long, unknown, and difficult journey which ultimately establishes the hero as unique in his search for a precious object or significant goal; the hero must do battle with guardians of the object or forces preventing him from reaching the goal.

In the mythical drama, pollution is a product of a set of circumstances beyond human control, unreasoned or overwhelming human or superhuman strength, or a profound ideological or religious conflict which admits of no compromise. In one of the shows surveyed here, for example, Steve's counteragent is an indestructible, self-protecting computer set to initiate a nuclear war automatically in the context of tense Soviet-American relations. To complicate matters further, an earthquake has both disrupted the timing of the computer and closed off circuits essential to shutting down the computer. These circumstances generate a set of

supernatural problems. Blame for these events cannot be placed on any human agent; guilt is beyond the limits of humans. Purification requires the strength, intelligence, and virture of a mythical Hercules or Jason, willing to undertake a dangerous journey operating, at best, with the aid of a select few who complement the hero's power. No predictable set of purifying acts exists; the hero's real powers may, in fact, surface only during the struggle itself. To get to the computer, Steve must, for example, pass through an underground research center which has been designed to protect itself; this center has been blown up and all its mechanisms are unpredictable. The hero alone controls the purification stage of the drama. Redemption occurs when the hero has accomplished the task and others are able to speak of the efforts employed to eliminate the pollution.

While the skills of the mythical hero and the completeness of the ritual vary from drama to drama, only a few popular televison series today employ even a variation of the mythical drama as the central vehicle to convey certain messages to the viewers; "Planet of the Apes" and "The Night Stalker" do contain some elements. In the past, various series such as "Superman" have also employed the form; generally at least one representative is found on television during any given time period. Problems which arise from overemphasis on the concept of the mythical hero seem too obvious to belabor; they relate clearly to the issues raised with respect to the romantic hero. The fact that the mythical drama does not appear extensively on television does suggest that our times are perhaps not conducive to the messages presented in such a form. The significance of this phenomenon is certainly worthy of further, in-depth speculation.

We readily acknowledge that popular television series function as entertainment; we have sought to offer an equally important but different conception of such programs. Essentially, we have suggested that such series are persuasive communications. As acts of communication, they represent choices about what to say and what not to say. Such choices reveal value judgments about what is important as well as what is "good" or "bad." The dramatic form controlling popular television series reinforce the tendency to highlight value judgments, since statements delineating "good" and "bad" are inherent in such forms and are revealed in plots, characters, settings, and themes. The messages conveyed to the viewers and the values they reinforce become credible because of the form and the content controlling each series. Form and content thus determine how values can subtly and effectively be conveyed to audiences.

While we may wish that we could dismiss such issues altogether, to do so is to ignore factors affecting thoughtful and insightful decision making. Therefore, we have been concerned primarily with the substantive relationships among popular television series, values, and communicative forms and content. We have argued that an intimate relationship exists among these three variables: television series function as persuasive acts of communication altering or reinforcing value systems.

One concluding methodological note regarding the interrelationship between content and form: early in our analysis, by way of our critical matrix, we suggested that content and form *could* be meaningfully related to reveal the persuasive styles of television series; in concluding, we would offer an even more powerful hypothesis—*content controls form and form controls content*. As we consider series after series, we were ultimately able to predict the content of a show if we knew its form; if we had determined the form, we could make reasonable estimates about the kinds of principles that could be conveyed on the show. Such an hypothesis clearly requires more direct assessment with appropriate methods; we believe we have provided a suitable heuristic base for this type of investigation.

Watching the Sit-Coms

Dorothy Rabinowitz

Amos n' Andy are long gone, but changing tastes, increased sophistication, and the jading plentitude that television has provided over the years seem in no way to have altered the capacity of American audiences to be held in thrall, week after week, by "shows." The shows Americans have liked the most recently have been staples of CBS television, the Saturday-night "situation comedies," as irrelevant a term for these programs as can have been invented. For it is not for anything as bland as the name implies that the Saturday night sit-coms have consistently drawn the highest Nielsen ratings. Comprising four half-hour segments, *All in the Family*, *The Jeffersons*, *The Mary Tyler Moore Show*, and *The Bob Newhart Show*, the Saturday night sit-coms have more often than not supplied a fare of a kind quite remarkable in the annals of commercial television. The departure this season of *All in the Family*, the most popular of them all, from Saturday night to Monday night offers as good an occasion as any for reflecting on the world of the sit-coms and their audience.

One begins by taking *All in the Family* (a Lear-Yorkin Production) for what it is, a weekly repository of our most fashionable pieties. The series is set in a lower-middle-class neigh-

Reprinted from *Intellect*—September-October, 1975.

borhood, its backdrop a lace-curtained, depressed, but impeccable two-story house of the kind one might find in working-class sections of Queens or Bay Ridge, Brooklyn. The head of the household, as everyone knows, is Archie Bunker, a bigot, an enemy of progress and of progressive thinkers of every stripe; a hardhat in short and in fact, Archie's employment being, vaguely, in the construction line. Ostensibly a member of the Wasp majority, albeit of its lower classes, Archie is hostile to blacks, Puerto Ricans, Jews, Catholics, atheists, homosexuals, and women's liberationists. Not that his crude assaults on these targets go unopposed, for his household is illuminated by the presence of a militantly progressive daughter and son-in-law (the latter to be sure, something of a sponger and a hothead), both of whom spring smartly into action whenever Archie opens his mouth.

An extraordinary number of words have been written about, and objections entered to, the "bigotry" of *All in the Family*. Civil-rights leaders have charged that the show disseminates racially and religiously biased attitudes, despite its clearly stated hostility to Archie's prejudices. Women's groups complain about the part of Edith, Archie's wife, a goodhearted but muddleheaded woman whom her husband refers to regularly as "the dingbat," and who accepts the role of loving servant to her husband. Nothing if not aware of these objections, the producers, writers, and directors of *All in the Family* have gone to great lengths to establish *all* of Archie's contentions as bigotry, up to and including his notion that black criminals might be a threat to one's life. Indeed, there is but one figure on whom the show's satire ranges entirely free and unselfconscious, and that figure is Archie himself and, by extension the hardhat type in general, a target of satire that has inspired more than one progressive sensibility since the days when construction workers fought student radicals in the street, and aligned themselves on the side of the President.

The first aim of this satire, it would appear, is to explode the myth of hardhat virility. Did you think that those strong, inarticulate louts were comfortable with their animal natures? You couldn't be more wrong. Archie's sex life is limited by inhibition and narrowness, as witness his discomfort when his wife proposes they return to their honeymoon hotel for a twenty-fifth wedding anniversary. Archie is futhermore, a blusterer and an ignoramus, who can get out no idiom but that it is mangled, no proverb but that it is turned upside down, no word of more than two syllables but that it is mispronounced. (Many of these manglings and mispronunciations are reminiscent indeed of the blackface violence perpetrated on the King's English by Amos n' Andy, back in that unenlightened past which is now to the enlightened an embarrassment to recall: "Wait a minute heah Andy! Whut is you doin? Is you mulsiflyin or reviding?") Archie is also a World War II veteran, a factor integral to his status as a reactionary. He has only to narrow his small blue eyes at his peace-marching son-in-law and deliver a prideful reference to "double-yew double-yew two" in order to induce laughter from a studio audience that *knows* how the failures of our past, of our elders, or everything we have become are inextricably linked with the proto-fascist type of the veteran.

Archie is not the only reactionary visible on *All in the Family*. Before their promotion to a series of their own, Archie's black neighbors, the Jeffersons, included in their long-suffering family circle a bigot almost as impossible as Archie, but one whose hatreds were directed against whites. This effort at balance aside, *All in the Family's* portrayal of blacks has reflected with some precision what the outer limits of comment are thought to be on that subject. The theme of black crime is particularly pertinent. In one episode, Archie confronts two black robbers, as verbal, elegant, and full of graceful effrontery as Archie is gauche and inarticulate. In addition to being cleverer than he (Archie has foolishly put his faith in a gun, while they rely on those typical weapons of the urban criminal, wit and cerebration), they are models of sensitivity—they indulge Edith's off-key singing, force Archie to be nice to her, and generally comport themselves like ambassadors to the Court of St. James. Elsewhere, Norman Lear, the "developer" of *All in the Family*, has developed other avenues for the treatment of this issue, notably in his black-family "spin-offs," whole series created around characters first established in other shows. In the immensely successful *Good Times*, shown on Tuesday evenings, a ghetto family comes to grips with black crime on several occasions, once in an episode during which the lovable teen-ager J.J. is forced to take part in a gang war against his will, and again when a black—and blind—salesman is presented as a bunko artist, an unscrupulous robber of poor ghetto dwellers and, the young militant of the family gives us to understand, of his own people.

"His own people" is the reassuring factor here. Lear's programs endorse the liberal answer to the high rate of black crime, the proposition that blacks are its chief victims. In addition, in all three of Lear's black-family programs—*The Jeffersons*, *Good Times*, and *Sanford and Son*—blacks alone pass judgment on black problems and on black attitudes in general. This enables a modest spirit of self-criticism to seem to prevail on these shows. On *The Jeffersons*, an upwardly-mobile anti-white George Jefferson is balanced off against his wife,

Louise, who is sanity and moderation itself. In one episode, George Jefferson and his son Lionel shower contempt upon Louise's elderly uncle, a retired butler whom they berate for having spent his life as an Uncle Tom in a white household and for being, clearly, an activist of the NAACP variety. "Listen, you!" the dignified older man roars at Lionel, "I used to spit out six like you before breakfast!" "I worked for many years to get from nigger to Negro, so you'll have to forgive me if it takes me a while to get used to calling myself a black now," the uncle concludes, with hauteur, to shrieks of applause from the audience for this defiance of the new by the old.

For airing sentiments like these, the producer of *All in the Family* has made a not inconsiderable name for himself as an entrepreneur of the controversial. On *All in the Family* alone, such subjects as menopause, miscarriage, and menstrauion have all been dealt with, if with the somewhat reverent air that inevitably seems to accompany the principle that all things having to do with our bodies are sacred. Next season, it is promised that *All in the Family* will venture a program on euthanasia. The decision to treat that theme was made, according to a New York *Times* piece, at what was presumably a typical conference between Lear and his story editor. "Can we find a way to do it without copping out?" Lear asks, "Maybe we can have the relatives agree to it and let the audience know they're not sure they made the right decision." It would appear that among "controversial" and pioneering types in the media, of whom Lear is so egregious an example, "no copping out" means that within the format of a show dealing with a morally questionable course of action, the principals decide *for* the action and carry it through: taking the negative side would be equivalent to "copping out." One of the possibilities that Lear and his fellow controversialists seem not ready to contemplate is the notion that moral courage might be more greatly manifested in a decision to defy, or even to ignore, some piece or other of the conventional wisdom.

Yet "controversial" themes have little, if anything, to do with the wide success of *All in the Family*. Its appeal is rooted not in the show's endorsement of liberal values, but, on the contrary, in its vivid, visual demonstration of the abiding attractiveness of the familiar as opposed to the strange, the old virtures as opposed to the new nonsense. The wirters who write the show, the actors who act in it, not to say the developer who develops and produces it, are all aware of the rule for success that politicians of every kind, including those in the entertainment business, understand very well—that it is easier to win by reassuring people than by trying to convert them. No matter how much "controversial" material *All in the Family* purveys, or how many progressive positions it endorses—no matter how many women get jobs in the construction firm Archie works for, or how many fine, manly homosexuals are trotted out for Archie's education—it is the fate of all of them to be rendered meaningless by reason of the show's main dramatic energies, which are bent precisely on establishing the irrelevance of the new and the progressive to the life and style of the lovable Bunkers: a life and style, we are given to understand, that are full of decency and worth.

Lear is not the first politician of his age to have read correctly the prevailing winds of the culture and to have perceived the wisdom in following *all* of them, though he may well be the first to have packaged that perception successfully for television. Nor is the package a small achievement, for there have been scenes on *All in the Family* equal to the best that commercial television has had to offer, most of them due to the skill of Carroll O'Connor, who plays Archie with a fidelity that has been the making of the show since its inception in 1971. To see Carroll O'Connor act this part is to have the pleasure of watching knowledge delivered. With his mastery of every inflection, every lift of the eyebrow, of a certain lower-middle-class type, O'Connor succeeds, in the face of all that rings false in Archie's lines, in making that which he knows so well, and which we, watching, know that he knows so well—namely, details—prevail over stereotype and caricature.

In one program, to cite but a single instance, Archie learns from his rich, despised, and much envied cousin Russell that Russell, a swinger, betrays his wife regularly. An appalled Archie sits in a bar and listens to Russell's cold-blooded talk about how uninteresting wives are sexually. At home, in a tearful scene, Archie's wife Edith (Jean Stapleton) is hearing the same sort of information concerning Russell from Russell's wife, a woman whose marriage the good-hearted Edith has always admired for its surface glamor. But when the cousins have gone home and Archie and Edith are alone, they cannot bring themselves to talk about what they have found out about the other couple. The camera zeroes in on the mute Archie and Edith, drawn close, suddenly, by an inexplicable current of feeling risen between them: on, particularly, the face of Archie, capably feigning indifference.

It is one of television's better moments, not only because the audience recognizes the truth of this silence—its legitimate observation of the way in which, except perhaps among the sophisticated, each sex still tends to reserve to itself what, for its own good reasons, it is judged the other need not know—or because the observation itself is an appealing one, but also because, in a medium whose chief terror has traditonally been any assay into the subtle, a highly condensed piece of shorthand has been permitted to stand without explication. Audiences have rightly perceived at such moments that in the "new breed" of situation comedy, they are indeed given something not accorded them on traditional programs. In the new programs writers and performers are not so much required to sustain a plot line—as is the case in more traditional shows—as to render social types, to satirize rather than to tell a story. It is required of the audience, in turn, that it know enough to recognize the types, that it follow the actor's shorthand, and that it become, in some measure, their partner and ally—for it is true of any

successful satire that it makes its audience a satirist by extension.

Thus, *The Mary Tyler Moore Show*, by far the most sophisticated of the sit-coms, requires that its audience recognize the puffery that goes into television news programs, enough at least to understand the character of Ted Baxter. The character of the silvery-haired Baxter is based on a type supposedly to be found in every newsroom in America: the newscaster hired entirely for the sake of his telegenic face, a vain, empty-headed show-business type with no comprehension whatsoever of the news he reads in so portentous and convincing tone. Ted knows that the only real news of consequence is his popularity ratings; even his honest and irascible producer, Lou Grant, in some degree shares this naively cynical attitude.

But if this sounds as if *The Mary Tyler Moore Show* is devoted to making "political" observations about life, the heart of the show is in fact elsewhere, try though its writers will, almost always unsuccessfully, to deal with such important "issues" as bigotry or women's rights. In one segment, the station-manager's wife decides, in the interest, vaguely, of "finding herself," to leave her husband and begin a new life alone, despite the fact that her marriage is an excellent one, and that she loves her husband deeply. This decision is a puzzle to her husband, and, it would seem, to the writers of the show as well, whose tortured efforts to make sense of it introduce a challenge greater than they are up to. The segment crawls to an end, finally, with the spectacle of the wife going out to hunt herself up, with none of the characters, least of all the departing wife, given a line that might impart a moment's conviction to the scene. The writers have, in their way here, made a discovery of the kind George Orwell recommended in "Politics and the English Language": in order to translate its meaning into activity they had to strip a politicized statement of its rhetoric, and they found themselves left with nothing.

Dedicated at its best, then, to satire and portraiture rather than to debate, *The Mary Tyler*

Moore Show concentrates its energies on rendering urban types, all of whom have their share of neurotic tendencies. The targets of their satire are the postures and compulsions of the workday consciousness. Lou Grant (Edward Asner), the producer, in broad outline a tough, straightforward newsroom type, speaks, within that "straight" portraiture, to the complicated, the inward, the quirky, the psychological. Mary Richards, the heroine, wages a continual war on her inhibitions, and a very contemporary war it is. A nice girl to the bone, gracious, well-bred, fair, and unwilling to offend, she has nevertheless absorbed the intelligence of an age which calls all her values into doubt, which instructs her to cast inhibition aside, and learn to be, among other things, aggressive, or be guilty of that worst of contemporary sins, the failure of self-fulfillment.

In sum, one of the reasons for the great appeal of *The Mary Tyler Moore Show* lies in its use of material that is as true a mirror of the preoccupations of our private lives as *All in the Family's* progressive issues are a false one. That material is primarily "relationships"—the very matter of the show, the action itself. When Mary's Jewish girlfriend, Rhoda, left the series, having been given a spin-off of her own, there was a considerable drop for a time in its pace and content, so much did the relationship between them carry the show. In addition to relationships, and in contrast to the sentimental *All in the Family*, which, in the oldest tradition of radio and television, illustrates the superiority of home and hearth over adventure, of the simple life over the grand, *The Mary Tyler Moore Show*, also deals with the delights of success, the energy of ambition, the pleasures of competition. And ambition is a ruling passion as well on *The Bob Newhart Show* (another Mary Tyler Moore Production), a program in which psychologists, urologists, dentists, and teachers all race about, testaments to the joy of professional life and to success.

Not surprisingly, there is comfort as well as fun in these comedies, which acknowledge that, in the service of ambition, in the operation of their most intimate relationships, all kinds of fine people are full of neurotic hungers, lying impulses, and shoddy vanities. Not only are the people in them successful, thereby proving that neurotic hunger and pretense might in fact function in a good cause, but they are appealing and wholesome as well. Rarely in popular entertainment, in fact, have the negative aspects of character played so heroic a role as in the sit-coms, *All in the Family* included. No wonder that we welcome them, that we are sorry when they end, for besides entertaining us, the sit-coms tell us what we had hoped all along was true: that it is *for* our faults we are loved, really, not in spite of them.

New! Improved! Advertising!

Ted Morgan

Uncle Sam belched. He was munching on his eighth Hebrew National hot dog. "A little more movement," said director Steve Horn (handlebar mustache and white suspenders). "You're anticipating by a hair." A production assistant picked the lint off Uncle Sam's satin suit, fluffed his long white beard and handed him another hot dog.

"Lift the frank a little higher," Horn said. "Turn it toward you. Look surprised at 'kosher.' The idea is that kosher blows your mind. At the word 'kosher' your eyes light up. It's kosher no less? Raise your eyes at 'higher authority.' At the word 'authority' you should have it in your mouth."

As Uncle Sam obeyed instructions, a bronze-toned, March of Time voice announced: "Government regulations say we can make our Hebrew National hot dog from frozen beef—we don't. They say we can add nonmeat fillers—we don't. They say we can use artificial coloring—we don't. They say we can add meat byproducts—we can't." Meaningful pause. "We're kosher." Meaningful pause. "And we have to answer to an even higher authority."

As the voice intoned, Uncle Same responded with growing interest, raising his eyebrows,

looking quizzically at the hot dog and sliding his lower jaw back and forth. At the word "kosher" he beamed, and at the mention of a higher authority he looked skyward, as a halo of sunlight formed around his head, and took a big bite out of the hot dog.

"Fantastic," Horn said. Actor William Newman looked relieved. After four hours on the set, he could take off the funny suit and the acrylic beard. The 30-second TV spot was in the can, at a relatively modest cost of $32,000. These days, a 30-second spot can range from $8,000 to $80,000, depending on the price of the director, the talent, and the cost of the location.

Dick Roth, beefy like his product, management supervisor for Scali, McCabe, Sloves, the advertising agency for Hebrew National, explained the strategy. "We're trying to take a product for Jewish people and give it a wider appeal. Our research showed that people were confused by what kosher was. Since we couldn't change the name of the product, we decided to meet the problem head on."

Roth and several of his colleagues had recently toured the Hebrew National plant. They were kidding around, asking each other where the snout trucks were. "But it's really a better product Roth said earnestly. "This isn't such a big account—about a million—but it's a show-case. It could be another Perdue."

One might think that the frankfurter commercial was a magnification of trivia, dignifying the lowly hot dog by tying it in with patriotism and religion. Actually, it was a momentous event Isidore (Skip) Pines, the president of the company, was on hand. So was Ed McCabe, 39-year-old boy wonder, multiple award-winning copywriter, and one of the reasons why his agency has become known as a "hot shop."

Founded in 1967 by five partners with zero billings (the amount of money spent on advertising by a company with a product to sell), the agency today has $40 million in billings and 120 employees. The partners have moved from a two-room hotel suite to three airy floors high above Third Avenue. They were named Agency of the Year in 1974 by Advertising Age, and they have a closetful of trophies. Their campaigns for Perdue chickens and Volvo are much admired in the trade. While other agencies have lost billings or gone under in the hard-times 70's, Scali, McCabe, Sloves have prospered and increased by 25 percent in 1974 and by 17 percent in 1975. Three-quarters of their business now comes to them, and they turn down accounts of less than $750,000 a year.

Success in advertising is hard to explain, but in the case of Scali, McCabe, Sloves it has to do with perceiving the 70's as a decade of lost illusions and tight money. To separate the consumer from his dollar, they have emphasized a kind of sardonic toughness. They have come to the conclusion that the consumer, like an insect that builds up resistance to DDT, is getting harder to fool. They have pioneered the era of "dog-eat-dog" advertising, in which the rival brand is the enemy and the market place is a no man's land.

Ed McCabe is a scrappy little Irishman whose first job after high school was in the mail room of a Chicago agency. The day of the hot-dog shooting, he was wearing jeans and a blue work shirt, and he held himself with his thumbs hooked into his jeans pockets.

McCabe and Roth huddled with Skip Pines, who said he really liked the commercial. It was merely great, Ed. They spoke in hushed tones. "CBS took a wait-and-see attitude," Roth said. "We got a rabbi to substantiate it. We wrote them a letter where we went back to Moses. We threw in the Torah, the Bible, the whole history of dietary laws."

"The networks are our biggest problem," McCabe said.

"You get a different response from each one," Roth said. "One accepted it, one said you've got a problem, and one said, you're commercializing God—that's a no-no."

Roth shook his head. He was genuinely grieved. "They set standards for taste and morality in the ads," he said, "and they destroy those standards in their programming!"

"You got to document every goddam comma," McCabe complained. "All you need is a confrontation with the networks to send you screaming to the booby hatch.

"They" are the networks' continuity clearance departments, which are responsible for making sure that commercials are not offensive or untruthful. "They" have a once-burned, twice-shy approach. Misrepresentation was rampant in the hard-sell 50's. What else could a company do when it was selling "parity" products? That is, stuff like soap, or margarine, or insurance, that is really no different from any of the other brands. So you have Anacin and its ingredient doctors recommend most. (You couldn't fault them—the ingredient was aspirin.) And you had a photographer dropping colorless glass marbles into a bowl of Campbell's soup to make the diced vegetables rise to the surface. And you had the man dressed in a white coat to make you think he was a doctor. And you had (and still have, in print) the outdoorsy look of Marlboro country and its rugged, clean-living, Stetson-hatted smokers, selling an implied health benefit for a product that poisons your lungs. And, because of heat and light requirements, you had TV studios using shaving cream for whipped cream and spiking coffee with molasses to give it body.

You can't blame the networks for screening

the commercials. But now, the agencies say, the pendulum has swung in the other direction. These days, you can spend $80,000 on a commercial and have no place to show it. Which is what happened recently to one of the country's largest corporations, whose agency came up with a commerical for a diet product showing a thin Santa Claus complaining that he'd lost his job. No one will ever see it. All three networks turned it down. You can't claim diet products cause weight loss.

WHEN YOU HIRE A NAPOLEAN, DON'T PUT HIM ON K.P.

Discontent, the midwife of new agencies, brought the five partners together. Four of them came out of Papert, Koenig & Lois, which was briefly a hot shop before dissolving. In its heyday, it was known as Stillman's Gym East, a place where people leaped across desks and threw things. One day, Marvin Sloves, an account supervisor, while walking in the street with Leonard Hultgren, the assistant research director, gave way to a feeling often expressed in his profession.

"I can't stand it anymore," he said, "I'd like to start my own agency."

"Why don't we?" Hultgren asked. They recruited two other disgruntled colleagues, Alan Pesky and Sam Scali, and moved into a two-room suite in the Gotham Hotel.

They needed a copywriter. Ed McCabe, in the meantime, had left the mail room and made a name for himself, eventually joining Carl Ally, a World War II and Korean War fighter pilot, known for his honest ads, who once remarked, "It's like selling a used car to a friend. I don't want to screw him—after all, I might see him again." Ed, who is forthright about his accomplishments, recalls that "Ally was doing $2 million when I got there, and three years later he was doing $23 million."

On the day in 1967 when Sam Scali asked him to recommend a copywriter, Ed had had a fight with Carl Ally over money. He recommended himself.

Volvo was Carl Ally's biggest account. Three months later, Ed ran into Carl, who told him, "I think I've blown the Volvo account." "Go on," Ed said, "you'll keep that account until your hair turns blue." Ed went back to the office to work on his only account, Citizens for a Quieter City—"it was something to do so I wouldn't attack people in the street out of frustration"—and heard to his susprise that Scali, McCabe had picked up Volvo's $10 million in billings.

After that, with their reputation growing, they picked up Barney's, three Revlon products, Savarin Coffee, Air-Wick, and the inimitable Frank Perdue, whom Ed McCabe made the tough man with the tender chicken. He knew Perdue was tough because Perdue had taken seven months to choose an agency, sitting through 47 presentations. Since the campaign began, his branded broiler business has doubled to $80 million a year, and Scali, McCabe are swamped with company presidents who want to be stars. They have since parted ways with Revlon, trading up to handle the full line of Prince Matchabelli products.

The five partners represent the invasion of the ethnics into a profession once dominated by Eastern Establishment Ivy Leaguers in J. Press suits. These old-line types got a little out of touch; they were still dropping nickels in subway turnstiles. The street-smart ethnics moved in, like Brooklyn-born Bill (You don't have to be Jewish) Bernbach, and George (If you've got it, flaunt it) Lois, a former semipro basketball player.

Marvin Sloves's office looks like boxing's hall of fame. The walls are covered with fight posters and ringside photographs, and original gloves from the Canzoneri-Al Singer fight, framed in a box. His father fought from 1916 to 1921 under the name Johnny Murray, "the Bronx Bonecrusher." "He was Jewish," Marvin explains, "but in those days a fighter had to be Irish." What happens to the son of a contending feather-weight? He becomes a Chinese scholar, of course. Marvin was doing graduate work at the University of Chicago's Chinese-Oriental institute, in the Eisenhower years, when he decided he did not want to serve in the State Department under John Foster Dulles. You could say that he backed into advertising as the result of an ideological commitment.

Actually advertising isn't one of those "what do you want to be when you grow up" professions. It's something most adpersons fall into, for one reason or another, like flunking out of dental school. In any case, 42-year-old Marvin Sloves would have made a swell ambassador. He strikes me as an unruffler of tempers, a disentangler of knots. I can see why the others made him president, aside from the fact that he can't write or draw.

Sam Scali can draw, and Ed McCabe can write, and they are both known as very tough. They say it helps in advertising to be known as a four-star bastard. Forty-year-old Sam Scali struck me mainly as a guy who enjoys his work "I like to do everything," he told me, from skywriting to matchbook covers." Ed McCabe is a driven man. Nothing is ever good enough. When the partners look at the agency reel (the showcase film of their best commercials) and everyone is chuckling and saying merely great, he is wincing and groaning. As a result, he's won more awards than he can remember, Gold Keys, Gold Medals, Andys, Clios, and he's the youngest member of the Copywriter's Hall of Fame (is there any other profession that hands out so many awards?). As a result, his staff once gave him a whip.

Leonard Hultgren, 44, head of research and accounting, and a Fordham graduate, came out of research and makes a point of getting his facts straight. When he gives you cost per mil (per each 1,000 persons reached) or production costs on a commercial, you believe him. Alan Pesky, overeducated like Marvin, the only Ivy Leaguer in the crowd, with an M.B.A. from Dartmouth, is a divided man. He loves the ad business, but he also loves the great outdoors, and wants to get into environmental work. That is something else about adpersons. In their heart of hearts, a lot of them nurture some private ambition that has nothing to do with their work.

Of the $40 million in annual billings, the agency grosses 15 percent, or $6 million. This covers a 15 percent commission on the cost of all the ads and commercials they place. It also covers a 17.65 percent mark-up on production costs. Everything is marked up—a TV commercial, plates for a magazine ad, retouching a photograph.

This system has its critics, particularly among print media men, who argue that agencies prefer television because there's more money in it. Tony Antin, an advertising expert put it this way: "They shoot a 60-second commerical, and it runs 50 times, at $100,000 a minute of prime time, and they get their commission each time it runs. It would take just as much work to write an ad for The Barber's Journal that cost $700.

"Take the management supervisor who wants to earn a profit for the agency. Where does he want his ads? In TV. Can you imagine a supervisor telling his boss at the agency: Last year I raised my client's sales by 10 percent. I took them out of TV and put them into print at a saving of 50 percent in their ad budget. That's marvelous, the boss says, you're fired.

"Also, it's easier to get a guy to spend on TV. He starts with a million, he gets sucked into three, he's like the guy who says I'll stay for one more hand. Clients like being in show biz. The guy goes home and tells his wife. I had lunch with Bob today. Bob who, she asks? Bob Hope, he works for me. What about the creative guy? Would he rather sit in the office and write ads or go out to the desert with a beautiful girl and sit in a car on top of a mesa and play Cecil B. De Mille? The account guy goes along, too, and everybody has a good time. But I'll tell you what. What is there between the edge of the screen and the cornea of your eye? Three yards of boredom."

Scali, McCabe, Sloves are screaming foul. They insist that they don't use TV because it's more profitable, they use it because it's best for the client. If they tried to sucker every client into million-dollar TV campaigns, they'd lose accounts. Sam Scali, the art director, wiry and gray-haired like a terrier, tells about a recent prospect. "It was a stockbrokerage house, they were enamored of TV, we told them it wasn't for them. With their size budget it was wasteful. What they wanted to say could best be said in print. We didn't get the account."

The get-rich-quick image of advertising (Mary Wells, at $325,000 a years, is said to be the highest-paid woman in the country), is dispelled by Leonard Hultgren, who slices the Scali, Mc-Cabe $6 million pie this way:

- ☐ 69 percent payroll (includes payroll taxes and fringe benefits).
- ☐ 6.8 percent rent and maintenance.
- ☐ 18.4 percent operating costs.
- ☐ 5.8 percent profit before profit-sharing.
- ☐ 1 percent net profit after profit-sharing, which means $60,000 divided among five partners, who also pay themselves salaries, of course. The salaries, says Sloves, were "in excess of $50,000" in 1975, a pay boost of about 20 percent over the previous year. But they claim that until 1974 other employees were getting higher salaries than they were.

BUILD A BETTER MOUSETRAP, AND IT WON'T MAKE A DAMN BIT OF DIFFERENCE

To understand what Scali, McCabe are doing right, why they are a "now" agency, you have to go back a bit, to the 50's, when the account executives who were tight with the clients dictated to the creative people. The 50's were product-oriented. It was the better-mousetrap era. They were looking, in Rosser Reeves's term, for a Unique Selling Proposition. At its best, this gave us David Ogilvy's "at 60 miles per hour, the loudest noise in the new Rolls-Royce comes from the electric clock." It sounds good, and who knows, it might even be true. At its worst, it was "our miracle suds get your clothes whiter than their miracle suds," or slice-of-life scenes on the order of "Oh, Maggie, how did you get your floors so sparkling clean?" which were models of humbug but seemed to

sell the product—so well that rival firms marketed me-too products.

In the 60's there was a turnaround. The idea became mightier than the marketing. Creativity was in the ascendant. Copywriters went from a rigid copy platform to a seat-of-the-pants approach. Bright 22-year-olds who were writing hernia ads for mail-order houses were suddenly promoted to creative director at $100,000 a year.

In the go-go 60's, adpersons pushed an image like the man in the Hathaway shirt and Commander Whitehead. It was the era of "everyone in the pool"—no idea was too wild. Take Mary Wells's campaign for Benson & Hedges. How to tell the world about those two extra millimeters? Research and marketing would have led to: Makes the Smoke Cooler, or More Imported Tobacco. Instead, she showed the cigarette breaking—Oh, the disadvantages of a longer cigarette! All the data said this won't sell cigarettes, but some obscure urge made the multitudes respond. In those days, you could sell a product by making people smile. Doyle Dane Bernbach adopted irreverence—in their Volkswagen ads, they took a position no other car wanted, the ugly position. Suddenly, clients told their agencies, give that Doyle Dane look.

At the same time, smart agencies were playing around with concepts like "accepted pairing" and "pre-emption." Avis was lagging behind Hertz. Doyle Dane realized that the simple negation of an unfavorable image doesn't pay. You don't deny the image, you make it work in your favor. The "We Try Harder" campaign was an example of "accepted pairing." After losing money for 13 years, Avis increased its share of the market from 29 percent to 35 percent, and Hertz dropped from 56 percent to 50 percent. And Doyle Dane's billings jumped from $50 million to $250 million.

Pre-emption means being the first to make a claim about your product (the more outrageous, the better), so that anyone else who says it is a me-too. When United Airlines used its "friendly skies" campaign, they pre-empted the air travel atmosphere. When market research showed that

20 percent of beer drinkers accounted for 80 percent of the beer consumed, Schaefer came out with "the one beer to have when you're having more than one," and pre-empted the heavy beer drinkers.

With the start of the recession in the late 60's, the creative approach was no longer enough. Ad budgets were tighter and people had less discretionary income. We had become an "overcommunicated society," polysaturated with messages. Some of the Madison Avenue's most cherished beliefs went up in smoke. Daniel Starch, a media analyst, spent 27 days in Atlanta covering audience response to 1,800 TV commercials. Only one viewer in six could identify the sponsor. One viewer in 12 misidentified him, saying Goodyear instead of Goodrich or Kellogg instead of Post. The days of "just put it on TV and you can sell it" were over.

In 1969, a fellow named Jack Trout wrote an article for the magazine Industrial Marketing, "Positioning is the game people play in today's me-too market place." Positioning became the magic word, the winning move in the kriegspiel. What was positioning? Essentially, it was like finding a seat on a crowded bus. You look at the market place. You see what vacancy there is. You build your campaign to position your product in that vacancy. If you do it right, the strap-hangers won't be able to grab your seat. "Campbell's in the cupboard is like money in the bank" was a good "hard-times" positioning for the 70's. Sports Illustrated positioned itself as a third newsweekly instead of just another sports magazine, and its circulation rose. Johnson & Johnson took a nothing brand, its baby shampoo, and turned it into a $20 million business by clever repositioning. The pitch was that because of air pollution you wash your hair more often, so you need a milder shampoo. Baby shampoo was positioned as a family shampoo.

Across the obstacle course that was advertising in the 70's sprinted Scali, McCabe, Sloves. They understood the strategy. According to Alan Pesky, they took it one step further, ushering in the dog-eat-dog era. Pesky said, "People

ask me, what makes your agency different? We firmly believe every client has an enemy. Our client is going to grow at the expense of the enemy. It's Volvo against Detroit. It's Savarin against Maxwell House. If you look at our ads, you'll see that we go for the jugular."

In the positioning war, half the battle is picking the right enemy. To sell Seneca's frozen apple juice, Scali, McCabe positioned it not against the $70 million fruit juice market but against the $480 million "bellywash" market. The commercial shows tousle-haired triplets drinking Hi-C, Hawaiian Punch and Seneca. The March of Time voice says, "Hi-C has 10 percent fruit juice, and kids love it. Hawaiian Punch has 11 percent fruit juice, and kids love it. Seneca has 100 percent fruit juice, and kids love it. Which one would you rather have your kids guzzle down?" Merely brilliant, Ed.

NOTHING'S WRITTEN IN STONE

One reason why Scali, McCabe is in a cold war with the networks is their shoot-'em-up approach. To launch a new Dictaphone gadget, for instance, they came up with "Bad News for I.B.M." But they don't shoot from the hip—they take careful aim in the research and media departments. When they landed the Barney's account, Leonard Hultgren started running "focused groups" in the big conference room with the oval butcher's-block table. Men were paid $10 or $20 to come in and rap about what they did or did not like about Barney's. The conference room was bugged and their remarks were taped for posterity.

Lo and behold, it came out in the focused groups that the location was bad. Seventh Avenue and 17th Street was not the corner you would choose to stroll by of a summer evening with your girl friend on your arm. Barney's lost the impulse buying. Also, the sales force was perceived as aggressive. "You put one foot in there and you walk out with a blue serge suit you didn't want." Scali, McCabe turned these problems into opportunities. The first full-page newspaper ad hit the multitudes with a Unique

Selling Proposition—a photograph of the street sign over the message, "We know you go out of your way and we want to pay you back."

To counter the image of pushy salesmen, they dreamed up a "Just Looking" button that a hostess pins on. I asked Marvin Sloves how the campaing was doing. He said, "The only reading we get is, business is terrific. It's become a $1.5 million account."

Michael Ephron, who has the permanently harassed look of someone who's always answering three phones at once, is Scali, McCabe's media director. He is the one who decides whether a product needs radio drive-time sixties (one-minute spots at peak commuting hours), a 1,200-line newspaper ad, or a 30-second TV spot (720 frames flashing by in one "memory scene").

I asked Michael Ephron how he decided what media to use. "You've got to be creative," he said. "Nothing's written in stone. Take Volvo. It now sells 75,000 cars a year in the American market, to a public disenchanted with Detroit. The consumer thought of the car as small and inexpensive. When the price went up, we had to reposition it as a luxury car. What was going to be our ultimate mix, in terms of different media playing different roles? Magazines fulfill the primary function of letting us provide someone in the market for a new car with a wealth of pertinent information. TV offers us a chance to maintain awareness of our product among the public at large, even though they're not in the market. Newspapers are an excellent retail medium, the closest one to the point of sale—we can get in dealer listings. We decided on a mix that was 50 percent TV, 35 percent magazines, and 15 percent newspapers. When you have a $10 million budget, it's bad to pinpoint your dollars, you have to use the buckshot approach."

ARE THEY OUR KIND OF PEOPLE?

The folks at Scali, McCabe work in a climate of constant self-congratulation: Inside Marvin Sloves there is a cheerleader going rah, rah, win team win. And Sam Scali chimes in, "Remem-ber that great Cadiallac ad? The penalty of leadership? Being in the forefront is a responsibility rather than a prize." But even the most successful agency is a place where nothing is safe or permanent. A lost account sends copywriters riffling through pages of the Advertising Agency Register and out of the office early, with their reel under their arm. It's not unusual for an account supervisor or a copywriter to have worked in a dozen agencies in six years.

A shadow crosses Marvin Slove's usually sunny face. "The worst thing about this business," he says, " is . . . there's no loyalty." A billion dollars' worth of business changes hands each year. What are the reasons? No one knows. They put out releases about irreconcilable policy differences, or basic disagreements in strategy, which means they zigged when they should have sagged. I.B.M. is said to have left Ogilvy because the people at I.B.M. were so computer-minded they wanted everything done yesterday; they felt Olgivy had too many clients and was too slow to respond to their needs. A departing account can start a stampede. When Needham, Harper & Steers lost Amtrak and the Post Office, other clients began to say, "There must be something wrong," and their billings went down, down, down.

"For us to lose an account is murderous," Marvin Sloves said. "It's like Lana Turner can't get a movie." After three years, he recently lost the Dictaphone account. "They were going out of business when they came to us," he said. "We got caught up in their internal battles. We wanted to put them on a fee rather than a commission basis, and they resigned on us." They also lost Jerry (What's the story?) Rosenberg, the discount furniture and appliance man, after a brief and fitful union. Scali, McCabe wanted to change the hardhat image. Jerry went back to his old agency, Marshall-Jordan.

Agency men usually profess to be baffled by client departures. Sam Scali says, "There's a lot of chemistry. Are they our kind of people?

IN AMERICA, EVERYONE IS HIS OWN BEST JUDGE OF HIS NEEDS

—Alex De Tocqueville

On balance, Marvin Sloves's permanent mood of elation seems justified, since there's far more new business than lost accounts. Ad agencies are obsessed with growth. Landing that new account is the great triumph, like storming the Nazi machine-gun nest.

Several years ago, American Can came to them. Someone over at American Can had a dream. It involved changing a basic American habit, but that's what progress is all about. You go from the thimble to the sewing machine. The dream was to replace a product that every American uses (except maybe a few rugged individualists), a product that adds up to a $788 million market in supermarket sales alone. The product was toilet paper, and the American Can people had produced lightly moistened tissue that would be sold in a dispenser, with refills. They had the product, but they had no name, no package and no advertising strategy.

They took it to Marvin Sloves, who swallowed hard, and accepted the account on a fee basis. He could see the pitfalls that lay ahead. You would have to educate the consumer. But the subject was a no-no. One of the three networks didn't allow the words "toilet paper" on the air—you had to say "bathroom tissue." And you couldn't tell people to "use" it—you had to ask them to "try" it.

On the other hand, it could be a wunderkind product. There was no market segmentation: It wasn't like a product for people who have hair with split ends or who want a soggy-proof breakfast cereal. And the demographics were great: Everybody's got a rear end, right? In marketing jargon, the product had "perceived value," as well as "dramatizable newness." Still, it was a big risk, both for American Can and Scali, McCabe. The road to early retirement is paved with new products that failed. Millions of dollars are spent in test marketing. If the tests are successful, and they go national, and the product bombs, you will see an item in the company's annual report that says: We are continuing to evaluate and test the opportunities for new products, with the normal occasional setback.

Between the birth of an idea and successful national marketing, only one new product in 50 survives. The other 49 are hastily buried in the potter's field of corporate struggle. Would American Can's lightly moistened tissues go the way of Raggedy Ann and Raggedy Andy disposable diapers which cost Scott paper $12 million, or Teal, the liquid toothpaste that turned customers' teeth gray, or Ken-L Ration's chorophyll-green dog food?

Scali, McCabe tested between 200 and 300 names before they picked the one that was the most favorably received: Fresh'n. Why the apostrophe? No one seems to know. They picked Omaha and Phoenix as test markets. Account men spent hundreds of hours listening to housewives rap about what toilet paper did or didn't do for them. They targeted Fresh'n for women 18 to 49. "But you want men to be aware of it too," Michael Ephron said, "so that when the wife comes home and says attach this to the bathroom wall, he'll be presold." They ran polls to measure brand awareness and repurchases. They became the world experts on toilet paper.

'People ask, what makes your agency different? If you look at our ads, you'll see that we go for the jugular.'

Alan Pesky and Dick Roth, who are handling the Fresh'n account, know that if they can change the toilet-paper habits of America, they're going to have company out there. "We can't reveal our copy strategy to our competitors," Pesky said. "Loose lips sink ships."

"We had to be specific and tasteful at the same time," Roth said. "Through research we arrived at a copy platform: 'Wet Cleans Better Than Dry.' We positioned ourselves against toilet paper and keyed our ads to people who were not afraid to talk about it."

"The person buys Fresh'n," Pesky said, "and thinks, I'm going to be cleaner and more serene with myself.'"

They started with coupon ads and went on to three-page magazine spreads. One ad shows a smiling couple on a couch announcing: "You know what? We don't use toilet paper." The ad explains that Fresh'n has been tested for flushability and biodegradability, and that two sheets can replace several feet of toilet paper—it discourages children from stuffing the bowl with wads of paper.

They used the same tag in the TV spots. One football player to another on the line of scrimmage: "I don't use toilet paper." One woman to another at the tennis net: "I've never played better since I stopped using toilet paper." And the March of Time voice says: "It's lightly moistened to get you cleaner. The cleaner you are the better you feel."

The American Can people checked the stores for shelf space and facings. Housewives seemed to be buying Fresh'n and coming back for refills. Share-of-the-market studies showed that Fresh'n was getting about 10 percent of the test cities.

It may be a while before all American is able to buy it. Testing will continue through 1976, Sloves says cautiously—extended, perhaps, to two more cities. If and when the product goes national, it seems unlikely that the TV commericials Scali, McCabe run on local stations will be acceptable to the networks.

WHAT GOOD IS HAPPINESS IF IT DOESN'T BRING YOU MONEY?

In a large, high-ceiling reception room at the back of the Four Seasons, the troops from Scali, McCabe gobbled down fancy hors d'oeuvres like fried oysters on toothpicks and sauteed duck livers with raisins. It was the eighth annual agency party held on Thanksgiving Eve.

Marvin Sloves, in his brown corduroy Barney's suit, made a little speech. Seventy-five was the greatest year ever, but '76 would be even better. In the next wo weeks there would be 10 major presentations. "We're going to give everybody 15 percent profit-sharing," he said, "We're going to give all of you a bonus." Faces beamed around the room.

Marvin announced the presentation of the president's award. "It could be anybody," he said. "It goes to someone who does something extraordinary. The prize, an attache case and a vice presidency, went to Jerry Mitty, a media man. He had heard that the Pioneer hi-fi account was up for grabs, which led to $4 million in billings for Scali, McCabe. Jerry's colleagues went up to him and clapped him on the back and said, "Well deserved, well deserved."

The party continued past the 7 P.M. deadline. Good cheer was much in evidence. Two soused copywriters came up to me and introduced each other, "I want you to meet Joe," one said, "he's the greatest writer in the United States."

"And this is Tom," Joe said, "the greatest writer in the whole world."

Joe stood in front of me, blinking, and waving like a flagpole in a stiff breeze. "Go ahead," he said. "Ask me a question. Ask me anything you want."

"O.K.," I said, "What do you want out of life?"

He stood there waving slowly for 10 seconds, and then said, "I want to write an ad that will blow the mind of the universe."

The Information Revolution and International Communication

Donald D. Day

As a result of the growth of the media, the on-rushing Information Revolution has forced man into a new era—an era in which the study of media and their effects is prerequisite to understanding interaction among people.

Revolution is the concept that has fired the imagination of generations the world over, a phenomenon whose dynamism and sense of manifest destiny have transcended barriers of time, language, culture, and race. A revolution which will turn history's national upheavals into mere ripples in time, by comparison, is beginning today on a world scale. It is the Information Revolution, a creature of this century's logarithmic growth in communication technology.

On the horizon are two-way television communication, via broadband transmission over extensive community antenna televison networks; visual telephones; computer-activated information and entertainment libraries, placing the aggregate wealth of man's knowledge on home television outlets at the flick of a switch: home entertainment and education of top quality, on videotape cassettes, viewed again through home TV; three-dimensional home movies; fac-simile printout—from home audiovisual terminals—of newspapers from around the world, including selective reception by subject indexing; mail transmitted as facsimile over telephone links; including sophisticated laser relays (replacing present microwave systems); voting and polling of the masses via home response units, making possible instantaneous referenda —and popular participation in major decisions of government; and home communications complexes which will facilitate decentralization of urban centers and repopulation of rural areas by making all business activities practical between one's home and the entire rest of the world.[1]

Also in the offing are communications signals with a terrain-hugging capability to flow over the usual visual-horizon limits of conventional microwave links, and thus make broadcast communication routine with the most isolated areas on earth.

A major factor in this Information Revolution has been satellite and related technology. A combination of new satellite and cable hardware already has mushroomed domestic and international communication channels. For ex-

[1] Joseph Newman, ed., *Wiring the World: The Explosion in Communications* (Washington, D.C.: U.S. News & World Report, 1971).

ample, a transistorized repeater cable to be laid between Britain and Canada will provide double the channel capacity now available from all six transatlantic cables currently in operation. The latest fourth-generation INTELSAT satellites will carry 6,000 channels each—25 times the capacity of the first telecommunication satellite orbited only a decade ago.[2]

The Explosion of Communications Technology

Development in communications engineering soon may make even 6,000 channels seem paltry, however. Conventional coaxial cables capable of 10,800 channels each soon are to be replaced by millimeter-waveguide systems of ultra-short frequency which can carry 250,000 channels. Beyond that, laser systems on the drawing boards and in preliminary testing could carry information in any conceivable volume. Even these quantum increases in channels understate the case, since channel *capacity* itself jumps from 648,000,000 bits per second per channel in coaxial cable to 15,000,000,000 per second in millimeter-waveguide, and an estimated 100,000,000,000 in laser systems.[3]

Coordination of the quickly expanding capabilities of satellite, cable, broadcast, and receiver hardware capabilities can have a resounding impact upon political, social, and economic institutions around the world. Even by itself, the orbiting of man's first direct-broadcast telecommunications satellite may drastically alter the prerogatives of national governments and seriously threaten nationalism. With the fact of direct broadcast from satellites to home receivers (eliminating the need for expensive—and easily censored—ground relay stations), authoritarian rule based upon strict information controls may become a thing of the past.

The scope of current developments in communication technology is not only broad, but

the pace is ever-quickening. Thirty-nine decades elapsed between the invention of movable type and the first rotary press; 39 years, between telegraph and telephone; 14 years, between crystal set and television; and nine years, from transistor to Sputnik.

As a result of the growth of media, the onrushing Information Revolution has forced man into a new era—an era in which the study of media and their effects is prerequisite to understanding interaction among people. Media have come to so permeate life that understanding them has become fundamental to responsible citizenship. In fact, mass media today are singularly distinguishable from earlier communication by their universal application to *all* classes and conditions of people. They are relevant to everyone—not only to a highly literate aristocracy.

Technology's International Impact

With a multitude of international editions by periodicals such as *Time* (6), *Newsweek* (19), and *Reader's Digest* (26); common global radio and TV relay via synchronous telecommunication satellites; and enormous increases in intercontinental telephone traffic, the Information Revolution is taking on a distinct international cast.

Little more than a century ago, all foreign news was several weeks old. Now, satellites make international communication virtually instantaneous. In the past quarter-century, news agencies have proliferated, industries have become more international; intergovernmental, UN, and other international organizations' affairs have greatly expanded; and air passenger traffic has exploded.

With this increase in international communication has come improved international collaboration—the technological realities of electronic media demand increased cooperation, for someone must want to (and be able to) receive that which is being sent. Nations are no longer so isolated, no longer operating solely on chance national stereotyping, with nearly all their so-

[2]Colin Cherry, *World Communication: Threat or Promise?* (London: Wiley-Interscience, 1971).
[3]John Pierce, "Communication," *Scientific American*, 227 (September, 1972), 31–41.

cial attitudes and international relations decided by elites and official institutions.

International Communication as a Field of Study

The escalating social and political complexity of international communication has brought about its institutionalization as an academic field of study, one which—because of its interdisciplinary character—may ultimately comprehend the entire scope of the behavior sciences.

IC, as it is known, has become the fracture zone—the meeting ground—of disciplines, because it is in the act of international communication that isolation is most dysfunctional and interdisciplinary cooperation most clearly advantageous. This convener function of IC is being accelerated not only by increased international travel and proliferating international media, but also by new, combined communications/cultural programs in universities and in business and government training.

The combination of increased travel, expanding media, intercultural training, and communication technology has produced a supra-culture of individuals who are more like each other than the typical "national character" of the states from which they come.[4] One of the common complaints of Third World states against international corporations is the companies co-opting of educated elites into "Western," multinational life styles and orientations.

Modern international media make possible increased non-physical intercultural contact, resulting in a convergence of social systems which requires an amalgamation of all the behavioral sciences if actors are to cope with increasingly complex relationships. The growing need to comprehend other-culture misunderstandings of intent forces interdisciplinary cooperation, so that communications may be molded to result

in intended impressions. The essence of the cross-cultural communications task is to anticipate both the nature of preconceptions in foreign systems and a message recipient's image of the institutions under discussion and the communicator. This calls for understanding a wealth of behavioral science aspects of the cultures involved.

Development of the Field

International Communication, then is a field without many of the barriers to interdisciplinary collaboration which often have inhibited intellectual growth. It encompasses three broad elements; communication theories and models, national mass media systems, and communications in national development.

Within each of these elements, numerous spin-offs from other disciplines have developed intriguing subfields. These include diffusion of innovation and information; national political, social, and economic integration; controls upon, and effects of mass media; communications; technology; stereotyping and imagery; cybernetics; socialization; gatekeeper studies of actors in mass media systems; public opinion and foreign policy; systems modeling; military strategy; international relations; comparative politics; decision-making processes; and interpersonal communication.

The field has not developed overnight, of course. What were later to be termed International Communication studies first appeared in appreciable numbers in the decade following World War I, when national media systems studies of Western Europe dominated the infant literature.

During the 1930's, public opinion and propaganda studies mushroomed. (Propaganda was to be a continuing fascination of IC scholars through the mid-1960's.) Gatekeeper studies of foreign correspondents also were numerous, and bibliographies made their first appearance.

In the World War II decade, IC studies continued to be dominated by propaganda concerns, although government regulation and free-

---

[4] Bryant Wedge, "Communication Analysis and Comprehensive Diplomacy," in A. Hoffman, ed., *International Communication and the New Diplomacy* (Bloomington: Indiana University Press, 1968), pp. 24–47.

dom of national media systems—and increasing area studies of the U.S. and Asia—made substantial contributions.

During the 1950's, the field saw the initial surge of what was to become its strongest element—communications in national development. Studies of national mass media systems, political integration, and economic development in Third World nations also made strong showings. Regulation of national media and studies of the international press—wire services, etc.— were major concerns.

By the 1960's, IC had developed into a comparative and integrated field centering upon social institutions and change, political behavior, public opinion, and mass media. Area and national development studies dominated the literature. Third World interest in the impact of media in national development, acceptance of communication analysis' ability to enable a better understanding of society, further expansion of education and business interests across national boundaries, and the sharpening of research tools and data management all contributed to rapid expansion of the field.[5]

The literature at present centers upon (in descending order) national mass media systems, communications and national development, regulations and law, and gatekeeper studies of international communicators. Many of the studies of national media systems involve the Third World, making national development the strongest sub-field.

The Contributions of Communications Modeling

Throughout the development of International Communication, modeling has been a continuing interest. Three types of models have been developed, each borrowed in some form from component disciplines—mathematical, social, psychological, and linguistic.

Paradigms of mediated stimulus, cognitive balance, and cybernetics were borrowed from psychology and related fields. A structural-functional attempt to equate performance elements of diverse national systems was integrated from comparative political science. Symbol and content analysis was taken from linguistics. The predictive ability of modeling is a major payoff of intellectual effort, and it is in this area that IC may make its most significant contribution.

In the cybernetic models of Karl Deutsch and Norbert Weiner lies a framework which integrates all the disciplines contributing to communication studies.[6] These models integrate the elements of psychology, sociology, anthropology, linguistics, etc., with computer science to create a reliable predictive tool based on the premise that an entity's reception and interpretation of, and subsequent reply to, stimuli are self-monitoring, self-controlling, and self-steering automatic processes.

Cybernetics suggests that this continual self-correction and self-steering is one of the most significant processes in the world, and that *all* organizations are held together by communication. In the cybernetic view, organizations— from amoeba to nations—react to their environment and the results of their own behavior by storing, processing, and applying information (communication). Cybernetics places communications at square one of all organized activity— no matter what the level—and posits behavioral analysis based upon a system's information-processing abilities.

Interestingly, the principles of the cybernetic model, although elaborated substantially through communication studies, were first taken from mathematical interpretations of natural processes in the biological sciences. The basic information-processing technique of selective attention, memory, recall, consciousness screens, and decision by will which are incor-

---

[5]Hamid Mowlana, "Trends in Research on International Communication in the United States," *Gazett*, 19 (1973), 79–90.

[6]Karl Deutsch, *The Nerves of Government: Models of Political Communication and Control* (New York: Free Press, 1966) and Norbert Weiner, *The Human Use of Human Beings: Cybernetics and Society* (New York: Avon, 1967).

porated into the cybernetic model are—in somewhat different perspective—the same techniques that operate in the natural and physical sciences.

Recognition of the Field

Offering promise of substantial return for investing disciplines—plus the possibility of a comprehensive theoretical framework for all organized activities—IC has been receiving increasing recognition with the onset of the Information Revolution (approximately since the mid-1950's).

Numerous universities have expanded media studies in traditional journalism to include cross-cultural communication and mass media impact upon society; corporations and higher education have begun to train businessmen, economists, educators, and technical experts in the multi-faceted aspects of international communication; government—notably in the U.S. Infor-

mation Agency—has begun to incorporate behavioral science and IC preparation in training for overseas assignments; and professional organizations such as the America Association for the Advancement of Science have included sessions in technological innovation, decision-making research, intercultural communication, science and international politics, and national development in their national conferences.

International Communication, then, has become an ongoing intellectual concern. Riding the wave of the Information Revolution and advances in communications technology, it has become a crossroads of intellectual pursuit. As a convener of integrated study from numerous other fields, it has produced solid evidence of the advantages of interdisciplinary cooperation—cooperation which some day may result in a long-anticipated merger of all the sciences—and a more complete understanding of the world around us.

Should These News Pictures Have Been Printed?

Malcolm F. Mallette

The subject is ethics and news pictures, and the pity is that we don't talk about it more. We talk about f-stops and forced developing and fisheye lenses, but we don't talk much about ethics.

A pretty good editor on a pretty good newspaper said recently, "What's to talk about? We don't print nudity—at least not frontal nudity, and we throw away most of those ridiculous cheesecake pictures. So what's to talk about?"

The answer is: plenty. Ethics is always a difficult subject. Even to read the definitions of ethics in the dictionary is to have one's eye glaze. Consider the definition: "The study of ideal human character, action and ends." I quote from Webster, who didn't use many pictures—and none wider than half a column.

The subject of ethics and news pictures has been passionately discussed at American Press Institute seminars for experienced newspapermen and women. I vividly recall one conference-table discussion at a Seminar for Picture Editors and Graphics Directors not long ago. For three days, as we discussed everything from techniques to motivation makeup, the subject of ethics flickered into the dialog. Like distant heat lightning, these were flashes of questioning

over ethics, flashes of uncertainty, and obvious disagreement.

One afternoon we tackled the subject head-on. "All right, gang, what do you print and what don't you print, and under what circumstances?" In turn, each of several members of the seminar eagerly told of pictures he had published—startling pictures, sexy pictures of gruesomeness and grief.

There was obvious pride in the narrations—and why not? On film they had captured a dramatic moment, and capturing dramatic moment is largely what news photography is all about. But notably absent in most of their accounts was a moment of judgment in the editing process—a pause to ask if the picture should be published. The feeling among this one segment of the seminar members seemed to be: "What's to consider? When you have a good picture, you print it."

The questioning was fervent. I am happy to say that the voices of responsibility were loud and clear. More heart-warming still was the reaction of members who had entered the discussion preaching an Eleventh Commandment for news photographers: "Thou shalt publish any picture that soothes your immortal ego." Almost unanimous conviction emerged that any

---

By permission of the author.

News and antiwar value of Eddie Adams' shot of Vietcong prisoner being executed brought wide use throughout world, won Pulitzer prize.

Edward Adams

newspaper of general circulation must deliberate carefully whether to print certain pictures of violence, suffering, and sex. Understanding also emerged that these decisions are seldom easy. And at no time was there a suggestion that we should protect the newspaper reader from all the stark realities of life.

Do we print the gruesome picture of the Buddhist monk who has set himself afire? Yes. Of course. And do we print the horrifying picture of the South Vietnamese military officer firing his pistol point-blank into the brain of a captive?

Startling, yes. Should they have been printed? Yes. Life is often startling and horrible. Only by knowing can readers seek a better existence for all.

But sometimes the line is very fine, and difficult judgments must be made. The fact that one shocking picture is printed does not mean that all should be. So let us consider now some news pictures and the circumstances in which they were printed—or not printed.

As I describe these pictures and the circumstances, ask yourself what *your* decision would have been had the responsibility been yours—to print or not to print. And remember: we are seeking guidelines for a newspaper of general circulation, a friend that should be welcome in your own home by readers of all ages.

Consider first Miss All-Bare America, wearing a costume appropriate to her title, after a press conference in Sardi's Restaurant in New York City. (Now I understand why it is often difficult to get a table at Sardi's.) Miss All-Bare America called the press conference to plead for "accepting our own bodies without either fear, shame, or disgust."

The caption of this United Press International picture begins: "Editors: Your attention is called to the contents of this picture." Know-

This 1942 photo showed *Life* readers U.S. dead for the first time in WW II. Its message and power overrode any objections to its use.

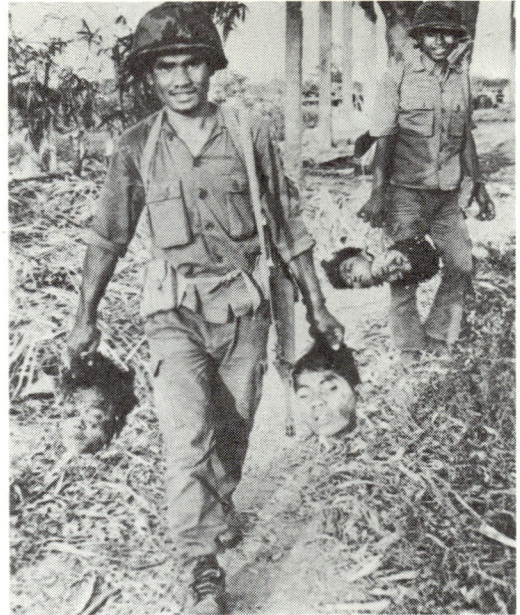

Although UPI wires moved this gruesome shot of Cambodian soldiers with enemies heads, no reports of use in U.S. papers were seen.

ing a little about editors, I would say the calling of attention was needless. Although this young woman may have a serious message we need to consider, the picture is obviously *not* for newspapers of general circulation.

Ah, but we seem to have some disagreement! At least one editor wanted to share this picture with others beside the snickering gang on the copy desk. A two-column picture of Miss All-Bare America, unretouched was printed in the Hong Kong *Standard*.

Now let us consider a case study provided by John C. Peterson, at the time Art Director of *The Toronto Star*.

The photograph shows the nude hockey goalie of Team Canada, which was on an international tour, in a sauna shower in Helsinki, where female attendants are employed. A female attendant is walking past the showering goalie and observing with only mild interest.

Team Canada was a big story, and upon the arrival of this picture, John Peterson faced a judgment. He reports that the issue was debated all the way to the publisher, with various editors suggesting treatment ranging from the front page to the wastebasket.

The Toronto Star decided on four-column display on the first sports page. *The Toronto Sun*, a tabloid sold only on newsstands, used the picture on page one, full-page width. Toronto's third newspaper, *The Globe and Mail*, used the picture four columns on the second sports page.

John Peterson's initial judgment was that the picture should go page one. After cooler thought, he says, "Understanding of the kind of paper we work for tells me the publisher's decision was correct." Peterson lists the factors for judgment. The picture is probably a setup, but illustrating a real situation. The pose is perhaps

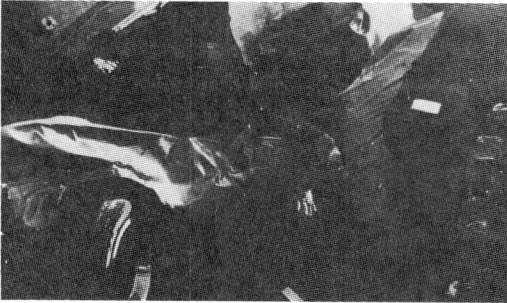

Craig Borck

Managing Editor of *St. Paul Dispatch* thought this strong but grisly car-wreck photo should not have run. Author agrees.

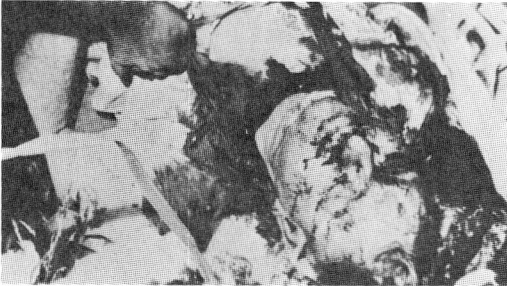

UPI Photo

U.S. Consul to Argentina was murded by guerrillas; UPI did not move it on domestic wires, but overseas press used it widely.

"dicey" (and not *totally* revealing . . . Ed.), but humorous rather than prurient. And the nudity is integral to the purpose of the picture.

So, perhaps John Peterson has given us some small pieces of the puzzle. A real-life situation, humor rather than prurience. And always very important, the kind of newspaper you publish.

Nudity is always a difficult question. Hal Buell, Executive Newsphoto Editor of The Associated Press, has stated the AP's working guidelines on transmitting nude pictures: "We will not carry full frontal views of nude men or women except in a most extreme case. Such a story has yet to occur. We will transmit pictures of bare bosoms when such pictures are

pertinent to the story. The hard-to-spell-out concept of 'taste' is always a consideration."

The bared female bosom has been carried on The AP wirephoto network on occasions, however—as during a protest demonstration while the 1972 political conventions were being held in Miami.

On another occasion The AP moved a picture of a topless girl strolling on a beach in Denmark. She goes unnoticed by other bathers. Why? Because scores of girls are going topless on public beaches in Europe. That was the editorial point of the picture, to illustrate changing values.

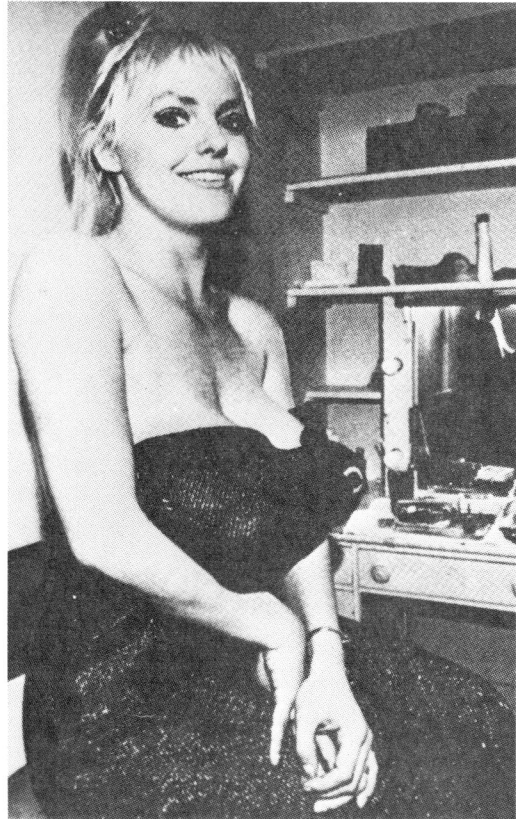

AP Wirephoto

Dancer Ann Marie's measurements are impressive (67–25–36) but news value of her photo was not. Picture wasn't used.

And then there was a revealing night at the opera in New Orleans, when soprano Carol Neblett disrobed at the end of the first act. The cutline on The AP picture said she was cheered and added: "Editors: please use this at your own discretion." The picture was used by a number of newspapers, and no doubt caused many readers to switch from country music to opera.

Of course, the ridiculous pictures are always with us, and a judgment not to use can be reached in five seconds—just before the picture is carefully stored in a desk drawer.

There was, for example, a picture of Miss Nude America, wearing only handcuffs. The UPI picture was datelined: Naked City, Ind. (The poor girl should have tried Sardi's.)

William Rose, Director of Photography for the *Ottawa Citizen*, found no redeeming news value in a picture of a go-go dancer who claimed body dimensions of 67–25–36, and with the picture as evidence, who was to doubt them?

Opera buff is displayed by soprano Carol Neblett during performance of *Thais*. Many papers used the photo, although caption had reference to editorial discretion.

But it was another one for the desk drawer, since it had no real reason to be printed in the public press.

However, William Rose did use a picture of high school students spelling out bent over, with pants pulled down, the name of an arch-rival by means of letters on their undershorts. One bare bottom was in the line of stooped-over students. That was the punctuation mark. Again, humor made the difference. No reader of *The Ottawa Citizen* reported an objection.

When a nightclub stripper jumped from the car of a powerful American Congressman and into Washington's Tidal Basin, we had a news story. When she danced in Boston to cash in on her new celebrity status and the Congressman watched from the wings, we had another news story. The AP moved several pictures of Fanne Fox, fully costumed and almost uncostumed. United Press International moved a picture that shows very much of a dancing Fanne Fox.

At most newspapers more revealing pictures

Keystone Press Agency.

Completely unauthorized photo of Britain's Princess Anne was widely used, thanks to its humor and changing public tastes.

of Fanne Fox went into the desk drawer, not the newspaper.

With—uh—hindsight, we might ask if there is humor in a picture of Princess Anne, royally exposed by the wind? "In years gone by," says Ted Majeski, Executive Newsphotos Editor of United Press International, "we probably would not have used this photo of Princess Anne's behind. But times have changed, and we *did* use it —worldwide. Despite protests from a few who thought it undignified the Royal Family, the picture was widely used in the American press."

All right, times have changed. But how much? Is there a fine line between a picture of a mischievous wind and a wire service picture that was *not* moved on the network? The picture, taken just after the swearing-in of an American diplomat, showed the diplomat kissing his wife and squeezing her bosom. The diplomat's hand may have been quicker than the eye, but not The Associated Press camera. The photographer who took the picture didn't notice the connubial squeeze. Tobey Massey, the Washington Newsphoto Editor, did—just as the picture was being prepared for transmission. He stopped the picture.

"This picture would have been in poor taste." says Massey. It would have made (the diplomat) a laughingstock and caused him much embarrassment."

The question of good taste is not limited to bare bottoms and bosoms. We also have pictures like one in which Kareem Abdul Jabbar, then with the Milwaukee Bucks basketball team, is conveying a nonverbal message. I am fairly certain he is not ordering two bottles of beer that made Milwaukee famous. These hand gestures were made before a crowd of ten thousand people in Milwaukee when Jabbar was the hero of the town, and it was not popular to show Jabbar as less than saintly.

On the sports desk of *The Milwaukee Journal* there were some who questioned whether the picture should be used. Chuck Johnson, the Sports Editor, reasoned that hero status was irrelevant. The gestures had been made in full view of the multitude. Dick Leonard, the *Jour-*

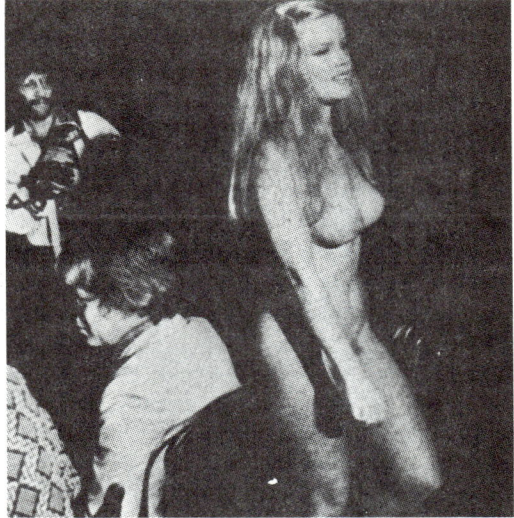

Hong Kong Standard regarded this picture of Miss All-Bare America leaving the press conference she had called as newsworthy enough to run. Family papers ignored it.

nal's editor, agreed with Johnson. The picture ran six columns.

"The readers took a dim view," Johnson recalls, "but not as dim as the Bucks. I was able to reason with readers who called in—that it happened in front of 10,000 persons, that they could explain (the gesture) to their children at home, rather than having them see it elsewhere. It all died down as fast as it flared up, and I think we did the right thing.

If we think of ethics as responsibility, we soon see that it must be exercised in many ways. William F. Cento, Graphic Arts Editor of the *St. Paul Dispatch* and *Pioneer Press* provides the example of a page-one picture showing two children climbing a wall in pursuit of a squirrel. One child is close to what may be dangerous electric wires. A reader wrote the *Pioneer Press* saying: "Please don't write stories like this without pointing out the dangers. Children looking at the picture will only think it is fun." The reader had a point.

Another judgment picture shows a man shooting a calf with a pistol during a mass killing of cattle to protest the cost of raising beef. Bill Cento says, "The story ran across the top of page one, but we ran the picture inside. A mistake, I believe. The words are needed to tell *why* it was done. The picture most forcefully tells that it *was* done—and that's the purpose of practically all news pictures."

That fine line is ever with us. *Newsweek* magazine carried a picture of the body of Roger Davies, the assassinated American ambassador to Cyprus. In a later issue *Newsweek* printed a letter to the editor that said: "What purpose could possibly be served by your printing the picture . . .? Why should Ambassado Davies' family and friends be made to suffer by chancing upon such a gruesome picture? As for the public interest, your picture was not news but sensationalist journalism . . ."

To which *Newsweek* replied: "*Newsweek* was one of a number of major publications that printed the picture of Ambassador Davies' body."

Are you satisfied with that answer if, indeed, it *is* an answer?

In 1966, UPI had to decide whether to use a vivid picture by Kyoichi Sawada, the Pulitzer Prize winner. The picture shows a dead Viet Cong soldier being dragged by an American armored vehicle to a burial site. UPI moved the picture, says Ted Majeski, knowing it would bring criticism. And it did.

Liberals, says Majeski, said this was typical of the horrors American forces were inflicting upon the Vietnamese; the Far Right saw it as an effort to picture the American soldier in a bad light.

UPI carried a picture of the blood-soaked body of U.S. Consul of Argentina, John Patrick Egan, assassinated by guerrillas. The picture, says UPI's Majeski, was not used on the domestic network because UPI believed few American newspapers would run a close-up of the bloody face. It did move on the European, Far East, and South American networks.

Says Majeski, "It was perhaps the best-played picture on the grisly story in the overseas press. An obvious difference in reader taste."

Or, I ask, does distance make the difference?

It is easier for American editors to run a picture of a dead and nameless Viet Cong than of a dead American? Probably so. Again, the thin line.

In 1974 a picture appeared in which Cambodian soldiers carry heads cut from Khmer Rouge soldiers after fighting near Phnom Penh. This was one of the widely played pictures in the foreign press. At UPI, Ted Majeski debated whether it was too gruesome to move in the United States. Since American forces were not involved, UPI decided to move it on the national network. The decision, says Majeski, was apparently wrong. He saw no reports of its use in American newspapers.

One photograph taken by an American newspaper showed the body and severed head of a man who committed suicide by placing his neck on a railroad track. The picture was not used because editors thought it would have been too hard on the family involved. I hope that everyone agrees with that decision.

Sometimes two professionals make their best judgment and come down on opposite sides of the fine line. Bill Cento of the *St. Paul Dispatch* illustrates this with a picture by Craig Borck in which the arm of a dead girl protrudes from a crashed car. Only the arm is visible amid the wreckage.

He says: "Grisly, yes. We used it, much to the displeasure of the Managing Editor, who saw it in the paper after it was too late to change. The limp arm and hand of the dead girl tells 'auto death' as forcefully as I've ever seen it told on film without ungodly blood and guts. I stand by use of this picture as being within whatever nebulous bounds we work within."

To which I add that it is so easy to be an expert in theory, and so difficult on the editor's desk. However, I think I would have spared the readers this one.

Bill Cento helps me to say how subjective judgment can be. In one dramatic picture, a drowned boy lies at the water's edge of a pond. The father and police restrain the grieving mother. A camera captured the heartbreaking scene. The *St. Paul Dispatch* ran the picture and received many calls objecting.

Cento asks: "Should we have intruded on this moment of grief? This is where I get inconsistent. I don't believe I'd use a picture like this again. At least I'd think long and hard about it."

There is no doubt in my mind. This is the kind of picture we can well do without.

When *do* we intrude on a moment of grief? On Veterans Day, a *Seattle Times* photographer snapped an anonymous mother in a military graveyard, her face contorted in grief. The woman did not know her picture was being taken. The photographer did not get her name, knowing he had a strong photo and not wanting to jeopardize it. *The Seattle Times*, says Jim Heckman, played the picture big on page one, but the Managing Editor worried about it all day.

A year later another photographer came across the same woman in the same cemetary. He talked to the woman and learned that she *liked* the picture. The picture won several prizes.

I don't mind declaring myself on this one. Perhaps all is well that ends well, but like the Managing Editor I would worry. And then I would have a long, long talk with the photographer who didn't want to jeopardize his picture.

On the other hand, many private moments might well be shared. For example: A husband and wife have just lost all their possessions in a fire. They embrace to comfort each other. The news camera clicks. Jack Burnett, Photographic and Engraving Manager of the London, Ontario, *Free Press*, offers the story, saying that he often wonders about invading people's privacy in moments of grief or tragedy. "And yet," he says, "every so often a picture (like this one) turns up that makes me realize we should continue. That does *not* mean that we should publish them all or be too callous or too aggressive."

Photographer Sam McLeod made the picture of the couple who had just lost everything in a fire. But it speaks of compassion and love The London *Free Press* played it big on page one. "I think we were right," says Jack Burnett. Of course they were right!

I present these case histories to chart the bends and wobbles of that fine line of judgment. Definitive statements are difficult to compose, but Russ Scott, Picture Editor of *The Flint Journal*, comes close in one sentence, "We base our picture usage on the premise that a family newspaper is seen by all members of the family."

But, as we have seen, there are times for exceptions. Judgments must be made one by one, since information, instruction, and news values must be considered in each case. Now let me summarize what I've tried to say.

Ethics *are* important. Editors (and photographers) must make careful judgments on when to use and when to throw away—at least into the bottom drawer. They cannot and should not shield readers and viewers from the stark realities of life. But the sensitive editor should ask: Is this a subject of importance, or are we offending unjustifiably?

The line is often thin. Given the best of judgment, we could disagree on whether to use certain pictures I have mentioned. And each of us might make different decisions under slightly different circumstances. I have declared myself on some of these pictures. Placed on the scene—who knows? I might have decided differently.

News pictures are a moment frozen in time. True, newspaper readers are conditioned by the televison camera that takes them to the battle front or the scene of the air crash. But the electronic image flickers and is gone.

Not so with the frozen moment of the news picture. It remains. It can haunt. It can hurt and hurt again. It can also leave an indelible message about the betterment of society, the end of war, the elimination of hunger, the alleviation of hunger, the alleviation of human misery. The mission of any good picture medium is to serve the reader. To serve, we must be credible, and so *credibility* is the media's most priceless asset. This credibility must be painstakingly established over a period of years.

So we must guard that credibility carefully. Poor judgement comes before the fall. And you know what the fall did to Humpty Dumpty.

Ten
Applying Communication

Introduction

In this last section of the book, we will explore a few of the many communication settings that exist. Communication can be applied to numerous fields that go beyond the contexts that were described in the last four chapters. In this chapter we will put all of the contexts and parts of the communication process together and apply them to three settings.

Rather than explore the traditional areas of education, religion, theatre, and the arts, we want to examine cross-cultural communication, political communication, and communication and law. We hope that you will have the interest to explore the role of communication in these and many other areas.

We will not attempt to describe all of the concepts that have been introduced in this book and apply them to each of the above areas. Rather, you will get an overview for each of the areas and then the articles will provide you with material pertinent to each topic. The bibliography will give you sources that you can turn to for a more in-depth look at each of the settings.

Cross-Cultural Communication

Although we have difficulty communicating with someone that we know quite well, this problem is compounded when we attempt to communicate with someone who has different attitudes and values. Cross-cultural communication is defined as communication between and among people with differing values and attitudes and usually different languages or language usage. If you have ever traveled abroad, you have probably already experienced the difficulty in communication with a person of another culture and another language.

Although Harms (1973) makes the following distinction between cross-cultural communication and intercultural communication, we are referring to the communication between individuals of two or more cultural backgrounds.

Intercultural Communication	Cross-cultural Communication
Two-way	One-way
Dyadic, small group	Large group
Mutual purpose	Individual purpose'
Unofficial	Official

Informal   Formal
Developed message   Prepared message
Interdependent   Hierarchial

We are considering both types of communication described by Harms to fit within our definitions. If you develop an interest in the area of cross-cultural communication, you will want to develop and refine your definitions.

The communication that takes place between members of two different subcultures fits within our definition. Communication between Mexican Americans and Anglos, native Americans and Anglos, and Blacks and whites would all be a part of the subcultural communication patterns.

We do not believe that you need a great deal of training in order to communicate with a member of another culture. In addition to communication skills, you need to know the values, attitudes, and language of another culture. Remember, it is in your self-interest to know the person with whom you are communicating. The more that you know about your audience, the easier it will be to communicate.

Crisis Communication

Have you ever had a personal crisis and not known how to talk about it? Have you ever had a friend confide in you about a personal problem and not known how to deal with the problem or with your friend? The study of crisis communication will help you deal with your own crisis communication situations and those of others. Crisis is defined as a turning point—when an individual is faced with an event that cannot be dealt with using the usual coping methods. This person, who could ordinarily deal with a problem, is in a crises state where the usual coping devices are unable to be used. For example, your girl friend has just called to say that she is through with you. This may leave you unable to cope and thus in a state of crisis. A crisis is usually a short-term event which leaves you without a means of resolving it without outside intervention.

If crisis is seen as an anti-growth-promoting behavior, then communication is an essential precursor of growth-promoting behavior. We believe that crises cannot be resolved without communication. The skills of communication that have been discussed throughout this book will be useful to you as you deal with a crisis setting. Toffler described what he called *future shock*. In essence, he was describing a crisis state when he talked about the effects of decisional stress combined with sensory and cognitive overload. Unless this state is dealt with effectively, the individual becomes maladaptive.

In Chapters V through VIII, the contexts for communication were discussed. Crises can develop in each of those contexts. On the interpersonal level crises can happen due to problems in dating, marriage, divorce, and family dysfunction, to name a few. At the group level, they can result from refusal to communicate, from strikes, and from other forms of protest. At the public level and through the mass media, crises can occur as natural disasters, in wars, or in riots.

Political Communication

Political analysts speculated that Hubert Humphrey could have beaten Nixon in 1968 if the election had been held later in

November. Obviously, it is easier to look back on a political campaign and see what went wrong than to look forward to an upcoming campaign and decide what to do.

All of the skills of communication are required to plan, develop, and conduct a campaign for political office. A political campaign requires knowledge of interpersonal, group, public, and mass communication if it is to be effective. Potential politicians are willing to spend large sums of money on campaign communication in the hope that they will be successful in a general election. It was estimated by Nimmo (1970) that at least $140 million was spent on all political campaigns in 1952, followed in 1956 by an expenditure of $155 million, $175 million in 1960, $200 million in 1964, and more than $250 million in 1968.

In his book, *The Political Persuaders*, Nimmo (1970) suggests several themes about political campaigns.

1. Modern political campaigns are based on application of the assumptions and techniques of the communication sciences.

2. The short-term effects of political campaigns on voter attitudes are greatest upon persons who are least interested in and committed to democratic electoral processes.

3. Campaigns permit voters to adjust their perceptions of political candidates long-term political prejudices.

4. Campaigns are a significant form of symbolic reassurance contributing to the stability of democratic regimes.

5. Professional expertise increasingly directs all phases of modern political campaigns.

6. Political scientists may well underestimate the impact of political campaigning on voting behavior.

The point is that communication plays a very important role in the campaign and election process.

Communication and the Law

With the popularity of the theme of law and order, communication experts are looking at the legal field as an area that applies many communication principles. Questions have been raised about jury selection, witness apparel, and defendant attractiveness. You should be able to apply all of the principles of communication to the court room. For example, witnesses are now being interviewed on videotape for playback to the jury. Likewise, police officers serving as witnesses are being interviewed on the job for later playback. A television tube may replace the witness stand.

Articles

In cross-cultural communication, Weaver looks at the American identity movements in an attempt to clarify some of the myths of the cultural melting pot. Kreyche looks at the impact of travel and communication on ethnicity and philosophy. Although he concentrates on philosophy, his observations are pertinent to the impact of culture on communication.

Arnold explores the role of communication in dealing with crises. In addition to his discussion of the nature of crisis and communication, Arnold examines two specific crises—suicide and organization dysfunction—and how communication can facilitate growth.

Nimmo examines the channels of communication as they impinge on the political campaign. He discusses all of the terms of communication, but you would need to read more before you planned your own campaign.

Finally, Welch describes the role of communication in the legal field. She compares many of the interesting applications of communication variables to the court room.

References

L. S. Harms, *Intercultural Communication* (New York: Harper & Row, 1973).

D. Nimmo, *The Political Persuaders* (Englewood Cliffs, N.J.: Prentice Hall, 1970).

American Identity Movements: A Cross-Cultural Confrontation

Gary R. Weaver

Today, large numbers of Americans refuse to give up their individual identities to become part of the larger abstractive society.

If we were to assess the significant, long-term results of the civil rights and anti-Vietnam war movements of the 1960's, we would probably place at the top of our list the numerous court decisions barring discrimination, the development of massive opposition to the Vietnam war, and the 18-year-old right to vote. While all of these developments are indeed important, I suggest that by far the most significant long-term consequence of both movements is the growth of popular questioning of cultural assumptions held by Americans for generations. Rather than having values of a subcultural group dissipated and absorbed by the dominant culture, these two groups have undermined the values and assumptions of the dominant culture.

The net results of these two movements has been a drive toward true pluralism of cultures and subcultures—including such "subcultural" identity groups as Women's Lib, Gay Lib, Chicano, American-Indian, and many other groups. No longer are individuals denying their identities to fit into an abstractive, Anglo-male society.

Reprinted from *Intellect*—March 1975.

They are asserting their uniqueness and wholeness while taking it for granted that they are entitled to their fair share of society's benefits.

The Melting Pot Myth

Foremost among the numerous assumptions which are now questioned by many Americans is the long-standing "melting pot" myth of cultural equality of people of all races. We would have to search diligently to find evidence of Chinese, Latin, Middle-Eastern, Indian-American, African, or of even Eastern or Southern European ethnic patterns of behavior and thought being absorbed into the American culture. The pot melted no further than corn, chop suey, spaghetti, pork chops, and shish kebab. Each ethnic group has not contributed its own cultural traits equally to the whole. Rather, there has been a cultural shaping by a white, male, Protestant, Anglo-Saxon cookie cutter. This leveling (not "melting") has now been challenged by numerous subcultural groups as they fight for their own life styles, values, perceptions, and interests, which are often contrary to the mainstream mold.

This cultural imperialism (not cultural pluralism) was a result of racism, liberalism, and rapid technological and urban growth. It was obvious-

267

ly easier to identify non-whites and to reject not only their cultural, but their individual, identities. The dynamics of racism are now apparent to most Americans. The more subtle effects of liberalism are less apparent. In fact, the community-focused, equality-directed characteristics of liberalism seem to be contrary to any sort of racism or cultural imperialism. Yet, the belief that all men are equal is perhaps as responsible for this cultural leveling as any sort of overt racism, primarily because it denies the reality of physical, cultural, and psychological differences among men.

Let us contrast the positions of the overt racist and the so-called liberal regarding racial attitudes. The racist would maintain that whites and non-whites are inherently different, and that non-whites are inferior to whites. The liberal would maintain that whites and non-whites are basically the same, except that non-whites have not been treated equally. This liberal contention appears very humane, yet could easily be translated to mean the only reason non-whites are different is that they are pathologically white. If their culture were the same as the white culture, everyone would be equal. This denies the very real fact that there are non-white subcultures and that non-whites are not only physiologically different, but also culturally different. Accepting these differences does not lead us back to racism, because there is no concurrent need to assume superiority or inferiority.

The break-up of fairly isolated communities and ethnic groups by industrialism, urban growth and technological advancement, especially in the mass media, has abetted the liberal drive for homogencity and the consequent imposition of an Anglo-Saxon cultural cookie cutter. This shaping and leveling is expressed by Daniel P. Moynahan as he suggests that the lack of a biological father in many black homes is responsible for much of the economic and social ills in ghettos around the country. The assumption is that the Western model of the family is ideal, and that the black model is pathological. There are literally millions of families around the world that do not have the biological father present, yet there is a low incidence of crime, few riots, and the social fabric seems quite healthy. Thus, it is anthropologically unsound to assume that the Western family model is "normal" or best. Indeed, numerous scholars are beginning to feel that the Western family model may be responsible for many contemporary ills in Western society today.

The Qualitative Revolution

Blacks and students towards the mid-1960's began to resemble each other in terms of opposition—they were against *the system*. Until then, this was not necessarily true—that is, the black civil rights movement was geared to allow increased participation in the system. To this extent, it was very much like the labor movement and previous revolutionary movements. Its objective was *quantitative*—a piece of the socioeconomic and political pie. The student movement, on the other hand, was primarily *qualitative*. For many, the pie was not worth eating in the first place. By the mid-1960's, however, black leaders began to question the quality of the pie and, indeed, began to develop cultural styles in opposition to the pie.

This opposition to the system extended throughout the student movement around the technologically advanced world. Regardless of nationality, students seemed to oppose any way of life or thought which appeared systematic, rule-bound, and impersonal, as opposed to the spontaneous, the free, the intensely and, therefore, personally felt. However, this opposition is true mainly of the technologically developed cultures. In the less technologically developed countries, student revolts were much less qualitative. For example, in January, 1972, there was a university student revolt in Sierra Leone, in which the major issues included ironing boards in the dormitories, more allowance, and better food. There was little effort to change "the system" of Sierra Leone.

Whereas the 1950's was the era of conformity, the 1960's was the era when nonconformity was paramount. In the late 1950's "everyone" smoked Marlboros, college men (black or white) wore Ivy League clothes, and, while McCarthy purged, the Korean War killed hundreds of thousands, an economic crisis pervaded, and Emmett Till was killed, young people ran through college dormitories yelling for panties before rushing to their favorite fraternity or sorority parties. In the 1960's, cigarettes became available for the *exceptional* man or woman, students could come to class nearly nude without arousing more than a hearty ho-hum, a President announced that he wanted to make the world "safe for diversity," and massive movements were led against racial discrimination and war. Students occupied the university president's office to protest discrimination, war, and lack of participation in decision-making. Fraternities and sororities were dying.

I suggest that many of these phenomena were not only reactions to the leveling process of the pre-1950's, but an effort to retain subcultural and personal identity, and to prevent the sense of meaninglessness and the rush toward an Orwellian *1984* from becoming a reality. That is, they were not signs of cultural disintegration, but, rather, efforts to truly maintain cultural integration of all ethnic and subcultural groups without the cultural imperialism of the past overwhelming individual and group identity.

No longer are various subcultural groups willing to pay the price of loss of individual and cultural identity to get their fair share of the systemic pie. If gaining a quantitative advance means qualitative loss in lifestyle to accommodate the mass-society cookie-cutter, then the alternative is no longer one of copping out, as the Beat Generation did, but one of altering the dominant cultural system to allow for retention and enhancement of cultural identity while offering a share of the pie. This new awareness may be termed "Consciousness Level III" or a "prefigurative culture," but the net result is that, with the 1970's, it has grown to include Women's Lib, Gay Lib, the Chicano movement, the American-Indian movement, and even various communal efforts.

The Associative vs. Abstractive Culture

What is the qualitative American cultural revolution all about? It is a struggle between two modes of thought, reflecting two cultures which seem in opposition. More importantly, it represents a struggle between two ways of organizing society, its values, and perceptions. It has been described as a struggle between associative and abstractive cultures, rational vs. analytic thought, or as a struggle between members of a *Gemeinschaft* or community and members of a *Gesellschaft* or more complex society.

The struggle is very much analogous to the culture clash of technologically advanced mass societies and non-technologically advanced, community-oriented cultures. Although this clash has been described as occurring between East and West, this is greatly oversimplified and misleading. In actuality, it has no absolute geographic parameters, but, rather, socioeconomic, philosophic, and experiential demarcations, with no sharp line dividing one culture into the associative grouping and another into the abstractive grouping. While the associative, non-Westernized grouping might include parts of Latin America, Asia, and Africa, there are "hybrids" of sorts—such as Japan, urbanized Latin America, and perhaps even urbanized Nigeria.

This oversimplified model of culture is intended to offer a way of contrasting and comparing two basic culture-and-personality systems. It is primarily descriptive, yet may lead us to understand that the clash between generations, races, and identity groups today is indeed a culture gap, not a generation gap. It is no accident that young people today have developed music styles similar to the realism of blues or the free-style of jazz, that youth prefer bright clothing, or that self-actualizing students use Eastern philosophies to guide their lifestyles while young blacks seek their African roots.

To illustrate this, let us consider the following

linguistic example. As an undergraduate, I often joined my fraternity brothers at Howard University as they met outside one of the women's dormitories to evaluate the quality and quantity of incoming coeds during the first few days of the fall semester. This was a popular male, chauvinistic activity which allowed the brothers to get together and talk. As we sat there, I noticed that a particular brother, John, was not with the group. I asked a fellow brother. "Where's John?" "Oh he's not hanging out. He's got a nose job." At the moment I thought it extremely odd that John, who was fairly handsome, would have his nose altered surgically. A few weeks later, I again noticed that John was not hanging out at a local bar with his fraternity brothers. Again, I inquired as to the whereabouts of John. Again, the reply was, "He's got a nose job." Finally, I broke down and asked, "What do you mean, a nose job?" "You know, a young lady has him by the nose." To have a "nose job" was to be deeply involved with a girlfriend, consequently being unable to hang out with his friends. Out of cultural context, and translated literally, the phrase made absolutely no sense.

Here we find a characteristic of associative or relational language. It is a product of small, intimate groups or people who subconsciously share similar experiences. For example, every language has a standard and nonstandard form—the so-called King's English and patois. The non-standard form is usually a subcultural form. In no way is the non-standard language a sign of lack of intelligence. In fact, it is often more sophisticated than the standard language in its verbal, spoken form. Seldom is it written, making it necessary to communicate face-to-face vocally, sharing more than simply words, but also the physical presence of another. Body language, tone of voices, and who is speaking to whom are all important. Everything is *associated* with everything. It is more intimate than standard language, which can be written and translated quite easily to everyone, regardless of who wrote it, where only *words* are relevant and *abstracted* or selected out of the communications scenaria.

Black Dialect: An Associative Language

Let us consider a non-standard form with which we are all somewhat familiar—black dialect, or black patois (sometimes termed ghettoese). Not only does it have a very consistent grammatical form, but, in terms of verbal usage, it is much more sophisticated than standard English. For example, if a teacher asked a child to have his mother come to school tomorrow, the child might respond, "No, she can't. She be sick." The teacher then asks, "Would you please have her come in next week, then?" The child responds, "No. She can't. She be sick." What is happening? Is the child making up an excuse? On the contrary, the child is expressing herself very clearly, using the verb "to be" in a tense which is no longer used in the English language, but is found in Shakespearean English, to indicate an ongoing process—that is, her mother is ill, and will be ill, an ongoing process. This verb tense is found in many non-written languages around the world and in many non-Western languages such as Greek. Interestingly, "to be" (ascription) is the most common verb in black dialect and many non-Western languages, while "to do" (achievement) is the most common verb in standard English.

Associative verbal interaction is highly developed. A popular activity among children in ghetto areas is an activity called Joning. the Dozens, or the Numbers. It is a form of interaction where one child tries to out-insult another, usually poetically, by referring to his mother. Often, this game can go on for hours and requires a good verbal command, the ability to tie words together associatively, use of vocal and body messages, and a very quick wit. Few standard-speaking children could handle the English language as deftly as these children do.

"Toasting" is another very common usage of non-standard English. A toast is a very long story in poetry fashion which is passed on and added to as it is passed along. Many famous toasts, such as "Stagger Lee," were developed in jail. Not only are toasts indicative of a highly sophisticated language form, they often have been passed down in perfect iambic pentameter form. The same is true of many of the lyrics to blues music.

In fact, all artistic work is, by definition, associative. That is, a work of art is meaningful because it sets off a series of emotional associations in the viewer/listener. It is somewhat misleading to term much modern art "abstract art." Although it does abstract from a totality of lines, colors, and forms only those which are basic to a particular theme, feeling, tone or mood, abstract art is art because the viewer can associate spontaneously with the message of the artist, without the clutter of extraneous lines, colors, and forms. To a great extent, this is perhaps the purest form of association, similar to the glass bead game of Herman Hesse.

Poetry and music are whole works which can not be divided into separate parts, however much pedantic critics might wish to do so. They ignite a series of deep associations in the listener's head, and he feels what the poet or composer felt. The words and sounds bring to his conscious mind feelings which were long buried in the unconscious. Is it any wonder that poetry is perhaps the most difficult written form to translate into another language?

A contrast of mainstream, white poetry and black poetry illustrates the associative element in the black culture. Black poetry is usually read aloud, and voice tone, gestures, and the presence of both poet and listener is essential (*e.g.*, Gil Scott Heron, Nikki Giovani). White poetry is usually not read aloud but, if it is, it is done in a monotone, non-emotional voice.

Lastly, we all speak associative languages with loved ones and friends. Labels we give loved ones have developed by usage and are intimate ways of expressing feelings. Most of us would be offended if a stranger called our wife "bunny," or our husband "sugar." Who says what to whom is vital, and the meaning is all in the situation.

Mass Society: The Abstractive Culture

Of course, we all can speak abstractive language.

It is technical and provides a common language for performing tasks without considering who is saying what to whom. The message, not the communicator, is all that is important. Thus, it can be easily written, but communicates little feeling. It is eminently rational, logical, practical, and simple. In fact, much of what the Anglo-male culture values is typically abstractive (objectivity, aloofness, rationality), and is exactly the opposite of what is considered associative—and often feminine (subjectivity, personally and emotionally involved).

These two styles of expression not only represent two ways of thought, but two ways of organizing society. The abstractive is typical of complex societies, where individual differences or subgroup differences are leveled to provide a common mode of communication. The associative represents a homogeneous community, where everyone shares the same collective unconscious, has similar values and perceptions, and has similar childhood experiences. The small, isolated village would be an associative community, while the larger urban areas or the total U.S. would be an abstractive mass society.

People come together in groups because they either trust each other or because there is mutual predictability. In a community, there is natural predictability, because all share the same collective values and behavior patterns. Everyone knows his or her place and belongs to the community. There are spontaneous similarities between all members of the community, and one can therefore infer from one's own behavior the behavior of others. This is very common in all homogeneous groups where there is no need for written rules to govern behavior, because what is proper is unconsciously known.

Ten years ago, in a small, white community, roles were *ascribed*. If you came from a wealthy, landed family or one with a long "noble" heritage, you could be the dumbest citizen in the community and still have the highest status. On the other hand, if you were the most intelligent black in the community, your role would be ascribed as having the lowest status. Communities are in-group oriented, unconsciously very tradition-directed, rigid, and difficult to belong to unless you were born into the culture. This is very illogical for organizing talents in the culture, but very *human*.

Abstractive societies are made up of groups of people who do not know each other well enough to trust one another spontaneously. People come from various ethnic groups, value systems, perceptual systems, etc. Status, ideally, is achieved generally in economic terms, and social trust is maintained through a system of explicit rules, which every member of the society must learn, and which must be enforced to protect the rights of all. Thus, what a person *is* becomes irrelevant to the system—only what a person *does is* important. This is much more logical and humane than the associative community, but much less human. In fact, it is a schizoid organization, where the totality of a person is discarded—whether he is Protestant, black, sad, happy, etc., is of no consequence unless it interferes with his task.

This schizoid nature of abstractive societies has led to the sense of alienation one feels. The boss really doesn't give a damn if your mother died last night. We have difficulty communicating feelings, and, in fact, we find we can not really feel anything. It has reached the point where the schizoid nature of the abstractive system has created inefficiency. Thus, businesses and government are supporting such devices as sensitivity sessions to break down the inability of people to relate as human beings, instead of merely as task performers.

In many ways, the abstractive society is more humane—that is, it is more objective and not as in-group oriented. A black would not be logically rejected simply for being black, because blackness is irrelevant to task performance. There is a larger and less rigid frame of reference, but, also, there is an inability to grant the wholeness of people and to take into account such supposedly irrelevant critera as ethnic identity, personal feelings, and individual egos.

The associative community is more human—it gives a sense of wholeness and belonging—but it also excludes the outsider and is often very inhumane. The abstractive society is more humane—it does not necessarily reject the outsider and allows for advancement in terms of achievement, but it is also less human, as it treats individuals in a schizoid manner. The associative community seems very illogical, because behavior is determined by custom and numerous factors are associated with particular behavior, whether logically or not. For example, a few years ago I was in Honduras, visiting a Peace Corps contingent there. Numerous women volunteers were having trouble in their village. The men no longer respected them, yet they had done nothing to earn this disrespect. Upon closer analysis, it was found that the American women chose to wear slacks, because they were much more practical in the jungle. However, the local culture frowned upon women who wore slacks. Generally, women who wore slacks were prostitutes. Thus, associated with wearing slacks was the suggestion of prostitution, and the American women are being associated with these so-called "bad" women.

True Plurality Today

Both the abstractive and associative cultures have their excesses. The associative community gives a sense of belonging, spontaneity, wholeness, predictability, ingroup identity, and is very human, but it also is often rigid, ascriptive, exclusive of outsiders, inhumane in extreme, and can even be turned fascistic. The abstractive society is very logical, achievement-oriented, and humane, but it also leads to alienation, lack of whole self-identity, a schizoid personality, and, consequently, is very inhuman. Economically (capitalism), politically (liberalism), and socially (mass societies of heterogeneous ethnic groups), the abstractive culture has clearly conquered most subcultural groups. However, the student movement was certainly a reaction to this system, as are the ethnic minority and various identity movements today.

Young people have asked themselves what price one has to pay to become a member of the abstractive system. Is life really meaningful if one earns $50,000 per year, but has sacrificed his individual identity and feels like an insignificant cog in a societal machine that determines his worth by what he *does* rather than who he *is*? Blacks and other minority groups have also asked themselves whether they must necessarily give up their individual and group identities to melt into the pot—can not one be black, and still be American? Was it an accident that other ethnic groups that melted so easily were termed Italian-American or Irish-American, while, until recently, those who could not melt were termed American Indians and American Negroes? Clearly, certain identifiable groups were treated as castes within the class system, and getting into the system seemed paramount. Thus, many blacks did straighten their hair and attempt to lighten their skin, many women did feel as if they must sacrifice their femininity to become achievers, and many homosexuals did marry and live miserable lives to keep their jobs and status in the society.

Presently, the qualitative demands that these groups participate with equal opportunity in the class system without giving up group or subcultural identity, because the white, male, Protestant, Anglo-Saxon mold is increasingly questioned and challenged in terms of its quality and worth. In fact, even white, male, Protestant, Anglo-Saxons have begun to join the Revolution.

Ethnicity and Philosophy

Gerald F. Kreyche

As travel and communications continue to give ready access to various cultures, they will bring mixed blessings to philosophy.

The purpose of this article is to suggest, rather than to define. It seeks to make explicit an implicit truth of which we are aware, but to which we pay little heed. In some ways, it is a plea for cultural pluralism as benefiting the cause of philosophy and philosophers.

The Thinker and His Environment

Philosophers have long been praised, if not for their solutions to problems, then at least for their objectivity in the quest for truth. Yet, it is strange that, to date, no serious study has been made in the sociology of philosophy which would put this in dispute. Such a study would likely indicate the considerable influence that ethnicity and the cultural *Umwelt* has upon the so-called objectivity of the philosopher.

An anecdote will illustrate this point. The story is told about the great musician, philosopher, and medical missionary, Albert Schweitzer, that he attended a concert in Berlin with a young French music critic. At its conclusion, the two

Reprinted from *Intellect*—September-October, 1975.

walked out and the young Frenchman exclaimed how terrible was the performance. Visibly upset, Schweitzer shook his finger at his companion and said, "Young man, you have no right to say that performance was terrible. I have attended the concert five times now and I say it was terrible!"

Recovering his wit and composure, the critic replied, "Dr. Schweitzer, as I recall, you were born in Alsace-Lorraine. Your French intuition told you the first time that the concert was terrible, but your German sense of scholarship made you go back four more times to confirm it!"

The incident may be apocryphal, but it points out a fundamental truth. That truth is that truth itself is strongly conditioned, approached, and confronted by the sociological background of the thinker. One might broaden this to include geographical, economical, physical, and psychological factors as well. Lumping them all together under the broad rubric of ethnicity, it is clear that, whatever models are proposed in philosophy, they will be partly lopsided. They are invariably the result of a cultural "tunnel vision."

Plato appreciated this limit situation in his famous analogy of the den. However, his philosopher-prisoner who escaped to the world of ideas (true reality) would be seen today as immersed in only another culture world among many. There is no real escape from the confines of the human condition. Francis Bacon himself is an object lesson. Brilliantly and literately, he describes the idols of the cave, marketplace, theatre, and tribe, only to fall victim to them himself.

The Afflectation of Culture

It is patent that each culture affects the values, outlooks, and moral views of its members. The culture is also largely determinant in selecting which problems will be central to the thought of its philosophers. If the medium is the message, then the approach to philosophy will have already narrowed the possible solutions to the problem being studied.

Even language considerably defines a way of thinking, and there is more truth than falsity in the Italian phrase that "The translator is a traitor." However, language itself is both a shaper and a product of a culture, both influencer and influenced by the ethnic values of a given people. Hence, to philosophize in another culture, in another language, is to philosophize differently. (If this is true, it boggles the mind to wonder what the philosophical situation in the West would be today, had not Charles Martel defeated the Arabs in the eighth century.)

Cultural Priorities

This thesis can be clarified with some concrete examples. The entire nature of truth, a phase which already presupposes a cultural context, will be approached differently and, therefore, understood differently, should one adopt the posture of a Biblical Jew, rather than that of a pre-Christian Greek. For the Jew, truth is *emet*, a rock foundation, whereas, for the Greek, it is *aletheia*, a kind of unconcealment of a hidden light. Paul Tillich exploited this distinction by stressing God as the ground of being, rather than its pinnacle of a Platonic supra-being, as hinted at in the *Republic*.

As great a difference can be observed in the Jewish notion of spirit as *ruah*, a kind of rushing, earthy wind, vs. *psyche*, an etheral principle more consonant with the Greek outlook on reality. The flesh and spirit of Biblical literature were no mere counterparts of Plato's body and soul or Aristotle's matter and form any more than were *Yaweh* and the *unmoved mover*.

Given this ethnicity, sight was and remains the greatest of the external senses for the Greek and most of us who follow in his Western tradition, but hearing and touch occupied that rank for the Hebrew. Accordingly, while the Greek looked for the *logos* and the light of truth, the Christianized Hebrew wanted to hear the *logos* and keep it for his own.

In fact, the ethnicity of the Hebrew made it difficult for him to be an achiever in philosophy at all—without, thereby, giving up his own ethnic traits of personalism and concreteness. This, in part, is the background for St. Paul's diatribes against the Greek philosophers, whose "wisdom was their folly." After all, for two millenia, philosophy has been geared to meet the demands of the Greek model, especially, as Hiedegger points out, of the post- rather than the pre-Socratic model.

Until recent times, the number of Jews who "have made it" in philosophy can be counted on the fingers of one hand. Those who did, often excelled at great personal sacrifice. In ancient times there was Philo, the Alexandrian Jew; in medieval times, Avicebron (Solomon Ibn Gabirol), who wrote in Arabic, and the famed Moses Maimonides; in modern times, Benedictus Spinoza. The explanation of this paucity of philosophers among a people who have otherwise distinguished themselves lies, in part, within the very culture. It was a culture which praised concrete, existential thinking as superior to abstract, categorical thinking. Because of this, religion almost singlehandedly provided all the answers to the problems of life which others were encouraged to seek in philosophy. It is related that, at the time of Maimonides, some Jews even petitioned the Spanish authorities to try him before the Christian Inquisition, for they feared his philosophical bent might lead Jews away from their own culture. One can also understand—from the then Jewish point of view—the contempt many felt for Spinoza, who "betrayed" his heritage.

Although a highly sensitive issue today, a similar situation often prevails with women and blacks in philosophy. Both strongly tend to be concrete thinkers, hence not the kind likely to be honored by those schooled in the norms of Western—*i.e.,* Greek—philosophical thinking. The few women and blacks who have succeeded in philosophy (and this is partly true in the sciences as well) are often accused *sub rosa* by their colleagues of having given up their femininity or blackness, respectively.

Other examples of the cultural shaping of philosophical outlooks can be found both near and far. Far, we discover the differences between Roman and Greek. The former was law-oriented, as befitted his practical bent. One calls to mind Cicero and other eclectics, who looked to philosophy more in search for rules of conduct than for solutions to highly theoretical questions. Romans never produced the "metaphysical" and "speculative" thinking so characteristic of Plato and Aristotle. However, the Roman development of jurisprudence is well known. It took their genius to get at the praxis which produced a long standing natural law philosophy growing out of their experience with the citizenry and that of the masses of foreigners coming into Rome and making their imprint on Roman ideals.

Closer at hand, we find typical differences between French and German modes of philosophizing. The very names of Kant, Hegel, Schelling, and Fichte call to mind a very different image of the philosopher than do Rousseau, Bergson, Voltaire, Ricoeur, Marcel, and Sartre. Since the times of Descartes, the French penchant has been for brilliant insight and gifted intuition in matters of life philosophy. The German predilection has been for the complete system philosophy, in all of its thorough-going detail. What comparison is there between the lucidity of the *Meditations* of Descartes and the obfuscations of Hegel's *Phenomenology of Mind?* Yet, both are great contributions to the field. Perhaps, to understand these differences,

we should recall the remark made by a German academician: "Why make it simple if it can be made complex?"

As might be expected, we could know, in the German sense of *a priori*, that British philosophy, like the Crown, would remain characteristically British throughout the centuries. The abiding interest would vacillate only slightly between philosophy having to do with the sciences or with political matters. Roger Bacon emphasized the former in the 13th century, while Francis Bacon gave play to both three centuries later. Hobbes and Hume are not far removed from each other's modes of philosophizing, and neither are Russell, Ayer, and Ryle. Most British thinkers have shown a strongly empirical and positivistic bias, coupled with a natural abhorrence for things metaphysical. Hume's admonition to throw anything dealing with the latter into the flames has not been lost upon the British.

Contrasted with the British, the Irish have produced no well-known philosophers—perhaps because the British have. More likely though, the economic conditions are responsible, being more conducive to producing playwrights, poets, and balladeers than philosophers.

Contemporary Spanish philosophy is typically people-oriented, whether turning inward, in the manner of Miguel de Unamuno (*The Tragic Sense of Life*), or outward, as in Orteg y Gasset (*Revolt of the Masses*).

Polish philosophy has always been strong in empirical areas. Hardnosed since Copernicus, it has gloried in the advance of science and logic. Its uneven national history has hurt the continuity of its thought, but, even today, the school of Polish logic is world reknowned.

American philosophy, although exhibiting a kinship to the Anglo-Saxon tradition, soon began adding its own temperament to its thought. American pragmatism and naturalism, to say nothing of "cash value" thinking espoused by William James, would hardly describe any philosophy except one that was thoroughly Yankee in outlook. It grew out of the needs of America, at a time in the 19th and 20th centuries when she was driven by manifest destiny to expand her horizons. Those needs of developing, consolidating, building bridges, and in general "getting the job done" were more favorable to a philosophy of doing than to one of merely speculating. Characteristically, American philosophy began to be shaped by American attitudes toward government, industry, education, and the life styles of its melting-pot population. John Dewey, William James, and Charles Peirce are as American as handguns and homemade apple pie.

Non-Cultural Influences

One might go on to build the case that ethnicity has a role to play in philosophy, but sufficient suggestions have been made to show this can be done. This, of course, is not to subscribe to the "nothing but" fallacy—namely, that culture is the only influence on philosophers. Nor is it to universalize from the particular. Because Hamlet and Kierkegaard were Danes and were melancholy does not imply that all Danes are brooders.

As indicated earlier, many factors share in the responsibility of stimulating philosophical thought. Among these might be listed the climate and geography of location (*cf.*, Tibetan gurus), the physiology of one's body (*cf.*, Nietzsche), the psychology of one's disposition (*cf.*, James distinction between the tough- and the tender-minded), the economics of one's life situation (*cf.*, Marx), etc. Mostly, of course, there is the philosopher's own freedom, but this too can be deployed only within the context of the above influences. This freedom is evidenced in the many exceptions to the general thesis of this article.

Some examples which immediately come to mind are the English Idealists, Bradley and Greene, who, like the American, Josiah Royce, and the Italian, Benedetto Croce, were heavily influenced by Hegel. All were momentary rejoiners who ran counter to the culture which gave them birth.

Another glaring exception to the influence of ethnicity on philosophy is the great success of Marx in Russia and the Eastern world. Althought Marx has been tempered by Lenin and Mao, among others, his style of philosophizing is more native to a Western than an Eastern mentality.

A Plea for Pluralism

As travel and communication continue to give ready access to various cultures, they will bring mixed blessings to philosophy. On the one hand, there will be a greater consciousness of one's own shortcomings and cultural myopia; on the other, there will be a greater homogencity of thought once the cultural differences have been assimilated or disintegrated. A general leveling process will take place, and we are already beginning to realize this. As Abraham Kaplan has pointed out, philosophy has become tedious and dreary. Some say it is in a state of paralysis by analysis. Variety is giving way to staid uniformity and technical agreement. Everything in it is becoming cut and dry.

If this be true, perhaps the promotion of pluralism in philosophy will be seen as a good in itself, needing no defense. The only caution which need be sounded is that, while pluralism should be introduced, recognized, and welcomed, its benefits can be had only so long as the pluralistic elements are in dialectical play with one another. If either gains an absolute ascendency, philosophy itself will suffer.

To claim that ethnicity should have some hold on the philsopher is not to diminish his genius nor his freedom. It is only to appreciate the realization that both can be exercised only in an historical situation. He can, at once, be an ethnic and a philosopher, realize that he has no corner on the truth, yet contribute substantially to it and see that his own growth stands in need of constant augmentation by others. As a philosopher, he will be able to agree with Aristotle that truth is like the broadside of a barn—easy to hit, but tought to score a bull's-eye.

Crisis Communication

William E. Arnold

In the song, GOODBYE MICHELLE, Jerry Jacks suggested that it was hard to die when all the birds were singing in the sky. Was he really planning to commit suicide? If we accept the song as a true desire to die, is the singer crying for help? What are the odds that he would be successful in committing suicide? Whether he intended to commit suicide or not, 83% of those who commit suicide have communicated such an intent within a year before the successful suicide. Suicide must be viewed as the antithesis of growth promoting behavior. Suicide is the result of a failure to resolve some form of personal crisis.

Another example of crisis was presented by Carkhuff (1969):

> It's not an easy thing to talk about. I guess the heart of the problem is sort of a sexual problem. I never thought I would have this sort of problem. But I find myself not getting the fulfillment I used to. It's not as enjoyable for my husband either, although we don't discuss it. I used to enjoy and look forward to making love. I used to have an orgasm but I don't anymore. I can't remember the last time I was satisfied. I find myself being attracted to other men and wondering what it would be like to go to bed with them. I don't know what this means. Is this symptomatic of our whole relationship as a marriage? Is something wrong with me or us? (p. 117)

Unlike the songwriter who planned to commit suicide, this woman decided that she faced a crisis and sought help of one trained in crisis intervention. More than one individual can face a similar crisis at a given moment. When tornadoes hit, many individuals including whole cities face singularly and collectively the same crisis.

The purpose of this paper is to examine the relationships of crisis, communication, and growth promoting behavior. While these concepts have been cross-referenced in the literature, they have not been explored for their commonality. This paper focuses on these interrelationships. To develop the commonality an exploration of the literature of crisis and crisis intervention is included.

While there is no agreement on the definition of a crisis, several versions emerge which have elements essential to the discussion. While the focus of each of these definitions is comparable, the emphasis is on a different stage of the crisis process. Caplan (1964) suggested that a crisis can be characterized as an emotional reaction to an external hazardous situation, with the possibility of ensuing disorganization of behavior. The emphasis in this definition is placed upon the external situation which creates the crisis. In a systems theory approach to crisis, this definition would be labelled a part of the input phase. Fink (1967) presented a process definition for crisis. He stated that a human system (individual, group, organization, or other) is assumed to be in a state of crisis when its repertoire of coping responses is not adequate to bring about a resolution of a problem which poses a threat to the sytem. He tied the definition into the input phase by suggesting that a crisis is precipitated by an indentifiable event either within or outside the system. Putting these together, crisis can be viewed as a hazard or threat which affects the problem-solving ability of the individual to resolve the issue in a normal manner. Erikson (1968) provided the output phase of our systems model analogy to crisis. He defined a crisis as a necessary turning point, a crucial moment, when development must move one way or another marshalling resources of growth and recovery and further differentiation. Thus, he was looking from a processing phase toward some output or final resolution of the crisis. Resolution could result in growth-promoting behavior. While more will be made of this point later in the paper, it is essential to emphasize the need for research on the nature of crisis, crisis formation, and the efficacy of communication as a process to facilitate crisis resolution and abatement.

As suggested above, a viable hope for growth-promoting behavior in an individual is through the development of ways of dealing with the problem through new resources and strengths within oneself and one's environment. When the individual has the capability either through one's own volition or with the help of a crisis interventionist to deal with the crisis and its ramifications, growth-promoting behavior has begun. Carkhuff (1969) extended this definition to a conclusion by suggesting that all processes that occur at crisis points in an individual's life can be deteriorative or growth-promoting by definition. Using our ethical standards, we would probably suggest that the song writer

in the introduction has decided on a behavior which would lead to death as the resolution of problems rather than through what we might perceive to be growth-promoting behavior. Suicide viewed in Carkhuff's terms, must be a deteriorative process.

Since these definitions explore the nature of crisis from a limited perspective, a more encompassing definition is needed. Crisis is defined as a decision-maker point when an individual, group, organization, state or nation is unable to cope without some form of assistance. When an organization is unable to cope with an important decision, this would be defined as a crisis. Watergate would be viewed as a national crisis; the Mideast situation could be seen as an international crisis. Each crisis leaves the respective agent unable to cope with a problem. This definition takes a process perspective in that the input is represented by all of the issues surrounding the event; the output—the ultimate decision; and the process phase—the steps necessary for resolution. While it would be possible for the person or agency in crisis to resolve the respective crisis, some help is usually necessary. As with all of the other definitions of crisis, communication is seen as an essential part of the process. Without communication, resolution would be impossible.

The primary assumption used by this writer was that communication is an essential precursor of growth-promoting behavior. The assumption is also made that communication can serve as an adaptive process to deal with crisis situations. This latter assumption was based on Fink's definition of crisis—a condition of an individual who is incapable of using his coping or adaptive responses to bring about resolution. Individuals who have faced a crisis and have resolved it have adapted to their environment. Communication must be seen as an integral part of this adaptive process. Brockopp and Hoff (1972) described a case which demonstrated the adaptive role of communication:

A girl called the crisis center upon the advice of her mother as she could not stop crying one morning following a suicide attempt with her mother's pills. Intake interview revealed a very depressed, anxious and desperate girl with a history of family conflict, drug involvement and a prior suicide attempt. After separate sessions with the girl and her divorced mother, family therapy was initiated with a total of six sessions including one with an older friend who allegedly initiated the girl into the drug scene. The focus in family crisis therapy was on the meaning of the girl's suicidal and drug behavior in relation to total family problems. By the end of the sessions there was evidence of marked improvement in communication between mother and daughter, relief of depression, crying and suicidal ideation of attempts. (p. 5)

Communication helped in the solution and was also the product of the crisis intervention.

Another assumption which served as a basis for this paper was that communication research on existing variables can help find answers to questions in a crisis and in crisis intervention. While it would be desirable to do research in the area of crisis intervention, it is not always possible to deal with individuals facing the crisis state. As a result, one must either deal with simulation exercises and their outcome, or apply the research of traditional communication to the crisis setting. Although further research must be encouraged in crisis, all current communication research must be examined for its relevance to crisis intervention work. For example, the research in credibility can have a great deal of application to the role of a crisis interventionist. Brockopp (1972) suggested that crisis centers must find individuals who are competent, able to respond to people in a positive way, are understanding, and can detect problems from the verbal and nonverbal cues. The last criterion suggests someone trained in communication. The literature of credibility including the many scales developed to measure credibility could be useful both for the selection of volunteers and for their evaluation.

The final assumption that this writer made in examination of the crisis literature was that

an individual who is in a crisis state seeks homeostasis through the resolution of his problem. Emmert and Arnold (in press) suggested that one of the basic needs of all individuals is to maintain consistency. Certainly a crisis can be viewed as a situation which arouses inconsistency or, in traditional terms, imbalance. The resolution of a crisis results in an equilibrium or a return to consistency.

Limitations

While it may be considered a disclaimer, several obvious limitations must be suggested at this time. Given the limitation of time and resources, this paper could not possibly be inclusive of all the areas of crisis or in all models of intervention. As a result, the paper will attempt to deal with some of the more basic issues of crisis and some of the more basic skills to ameliorate the crisis state. Readers are invited to turn to Cowen (1973) and Back (1974) for a more thorough review of the literature in the psychological area of social and community intervention and specific intervention techniques. These writers have annotated the current literature in the area of crisis intervention. One source which describes crisis intervention and intervention training is Carkhuff (1969).

The final limitation of this paper must be in the scope to which any given crisis is examined. For example, the development of an interpersonal crisis can result in numerous levels and areas in which the person is affected. Only the areas of suicide and organizational crisis are dealt with in any depth. The Watergate crisis would have been an interesting case for exploration in this paper, but we need a perspective that only time can provide.

Categories of Crises

To understand the role of communication as an adaptive process in crisis, the different types of crises are delineated. Writers in the field have attempted to differentiate types of crises from numerous perspectives. This paper will examine the category systems of Caplan (1964), Hill (1958), Eliot (1949), and Ruesch (1961).

Caplan (1964) was able to develop two broad categories of crises which he felt explained most circumstances. The first group included those crises which were a result of changes in the everyday environment. These included such things as attending school for the first time, the birth of a sibling, and the emergence of heterosexual interests, marriage, retirement, death, and divorce. These events were perceived as commonly occurring or expected in most everyday living. They could also be viewed as crises that would affect an individual and, to a limited extent, groups of individuals. While many individuals might feel grief associated with death, each grieving person would face the crisis individually. The second category included crises which were a result of unusual events, such as chronic illness, accidents, or family dislocations. These crises could be viewed as unexpected. These crises, while most often affecting an individual, could also affect the members of the immediate or extended family. However, Caplan's system must be viewed as limited in that it dealt primarily with the individual crisis, rather than the broad crisis which could affect an organization, group or state.

Hill (1958), like Caplan, saw crises basically in two categories. He placed greater emphasis on the family as the focus of crisis. His first category included those crises precipitated by extra-familial events. These events included war, floods, economic depression, and other forms of natural disaster. Hill's secondary category of crises were those precipitated by intra-familial events or circumstances. Hill's second category then, would include most of the crises elaborated by Caplan. Hill felt the intrafamilial situation such as desertion, alcoholism, and infidelity could result typically in the demoralization of a family, whereas extra-familial crises would tend to solidify the family. Although Hill's category system broadened the basis for crises to include a group, or in his system, a family, his perspective was limited as Caplan's in that he did not

include a societal based categorical system for crises.

While Hill's system broadened the base for a delineation of crises, Eliot (1949) provided an in-depth consideration of the intrafamilial circumstances. Eliot labelled the first of these circumstances *dismemberment* which would include the loss of a family member either through death or extended separation because of war, imprisonment, economic dislocation, or hospitalization. He labelled the second category *crises of ascension* which included unplanned additions to the family. These would range from unwanted pregnancies to the unwanted addition of a step child or step parent. In the third category of crises, *demoralization*, the family was faced with an undesirable event which affects one or more members. These would include nonsupport by a divorced spouse, infidelity, alcoholism, unemployment, and mental disorders. These, of course, were quite similar to the situations described in Hill's category of crises. In his final category, Eliot lumped all crises that would be a combination of the three. Thus, it was possible to have demoralization accompanied by dismemberment or association. Typical examples of these would include a runaway adolescent, a suicide, or a homicide. Like Caplan, Eliot did not provide a category system which would include all types of crises. While he should not be faulted for this omission, a broad based definition is needed for our discussion.

Following the systems model analogy provided earlier in this paper, Ruesch (1961) suggests that crises can be explored from an individual or group viewpoint and that these crises can occur at different stages in the systems model. He suggested several crises which would occur at the input stage when an individual might be overstimulated with a rapid bombardment without pause or with intense stimulation which exceeds the tolerance or limits of the individual. Scott and Lashbrook (1974) suggested that one of the major problems facing the communication field was to deal with this very condition. Together (1970) they coined the phrase, *future shock*, to describe this condition. Society now faces a time of information overload so that we are no longer able to cope. This point was not new and was suggested in the original Shannon and Weaver discussion of information theory (1949).

A second example of an input crisis would be the opposite of information overload. Understimulation could be a crisis which would include voluntary or forced sensory deprivation. Buley (1973) looked at the effects of the combination sensory deprivation and/or information overload on the communicative network of an individual. These input crises as described by Ruesch are central to the study of communication. We have yet to scratch the surface of the effects of sensory deprivation and information overload as it relates to the whole system of communication. Toffler (1970) also discussed this crisis when he stated that when we combine the effects of decisional stress with sensory and cognitive overload, we produce severe common forms of individual maladaptation.

Ruesch's second level of individual crisis was labelled *anticipation* or *recollection*. These included circumstances where statements were shown to be at variance with actual events or when the anticipation of a future state is no longer possible and the individual faces depression. The inability of an individual to predict future events typified the crisis that Ruesch was talking about at the second level.

Within the processing stage, Ruesch labelled his crisis as decision-making. When decisions did not solve the problem or when the circumstances changed so rapidly that decison often came too late, a crisis often occurred. We have all faced such decision-making crises when we had to select among numerous job opportunities, each with a different time for decision (at least during the prosperous years of the 60's). Soldiers are faced with these forms of crisis in every battle. As soon as a decision is reached, new information arrives and forces a new decision. Kissinger's hopping from Mideast capital to Mideast capital could result in such a crisis if one nation changes its mind while he is talking

to the other. All research on decision-making and problem-solving methods is relevant to this level of crisis.

Output was Ruesch's final level of individual crisis. A convention-goer, because he engaged in over activity with insufficient rest and/or sleep deprivation, would suffer this type of crisis. In all cases, Ruesch was suggesting a crisis which affects an individual when faced with quantitative alterations in a relationship with one's surroundings. It must be underscored that most of these crises resulted from some kind of communication activity, be it an incomplete process or a quantitative deviation in communication itself.

In examining crises which affect a group, Ruesch suggested that these occurred either when communication within a group was disturbed or when communication with other groups was disturbed. While he did not explore these from a systems theory analogy, they seemed to be amenable to categorization at three levels. One level concerned the nature of the group in its composition, relationship, organization, or value system. A second level concerned the messages which flow within and between the groups. The third level concerned the contact of the group either with disturbed individuals, or with catastrophic situations occurring from such things as hurricanes and earthquakes. Later we will explore the role of communication in the reduction of crises. Thus far communication has been viewed by Ruesch as a major part of the process which disturbs groups causing them to face a crisis.

To overcome the shortcomings of the previously suggested categorical systems for crises, a broad model was developed for the elaboration of crises as well as the suggested types of intervention for dealing with the crises. (See Figure I.) Close examination of this model shows that it parallels our communication paradigm. Rather than viewing some psychological and physiological crises as interpersonal, they were viewed as intrapersonal or crises of the individual. No attempt was made to provide a complete delineation of all crises affecting us on an intrapersonal, interpersonal, group or organization, community, or societal level. Likewise, the intervention systems were also not completely delineated. This model provides a framework for further elaboration and discussion.

Figure I

CRISIS	INTERVENTION

INTRAPERSONAL

Psychological

Anxiety	Telephone Service
Stress	
	Therapy

Physical

Suicide	Therapy
Drugs	Drug Rescue
Medical	

INTERPERSONAL

Dating	Telephone Service
Marriage	Counseling
Divorce	Psychotherapy
Family Dysfunction	

GROUP

Protest	Arbitration
Strikes	Negotiation

ORGANIZATION

Declining Market	Counseling
Bankruptcy	Legislation

COMMUNITY

Disaster	Community Relief
	Community Mental Health Programs

SOCIETY

War	United Nations
	Negotiation

Stages of Crises

Both Pasework and Albers (1972) and Fink (1967) have developed models for exploring the stages of an individual crisis. Their models were quite similar. However, the Fink model differentiated the experience in an individual while passing through the stages of an individual crisis. Figure II presents the psychological phases of crisis as an individual faces them. Fink postulated four sequential phases that the individual goes through in order to cope with the crisis situation in a constructive manner. These are: 1) shock, 2) defense retreat, 3) acknowledgement, 4) adaptation. Similarly, Pasework and Albers defined phase one as a period of disorganization where an individual would withdraw or experience heightened anxiety as a result of the crisis event. An advantage of the Fink model was that it described the effect of the four phases on different components of the individual, i.e., self-perception, perceptions of reality, emotional experiences, and on the cognitive structure of the situation. His last category of physical disability would apply only as a prototype for those circumstances when an individual was faced with a crisis of genetic disability, disabling injury, or a disease. Communication plays an important part of the development of self-perception, of our perceptions of reality around us, and how we emotionally or cognitively respond to a circumstance.

Gottschalk and Gleser (1969) developed a measuring instrument for the transient emotional motivational and cognitive states. This approach uses lexical aspects of verbal communication rather than vocal or paralanguage cues. Their scales, which have been tested on verbal behavior, are composed of items which measure anxiety, hostility, social alienation-personal disorganization, capacity for human relations, cognitive and intellectual impairment, hope, sickness-health. The implications of their measurement of psychological status through content analysis of verbal communication behavior have not been explored by the communication field or applied to crisis and crisis intervention.

In reviewing the stages of a crisis, Pasework and Albers (1972) drew two conclusions which seemed appropriate to communication's role

Figure II

Psychologic Phases of Crisis

TIME Phase	Self Experience	Reality Perceptions	Emotional Experience	Cognitive Structure	Physical Disability
Shock (stress)	Threat to existing structures	Perceived as overwhelming	Panic; anxiety; helplessness	Disorganization-inability to plan or to reason or to understand situation	Acute somatic damage requiring full full medical care
Defensive retreat	Attempt to maintain old structures	Avoidance of reality; "wishful thinking"; denial, repression	Indifference or euphoria (except when challenged, in which case anger); (low anxiety)	Defensive reorganization; resistance to change	Physical recovery from acute phase; functional return to maximum possible level
Acknowledgment (renewed stress)	Giving up existing structure; self-depreciation	Facing reality; facts "impose" themselves	Depression with apathy or agitation; bitterness; high mourning; high anxiety; if overwhelming, suicide	Defensive breakdown: (1) disorganization; (2) reorganization in terms of altered reality perceptions	Physical plateau; gradual slowing of improvement until no change is experienced
Adapation and change	Establishing new structure; sense of worth	New reality testing	Gradual increase in satisfying experiences; (gradual lowering of anxiety)	Reorganization in terms of present resources and abilities	No change in physical disability status

in crisis resolution. First, an individual needs and may require assistance in surmounting the crisis. These persons can be members of the immediate family, friends, or social workers. Second, facilitating communication between the individual and these helper individuals mitigates the severity of the crisis. While both of these conclusions drawn from literature, it would certainly be appropriate to test these in actual crisis situations. Particularly, studies should be conducted on the role of communication, in its facilitating dimension, as a reducer of crisis. The second conclusion of Pasework and Albers supports the earlier assumption that communication serves an adaptive role in the amelioration of crisis.

Intervention Strategies

For any intervention strategy to work, the individual experiencing the crisis must be aware that such intervention is available. Frequently, individuals in crisis have had no previous knowledge of, let alone contact with, organizations designed to provide intervention services. Having developed a crisis center, this author is aware of the difficulties in establishing the center as a viable option for crisis intervention. Much research has been conducted on the community's awareness of new services for the purpose of crisis resolution. See, for example, the research of Gaullorakis (1971) Arnold (1972) and Arnold, Liddell, Findling (1974) for an elaboration of three studies designed to determine communication networks for an emerging crisis center.

The success of any intervention strategy rests on the credibility of the interventionist with the person in crisis. While many communication principles can be used to facilitate resolution of the crisis, basic trust and confidence of the interventionist is paramount in the crisis relationship (Brockopp, 1972). While the severity of the crisis would mitigate against the elaborate building of a therapist's credentials, some effort must be made either prior to or during the crisis interaction to establish the credibility of the interventionist. Rusk (1971) suggested that the golden rule for the helper in crisis intervention is to do for others that which they cannot do for themselves and no more. The helper provides a coping behavior for the helpee* so that the helpee might see the way out of the crisis and forward toward continued growth-promoting behavior.

Rusk (1971) suggested several skills or approaches to deal with the helper/helpee relationship. These are: 1) calm confidence, 2) hopefulness, 3) active leadership, 4) intrusiveness, and 5) explicit empathy. The first two, which represent attitudes of the helper, could be developed and tested through the communication analysis suggested by Gottschalk and Gleser. Besides reducing the anxiety of the individual in crisis, the outward manifestations of these attitudes should assist in establishing the credibility of the helper. Unlike forms of psychotherapy, active leadership suggests that the crisis situation is so unique that the helper must apply control and assist the helpee develop a specific coping behavior. The helper must assist the individual in focusing on the appropriate behavior to resolve the crisis. This would be the opposite of non-directive therapy. Rusk suggested that empathy, which is a key to the therapeutic relationship, can awaken feelings akin to the mother-child symbiosis. In fact, he would probably suggest that empathy is the basis for the establishment of what we would call high credibility. The helper who refuses to

*helpee—one who faces the crisis.

share the distress will find the patient reluctant to confront reality and will usually dismiss the helper as one who does not care about the individual or the crisis. The verbal behavior of the helper should be subjected to content analysis to determine the ability to empathize with the helpee.

Each of these skills suggested by Rusk was based upon communication as an adaptive behavior. Each, however, should be tested for its ability to not only resolve the crisis, but to establish a meaningful intervention relationship.

Carkhuff (1969) developed five scales to measure skills for the helping relationship. These skills included empathic understanding of interpersonal process, communication of respect in interpersonal processes, personally relevant concreteness or specificity of expression in interpersonal processes, facilitative genuineness in interpersonal processes and facilitative self-disclosure in interpersonal processes. Again, each of these represents a dimension of therapeutic communication as a means of dealing with an individual in crisis. Each of these skills was developed on five levels in order to determine the degree of effectiveness of the helper. These range from verbal and behavioral expressions of the helpee to level five where the helper's response adds significantly to the feelings and meanings of expressions of the helpee. Again, these skills must be elaborated and tested for their effectiveness in dealing with the crises that individual, group, or organizations face. Time does not permit an elaboration of Carkhuff's system for communication training to develop these skills in the helper. It is obvious that research is needed to determine the effectiveness of his skills in the crisis interaction.

These skills and strategies could be employed to serve four functions in the crisis intervention. First, the helper could provide an empathetic response to the person in crisis. While this would not be complete in itself, it is perhaps a sine qua non in crisis intervention. Second, the helper must provide an accurate reflection of ideas and feelings of the helpee. Such an objective demands skills in critical listening both for the verbal and the paralanguage of the helpee. Third, the interventionist must be able to provide information for the immediate resolution of the crisis. This demands of the helper not only communicator credibility, but competence to express a variety of behavioral options to the helpee. Fourth, a helper must be able to convince the helpee of the need for a plan of resolution and to put it into effect. Certainly all the literature in persuasion, attitude and behavioral change theory would be appropriate to develop this skill.

Rusk (1971) suggested some advantages which amortize the effectiveness of immediate crisis intervention. The helper must make intelligent decisions based upon very incomplete information. Usually, there is little time available to accumulate the information in order to make these decisions. Another disadvantage is that in crisis situations, the helper usually deals with less adaptable, less healthy people who have difficulty adjusting to life. Follow-up is also very difficult to arrange in emergency intervention relationships. Finally, limited resources tend to force a crisis resolution into less than an ideal compromise. These disadvantages should be considered as hurdles which make the interventionist's job more difficult, but not as a self-fulfilling prophecy for the failure of intervention techniques. Research could be conducted by communication scholars to determine the degree to which they prevent the facilitative communication for crisis intervention.

Brockopp (1972) developed specific criteria for intervention which relate to the above functions and disadvantages suggested by Rusk. These criteria were developed to help the crisis worker determine which individuals would be appropriate for crisis intervention:

A. Recognition by the crisis intervener that the person is in a state of impending active crisis.
B. Determination of the severity of the crisis; i.e., whether the person is able to benefit from assistance outside of a hospital setting.
C. Recognition of suicidal and/or homicidal impulse in the client.
D. Motivation and ability of the client to use his personal resources and the resources of his neighborhood and community.
E. Acceptance by the client and worker of a treatment plan which is achievable within a four to six week time period.
F. Probability that he will be able to enlist appropriate referral sources for treatment of his client's problem. (p. 5)

Thus far we have examined the crisis in its broad categories as well as the specific stages and techniques and skills used to intervene and thus resolve the crisis. The remaining portion of this paper will turn to an examination of two specific crises as they relate to the previous discussion and to communication and growth-promoting behavior.

Case Study—Suicide

This paper began with a question concerning whether or not the songwriter was planning to commit suicide. The underlying questions, of course, are why do people commit suicide and how crisis intervention relates to it? One could view it as a sociologist and say that suicide is a result of the inability of the individual to integrate with the social milieu. Psychiatrists or psychologists, on the other hand, might attribute it to some deep personality characteristic or childhood experience which disposes an individual toward suicide. Our question here is not why people commit suicide, but what is the relationship of suicide to crisis intervention and communication.

Miller (1967) developed a model of suicide based on three components which she labelled commitment, crisis, and communication. Commitment is a process by which an individual fixes on one self-concept to the exclusion of others and is unable to change when differing situations occur. The more narrow or rigid the self-concept, the more likely other forms of coping behavior cannot be accepted and thus, suicide might be viewed as the only way out of this very tight commitment. Communication, as viewed by Miller, is a process whereby individuals communicate with others openly and clearly in order to satisfy both the exchange of ideas, to test reality, and to test our own self-concept on others. Her view of crisis is similar to Caplan and others in that she defines it as a turning point which could bring about despair. If the functions of communication are not served, the individual is faced with incomplete information and the possibility that distortions may occur. Ultimately, withdrawal, isolation, and anxiety may result. Miller concluded this point by saying that the individual begins to doubt his self-concept, feels worthless, and begins the downward spiral into a suicide condition. For her, communication or the lack thereof, plays a significant role in the emergence of suicidal threats or behavior.

The writer has received several letters which may be a cry for help and/or a sign of a potential suicide. The first letter expressed despondency over the suicide of a brother and the serious illness of a father. The second letter contained the following paragraph:

> I have two main concerns now. To be at peace with myself, and to be happy. The only trouble with having goals like this is that you want to wish them for everyone else. Most of us are still trying to find it and some of us have some of the answers. This concern for peace of mind and happiness is so basic that most people prefer to ignore it for financial security, or job accomplishments. I feel that without peace of mind and happiness, nothing makes any sense!!!!!

The third letter contained an itinerary of what had been labelled in all letters as the "Last Trip Home." Will it be the last trip? No, if further communication can produce other adaptive behavior; attempts will be made to accomplish this behavior. As of this writing, other adaptive behaviors have prevented a potential suicide.

Breed (1972) suggested an elaboration of the Miller model in the form utilizing five components: (a) commitment; (b) rigidity; (c) failure; (d) shame; (e) isolation. These five components

were based upon several years of research on individuals who either knew people who had committed suicide, or had a very close relationship with them. Breed's introduction of the fourth component, shame, provides a different perspective than the Miller model. This includes the prospective suicide victim's response to failure in some major role. Breed's social isolation can be considered similar to Miller's rubric-communication. To prevent social isolation, the individual has a need to receive the approval of other persons. This point came close to home as the writer was reminded by a colleague of the need to praise actors and actresses upon the completion of a production after he had failed to do so. Such approval would provide for legitimization and validation of the individual's identity. The presence of these five characteristics in 137 suicide cases can be seen in Figure III. This figure is not only useful for its comparison on each of the items, but as an elaboration of the definition of each of the five components.

In addition to these components of suicidal behavior, certain specific behaviors can be noted for their relationship to communication. As stated in the beginning of this paper, approximately 83 percent of those who commit suicide, communicate that intent beforehand. The difficulty with communication of intent and actual suicide behavior is that noncomitters as well as committers communicate. Dorpat and Boswell (1963) reported that 83 percent of committers had previously within one year communicated their intent, whereas 78 percent of those who had only made suicidal gestures had not so communicated. Thus, communication of suicidal intent is one of those suicide specific signs that may exclude many persons who are suicidal but will never commit, while including those who eventually do so. Further research must be done in order to delineate between those who communicate an attempt to commit suicide and those who only make gestures toward suicide. When we know who is likely to be a committer, we can then attempt to develop growth-promoting behavior.

The communication of an intent to commit

Figure III
Presence of "Basic Suicide Syndrome" Characteristics in
137 New Orleans Suicides, by Sex
(Presented in Percentages)

	Male (N=52)	Female (N=85)
Commitment		
1. Internalized cultural roles and goals very strongly	87	87
Rigidity		
2. Did not change goals	75	85
3. Did not change roles	67	82
4. Rigid on roles and goals, brittle cognitive and affective orientation	81	67
5. Pattern oriented, not person oriented	77	72
6. Failed to use ego defenses available to him	92	82
7. Had tunnel vision	81	87
Failure		
Males only		
8. Downward vertical mobility of any sort (work-life, inter-generational, or financial)	75	
9. Unemployed or not working full time	50	
Females only		
10. Major problem was with husband or mate		41
11. Was not living with husband at time of death		47
12. Never had a child		35
13. No child in household at time of death		62
14. Facade of feminity-wife, mother, etc., more of a role than an identity		58
Shame		
15. Low self-esteem (grades 3 and 4 on 4-point scale)	83	81
16. Depressed and felt worthless	83	78
17. Felt others "labeled" him as failure, "took the attitude of the other"	64	44
18. Felt shame, from failure	37	32
19. Goals lost their meaning	98	37
20. Loss of hope	83	70
Isolation		
21. Relatively few social contacts with others (grades 3 and 4 on 4-point scale)	43	41
22. Alone or felt alone	65	76
23. Felt like a "foreigner in life"	65	66
24. Kept problems to himself	69	56
25. Frustration of dependency needs	33	54
26. Problems with identity and independence	65	67
27. Part of him (her) is gone	27	57
28. Difficulties with disclosing self	44	42
29. Suicide intent communicated	44	47
30. Withdrew markedly from social relations during last year of life	29	36
31. Defensive about getting help	60	54
32. Showed all components of basic suicide syndrome	50	40

suicide was one type of crisis discussed by Lester and Lester (1971). Sometimes an individual does not really wish to die, but only wants to change the way other people act. An example of such a communicative intent that backfired was described at a recent suicidology meeting. A young lady had indicated to her husband many times that she was going to commit suicide if things didn't change. Her husband adopted a ritual of coming home and immediately going to the refrigerator for a can of beer. The woman, counting on such behavior, placed a note on the refrigerator saying that she had taken a quantity of sleeping pills. Her intent was that her husband would come home; find the note; rush to the bedroom; and take her to an emergency room before the pills had a chance to be fatal. Unfortunately, her husband decided to work late at the office, and her message was not received in time to prevent her suicide.

Lester and Lester suggested other suicidal crises including impulsive suicide behavior which results from anger, disappointment or frustration. This crisis can be perceived as highly temporary, but could lead to a dysfunctional end.

A third crisis could be described as the individual who feels that life is no longer worth living and goes into a period of serious depression. The last form of suicidal crisis results from very serious illness such as cancer or some other terminal disease. This suicidal crisis emerges as a result of the individual trying to spare the loved one the difficulty of caring for him during his terminal disease.

Each of these crises represents different needs with regard to intervention strategies. While the impulsive can be dealt with on an empathetic level, attempts to counsel a potential suicide whose problem is serious illness calls for a thorough grounding of pertinent information, as well as the ability to convince the helpee that other viable alternatives are available for coping with the crisis. Research is needed that tests the effectiveness of particular intervention strategies and techniques with each form of suicidal crisis.

As suggested earlier, we know the percentage of people who cry for help by forewarning through communication of their intent to commit suicide. Unfortunately, we are not sophisticated enough to decipher those who simply want to make a suicidal gesture through communication, and those who are actually serious in their intent, and who will ultimately commit suicide. What is lacking is a regression model which would help us distinguish between those who are suicide-prone and those who would ultimately commit suicide.

We have explored suicide as just one crisis of the multitude that is present each day. While it is suggested that suicide is the antithesis of growth-promoting behavior, we can conclude that the adequate resolution of crisis at any level can be considered growth-promoting behavior.

Case Study-Organization

As suicide was an example of an intrapersonal crisis, organizational crises can be viewed as either group and/or interpersonal crisis. Lippitt and Schmidt (1967) discussed six types of crises which they felt an organization could face. These occur anytime from the birth of the organization through its maturity. First, entrepreneurs must answer the question, how much are they willing to risk as they gamble on a new business? For example, potential land barons in Arizona face the problem of deciding whether or not land purchases in the White Mountains would be a viable venture. In line with our earlier definitions of crisis, these individuals are faced with a decision as to whether or not to risk dollars, time, energy, and their reputations in order to invest in land.

Having made the decision to launch a business venture, the second major crisis concerned the organization's ability to survive as a viable system. This raised the question, how much is the organization willing to sacrifice? With three-fourths of all new businesses in the United States failing to survive their first year of operation and less than half of the remainder contin-

Figure IV

Phases of Organizational Crisis

PHASE	INTER-PERSONAL RELATIONS	INTER-GROUP RELATIONS	COMMUNI-CATION	LEADERSHIP AND DECISION-MAKING	PROBLEM HANDLING	PLANNING AND GOAL SETTING	STRUCTURE
Shock	Fragmented	Disconnected	Random	Paralyzed	None	Dormant	Chaotic
Defensive Retreat	Protective Cohesion	Alienated	Ritualized	Autocratic	Mechanistic	Expedient	Traditional
Acknowl-edgement	Confrontation (supportive)	Mutuality	Searching	Participative	Explorative	Synthesizing	Experimenting
Adaptation and Change	Interdepen-dent	Coordinated	Authentic Congruent	Task-centered	Flexible	Exhaustive and Integrative	Organic

uing in operation, this question becomes paramount.

If this crisis is dealt with effectively, the organization can then be confronted by a third crisis. Lippitt and Schmidt labelled the third crisis as the achievement of stability. The question raised by this crisis is: how willing are the individuals involved to be organized and accept enforce discipline? In the sense, the question is: are they willing to be institutionalized?

The fourth crisis was labelled one of pride and reputation: This crisis suggested that management of an organization must face up to the constant need for monitoring, reviewing, evaluation, and ultimately improvement. Most often, this crisis would probably not occur until one realized that the opposition had done something to improve their image and thus the marketability of their product. Alka Seltzer faced this crisis when they discovered that their commercials, while interesting, funny, and winning Clio awards, were failing to sell the product to the American public.

The fifth crisis for an organization was that of developing uniqueness. How willing is an organization to adapt or cope with change? A certain Midwestern university failed to listen to their president when he suggested changes that would make their organization unique in higher education. This crisis, of course, is always balanced by the other crises already discussed. Thus, the fear of change overcame the potential for uniqueness of that school.

Finally, a sixth type of organizational crisis was labelled, contribution to society. The question that executives must face is: What are we willing to give to society without expecting a direct return? Not all organizations believe that this is something that should even concern them.

Not all organizations face these crises nor do they all suffer the same severity. Much depends on the extent of the conceived organizational need and on the organization's financial status with regard to those needs. These are, however, crises that each organization can and probably does face.

Fink, Beak, and Taddeo (1971) modified the

Fink model of an individual crisis and adapted it through extrapolation for an organizational crisis. Figure IV presents the parameters of this model as it relates to the phases of crisis. Unlike the individual crisis model, this model can be tied to communication immediately. The categories on interpersonal relations, intergroup relations, problem-solving, and leadership and decision-making all relate to various forms of communication. Obviously, research should be conducted to see whether or not the results suggested by the authors can be found in each of the four phases over time.

Returning to that Midwestern university, as an example, the author was present when the Higher Board of Education for the state demanded that each university face a potential 15 percent cut due to declining enrollment. While each of the schools in the state went through the various phases suggested by Fink, *et. al.,* not all of them remained in each category for any length of time. The Midwestern university with which I was most familiar, passed quickly from the shock and defensive retreat stage into the acknowledgement and adaption portion of the model. Other schools remained in the shock period or defensive retreat period for much greater lengths of time. The behaviors found in each of the categories can be attributed to each of the universities. While the Fink, *et. al.,* model was not used for the basis of a new volume on that university crisis, see Berlo (in press) for a detailed elaboration of the event.

Figure V presents the requirements needed by an organization in order to effectively deal with the crises. Although the crises discussed were developed by Lippitt and Schmidt, they should apply to an organization whether or not the product is the most important aspect of the company's existence. It should be noted that communication is seen to be a major part of the skills necessary for the amelioration of each of the crises.

Conclusion

Throughout this paper we have seen examples of where communication has led into a crisis

Figure V

Requirements to Meet Crises

CRITICAL CONCERN	KNOWLEDGE	SKILLS	ATTITUDES
To create a system	Clearly perceived short-range objective in mind of top man	Ability to transmit knowledge into action by self and into	Belief in own ability, product, and market
To survive	The short-range objectives that need to be communicated	Communications know-how; ability to adjust to changing conditions	Faith in future
To stabilize	How top man can predict relevant factors and make long-range plans	Ability to transmit planning knowledge into communicable objectives	Trust in other members of organization
To earn good reputation	Planning know-how and understanding of goals on part of whole executive team	Facility of allowing others a voice in decision making, involving others in decision making and obtaining commitments from them, and communicating objectives to customers	Interest in customers
To achieve uniqueness	Understanding on part of policy team of how others should set own objectives, and how to manage subunits of the organization	Ability to teach others to plan; proficiency in integrating plans of subunits into objectives and resources of organization	Self-confidence
To earn respect and appreciation	General management understanding of the larger objectives or organization and of society	Ability to apply own organization and resources to the problems of the larger community	Sense of responsibility to society and mankind

when it became dysfunctional. On the other hand, it is perhaps one of the only ways which allows us to deal with crisis. Research in crisis and crisis intervention, while thoroughly documented in the psychological and psychiatric literature, is certainly an area on which our field has yet to focus its attention. We have neglected our responsibilities for research in crisis intervention. Members of the International Communication Association have recently recognized a need for a concerted effort in this direction when they formed a division of therapeutic communication. While we should be utilitarian in our approach to psychological and sociological literature on crisis, we should be perceptive enough to realize that communication scholars must make a concerted effort to provide a basis for essentially what is a communication skill—crisis intervention.

References

W. E. Arnold, "Diffusion of Information About Crisis Centers," *Crisis Intervention*, 4 (1972), 7-13.

W. E. Arnold, C. Liddell, and J. Findling, "Diffusion

of Information About Crisis Intervention," *Crisis Intervention*, 5 (1974), 2-11.

K. Back, "Intervention Techniques: Small Groups," *Annual Review of Psychology*, 25 (1974), 367-87.

D. Berlo, "University in Crisis." Unpublished manuscript, 1974.

W. Breed, "Five Components of a Basic Suicide Syndrome," *Life-Threatening Behavior*, 2 (1972), 3-18.

G. Brockopp, "Selecting the Crisis Intervener," *Crisis Intervention*, 4 (1972), 33-9.

G. Brockopp and L. Hoff, "Crisis Intervention Services and Community Mental Health Programs," *Crisis Intervention*, 4 (1972), 1-7.

J. Buley, "Information Restriction and the Duration of the Initial Contact Between Strangers." Unpublished paper, 1973.

G. Caplan, *Principles of Preventive Psychiatry* (New York: Basic Books, 1964).

R. Carkhuff, *Helping and Human Relations* (New York: Holt, Rinehart, Winston, 1969), 2 vols.

E. Cowan, "School and Community Interventions," *Annual Review of Psychology*, 24 (1973), 423-72.

T. Dorpat and J. W. Boswell, "An Evaluation of Suicidal Intent in Suicide Attempts," *Comprehensive Psychiatry*, 4 (1963), 117-25.

T. D. Eliot, "Handling Family Strains and Shocks." In H. Becker and R. Hill (eds.), *Family, Marriage and Parenthood* (Boston, Mass.: D. C. Heath and Co., 1949).

P. Emmert and W. E. Arnold, "Persuasion." Unpublished manuscript, 1973.

E. Erikson, *Identity and the Life Cycle* (New York: International Universities Press, 1959).

S. L. Fink, "Crisis and Motivation: A Theoretical Model," *Archives of Physical Medicine & Rehabilitation*, 48 (1967), 592-97.

S. L. Fink, J. Beak, and K. Taddeo, "Organizational Crisis and Change," *Journal of Applied Behavioral Science*, 7 (1971), 15-41.

M. Gaullorakis, "The Diffusion of Information About PATH at Illinois State University." Unpublished thesis, Illinois State University, 1971.

L. Gottschalk and G. Gleser, *The Measurement of Psychological States Through the Content Analysis of Verbal Behavior* (Berkeley: University of California Press, 1969).

R. Hill, "Genetic Features of Families Under Stress," *Social Casework*, 39 (1958), 139-50.

G. Lester and D. Lester, *Suicide: The Gamble with Death* (Englewood Cliffs, New Jersey: Prentice-Hall, 1971).

G. Lippitt and W. Schmidt, "Crises in a Developing Organization," *Harvard Business Review*, 45 (1967), 102-12.

D. H. Miller, "Suicide Careers: Toward a Symbolic Interaction Theory of Suicide." Unpublished dissertation, University of California at Berkeley, 1967.

R. Pasework and D. Albers, "Crisis Intervention: Theory in Search of a Program," *Social Work*, 17 (1972), 70-7.

J. Ruesch, *Therapeutic Communication* (New York: W. W. Norton, 1961).

T. Rusk and R. Gerner, "A Study of the Process of Emergency Psychotherapy," *American Journal of Psychiatry*, 128 (1972), 882-86.

M. Scott and B. Lashbrook, "Man-machine Interface: A Reconceptualization of Communication Education." Unpublished paper, 1974.

C. Shannon and W. Weaver, *The Mathematical Theory of Communication* (Urbana, Illinois: University of Illinois Press, 1949).

A. Toffler, *Future Shock* (New York: Bantam Books, 1970).

Channels of Campaign Communication

Dan Nimmo

The media used by political campaigners ranges from the most tacky of signs erected in a neighbor's yard to slick television commercials that sell by understatement. We shall look at five categories of communication channels employed in American campaigns—personal appearances, the campaign organization, displays, the printed media, the auditory media, and television. The professional campaigner's selection of a particular media, or combination of media, to carry the candidate's appeal depends on the audience sought and the purpose of the message. If, for example, the target audience consists of the uninformed, uninterested, and independent voters, television plays a prominent role. For such targets the mass media are helpful in promoting name recognition (making a candidate know to large numbers of people), projecting an appealing image, or turning out voters on election day. Some aspects of campaign communication, however, are directed not at the mass but at differentiated groups with special concerns in hopes of getting endorsements, financial support, and votes. Direct mailings, door-to-door canvassing, newspaper

Dan Nimmo, *The Political Persuaders*: The Techniques of Modern Election Campaigns, © 1970 pp 118–40. Reprinted by permission of Prentice-Hall, Inc., Englewood Cliffs, New Jersey.

advertising, and regional televison are adaptable to these more selective appeals. As needed, they can provide special literature for medical doctors or a taped radio program for farmers. Selective media differ from the mass media as a rifle might differ from a shotgun. Finally, the candidate has the audience of his own supporters, volunteers, and workers. Constant attention must be paid to lifting their sagging morale. Much of the typical paraphernalia of campaigns —billboards, yard signs, bumper stickers, buttons, and so forth—are designed more to counter the lethargy of the committed than to influence undecided voters.

Personal Media

Even in the age of televison public appearances by a politician carry his message to voters. A candidate for a lower-level office (legislative seat, city council, or school board, for example) frequently builds his entire campaign around relatively inexpensive appearances; candidates in congressional and statewide districts take pains to assure that their public presentations mesh well with sophisticated media techniques.

The candidate's appearances take various forms. The prepared speech repeated endlessly is perhaps the most common. Campaign mythology says that the purpose behind these formal presentations is to enable the candidate to "speak out on the issues." But, the speeches are not designed to change people's minds or even to give an in-depth view of the candidate's position. The function of discussing issues is more latent than manifest. By quoting facts and details on a variety of issues the candidate leaves the impression that he possesses the knowledge, sophistication, and acumen to hold public office. Indeed, rather than trying to communicate the content of his speech to his audience, he may purposely talk above them and create the aura that he is prepared to deal with highly complex matters. In 1968 Richard Nixon had a set presentation, "The Speech," delivered extemporaneously, as if unprepared; actually the address had evolved gradually during the primaries and was much the same message in September that it had been in January, but to small-town audiences it was a natural, unrehearsed statement from the heart.[16] In sum, candidates endeavor to communicate not substance, but style and image in their speeches.

Staged rallies also occupy an important place in any campaign. In shopping centers and factories, in football stadia and baseball parks, opening campaign headquarters and dedicating statues, at whistlestops and airport fly-ins these appearances stimulate supporters turned out by professional managers. (Spencer-Roberts prepared innumerable rallies for Nelson Rockefeller in 1964.) The professional managers plan minute details of rallies, including who sits on the platform with the candidate, who introduces him, the number of noisemakers that should be available, the exact moment to release balloons, and whether each reporter covering the event prefers a 7-to-1 or 12-to-1 martini. Again, this maximum contrivance of setting is designed to publicize style, not substance.

Press conferences are handy ways of exposing candidates to the fourth estate, usually un-

der favorable conditions. Candidates traditionally grant several "background" interviews to permit reporters to probe them on salient issues. Some candidates, particularly those who think the reporters covering their campaigns secretly favor the opposition, avoid such conferences. The Spencer-Roberts firm, for example, banned any press conferences with Ronald Reagan in the 1966 California gubernatorial election. Reagan was suspicious of and hostile to the press; his managers feared an outburst from their star that might alienate the journalists. Richard Nixon's managers in 1968 courted the working press assiduously by caring for reporters' creature comforts with hotel accommodations, yacht trips, water-skiing, limousine transportation, and endless rounds of cocktail parties. Nixon himself, however, remained aloof and granted only brief interviews as he stepped from his airplane, limousine, or hotel. By holding the press at arm's length Nixon's managers sought to convey the image of a calm, efficient, deliberate, and cautious approach to the crises of the times.[17]

Personal appearances in local elections frequently take the form of coffees with the candidate. Acquaintances of the candidate invite friends, usually on a neighborhood basis. Beyond a light discussion of issues these coffees serve the more important function of recruiting campaign workers. Formalized coffees are frequently filmed for television. The result is a seemingly leisurely approach providing the candidate the opportunity to field, usually flawlessly, the inquires of housewives, dowagers, and coeds.

Formal speeches, rallies, press conferences, and coffees are traditional ways of exposing the candidate to the public, primarily to convey a positive impression of his personality, manner, and sincerity. In recent campaigns professional managers have developed a variation that brings

---

[16] Theodore H. White, *The Making of the President 1968* (New York: Atheneum Publishers, 1969), p. 378.

[17] Lewis Chester, Godfrey Hodgson, and Bruce Page, *An American Melodrama: The Presidential Campaign of 1968* (New York: The Viking Press, 1969), pp. 677–89, discusses the Nixon treatment of the press in detail. For a comparison, see White, *The Making of the President 1968*, pp. 381–82.

date. Speeches and rallies are risky if the candidate, faced with a hostile audience of militant students or racial minorities, might "blow his cool" and show anger, outrage, or lack of sympathy. When the audience cannot be selected to the candidate's advantage, campaign managers employ a new tactic of "confrontation." The candidate facing a hostile crowd simply challenges one or more of his hecklers to share the rostrum. If he has the native talent and has been properly coached, he convinces detractors that he is sincerely interested in a rational discussion of the militants' grievances, that he understands their plight, and that he is courageous and spontaneous. Governor Claude Kirk managed to win election in Florida as a Republican by confronting his detractors in this fashion. After his election, and on the advice of professional managers, he continued the confrontation tactic and won nationwide acclaim when he successfully "faced down" black militant leader Rap Brown. In the 1968 presidential contest the Democratic nominee for vice-president, Senator Edmund Muskie, confronted numerous student militants at rallies on college campuses. Muskie maintained control in each situation and usually won the respect of his audience. The novelty of the technique guaranteed valuable television exposure on evening news programs.

Organizational Media

By organizational media we refer to the offices within the campaign organization that communicate with voters on the candidate's behalf—precinct workers, speakers' bureaus, and endorsement groups.

We observed (previously) that research into voting behavior has indicated that some voters decide to vote for candidates because they have been influenced by friends. Since the enthusiasm of an amateur volunteer wins votes, candidates at all levels rely heavily on grass-roots workers to carry their message, particularly in primaries, where turnout is small and the number of candidates usually large. It is impossible

to measure precisely how intricate the network of grass-roots volunteers is in any election, but the evidence suggests that it is extensive. In September, 1964, for example, a Gallup poll reported that Republican party workers had contacted 7,100,000 households on behalf of the Goldwater candidacy; Democrats had contacted 3,800,000 for the Johnson-Humphrey ticket.[18] If party workers contact only their own sympathizers, of course, the extensive network indicated by these figures is meaningless; Republicans who had already decided on Goldwater and were later contacted by volunteers on Goldwater's behalf would add nothing. There is evidence, however, that in 1964 Republican workers had an effect on voting decisions that was independent of voters' party loyalties; one survey indicates, for example, that of Independents contacted by Republicans, one-half voted for Goldwater and of Independents not contacted only 29 per cent chose Goldwater. Similarly, of Democrats contacted by Republicans 15 per cent voted for Goldwater; of those Democrats not contacted only 9 per cent chose Goldwater. In sum, "we can conclude that this organizational work did influence votes, and that it represented genuine Republican success."[19]

Speakers' bureaus contribute relatively little to the drive to win converts. In a television era only the candidate can really speak for himself as far as the audience-electorate is concerned. But the speakers' bureau (a staff of individuals ready to speak anywhere at any time for the cause) does serve a purpose. Speakers travel to local headquarters to raise the morale of workers. In presidential elections the Republican party has a "truth squad" consisting of Republican congressmen who follow Democratic candidates from town to town. The device garners publicity which undercuts the appearance of the Democratic standard-bearer and the Republican speakers stir up local supporters with arguments

[18]Thomas W. Benham, "Polling for A Presidential Candidate," *Public Opinion Quarterly*, XXIX (Summer, 1965), 192.

[19]John H. Kessel, *The Goldwater Coalition* (New York: The Bobbs-Merrill Co., Inc., 1968), pp. 287–89

to counter the Democratic presence. The staff of a speakers' bureau is more effective in local referenda than in partisan elections. Prestigious citizens armed with slides, charts, films, and other material to sell a bond issue, a charter amendment, or a tax increase speak at Rotary or Lions Club luncheons. The speakers endeavor to convert highly impersonal propositions into personal issues.[20]

Many voters judge a candidate by the people who endorse him. Consequently, campaign managers seek endorsements from prestigious groups not so much because of the votes represented by group members but because the endorsing groups can be added to the general network for delivering the campaign message. Whitaker and Baxter, the campaign managment firm, always seeks endorsements for candidates and causes from a wide variety of groups. In their planning the mobilization of "natural allies" is an essential feature of the campaign.[21] Managers publicize the endorsements through news stories and attempt to prompt new endorsements from other organizations. Sometimes, however, it is best to keep endorsements quiet. Spencer-Roberts, for instance, walked a delicate line in electing Ronald Reagan govenor of California in 1966. Spencer-Roberts had to win endorsements from moderate groups without alienating the members of the right-wing John Birch Society which supported Reagan. To accomplish this Reagan had to disavow certain aspects of the Birch philosophy, so Spencer-Roberts issued a mimeographed statement that criticized Robert Welch, the society's founder but avoided indictment of the Society or its members. The charge against Welch helped mute the extremist label pinned on Reagan by Democrats, yet retained the votes and money of Birchers.[22] Edward Kennedy's managers recognized the value of individual endorsements in his 1961 campaign for the U.S. Senate. Prior to the Democratic primary the Kennedy team conducted a door-to-door signature drive to obtain the endorsement of Democrats, Republicans, and Independents. The 200,000 pledges permitted Kennedy's managers to publicize the broad endorsement by members of all parties in Massachusetts.[23]

Display Media

Any discussion of campaign media would be remiss to ignore such items as bumper stickers, billboards, yard signs, placards, buttons, and other visual aids. Candidates distribute propaganda novelties to build morale and to promote name recognition. Edward Kennedy's campaign for the U.S. Senate in 1961 suggests the magnitude of these operations. Kennedy forces purchased 500,000 bumper stickers, distributed a million tri-color printed handouts, spent $47,000 on billboards and another $43,500 on bumper stickers, buttons, lapel tabs, streamers, ribbons, and other novelties. A further indication of the importance politicians place on such media is the fact that the twenty candidates for Congress in the bay area of California in 1962 devoted 16 per cent of their campaign budgets to signs, billboards, and the like.[24]

Display messages such as "Dump the "Hump," "Clean Gene," "Make Love, Not War," or "We Try Harder," are really directed at the in-groups who already sympathize with the purposes of the campaign. Few opinions or votes are changed by such displays. But they do put supporters (and the opposition) on notice that the campaign is under way. Sympathizers feel they are effective (even though they may not be) when they distribute pencils, bumper stickers, buttons, and cards bearing their candidate's name. The opposition, particularly amateurs, are intimidated by elaborate displays into fearing they may be "outspent."

Outdoor advertising—billboards and placards

[20]Baus and Ross, *Politics Battle Plan*, p. 360.
[21]Kelley, *Professional Public Relations*, pp. 58–59.
[22]Joseph Lewis, *What Makes Reagan Run?* (New York: McGraw-Hill Book Company, 1968), p. 131.

[23]Murray B. Levin, *Kennedy Campaigning* (Boston: Beacon Press, 1966), pp. 175–76.
[24]Ibid., pp. 276–79; David A. Leuthold, *Electioneering in a Democracy* (New York: John Wiley & Sons, Inc., 1968), p. 104.

—dots the landscape in every election. Many campaign managers swear it is effective not only in raising the spirit of the troops but in advancing name recognition. At a cost of but 8–18¢ per 1,000 voters reached, billboards are an inexpensive channel of mass advertising. Placards on telephone poles, fence posts, and tree trunks are even cheaper. If properly tied into the overall campaign theme, billboards give a rationale for voting for the candidate that lingers in the voter's mind. In his successful campaign for Congress in 1966, for example, Republican George Bush in Texas effectively combined the use of billboards and television. Measurement of the effects of the outdoor displays revealed that voters surveyed had not only noticed the principal theme, "Vote for Bush and Watch the Action," but were able to recall it long after the campaign.

An effective display format for reaching the informed and involved voter who is not yet committed is the visual aid. The first systematic employment of visual aids as a nationwide campaign technique occurred in the 1952 presidential election. Republican strategists developed films, slides, and taped presentations for service organizations, businessmen's clubs, women's associations, church groups, and employee organizations. Particularly effective were cartoons that carried the Republican message in a light vein. These visual aids appeared throughout the country and reached an estimated audience of 3 million. One firm, the John Deere Company, provided a crew to show such films on a full-time basis (thus making a non-monetary but substantial contribution to the Republican effort).[25]

Printed Media

The most widely used of the printed media are campaign literature, political biographies, and newspaper publicity and advertising. Each possesses useful features as a campaign technique.

[25] Kelley, *Professional Public Relations*, pp. 164–65.

Campaign Literature

Campaigners spend a sizable portion of their time and money distributing literature about the candidate and his cause. In 1962 26 per cent of all expenditures by congressional candidates in California's bay area went to print, distribute, and mail literature and handouts.[26] Similar levels of expenditure for propaganda leaflets occur in other winning and losing campaigns. Pierre Salinger, once President John F. Kennedy's press secretary, sought the Democratic nomination for the U.S. Senate from California in 1964. Salinger had never held elective office and faced a formidable opponent in State Controller Alan Cranston. To capitalize on his association with the popular Kennedys, Salinger's managers allocated funds to prepare and distribute a black-bordered picture of Jack Kennedy carrying a plea to support candidates "in the tradition of our martyred President." Although in questionable taste, the tactic helped Salinger defeat Cranston by 140,000 votes.[27] In Nelson Rockefeller's unsuccessful effort to win the 1964 California Republican primary the Spencer-Roberts firm relied heavily on printed material; they spent $120,000, for example, on a single mailing of quotes from Barry Goldwater (entitled "Who Do You Want in the Room with the H Bomb?") to demonstrate the Arizona Senator's "trigger-happy" approach to foreign affairs, they also distributed a regular pro-Rockefeller newsletter with a circulation that rose to 25,000.[28]

There are two basic types of printed literature. The first carries general appeals aimed at a mass audience through direct mail techniques. In a highly mobile population like that of America, candidates seldom rely solely on personal contact with prospective voters (either direct or through their organized workers). Radio and television are the most publicized ways to reach

[26] Leuthold, *Electioneering in a Democracy*, p. 101.
[27] Lewis, *What Makes Reagan Run?*, p. 83.
[28] Theodore H. White, *The Making of the President 1964* (New York: The New American Library, 1966), pp. 150–53.

a mass electorate, but direct mail can also be significant. If professional campaigners specialize in direct-mail techniques, the results can be startling. Direct mail figured prominently in the upset when write-in candidate Henry Cabot Lodge, then in Saigon as ambassador to Vietnam, defeated Barry Goldwater, Nelson Rockefeller, and others in the 1964 New Hampshire Republican presidential primary. The Lodge effort was managed by Paul Grindle, a New England businessman who had used direct-mail techniques to build a successful scientific instrument firm. Grindle turned his professional talents in direct mailing to the task of distributing 96,000 letters in a first mailer and obtaining 8,600 pledges of support in return. A second mailer drew an even larger response. Lodge ultimately received 33,000 write-ins in the primary of which as many as 26,000 may originally have been contacted through mailings.[29] Direct mail played a similar role in the 1966 Democratic gubernatorial primary in Pennsylvania. The imaginative merchandising techniques of professional campaigner Joseph Napolitan converted an unknown, Milton Shapp, into a credible candidate. Napolitan distributed 1,000,000 sixteen-page brochures entitled "The Man Against the Machine" (the central theme of Shapp's campaign against the Democratic organization). At a cost of seven cents to produce and distribute, these general audience brochures were an economical way to gain access to a vast constituency.[30]

The second type of printed literature is aimed not at the mass audience, but at specific interest groups. This clientele literature frequently is distributed by direct mail (as in Winthrop Rockefeller's campaigns for the governorship of Arkansas discussed in Chapter 3), but is hard to distinguish group members when managers have only general mailing lists. Hence other means are needed to reach sectional, religious, occupational, racial, economic, and professional audiences. One technique is to have the interest

group itself do the distributing. In the 1968 presidential campaign the AFL-CIO's Committee on Political Education (COPE) distributed a brochure on behalf of the Democratic party to union members. The tri-color brochure countered the rising support for third-party candidate George Wallace by recounting that "George Wallace's Alabama" ranked forty-eighth among states in per capita income and per pupil expenditures on schools, forty-ninth in welfare payments, and had one of the highest illiteracy rates in the nation. In his term as governor, the union brochure noted, Wallace had not changed these conditions yet he wanted to be president. One cannot say whether the leaflet was effective but it did reach its intended audience. Another way for distributing clientele literature is to use a large mercenary or volunteer organization to distribute pamphlets in person. In winning his reelection as governor of New York in 1966 Nelson Rockefeller's managers prepared brochures on the governor's programs for mental retardation, labor, the arts, and so forth. For each kind of brochure a worker was paid to see that it reached the intended audience. Similarly, Spencer-Roberts flooded low-income white areas with a brochure reminding voters that Ronald Reagan had once been president of the Screen Actors Guild and asking, "Can a Union Man Be Elected Governor?" The leaflet helped counter the charge that Reagan was anti-union; it adroitly ignored Reagan's support for Section 14B of the Taft-Hartley Act permitting states to pass "right to work" laws, which was opposed by labor unions.[31]

Richard Nixon's 1968 campaign had a "participation mailer" to give the citizen the impression he was actually influencing the candidate's thoughts. In Republican headquarters throughout America visitors were encouraged to ask questions, recorded on tape, to be sent to the candidate. Then a computer programmed with Nixon's positions on significant issues would prepare a "personalized" letter to be mailed to the questioner.

[29] Ibid., pp. 136–38.
[30] James M. Perry, *The New Politics* (New York: Clarkson N. Potter, Inc., 1968), pp. 59–64.
[31] Lewis, *What Makes Reagan Run?*, pp. 149–50.

There is little evidence available on the effectiveness of general audience and clientele literature delivered by direct mail, special groups, or the candidate's organization. American's mail boxes are certainly glutted with "junk" advertising; much of it is thrown away, despite a survey conducted by the Direct Mail Advertising Association which reported that 85 per cent of those questioned had "no general dislike to direct mail."[32] We have no reason to believe that campaign literature wins votes, although emotional appeals in printed materials have proved effective in limited cases.[33] Yet campaign managers rely on printed materials, particularly to promote name recognition and to reinforce the themes touted by personal appearances, campaign workers, and radio and televison messages. There is evidence that literature promotes voter turnout. One study of a local charter revision election revealed that of persons not contacted, only one-third voted; of those contacted by mail, 60 per cent voted; and three-fourths of those contacted personally voted.[34]

Campaign Biographies and Tracts

In every political contest, particularly those for the presidency, books detail the lives of respective candidates. Sometimes the content is laudatory, sometimes it is critical, but in either event the biographies are intended not only to make money for the author, but also to shape the image of the office-seeker, to reinforce loyalties, and to condition voters' perceptions.

Campaign biographies played a prominent role in the presidential election of 1964. For example, six million copies of J. Evetts Haley's anti-Johnson diatribe, *A Texan Looks at Lyndon*, were published and distributed; seven million copies of John Stromer's *None Dare Call It Treason*, also anti-Johnson, were printed. In general the 1964 election witnessed the publication of an unprecedented number of books and pamphlets designed to criticize or expose.

Political tracts also carry candidates' messages. In 1964 Barry Goldwater's *Conscience of A Conservative* was a best-seller; Johnson forces countered with the president's *My Hope for America*. It is doubtful that either book changed voters' minds or constituted a lasting addition to the literature of American political thought. In most cases such books reach the already informed and committed and merely reinforce the direction and intensity of their predispositions.[35]

Newspaper and Political Campaigns

Professional campaigners use newspapers for image-building publicity, advertising, and editorial endorsements. We said in Chapter 1 that campaign managers promote a positive image of their candidate. Recall we likened a candidate's image to the impression voters have of his inner character, an impression constructed from his physical appearance, style of life, bearing, conduct, and manner. A man displays an image by assuming a role in life. Selective aspects of his personality suitable to that role are emphasized and permitted public exposure; those not so suited are underplayed, compensated for by revealing "other sides" of the man, or simply ignored. The image is not, therefore, that of the "whole man," but of dimensions of personality appropriate to the role and its setting. All the mass media may be used to portray candidate images, but professional campaigners charged with the task of conveying positive pictures of their candidate—the image specialists[36]—are particularly fond of newspapers, radio, and television for this purpose.

[32]Baus and Ross, *Politics Battle Plan*, p. 339.

[33]G. W. Hartmann, "A Field Experiment on the Comparative Effectiveness of 'Emotional' and 'Rational' Political Leaflets in Determining Election Results," *Journal of Abnormal and Social Psychology*, XXXI (1936), 99–114.

[34]Samuel J. Eldersveld and Richard W. Dodge, "Personal Contact or Mail Propaganda?" in Daniel Katz et al., eds., *Public Opinion and Propaganda* (New York: Henry Holt and Co., 1954), pp. 532–42.

[35]Charles A. H. Thomson, "Mass Media Performance," in Milton C. Cummings, Jr., ed., *The National Election of 1964* (Washington, D.C.: The Brookings Institution, 1966), pp. 138–42.

[36]Wyckoff, *The Image Candidates*, p. 11; Joe McGinniss, *The Selling of the President 1968* (New York: Trident Press, 1969), pp. 26, 38.

Newspapers publicize candidates in ways that convey to the reader an impression of the candidate's credibility and character. In covering opposing candidates, for example, the placement of the news stories about each make a difference. A critical story on a front page one day is not easily offset if a candidate's denial appears on a back page. Headlines also make a difference; "Humphrey Picketed" leaves a different impression than "Humphrey Speaks." The types of stories about candidates contributes to their images. Citizens are pleased to know their would-be mayor visited a children's hospital but seldom approve of his failure to pay a traffic ticket when he was in law school. The tone and content of news stories subtly build or destroy a reputation while reporting the candidate's deed and misdeeds, describing his appearance or style, and extolling or lamenting his character.

All this is not to suggest newspapers characteristically distort their electoral coverage in deliberate attempts to favor one candidate over another. Analysis of America's fifteen most prestigious dailies in the 1960 and 1964 elections indicate that they devoted almost equal space to both sides even though nine of the fifteen supported Nixon editorially in 1960 and eleven endorsed President Johnson in 1964. No clear coloring of coverage emerged in story content in either year, although there is some suggestion that editorial positions on foreign affairs worked to Johnson's advantage in ten of the prestige papers in 1964.[37]

Columnists are particularly adept at image-building. In major New York City dailies, for example, they played a major role in advancing John Lindsay's candidacy for mayor. A content analysis during the 1965 election reported that thirty-seven of fifty-seven columns were either favorable to Lindsay or against his opponents. His positive reputation soared as columnists described him as the potential Republican candidate for president in 1968, as vying for governor of New York with Robert Kennedy in 1970, as representative of "a new generation of educated and public-spirited men," and as probable "landslide" victor.[38]

Campaign managers recognize the image-building potential of newspaper publicity and cultivate every opportunity to present their candidates in favorable lights to publishers, editors, reporters, and columnists. Sometimes, however, their candidate makes the wrong kind of news. Reporters covering Barry Goldwater in 1964, for example, found him personally attractive, but his policy pronouncements and his off-the-cuff remarks at news conferences always caused difficulty. If the journalists reported accurately his quick rejoinders (like his statement that the U.S. should bomb North Vietnam), they knew they were not doing justice to the candidate's total stand. For a period they probed for safe questions to report what they thought he had meant in a belligerent remark, but they turned ultimately to direct quotes. This proved devastating and the Goldwater camp soon avoided frequent meetings of their candidate with the press. Goldwater had won the battle for exposure but the effects of his remarks were causing him to lose the war.[39]

Image-building publicity is not sufficient to communicate the candidate's message in newspapers, particularly if the publicity is not favorable. Consequently, campaign expenditures for paid newspaper advertising are heavy. Such expenditures are justified by campaigners on the basis of studies indicating that 80 per cent of pages carrying national advertising, for example, are opened and scanned by the average reader and that men and women of all ages, incomes,

[37]See Guido H. Stempel III, "The Prestige Press Covers the 1960 Presidential Campaign," *Journalism Quarterly*, XXXVIII (Spring, 1961), 157–63; Guido H. Stempel III, "The Prestige Press in Two Presidential Elections," *Journalism Quarterly*, XLII (Winter, 1965), 15–21; Jim A. Hart, "Election Campaign Coverage in English and U.S. Daily Newspapers," *Journalism Quarterly*, XLII (Spring, 1965), 213–18; and David S. Myers, "Editorials and Foreign Affairs in the 1964 Presidential Campaign," *Journalism Quarterly*, XLV (Summer, 1968), 211–18.

[38]Donald R. Shanor, "The Columnists Look at Lindsay," *Journalism Quarterly*, XLIII (Summer, 1966), 287–90.

[39]White, *The Making of the President 1964*, p. 133.

educational attainments, and regions pay atten-tion to newspaper ads.[40] Whereas newspaper advertising normally has been employed for di-rect appeals to voters, specialists make increas-ing use of space for image-advertising. Picture material is well suited to image projection. In a sample of ninety newspapers during the 1960 presidential campaign, for instance, Democrats used pictures in almost 60 per cent of their advertising. Most of the ads were directed sim-ply at promoting name recognition, but almost one-fourth had an image appeal as well. One ad pictured Jacqueline Kennedy on the phone re-minding all women to listen to a special broad-cast for wives and mothers. Republicans used fewer image ads, but a prominent one captured a principle theme of Nixon's managers, it por-trayed Nixon pointing a finger at the Soviet Union's Premier Nikita Khrushchev during their "debate" in Moscow when Nixon toured that country and left the impression that Nixon was master of the situation.

Other advertising formats include endorse-ments of the candidate by prestigious persons, linking the presidential candidate to local office-seekers, and ads directed to special interests. To appeal to special interests, candidates always place advertising in Negro and foreign language newspapers. Newspaper advertising, at least in presidential elections, is usually concentrated in the last two weeks of the campaign.[41]

Editorial endorsements typically favor Re-publican candidates, particularly in presidential contests or in gubernatorial, senatorial, and congressional races outside the South. From 1940 to 1960, for example, from one-half to two-thirds of the dailies in the United States (with from 70 to 80 per cent of total circula-tion) endorsed the Republican presidential standard-bearer. In 1964 there was a sharp re-versal as only 35 per cent of dailies endorsed Barry Goldwater, 42 per cent endorsed Lyndon Johnson, and 23 per cent remained uncommit-ted.[42] The normal pattern returned in 1968. That editorial endorsements are neither a neces-sary nor sufficient conditon for election victory is demonstrated by the many candidates at local, state, and national levels who win over editorial opposition. This is not to say that en-dorsements or newspaper coverage has no in-fluence. Indications are that editorial endorse-ments provide cues for voters, especially in nonpartisan local elections and in state and local referenda where party loyalties are less rel-event. In California elections held between 1948 and 1962, for example, newspapers en-dorsed the winning candidate in local elections 84 per cent of the time, for state senate 65 per cent of the time, and in 63 per cent of elections for the state assembly.[43] Indeed, the principal proposition that emerges from studies of the campaign effects of newspaper readership is that newspapers influence (through stories, advertising, and editorials) the marginally inter-ested voter. Under conditions of low involve-ment the voter has few guidelines for what to believe or how to vote. In these circumstances readers frequently acquire knowledge of issues, form attitudes, and vote on the basis of news-paper content.[44]

[40] The Newspaper Information Committee, *A Study of the Opportunity for Exposure to National News-paper Advertising* (New York: Bureau of Advertising, ANPA, 1966).

[41] James J. Mullen, "Newspaper Advertising in the Kennedy-Nixon Campaign," *Journalism Quarterly*, XL (Winter, 1963), 3–11; James J. Mullen, "Newspaper Advertising in the Johnson-Goldwater Campaign," *Journalism Quarterly*, XLV (Summer, 1968), 219–25; James J. Mullen, "How Candidates for the Senate Use Newspaper Advertising," *Journalism Quarterly*, XL (Autumn, 1963), 532–38.

[42] Edwin Emery, "Press Support for Johnson and Goldwater," *Journalism Quarterly*, XLI (Autumn, 1964), 485–88; Richard L. Bishop and Robert L. Brown, "Michigan Newspaper Bias in the 1966 Cam-paign," *Journalism Quarterly*, XLV (Summer, 1968), 337–38.

[43] James E. Gregg, "Newspaper Editorial Endorse-ments and California Elections, 1948–62," *Journalism Quarterly*, XLII (Autumn, 1965), 532–38; Jules Beck-er and Douglas A. Fuchs, "How Two Major California Dailies Covered Reagan vs. Brown," *Journalism Quar-terly*, XLIV (Winter, 1967), 645–53.

[44] James E. Brinton and L. Norman McKown, "Ef-fects of Newspaper Reading on Knowledge and Atti-tude," *Journalism Quarterly*, XXXVIII (Spring, 1961), 187–95.

Auditory Media

We have said that the modern political campaign is a mediated one; instead of direct contact with the electorate, the candidate's character and appeals reach voters through organized partisans, displays, and the printed media. Even more significant in this century are the electronic media: radio and the telephone channel the candidate's words; televison adds the illusion of the candidate's presence.

Campaigning By Radio

With the advent of radio in the 1920s politicians gained a means of achieving instantaneous transmission of appeals to individual members of a mass electorate. No longer did they have to wait for staged rallies, recruited volunteers, billboard erection, and the publication or distribution of literature and newspapers. Now they could speak directly to the people. The first candidate to use radio effectively was President Franklin Roosevelt in 1936. The addition of radio to campaigns was followed by significant increases in turnouts in presidential and congressional elections.[45] By the second decade of radio's popularity it seemed destined to play the dominant role in future elections. Then, with the emergence of television, politicians ceased to emphasize radio as a campaign medium. Only in recent elections has its utility been rediscovered by professional campaigners.

In recent presidential contests Republicans especially have re-emphasized radio as a campaign medium. Barry Goldwater's managers in 1964 broadcast a five-minute "Goldwater Report" each evening from October 28 to election eve on 300 stations of the Mutual Broadcasting System. In addition radio spot announcements were used extensively for national, state, and local tickets urging citizens to vote a straight Republican ticket "From Goldwater to_____" (the name of the last-named local candidate on the ballot in a particular area).   But John

Mitchell, Richard Nixon's campaign manager in 1968, exploited radio more fully than in any campaign to date. He found the medium so effective that he remarked after the campaign that if it were to do over again, his only change would be to spend more money on radio. Among Mitchell's techniques were rebroadcasts of five-minute excerpts from Nixon's acceptance speech before the Republican convention calling for "New Leadership"; the presentation of long, detailed speeches on key issues that were not well-adapted to televison, but that sounded tightly reasoned and well-informed on radio; the broadcast of radio messages from Nixon's campaign plane while the candidate was flying over a particular region thus permitting Nixon to tailor his remarks to special clienteles; and numerous appearances by key Republicans on interview programs, call-in shows, and talk programs.

Radio has certain advantages over other campaign media. It reaches an audience largely missed by either newspaper or television. The average suburban commuter spends ninety minutes of every working day isolated in his automobile. Radio is his link with the world. Millions of housewives listen to radio during their daily chores. The elderly, who grew up with radio, depend on news broadcasts for information about politics. And the transistor has a sizable audience of young adults still "hooked" on radio as they grow out of their rock-and-roll teens. Radio is also far less expensive for political advertising than is television. Candidates for minor offices find it more economical to reach their limited electorate by radio than to pay exorbitant television rates to carry their message to counties in which they are not running. Radio often provides free image-building publicity. Interview and "talk" shows are the staple of public affairs programming on radio. Managers exploit radio shows that rely on listeners to phone in their views by organizing volunteers to flood the station with calls favorable to their candidate. And candidates not particularly marketable on television may come off well as radio performers. In 1960, for example, viewers of

[45] Angus Campbell, "Has Television Reshaped Politics?," *Columbia Journalism Review*, I (1963), 10–22.

the Kennedy-Nixon debates on television generally credited Kennedy with "winning"; but persons who had listened only to radio thought Nixon had done the superior job. Since radio news programs depend heavily on taping "actualities" (the voices of persons in the news), candidates try to make news for stations. In his first campaign for mayor of Los Angeles in 1961 Sam Yorty bought little radio time but had taped interviews played on numerous public affairs programs. Since his opponent Mayor Norris Poulson, was supported heavily by the metropolitan newspapers, the free radio time was exploited by Yorty as an essential communication channel to his campaign audience.[46] Finally, one professional campaign manager argues that radio is the best place for the "hard sell," particularly when that includes attacks on an opponent that a candidate does not want answered—the "hit and run." Missouri Senator Stuart Symington faced such a radio attack in his first campaign for the U.S. Senate in 1952. His opponent's radio advertising charged that Symington's position on issues paralleled that of Viot Marcantonio, a New York congressman. Marcantonio's position was labeled the "Communist line." The link of Symington to communism, however, proved too tenuous for voters; they elected Symington even though Eisenhower carried the state for Republicans.

Telephones and Turnout

So well publicized is the role of the newspaper, radio, or television as a medium of mass communication that we overlook the most popular channel for conducting business, transmitting information, providing entertainment, and influencing opinions—the telephone. Professional campaigners, however, do not overlook it. Indeed, campaign managers who specialize in organizing telephone campaigns are well paid; they compile lists of telephone subscribers (both general lists and lists for special clienteles), es-

tablish central headquarters, and recruit personnel for round-the-clock manning of phones. Using arrangements with phone companies to place unlimited numbers of local and long distance calls for a set fee (the WATS line or Wide Area Telephone Service), the specialists try to influence voters and get them to the polls.

The principal technique using the telephone to survey voters is the playback of a recorded message. Here an operator dials a number, gets an answer, and switches on a recorded message by a candidate. If the listener has been notified to expect the call (perhaps by letter), he may have the illusion he is actually speaking with the candidate; even in the absence of this illusion he is flattered by the attention. George Romney's managers in Michigan market-tested several variations of the basic technique including a message from Romney alone, one from Romney introducing a congressional candidate who would speak to the phone listener, and one providing a number to be called should the citizen have any questions or complaints. In the 1966 election the Romney organization completed calls to 145,758 households in three key congressional districts. Romney's managers felt that the calls supplied the margin of victory for their candidate in two of those districts. At a cost of 4–5¢ per call the telephone could play an even greater role as a relatively inexpensive campaign medium in the future.[47]

Recent campaigns provide examples of how effective the telephone can be in getting voters to the polls. In the 1968 Democratic gubernatorial primary in Texas eleven candidates vied for the nomination. The leading contenders were the current lieutenant governor (Preston Smith), former ambassador to Vietnam (Eugene Locke), and a twice-defeated candidate for governor in past elections (Don Yarborough). Far down the line was a politician-rancher, Dolph Briscoe, who had been out of elective politics for several years. Briscoe's managers hired an eastern firm which specialized in telephone campaigns to conduct a "blitz" on elec-

[46]Charles G. Mayo, "The Mass Media and Campaign Strategy in a Mayoralty Election," *Journalism Quarterly*, XLI (Summer, 1964), 353–59.

[47]Perry, *The New Politics*, pp. 102–3.

tion eve. In the counties in which the blitz was conducted the turnout for Briscoe exceeded all poll predictions by significant margins and Briscoe finished fourth among all candidates, missing the run-off primary.

The telephone blitz was not a new technique. It had been particularly effective on a national scale in Richard Nixon's 1960 presidential campaign. Since then it has become a standard method of achieving high voter turnouts in "soft areas." Nixon managers used the technique on behalf of his write-in candidacy in the 1964 Oregon presidential primary and Spencer-Roberts employed the blitz for Nelson Rockefeller in the 1964 California Republican presidential primary.

The telephone is a tool for campaign research as well as for stimulating turnout. In seeking the Republican nomination to win his reelection as mayor of New York City in 1969, John Lindsay's managers established a phone brigade to make calls to 100,000 registered Republicans. Each Republican rated Lindsay and his opponent; John Marchi, on a scale from one to five; names of persons giving Lindsay positive ratings were stored in a computer with addresses, telephone numbers, ages, income, and ethnic backgrounds. The computer printout was used to provide lists of voters to contact on election day. One estimate placed the pro-Lindsay responses at only one of every three, a portent of his ultimate loss to Marchi in the Republican primary.[48]

Television Media

Despite the increasingly imaginative use of direct mail, image-advertising in newspapers, radio publicity, recorded messages, and telephone blitzes, it is televison that distinguishes modern campaign communication from that prior to the invasion of the professional campaigners. We will focus on two aspects of the television revolution in campaigning—the con-

[48]James M. Perry, "Politically, The Mayor Is Not Doing So Well,'" *The National Observer*, June 9, 1969.

siderations in its selection as a campaign medium and the professional approach to image-making on television.

The Uses and Costs of Televised Campaigning

Professional managers cite several instances where television is the only appropriate media around which to organize a campaign. The most universally cited is the election involving an unknown candidate running against an incumbent. The newcomer must rely on normally inactive citizens to overcome the traditional support that regularly elects the incumbent. Because the newcomer is unknown and is appealing to persons with little active interest in politics, his managers know that voters will not come to his public appearances, peruse his literature, note his displays, or read about him in newspapers. He must therefore wage his campaign in the voters' homes when residents settle down to be entertained. As the great entertainer television provides the political neophyte a means for shattering the inattention of his desired audience.

But incumbents also use television extensively, particularly the incumbent who has not made a strong impression (or has made a negative impression) on his constituents and faces still opposition. In Senator John Tower's reelection campaign in 1966 (see Chapter 3) a television campaign was designed with precisely these goals in mind—to awaken Texans to Tower's accomplishments and to replace a negative image with a positive one. The result was a slick and successful advertising campaign (prominently featuring the candidate and his attractive family) planned and executed by the Rives-Dyke advertising agency of Houston.

Primary elections are particularly well suited to television campaigning. In the absence of anchoring partisan loyalties and clear-cut issues, most candidates who enter the campaign as relative unknowns. Recent American political history is replete with examples of men who have become credible candidates because of clever television campaigns in primaries; Milton Shapp in his 1966 bid to become the Democratic nominee for governor of Pennsylvania, Ronald Reagan in his triumph over San Francisco Mayor George Christopher in 1966, and the case of Don Tabbert of Indiana are illustrative. Sometimes similar conditions prevail in general elections, particularly in contests for lesser offices. A new star appeared on the Missouri political horizon in the 1968 election for attorney general when John C. Danforth, a Republican, upset the Democratic candidate by massive use of well-produced television spots in the final two weeks of the campaign. His victory made him the first Republican to win statewide office in Missouri in two decades and resulted in a *Newsweek* designation as one of the four most promising politicians for the 1970s.

One final instance when television campaigning seems most appropriate occurs when a candidate faces a hostile press (or when it seems to him that the press is hostile). Televison permits him to hurdle reporters or editors and reach voters directly. We described earlier how the Spencer-Roberts firm deliberately shielded Ronald Reagan from reporters, preferring Reagan's presence on televison to outline his positions. Similarly, Sam Yorty's managers hurdled hostile editorial writers by taking advantage of television in the Los Angeles mayor's race of 1961 against Norris Poulson. In addition to paid half-hour talks by Yorty on camera, his managers missed no opportunity for publicity through televised news conferences, interviews, and panel shows.[49]

Televison is not always appropriate, especially for those candidates who leave a poor television impression. In the Yorty-Poulson race, Poulson's managers—the Baus and Ross agency—discouraged televised appearances of their candidate because his voice was scarcely audible as a result of a throat ailment. Ultimately Poulson went on television despite his managers. An impression of the showing can be gained from a survey of voters undertaken by a commerical polling organization after the election. Of Yorty voters 73 per cent said they felt television was the most effective medium in winning votes for their candidate, but only a bare majority of the Poulson voters thought that television had assisted his campaign.

Whether a candidate uses television or not depends in large measure on the costs of producing the television package, buying television time, and preempting other programs. Production costs alone are sizable. Professional campaigner Joseph Napolitan allocated $120,000 alone to Guggenheim Productions for spots and films used in Milton Shapp's campaign in Pennsylvania in 1966. Napolitan easily surpassed that cost in the documentary about Hubert Humphrey which he commissioned to be shown on election eve in 1968. But the high production costs resulted in equally high quality and effectiveness, like that of the segment in which Humphrey played with his mentally retarded grandchild and observed in tears that through her affliction he had learned the power of human love. Skimping on production costs, suggests Napolitan, is false economy: "The truth is that you just can't make good, cheap films."[50]

Television time is also expensive. Rates depend on the time-period purchased. The larger the number of viewers likely to be reached at any given hour, the higher the cost. A full hour on network television would cost no less than $100,000 during prime viewing hours. A one-minute spot announcement during NBC's series, *The Virginian*, would cost $23,000. In New York City twenty seconds of prime time costs in the neighborhood of $3,000 but in Los Angeles "only" half as much.

And campaigners pay for the right to preempt programs normally shown in the desired time period. Campaigners usually pay the production costs of the programs they preempt, a cost that can easily exceed the production figures for the candidate's own film and the original costs for air time.

[49]Mayo, "The Mass Media," p. 358.

[50]Chester et al., *An American Melodrama*, p. 754; Perry, *The New Politics*, p. 54.

Potential in Legal Communication: What's the Verdict?

Caroline Welch

Recently, research both in laboratory settings and in the "real world" of trial by jury, has seen the application of certain components of speech communication and other social sciences to law. The increasing number of studies in legal communication is especially timely. It is difficult to name a period in American history when more attention has been focused on the judicial process and communication.

Evidence of the usefulness and need for further research in the area of legal communication will be demonstrated in this paper from two perspectives: First, from the consideration of potential methods of improving court procedures, including specifically the use of videotape and a re-evaluation of the traditional order of presentation at trial; and secondly, from the consideration of previously unchallenged assumptions concerning the jury, specifically including aspects of jury selection and juror response. These perspectives are not designed to be representative nor all-inclusive of current research in legal communication. Rather, they are two of the most dynamic and potentially use-

ful areas of current study which clearly illustrates the importance of legal communication to speech communication and to the judicial system in this country.

The search for improving court procedures has been undertaken on several levels. An increasing number of legal professionals have endorsed the use of videotape in courtroom trials. Their support ranges from taping individual witness testimony to prerecording of entire trials for presentation to juries. Given the problems of crowded court agendas, dead or disappearing witnesses, and unmangeable defendants, the advantages of videotape are important ones. Not only would the number of cases tried be expedited, but videotape also permits deletion of legally inadmissible materials so that they do influence jurors.

Miller and others were able to build a realistic re-creation of an actual trial and found that the responses of jurors exposed to a live trial do not differ significantly from those exposed to a videotaped trial.[1] Likewise, Anapol confirms that "A jury watching a videotaped trial will ar-

Caroline Welch, "Potential in Legal Communication: What's the Verdict?" Journal of American Forensic Association, XII (Winter 1976), 138–43.

[1]Gerald Miller, David Bender, Thomas Florence, and Henry Nicholson, "Reel Versus Reel: What's the Verdict?," *JC*, 24 (Summer, 1974), 99.

307

rive at a verdict not significantly different from a jury watching an actual trial."[2] However, as a study undertaken by the National Center for State Courts in Denver, Colorado concluded: "The use of the video medium in criminal courts raises many issues and questions which are yet to be resolved."[3]

The central Constitutional issue to be resolved in the videotaping of testimony is the Sixth Amendment right of the accused to confront witnesses against him. The key issue is whether the video medium provides the right of confrontation or whether physical face-to-face confrontation at trial is required.[4]

A second Constitutional question which concerns the use of videotaped testimony for trial is its effect on the accused's Sixth Amendment right to counsel. One aspect of the right to counsel considers the effectiveness of counsel's cross-examination and opening and closing arguments when all of these are on videotape and counsel must address a jury which he cannot see or know the composition of.[5]

In most states, the use of videotape as a record of trial proceedings will require a revision of statutes and court rules. To insure proper use of the medium, further studies in legal communication are essential.

Another level on which recent study has been done to improve court procedures is in the area of order of presentation of evidence. Thibaut and Walker at the University of North Carolina have used elaborate laboratory methods to examine the order of presentation at trial. In the traditional adversary process, the prosecution (or plaintiff) usually has the right to make the first opening statement present evidence first, and make both the first and final closing arguments. The common justification for this ordering is that the burden of proof should have the advantage of making the first and last presentation. Although there is no established "internal order," some attorneys normally save their strongest, most convincing evidence for last—both for dramatic effect and to assist the jury in remembering the strongest evidence most vividly.

The North Carolina study examined these assumptions and concluded that it does make a difference who goes first or second in the adversary presentation of legal materials, and the second position is the more advantageous. The traditional weak too strong (climatic) ordering of arguments is the more effective only for the plaintiff or prosecution. The climatic order is advantageous for the defense only when the defense's presentation comes after the prosecution's, and there only to a relatively minor degree. Thibaut and Walker conclude:

> If the ideal order of evidence presented is one that eliminates any advantage gained solely because of order, the ideal sequence for an adversary system would be: The advocate asserting guilt or fault should go first and present his case in climactic order; the advocate defending should follow and do likewise. This gives a gross order advantage to the defense, offset by the climatic order advantage given the prosecution.[6]

In addition to the Thibaut and Walker study, others such as Shaw[7] and Stone[8] have also taken a second look at previously unquestioned courtroom proceedings which have been pre-

[2]Malthon Anapol, "A View From Inside the Jury Room: An Analysis of the Verdicts and Decision-Making Variables of Simulated Juries," Unpublished Report, Univ. of Delaware, (1974), 15.

[3]Francis Taillefer, Ernest Short, Michael Greenwood, and Grant Brady, "Video Support in the Criminal Courts," *JC*, 24 (Summer, 1974), 114; see also "Symposium: The Use of Videotape in the Courtroom," *Brigham Young U. Law Rev.*, (No. 2, 1975); Sherwood, Salvan, "Videotape for the Legal Community," *Judicature*, 59 (Dec., 1975), 222–29; Irving Kosky, "Videotape in Ohio," *Judicature*, 59 (Dec., 1975), 231–38.

[4]Kosky, pp. 236–37.

[5]*Ibid.*

[6]John Thibaut and William Walker, "Going to Court," *Mosaic*, 5 (Summer, 1974), 27.

[7]Lew Shaw, "Trial By Jury: An Analysis of the Jury's Verdict," Unpublished Ph.D. dissertation, Rensselaer Polytechnic Institute, 1975.

[8]Vernon Stone, "A Primacy Effect in Decision Making by Jurors," *JC*, 19 (Sept., 1969), 239–47.

sumed to be objective and fair over the years. A second perspective in demonstrating the usefulness and need for further research in legal communication is the jury selection process. In recognizing the importance of personality traits and mental attitudes in determing the verdict, defense lawyers have been enlisting the help of social scientists in selecting jurors.[9] Although sophisticated, new theories and techniques are used in the process of jury selection, lawyers, over the years have accumulated several stereotyped beliefs about people who will make good or bad jurors.

Tate very generally described some of the stereotyped beliefs of lawyers on who will make good or bad jurors:

> They feel that persons of Latin descent are emotional, while German, British, and Scandinavians are conservative and will support the prosecution more than the defense. Blacks, Italians, Jews, Frenchmen, and Spaniards are expected to support the defense more than the prosecution. Waitresses, bartenders, artists, actors, social scientists, and persons with more experience "in the world" are thought to make better jurors than engineers and accountants.[10]

Some lawyers have gone well beyond the use of such stereotyped beliefs and large sums of money are paid to compile statistically sound profiles of the "ideal juror" and then challenges are made during the jury selection accordingly.[11] Presently, such data is used primarily to counter publicity to obtain jurors not already convinced. Watergate is one such example.

William J. Bryan, Jr., an attorney and physician who has helped select juries for Melvin Belli and F. Lee Bailey, stated in early October of 1973 that "... for all intents and purposes the Watergate coverup case will have been decided with the selection of the final juror. ... If you get the right jury the ordeal should benefit the defense.[12]

What is the right jury? In this case, the right juror for the defense in Bryan's estimation is a true believer in the old American axiom, "you don't kick a man when he's down." Sex, too, is an important factor here, as Bryan explains:

> Women, providing they are not male haters, tend to be rather forgiving of men. This is especially true if the men in question have presence and substance—something all of the Watergate defendants have in common. Even John Mitchell, despite his baldness and paunch, looks benign and relaxed when clutching his pipe.[13]

From the prosecution's standpoint, the "ideal juror" is a young man, actively concerned with cleaning up the political system. Bryan further specifies that:

> Engineers and accountants, as groups, are likely to be prosectuion-minded in this trial because they are most likely to have faith in the tapes—products of engineering science and analogous to the adding machine tapes on which accountants rely.[14]

Many lawyers agree that these social science techniques ultimately will be used in trials where publicity is not an issue. Whether these techniques really advance the cause of justice is a matter of intense debate. Some doubt the extent of their impact, while others argue that the techniques are too effective and should be avoided.

[9]Amitai Etzioni, "Creating an Imbalance," *Trial*, 10 (Nov./Dec., 1974), 28–30; Howard Moore, Jr., "Redressing the Balance," *Trial*, 10 (Nov./Dec., 1974), 29+; and Michael Saks, "Social Scientists Can't Rig Juries," *Psy. T.*, 9 (Jan., 1976), 48–57.

[10]Eugene Tate, Ernest Howrish, and Stanley Clark, "Communication Variables in Jury Selection," *JC*, 24 (Sept., 1974), 132; see also Harry Kalven, Jr. and Hans Zeisel, *The American Jury*, (Boston: Little, Brown, 1966), 193–218.

[11]Jay Schulman, *et al.*, "Recipe for a Jury," *Psy. T.*, 6 (May, 1973), 37–44.

[12]William J. Bryan, "An Experts Advice to the Watergate Defense: How to Pick a Winning Panel of Jurors," *Los Angeles Times*, (October 15, 1974), 1; see also William J. Bryan, Jr., *The Chosen One*, (N.Y.: Vantage Press, 1971).

[13]Bryan (1974), p. 13.

[14]*Ibid.*

Sociologist Amital Etzioni is concerned about the potential threat to a fair trail posed by the availability of sophisticated social science techniques. He believes that a team of social scientists can exercise excessive control over a jury and allow lawyers to pick juries partial to their cause. Since states do not provide district attorneys with such teams. Etzioni warns that defendants have the edge—and the wealthier the defendant, the greater the edge.[15] Such arguments add new fuel to the case for limiting lawyers' role in jury selection.[16] Further research in this area can determine whether these social science techniques and the stereotyped beliefs of lawyers, are impairing the proper operation of the jury system. Ultimately, such research may be the catalyst for reform of our jury selection process.

Several communication aspects of juror response raise important questions which reflect upon our judicial system. Four of the more important are: the effects of defendant's attractiveness, note-taking, language, and time on juror response.

Landy and Aronson's experiment which showed that discrepancies in sentencing can result from varying the characteristics of the defendant. They found that simulated jurors were significantly more lenient with the attractive and neutral defendants than they were with the unattractive defendant: the unattractive defendant was sentenced to more years in prison than both the attractive and neutral defendant.[17]

In another study of a similar type, Friend and Vinson confirmed their predictions that judges and jurors, when consciously attempting to be "impartial" in their decisions, may actually "lean over backwards" to offset their biases. Friend and Vinson suggest that "socially and physically unattractive defendants may receive less severe sentences than attractive and neutral defendants."[18] These findings suggest the presence of certain variables which may be operating in the courtroom and possibly interfering with the effectiveness of the judicial system.

In exploring another aspect of juror response, Anapol tried unsuccessfuly to determine the origin of the almost universal rule against note-taking among jurors. He states:

> We can specualte that it stems from a period when literacy wasn't common and a fear that if one or two jurors were able to take notes they would wield disproportionate power among the illiterate jurors.[19]

Anapol emphasizes that more research is needed in this area because he has found that for simulated jurors who took notes, the events of the trial were more vivid and more clear, which in turn, influenced the verdict which they brought forward.

In considering the aspect of language, psychologist Elizabeth Loftus has studied the effect of substituting one word for another on quantitative judgments. After showing a traffic accident film, varying forms of critical questions were asked the simulated jurors. For some the question was "About how fast were the cars going when they hit each other?" Other questions replaced the verb *hit* with smashed, collided, bumped, or contacted. The words imply

[15] Etzioni, pp. 28, 30.

[16] For an opposite point of view see Moore, pp. 29+; and Alice Padawer-Singer, A. Singer, and R. Singer, "Voir Dire By Two Lawyers: An Essential Safeguard," *Judicature*, 57 (April, 1974), 386–91.

[17] D. Landy, and E. Aronson, "The Influence of the Characteristics of the Criminal and His Victim on the Decisions of Simulated Jurors," *J. of Exp. Soc. Psy.*, 5 (1969), 150.

[18] Ronald Friend, and Michael Vinson, "Leaning over Backwards: Jurors Responses to Defendants' Attractiveness," *JC*, 24 (Sept., 1974), 124; see also Joan Kessler, "The Social Psychology of Jury Deliberations," in Rita James Simon, (ed.), *The Jury System in America: A Critical Overview*, 4 (Sage Publications, 1975), p. 78 and R. Kulka and J. Kessler, "The Influence of Physical Attractiveness on Decisions of Simulated Jurors," Presented to the Speech Comm. Assoc. Convention, New York, Nov., 1973.

[19] Anapol, p. 11; see also Robert Forston, "Sense and Non-sense: Trial Communication," *Brigham Young Law Rev.*, (No. 3, 1975), in Press.

different things about speed and force of impact. These differences affected judgment about velocity. The estimates varied considerably, depending on which question has been asked. Average speed estimates for different verbs ranged from 40.8 when the verb "smashed" was used, to 31.8 when the verb "contacted" was used.[20]

A week later, the subjects were called back and asked if they had seen any broken glass, although, in fact, there had been none in the film. The results showed that more than twice as many individuals questioned with "smashed" reported seeing the non-existent glass as those questioned with "hit." Loftus suggests that the word "smashed" influenced the individuals to remember the accident as more severe than it had been, and it follows, then, that they might also "remember" details that were not shown, but were consistent with an accident occurring at high speed—like broken glass. It seems logical to conclude that a certain suggestibility accompanies certain words which can influence not only our juror response but eyewitness testimony as well.

Studies on the effect of time on an individual's memory cast serious doubts on eyewitness testimony, which has traditionally been held in high esteem by the courts. Between the time that an event is witnessed, and told to someone else, the memory of the event may change drastically.[21]

Loftus used a study and several examples as evidence to substantiate problems involved in the lapse of time and witness identification. In one study 141 students witnessed a staged assault on a professor. Seven weeks later they were asked to identify the assailant from a group of six photographs. Although the episode had been a dramatic one, 60 per cent of the witnesses, including the professor who had been attacked, chose the wrong man. Twenty-five

per cent selected an individual who had been at the scene of the crime but as an innocent bystander.

The results of the above kind of experimentation may be somewhat entertaining, but situations in real life are serious. Loftus wrote of a *Los Angeles Times* report about the mistaken conviction of a man whom seven witnesses had identified as the robber of a bank. In a similar case but different newspaper report, seventeen witnesses identified a man as the person who shot a police officer; later it was verified that the man had not been in the vicinity of the crime during its occurrence.[22]

Consideration of the effects of defendant's attractiveness, note-taking, language, and the lapse of time on the testimony of eyewitnesses are areas which need further study. Further research may suggest the need for a reevaluation of some of our traditional practices and basic assumptions which have been prevalent in our judicial system.

As suggested earlier, the material presented here deals with only two perspectives of legal communication: methods of improving court proceedings and unchallenged assumptions concerning the jury. While there are numerous other aspects of legal communication, the above studies cast doubt on the effectiveness and fairness of traditional courtroom procedures and demonstrate the need to seriously examine the law in terms of speech communication. Numerous other aspects of legal communication not discussed here add to the doubts expressed by this author. For example, consider the following legal communication issues: confusing judge's instructions to jurors,[23] the timing of judge's instructions,[24] the use of written jury instructions,[25] the size of juries—twelve or six

---

[20] Elizabeth Loftus, "Reconstructing Memory: The Incredible Eyewitness," *Psy. T.*, 7 (Dec., 1974), 119.
[21] *Ibid.*, p. 117.

[22] *Ibid.*
[23] Kalven and Zeisel, pp. 149–62; and Robert Forston, "Judge's Instructions: A Quantitative Analysis of Juror's Listening Comprehension," *Today's Speech*, 18 (Fall, 1970), 34–8.
[24] Forston (1975).
[25] *Ibid.*

members,[26] the acceptance of less than unanimous verdicts,[27] and the influence of trial judge's nonverbal demeanor on juries.[28] The assumptions and issues discussed here indicated, on many of the questions concerning legal communication, that the jury is still out.

[26] See William Arnold's article in this issue.

[27] Alice Padawer-Singer, "Less than Unanimous vs. Unaimous Jury Verdicts," Unpublished paper presented to the Speech Comm. Assoc. Convention, Chicago, Ill., Dec. 1974.

[28] Leslie Conner, "The Trial Judge's Demeanor: Its Impact on the Jury," *The Judge's J.*, 13 (Jan., 1974), 2–3.

Index

†